FASHION SKETCHBOOK

Male Figure Template

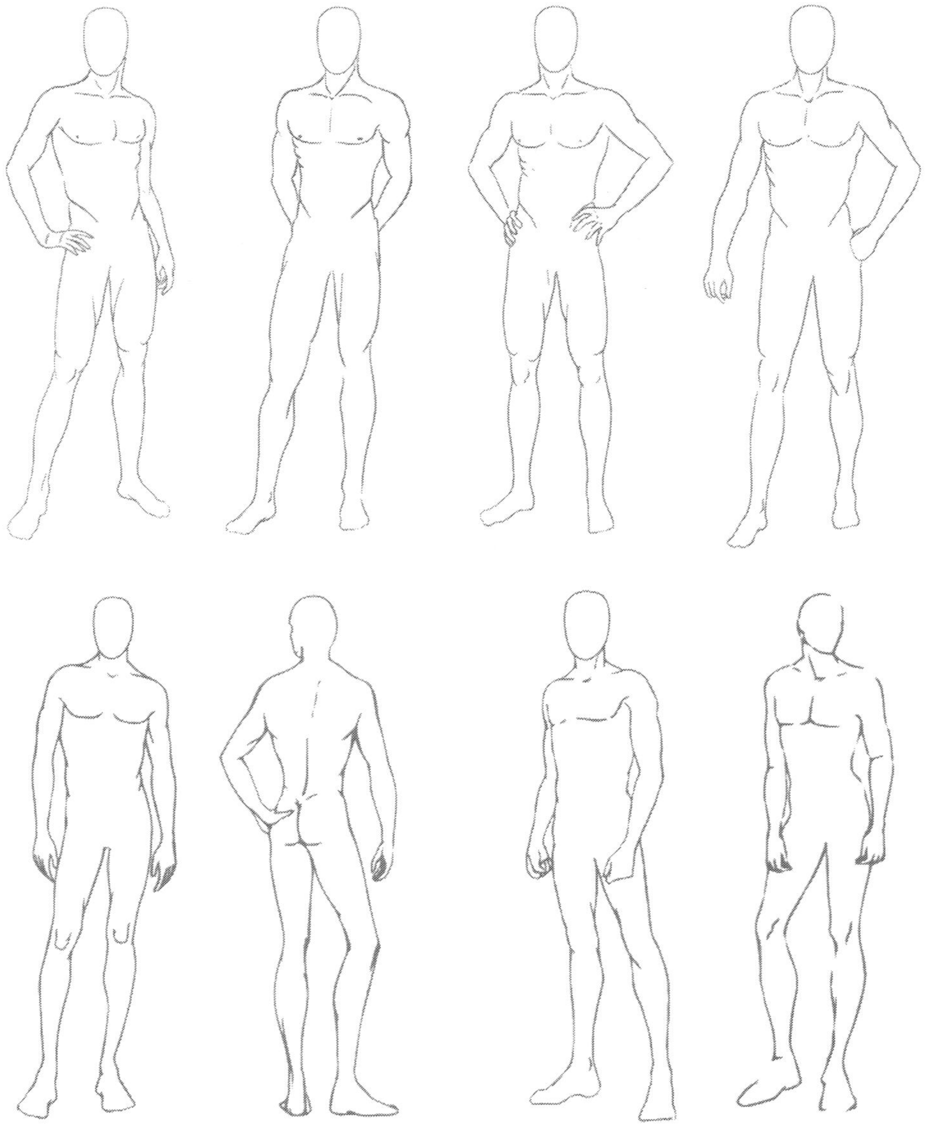

Lance Publishing Studio

Lance Derrick

lancepublish.com

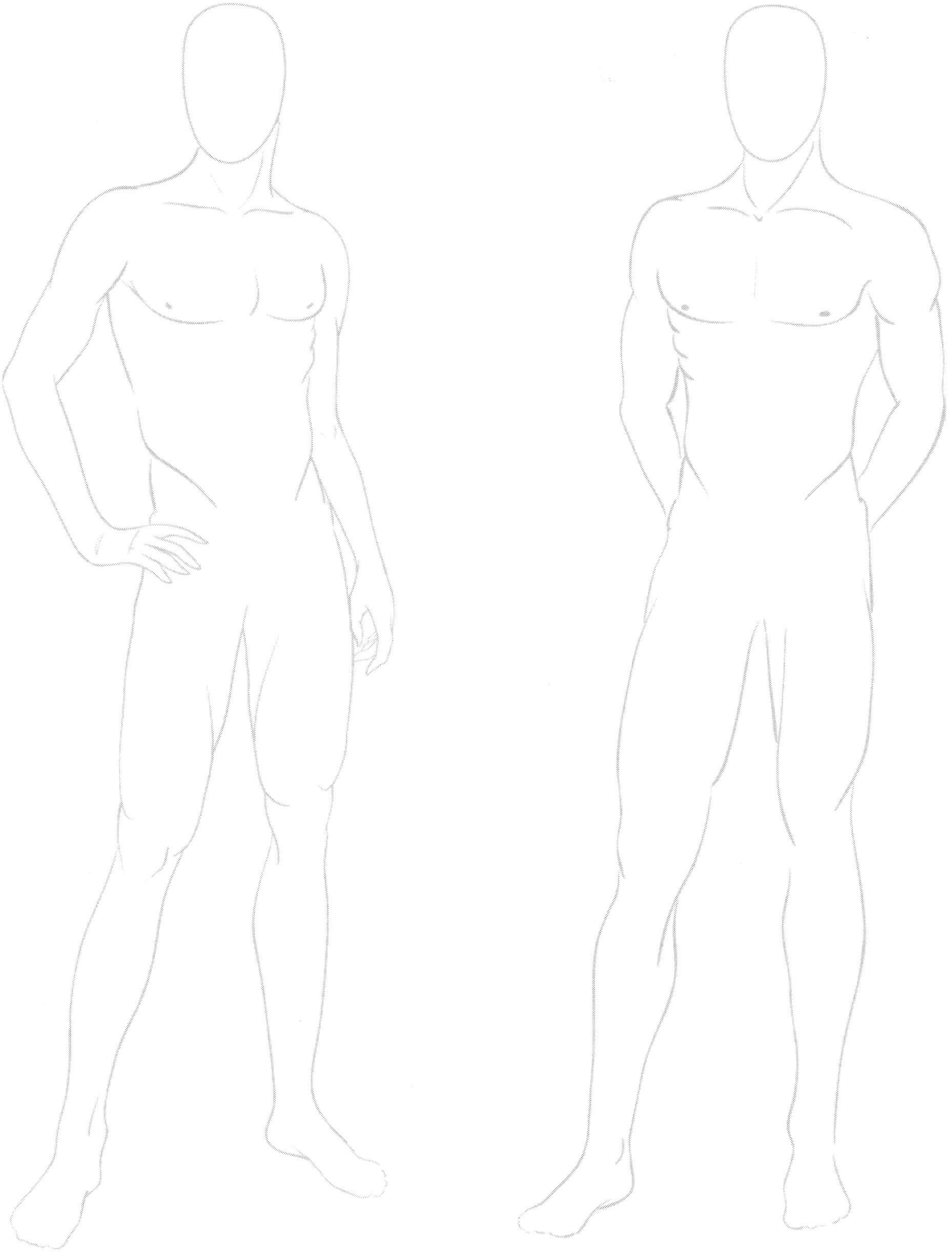

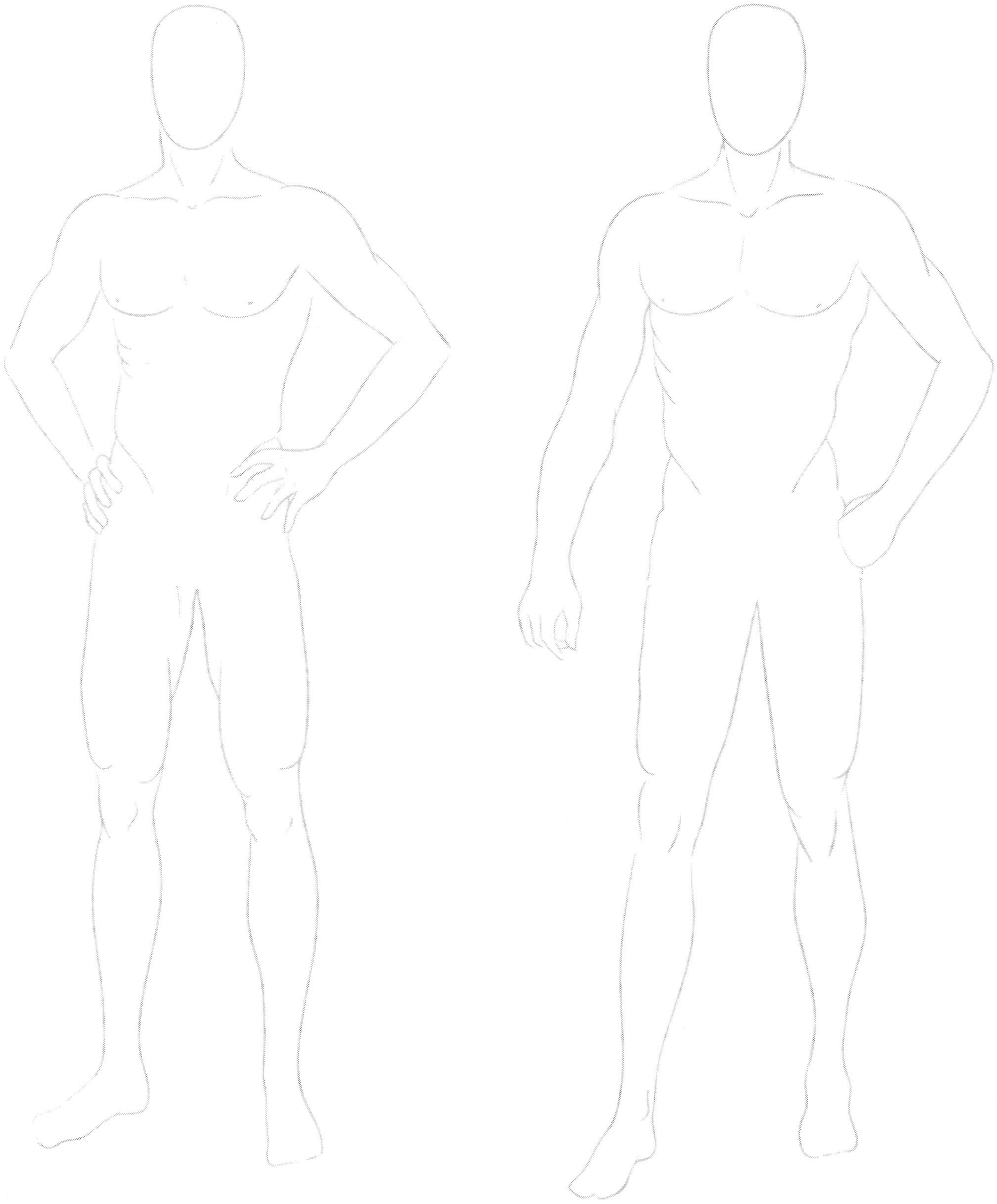

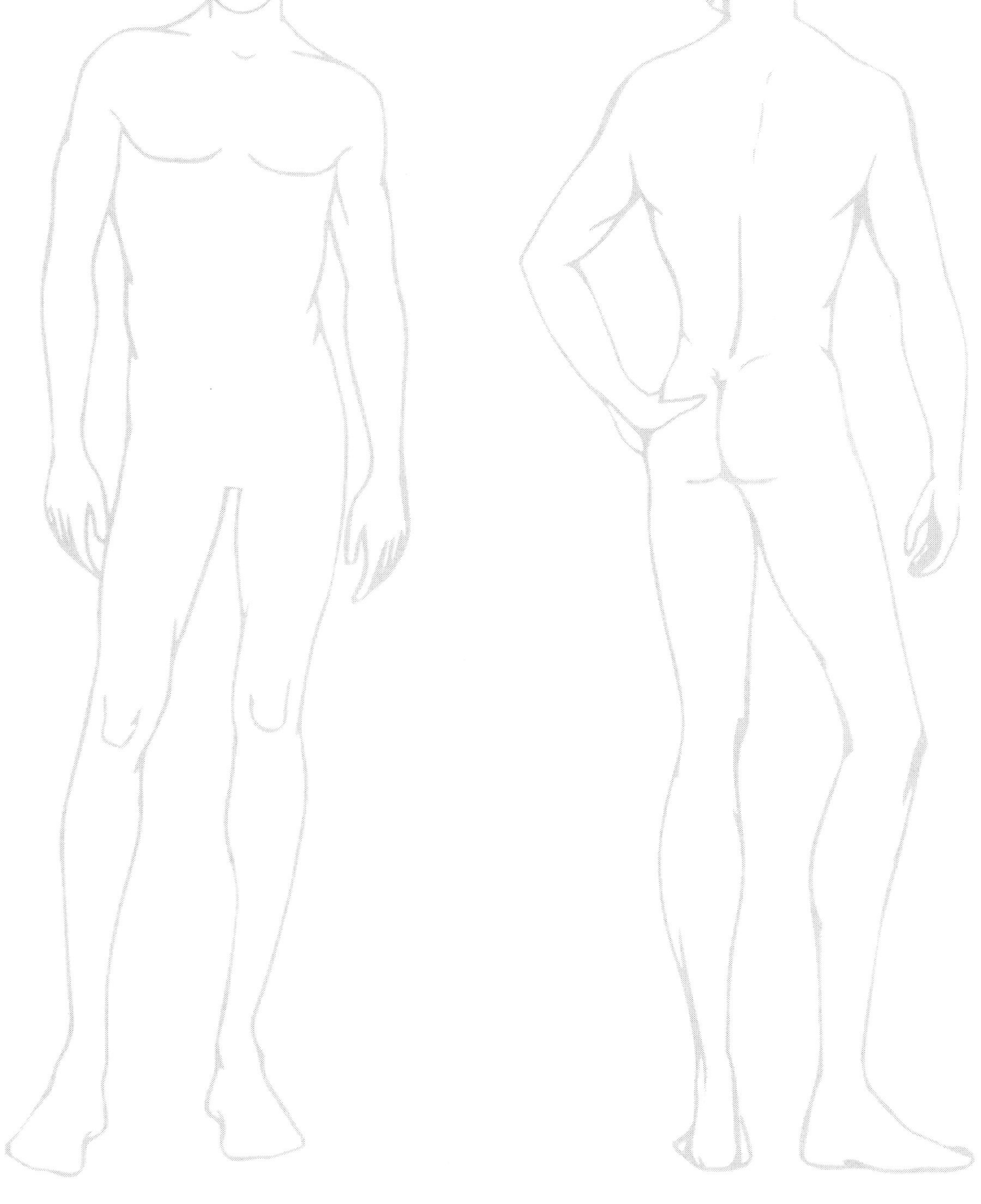

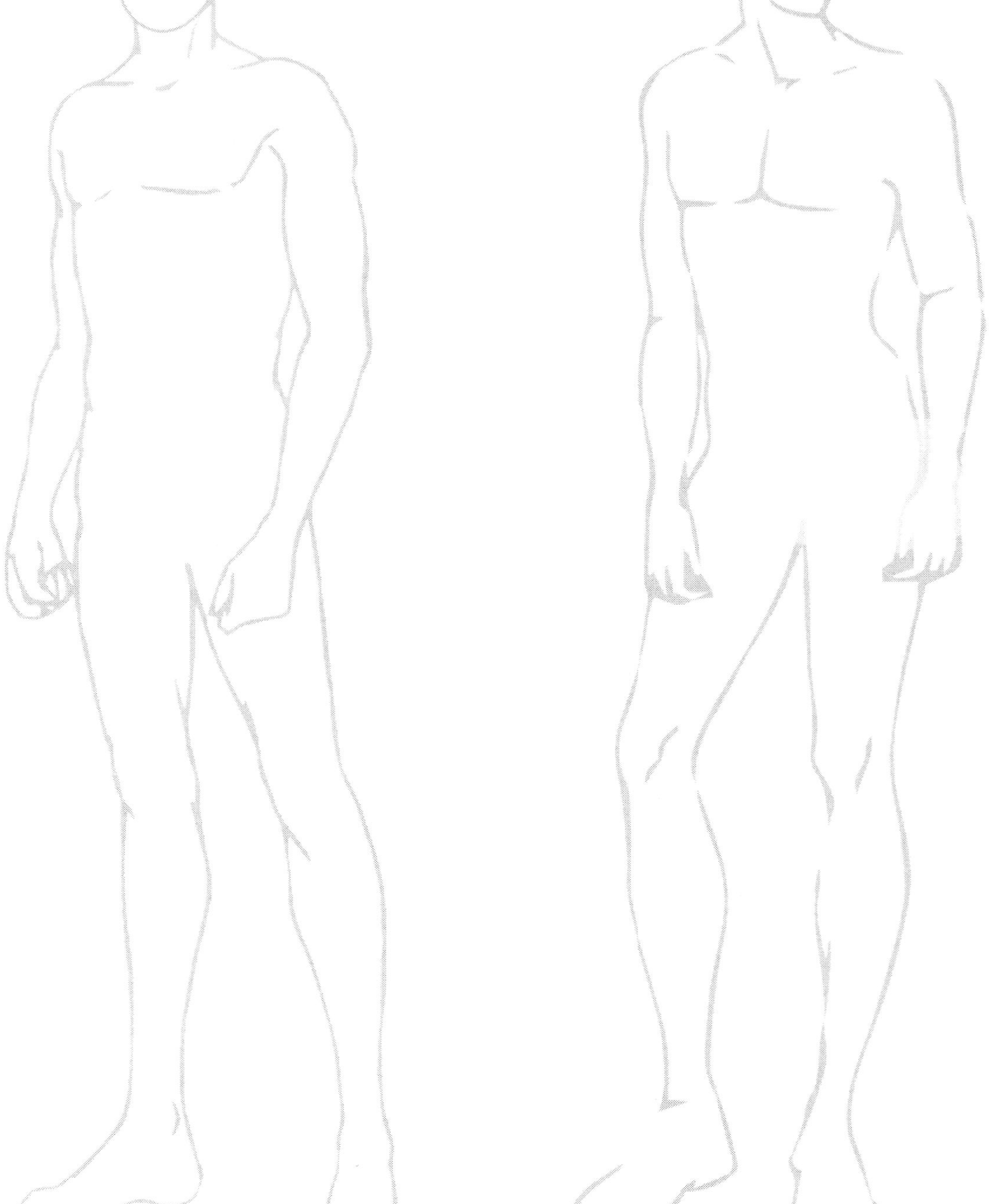

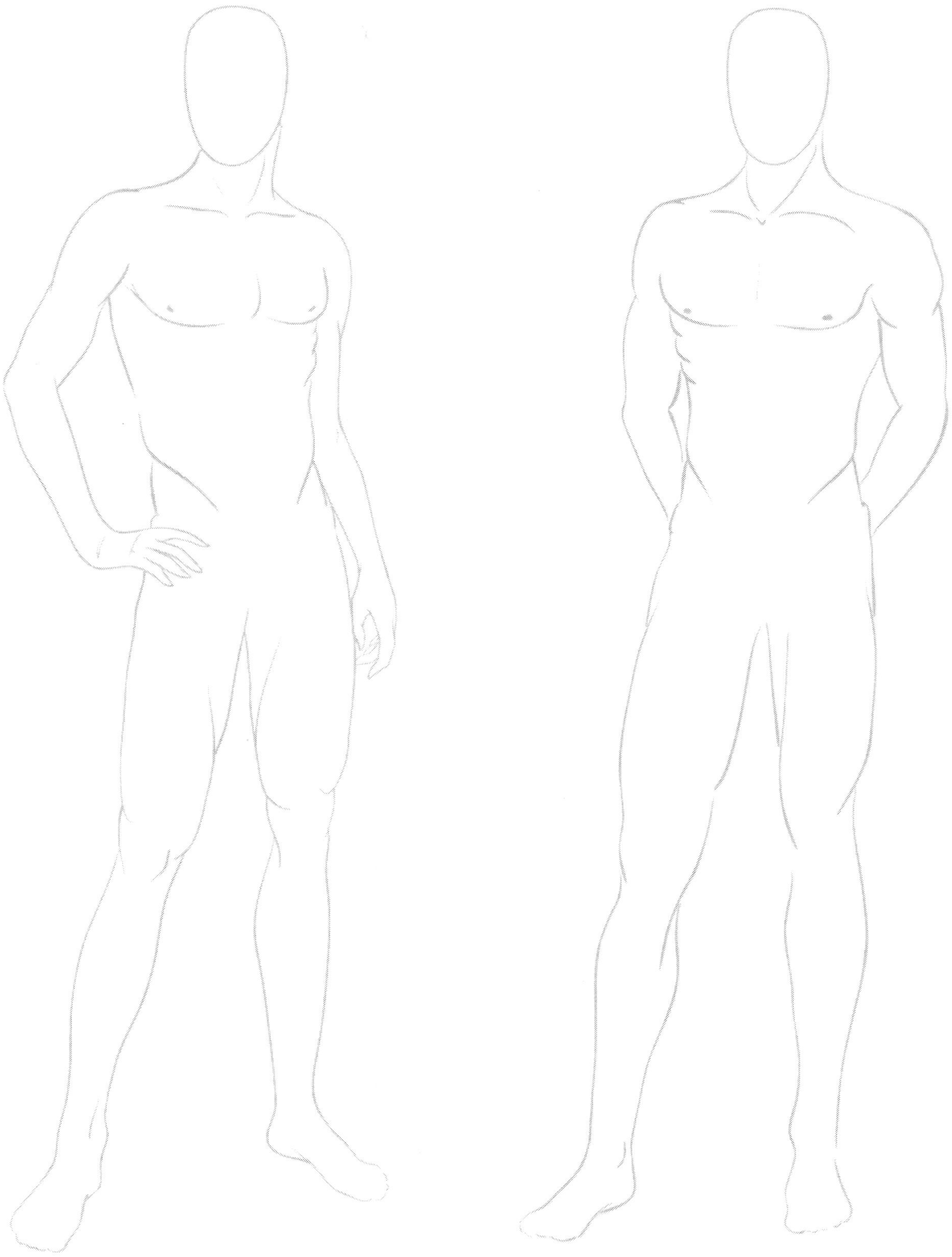

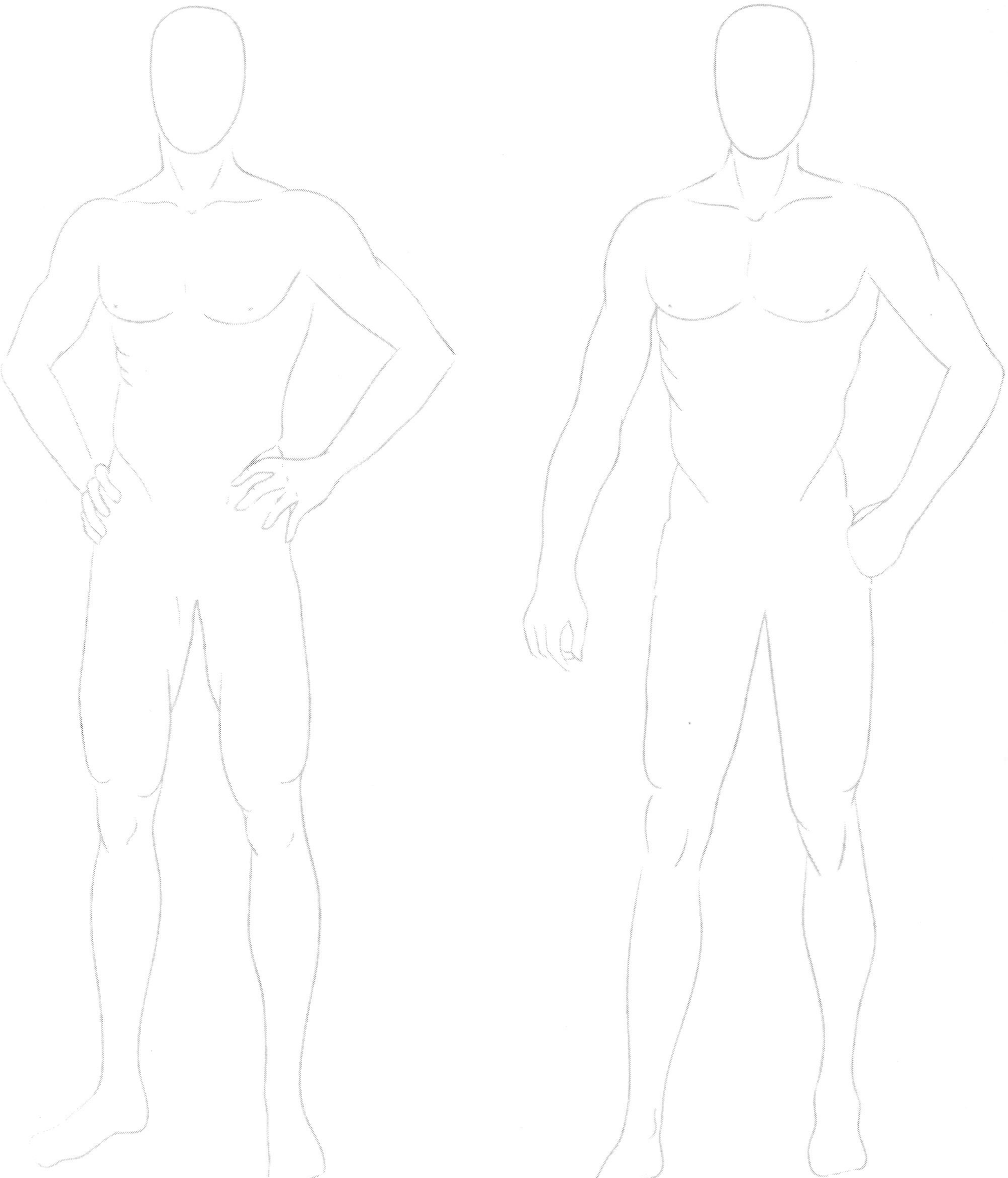

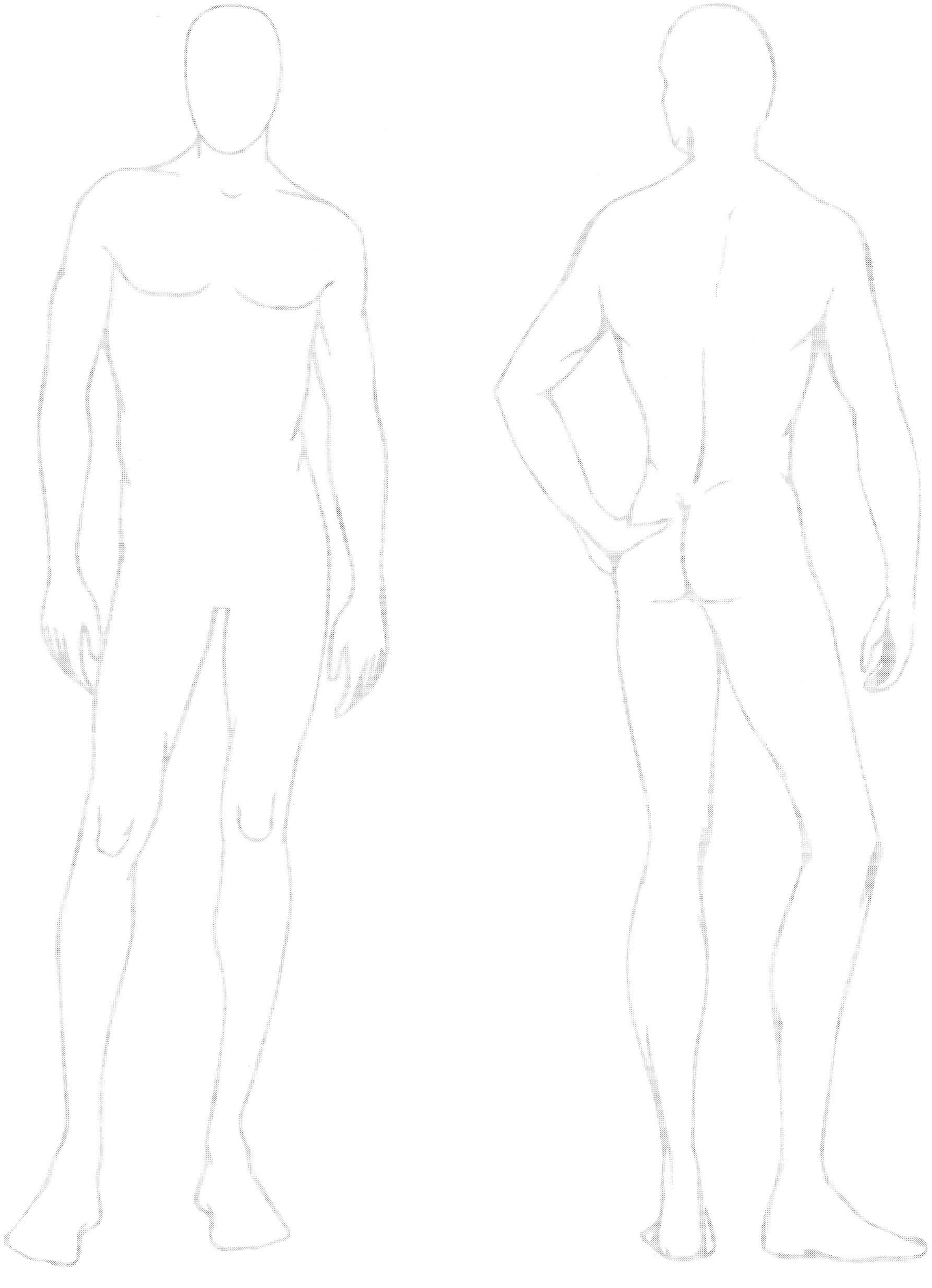

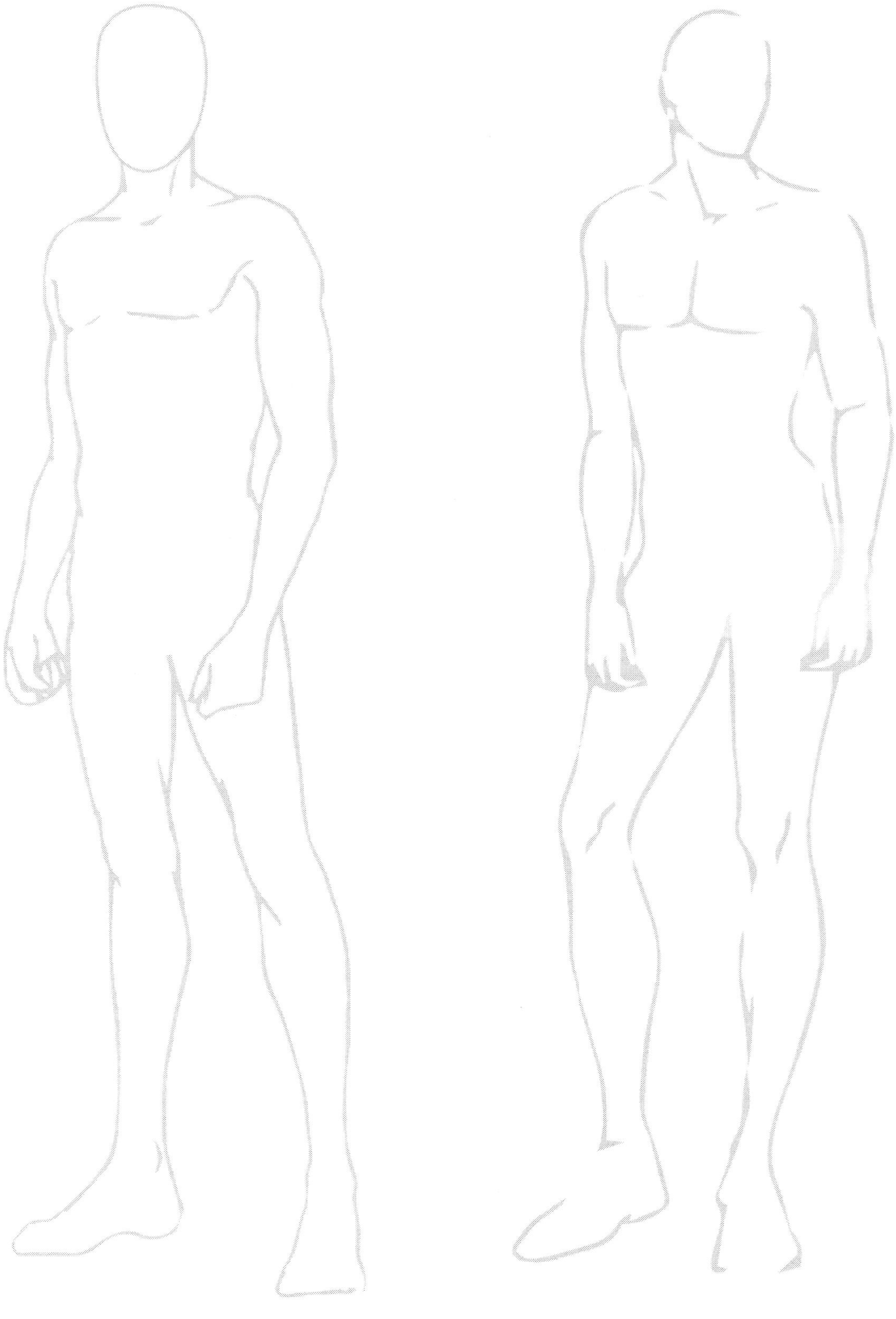

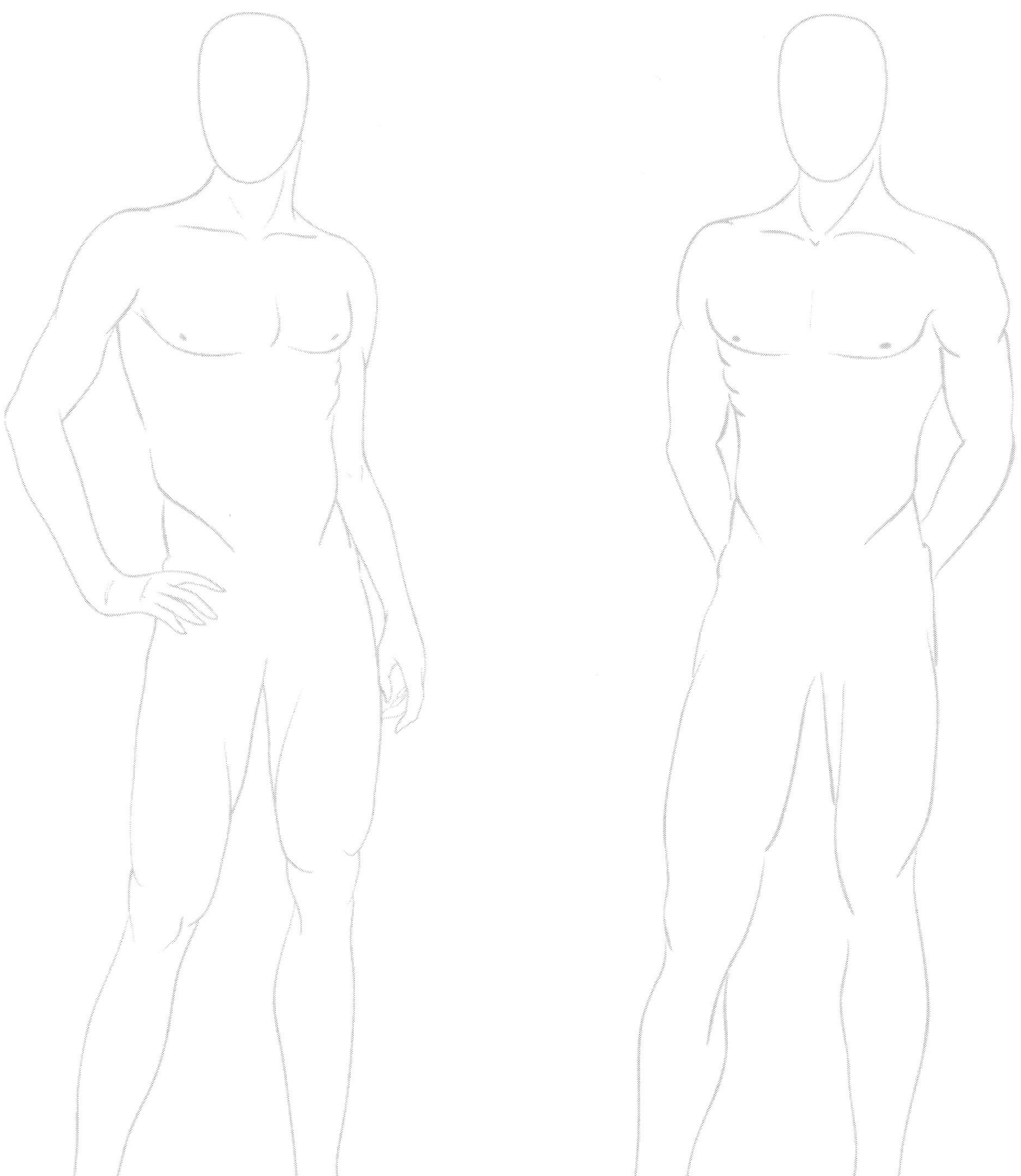

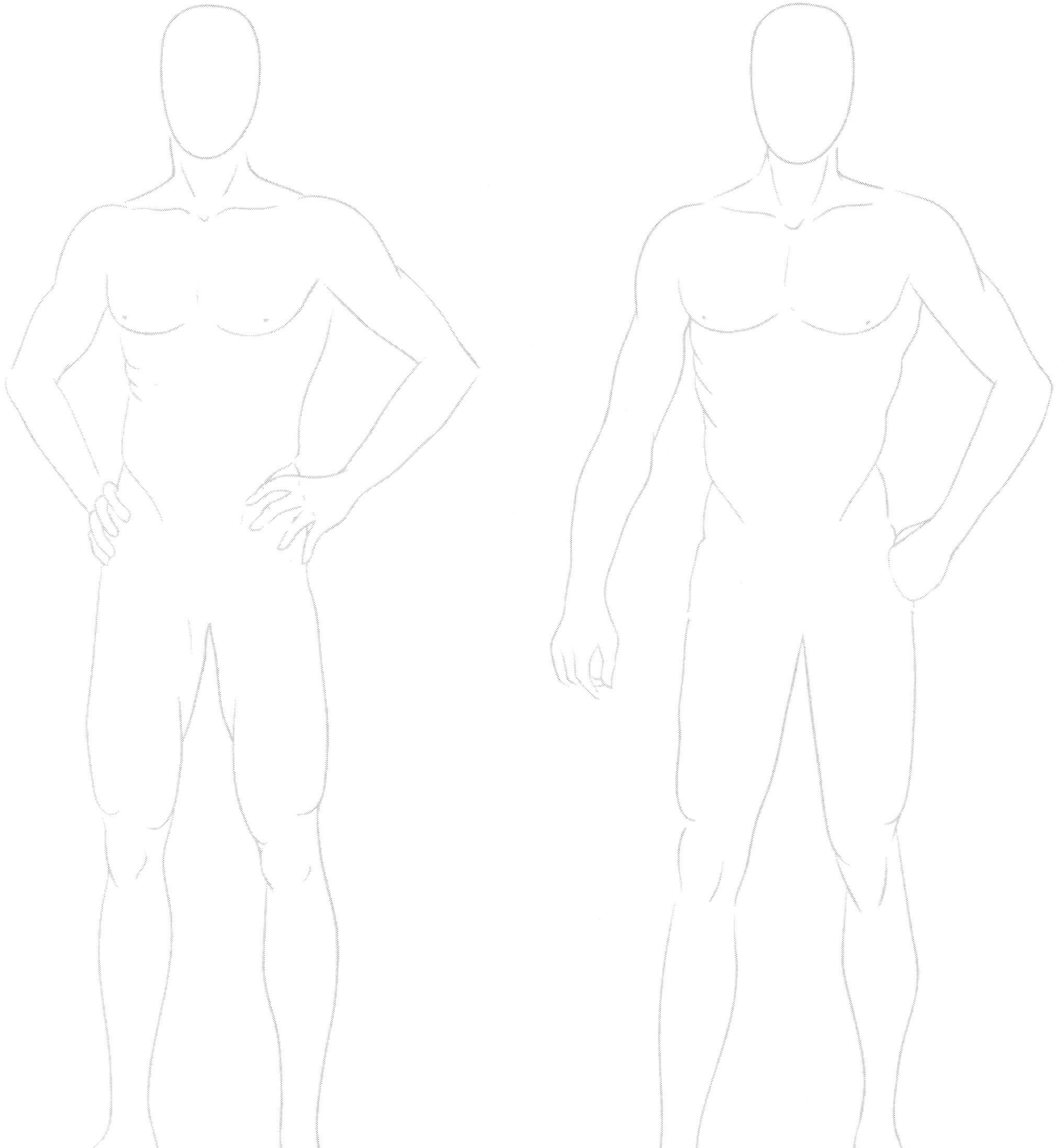

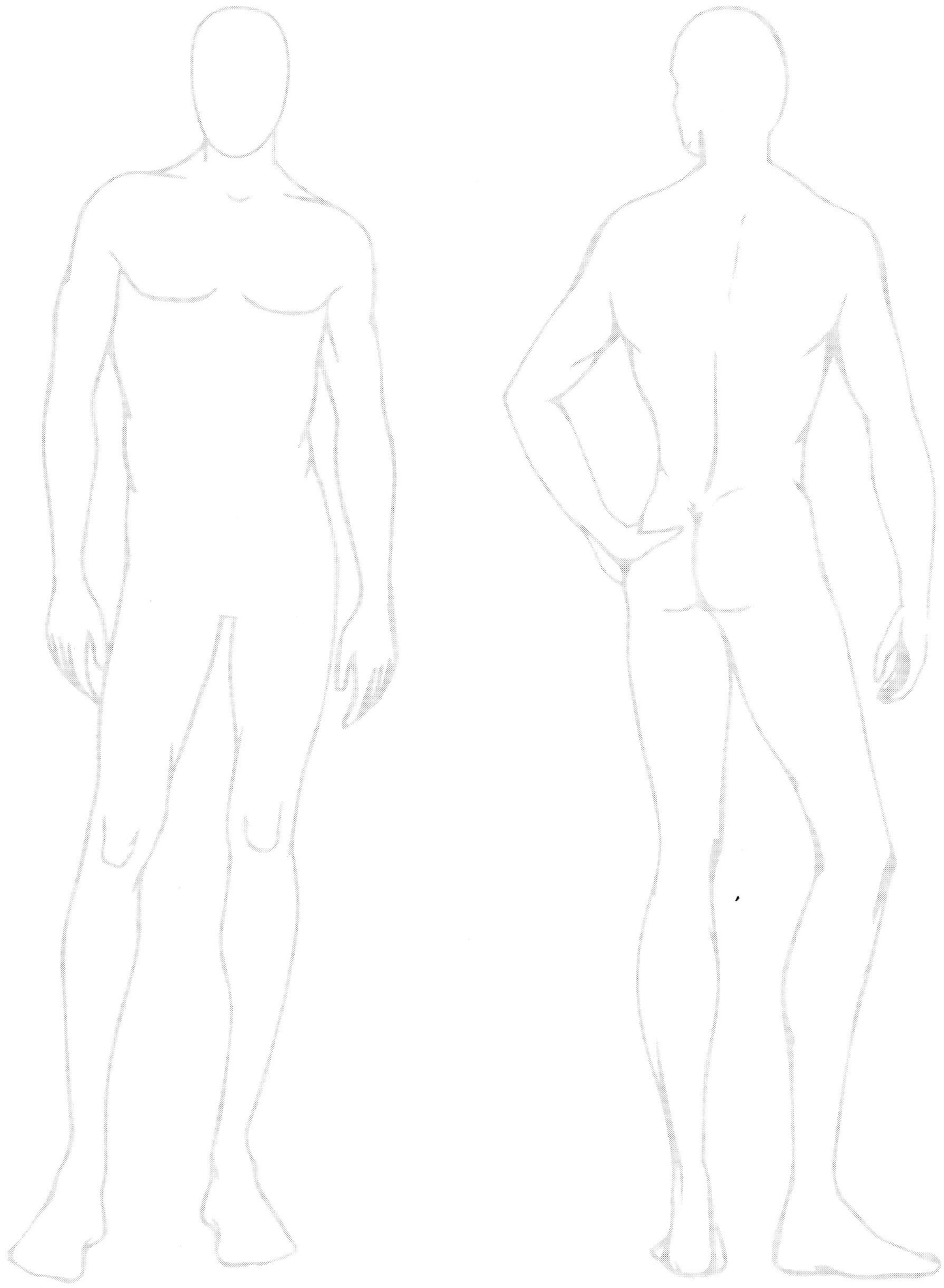

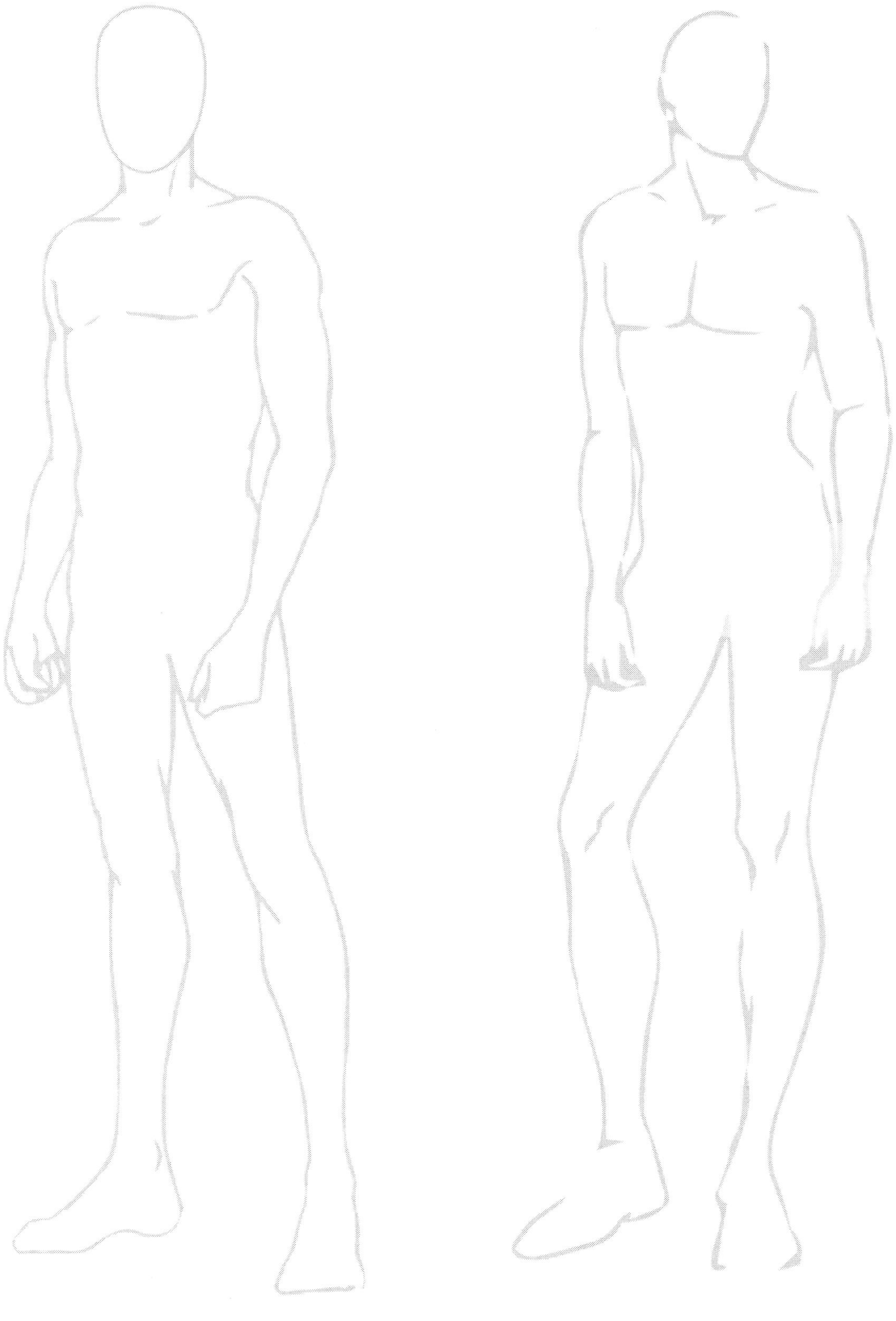

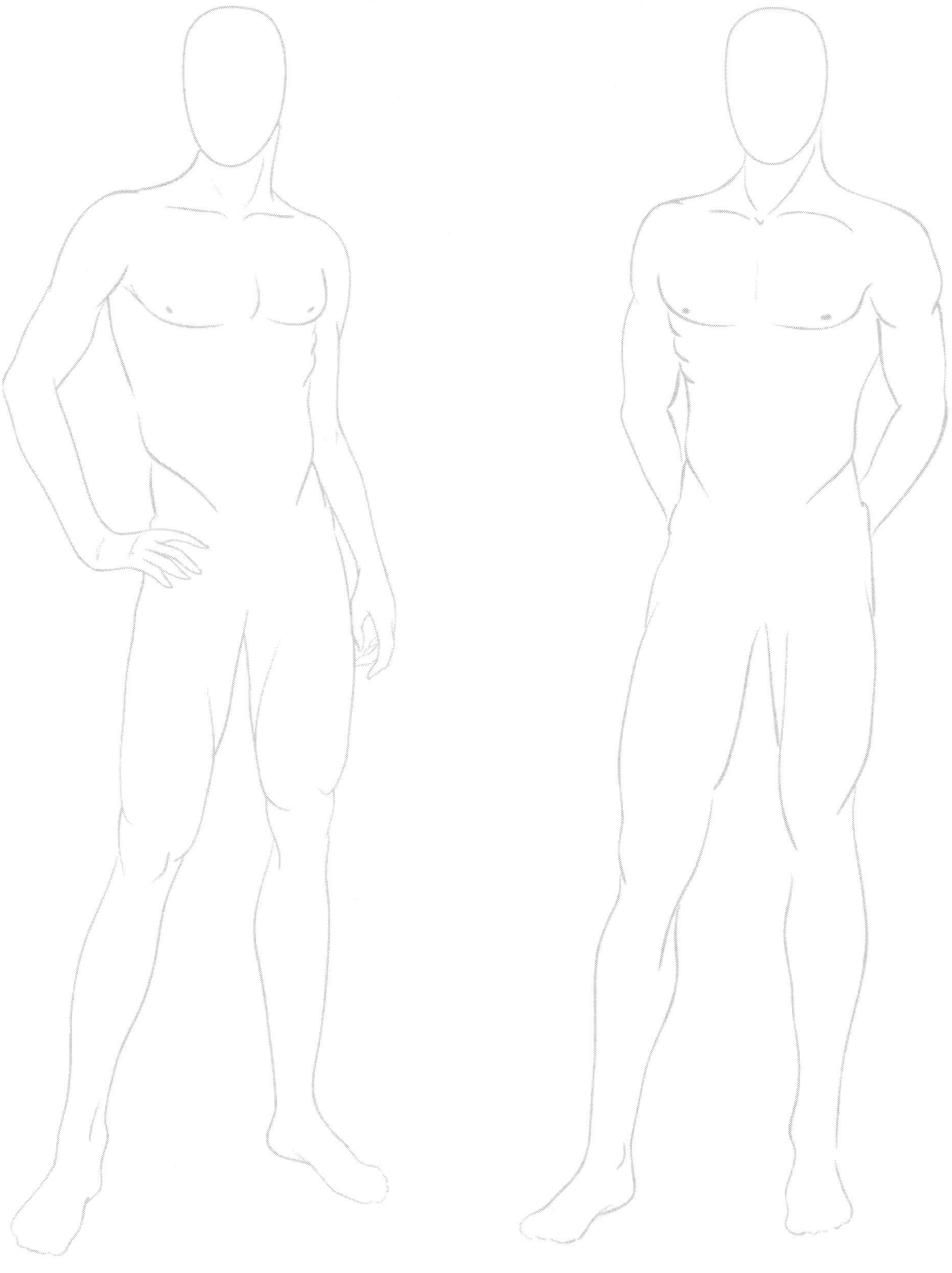

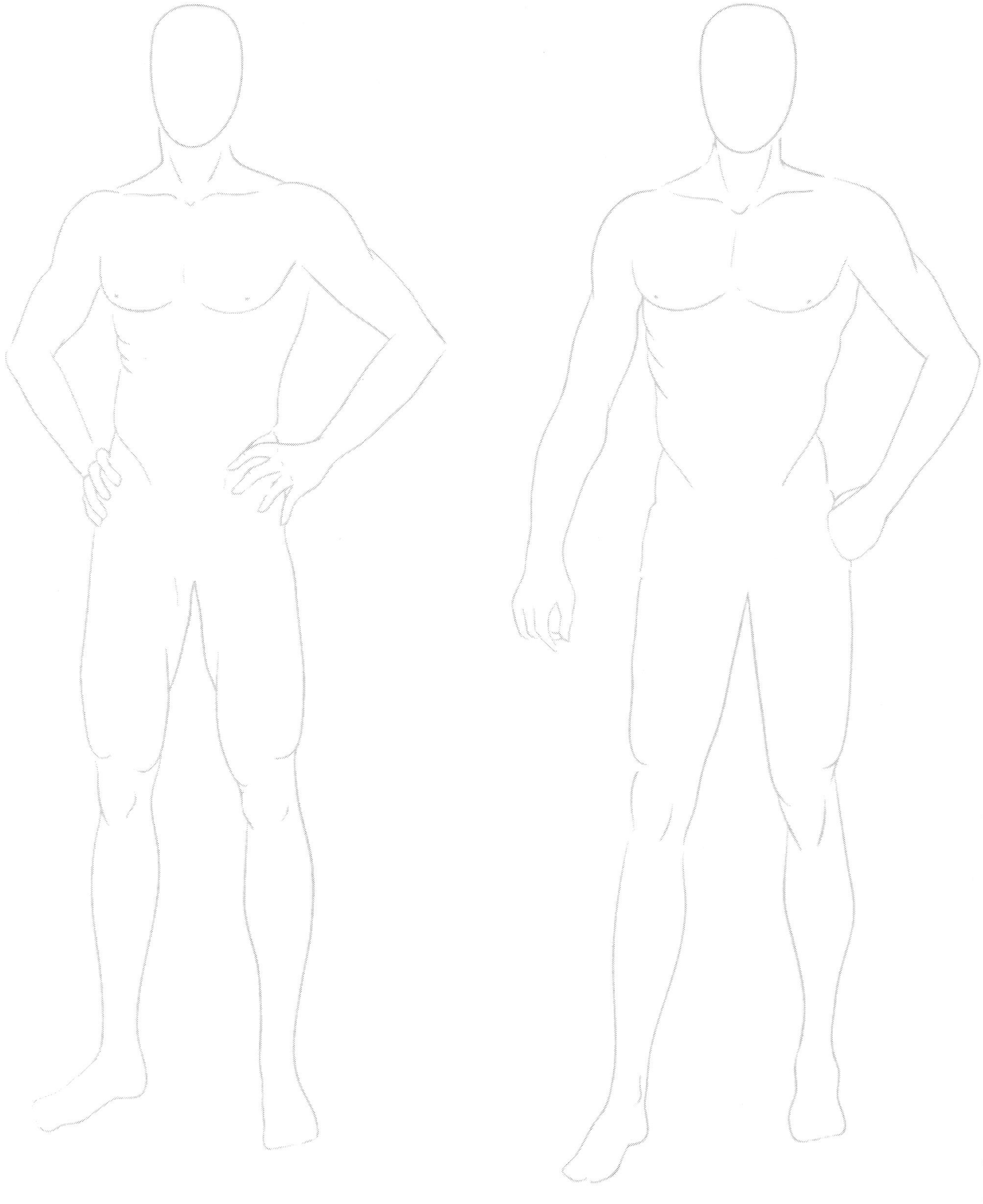

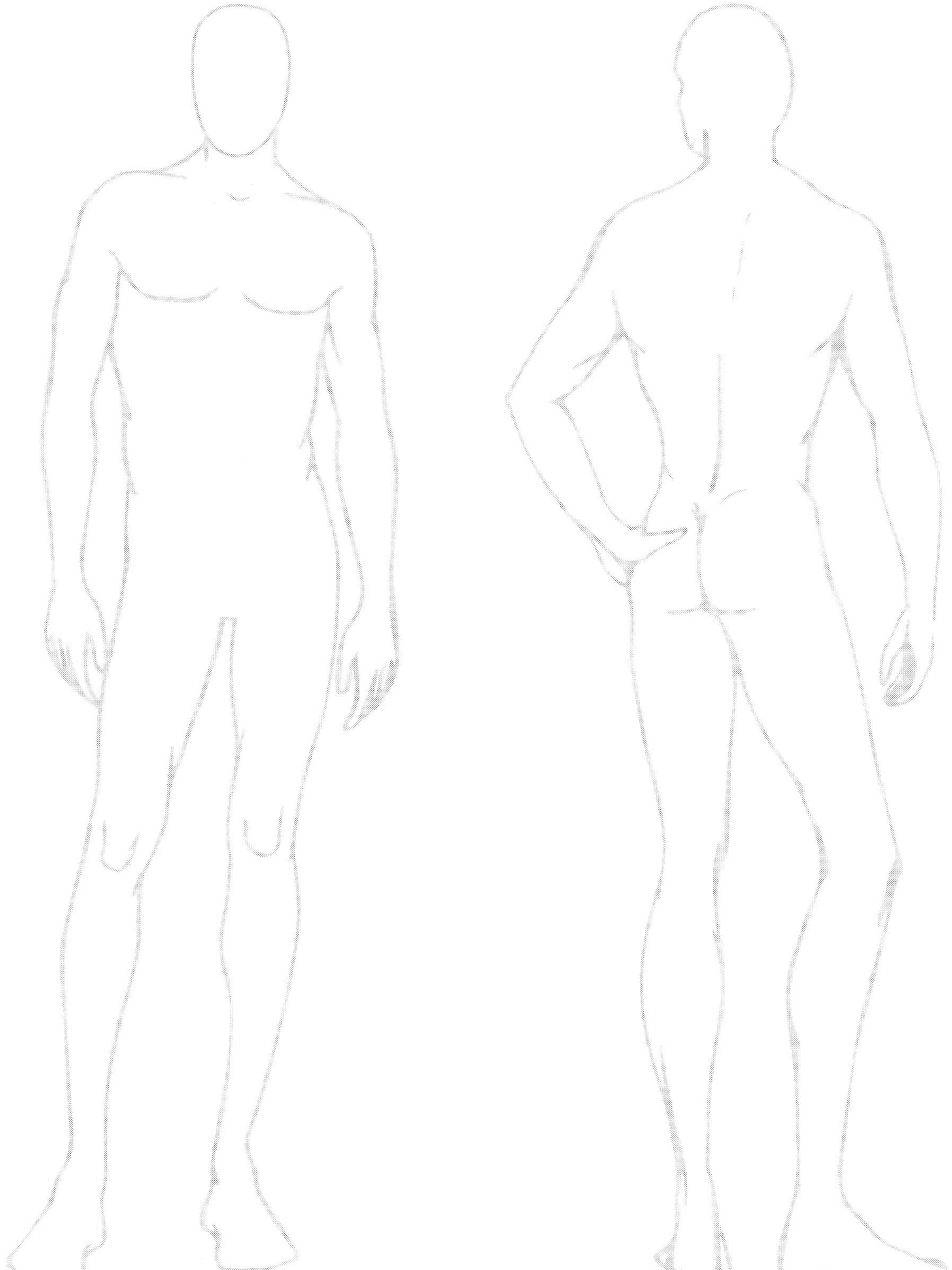

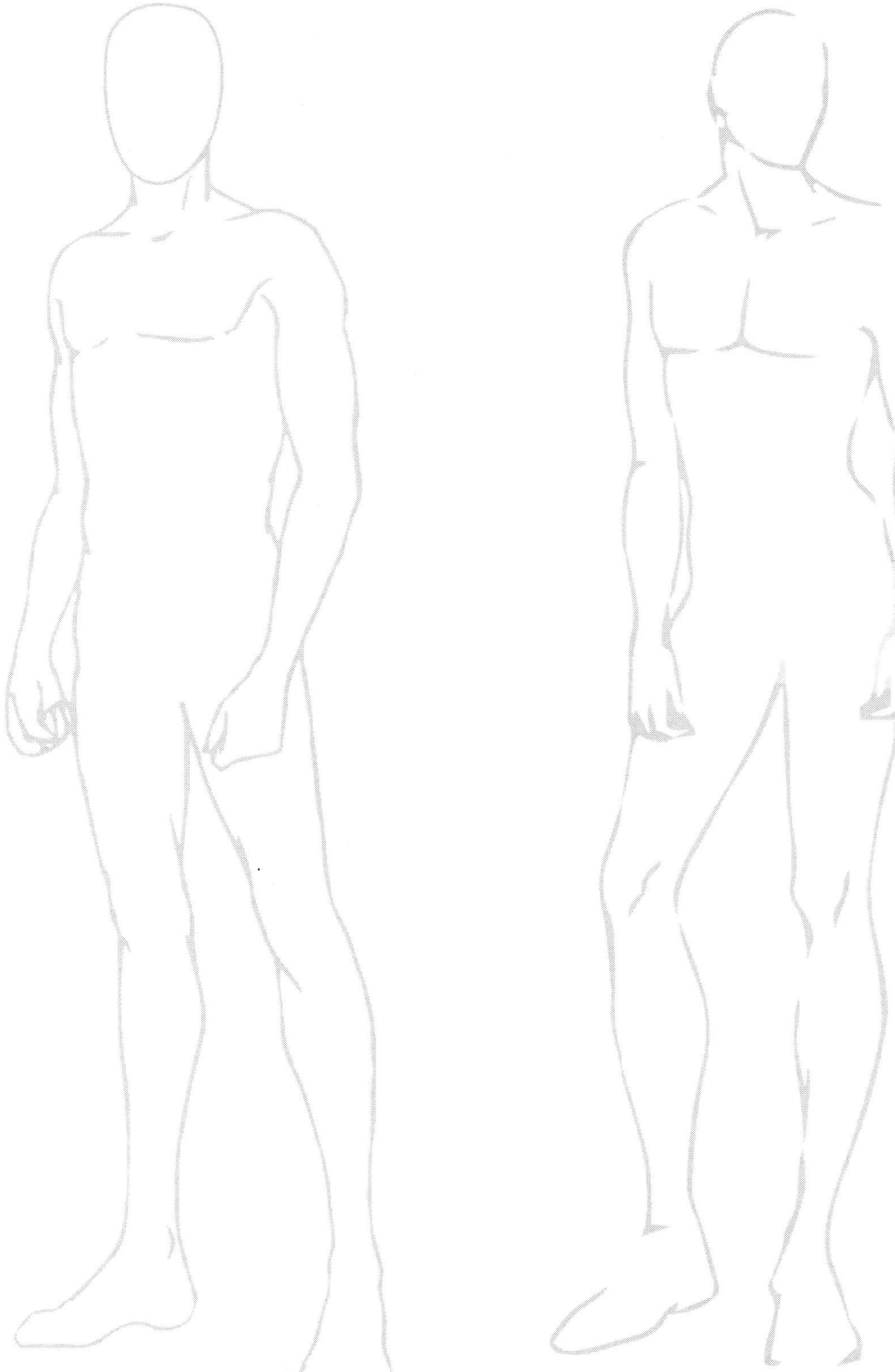

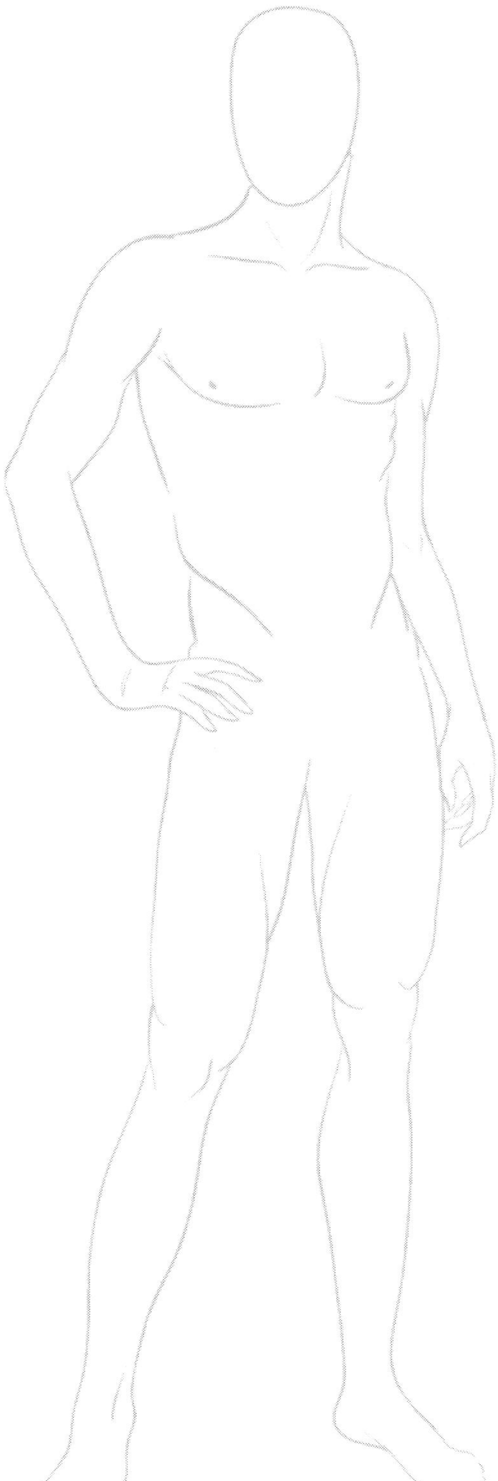

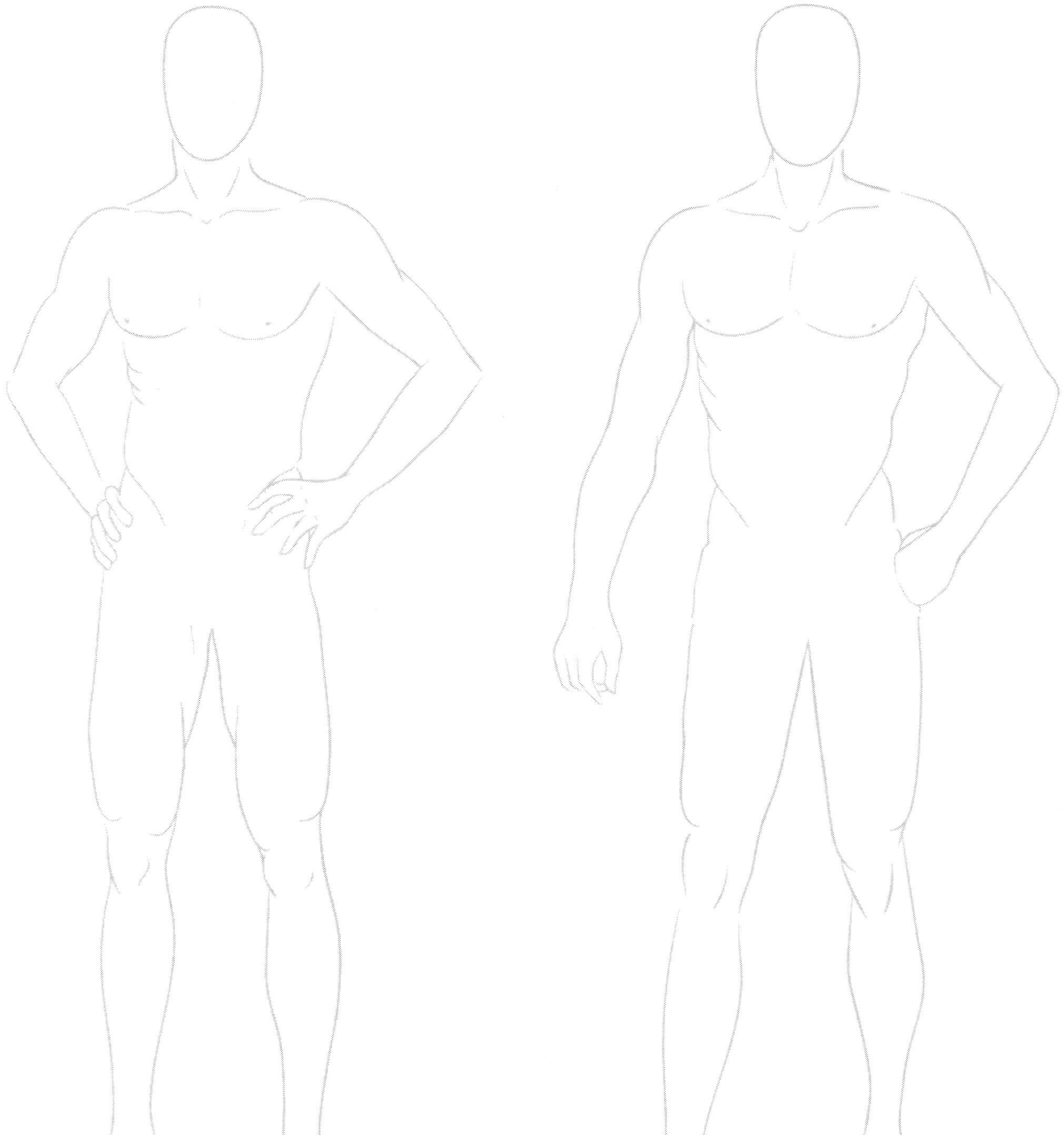

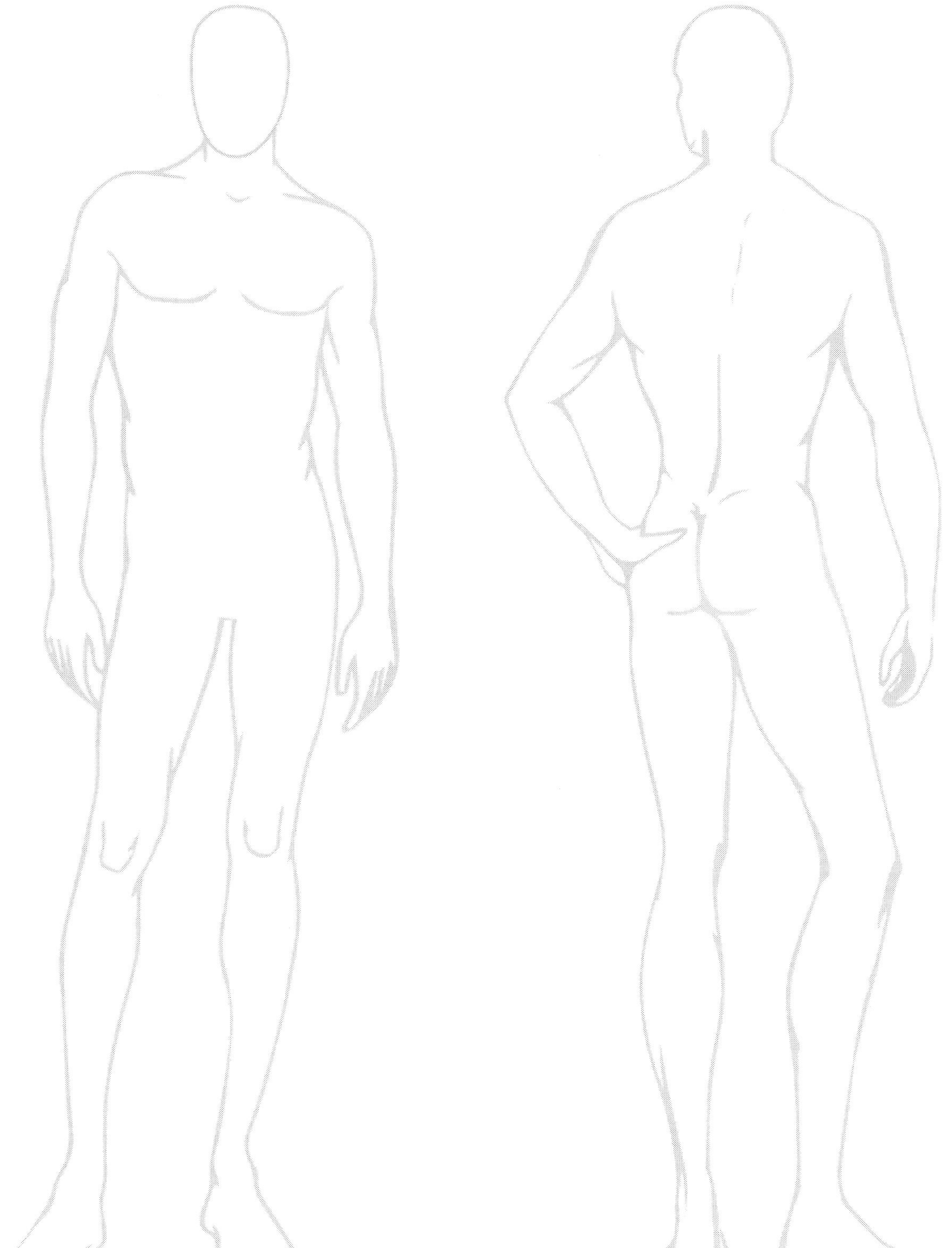

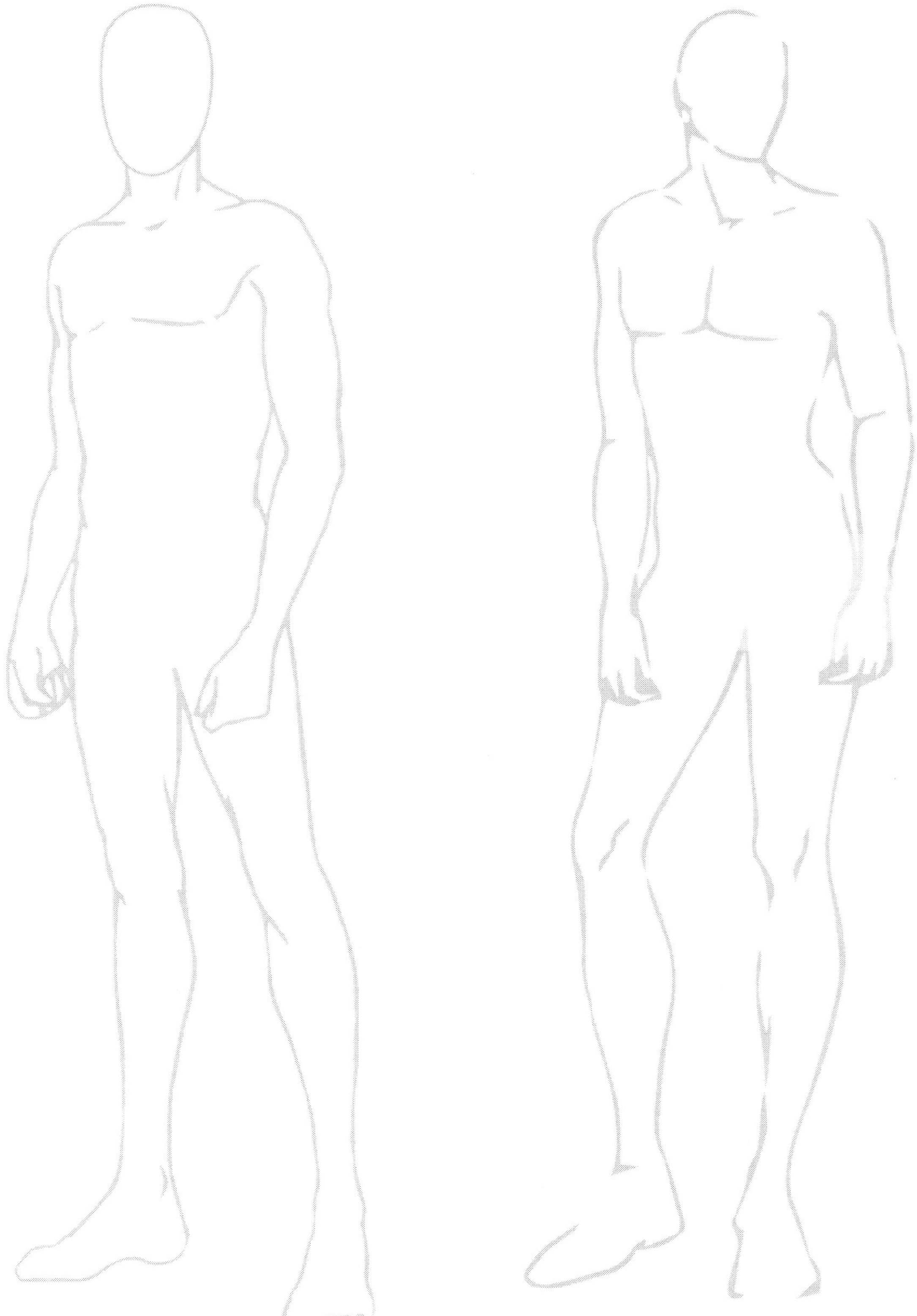

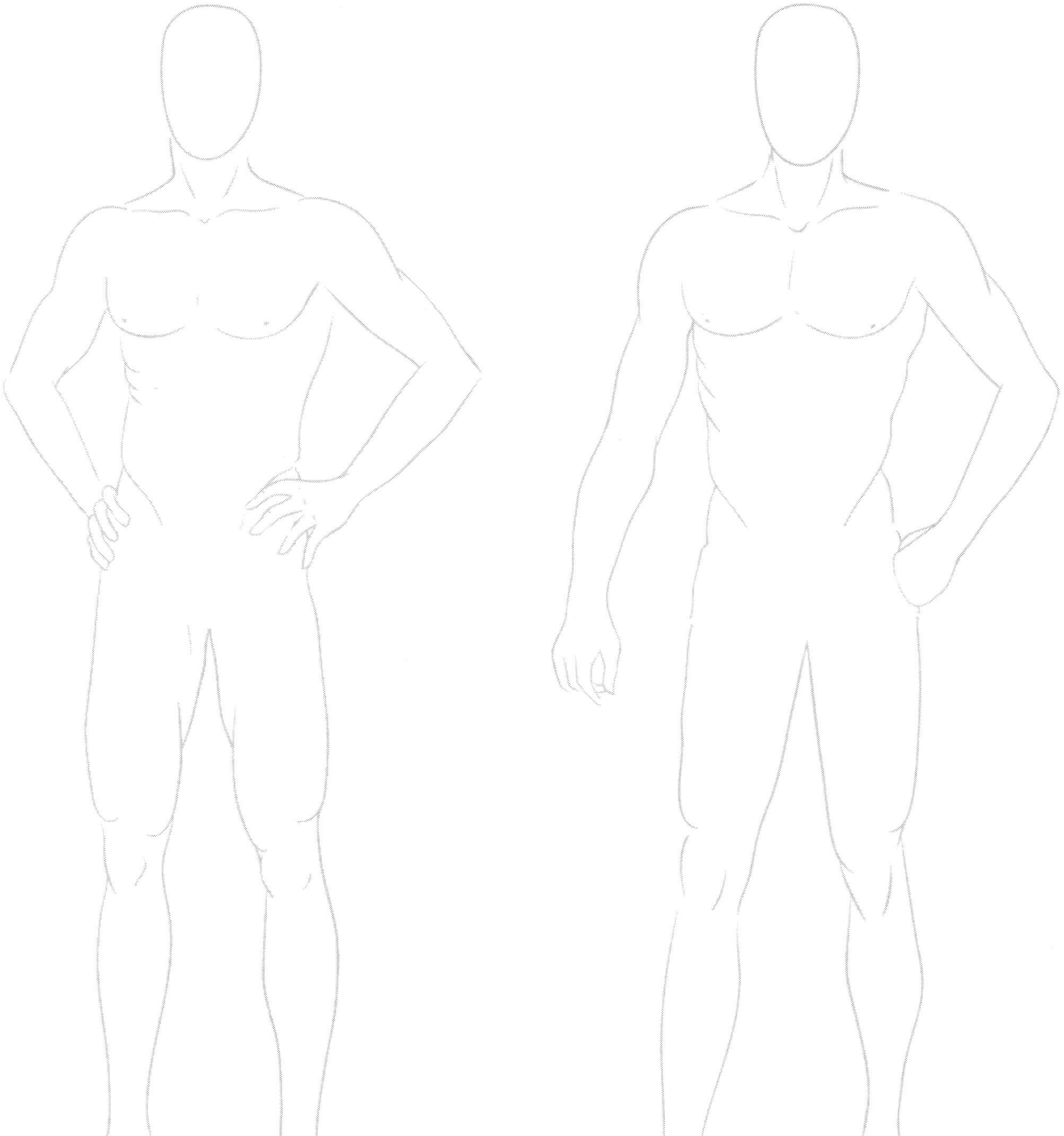

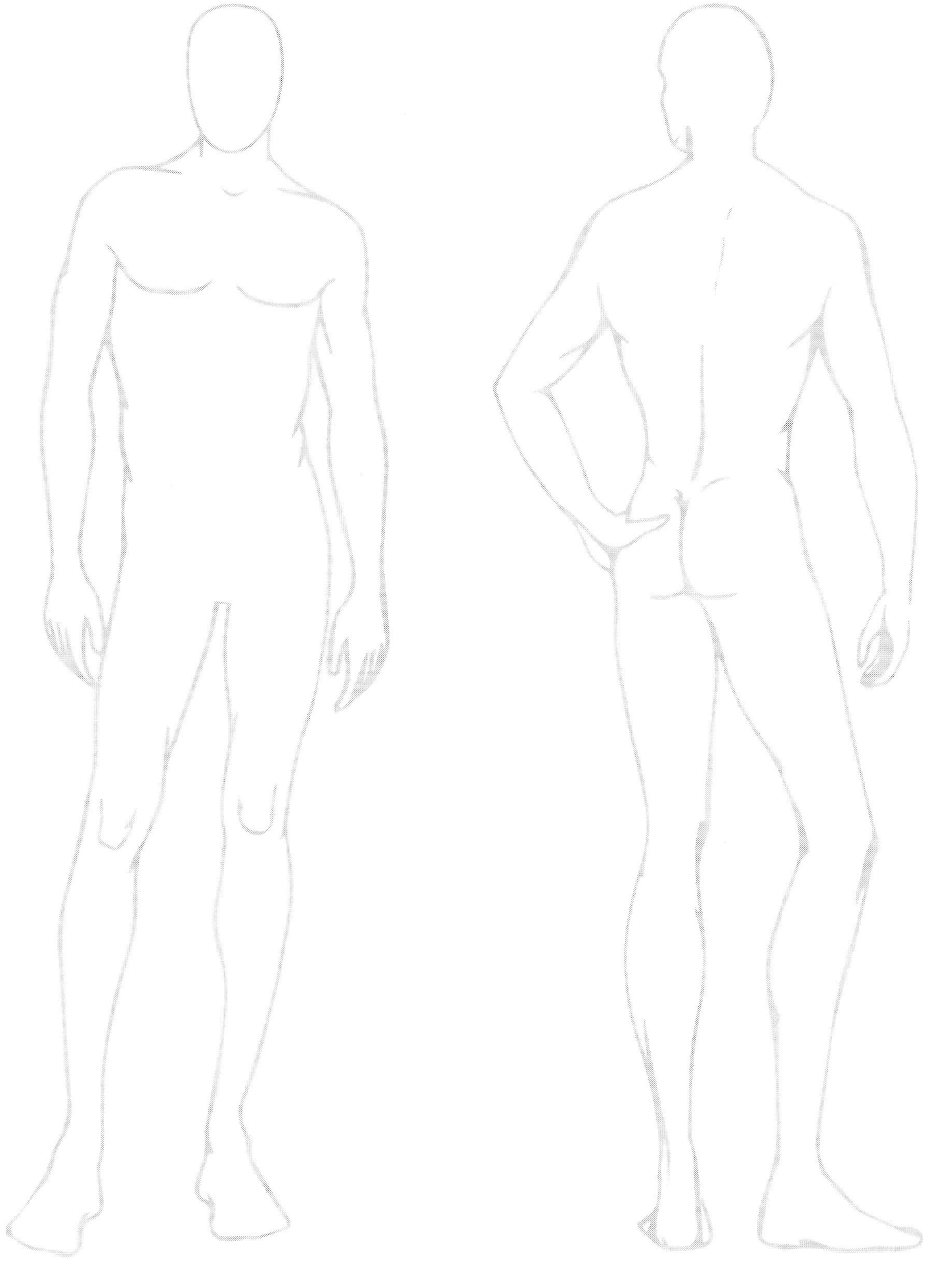

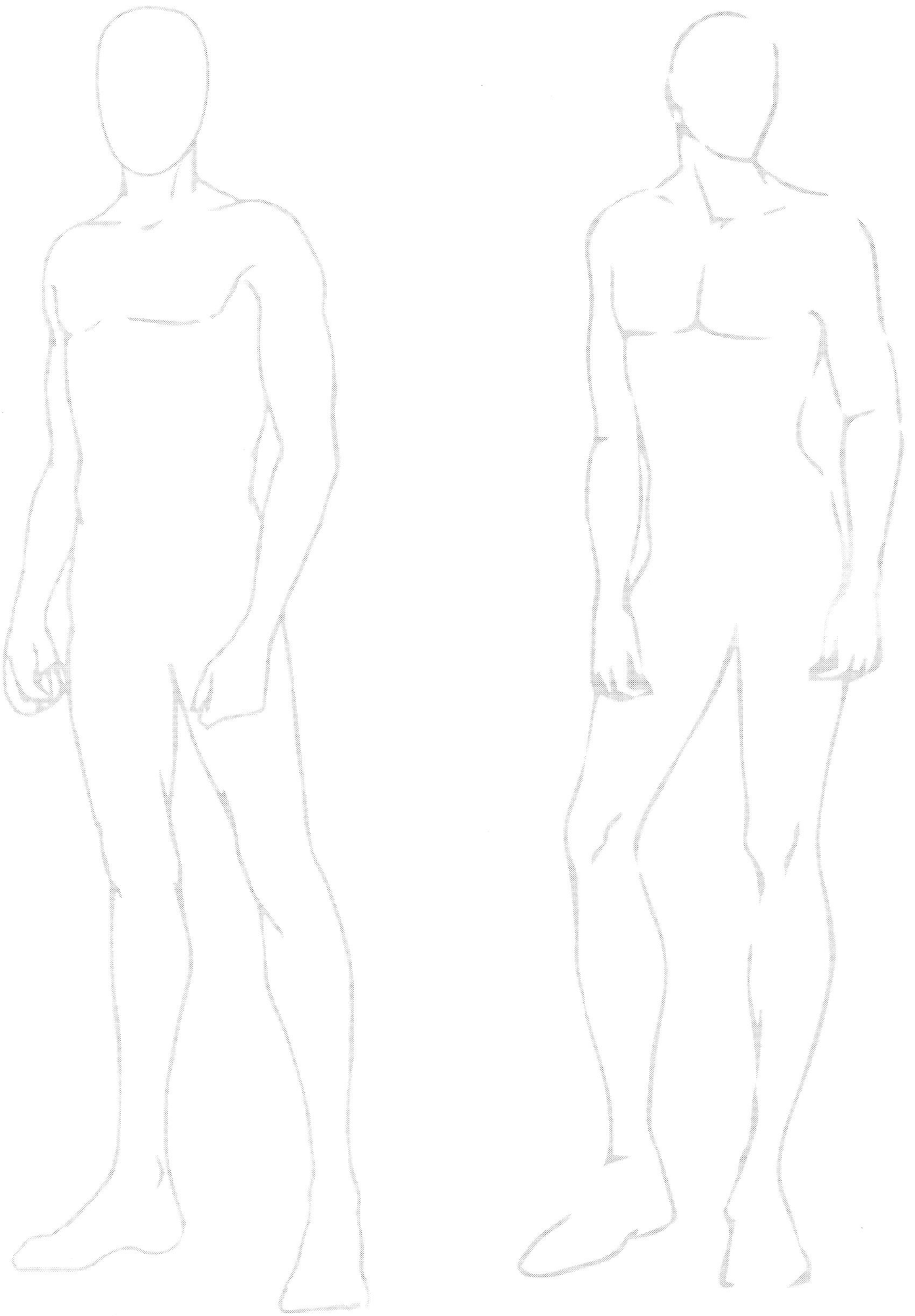

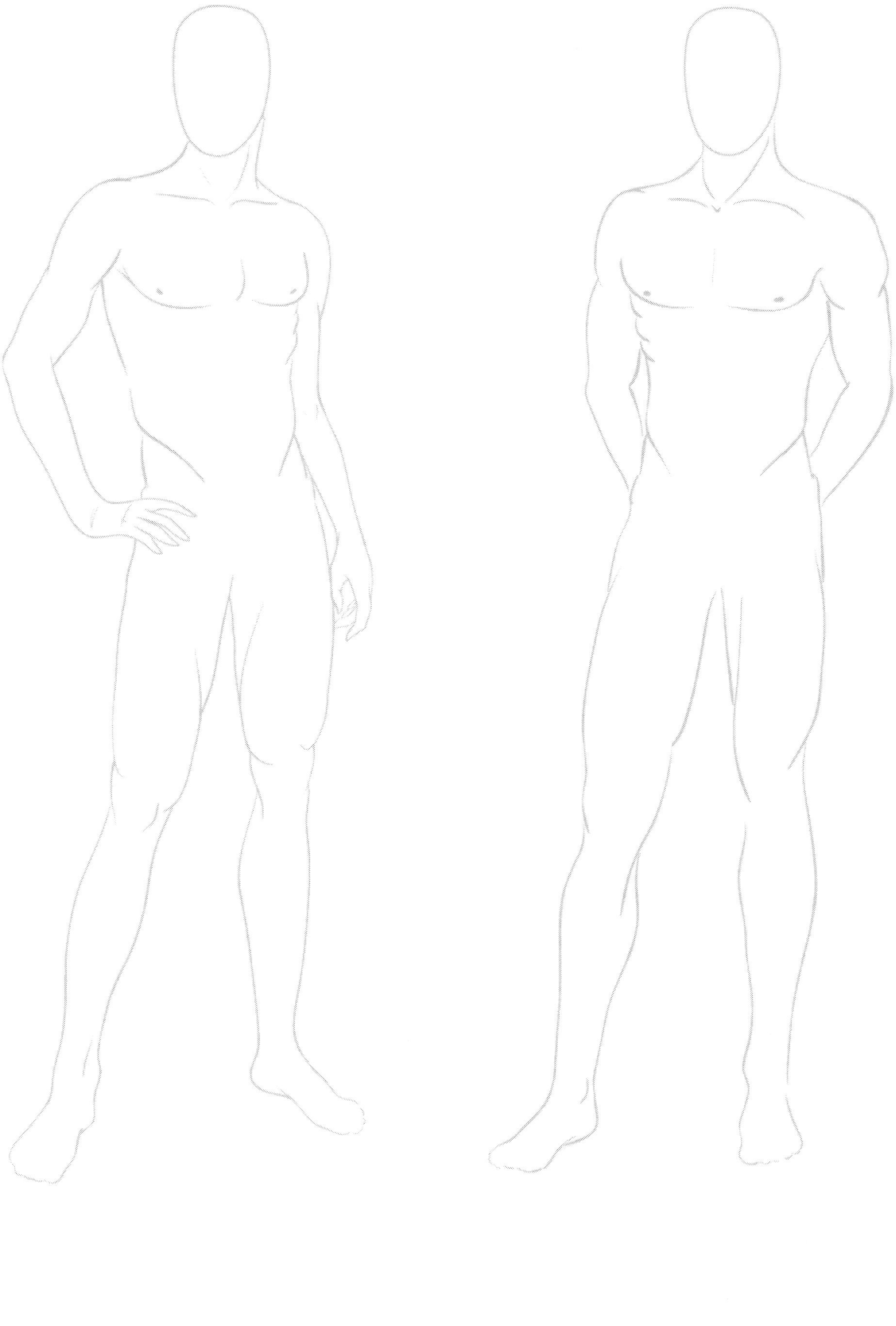

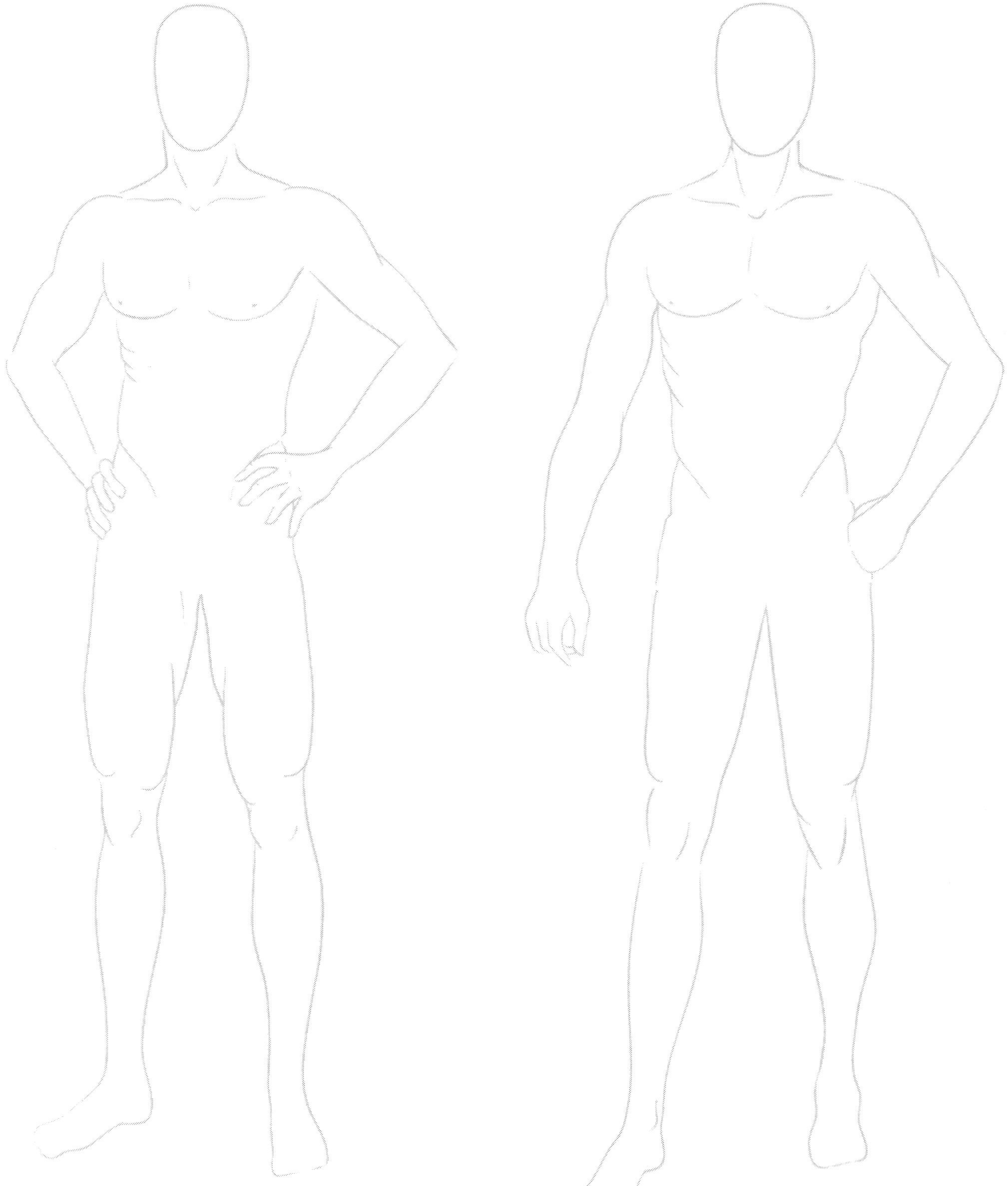

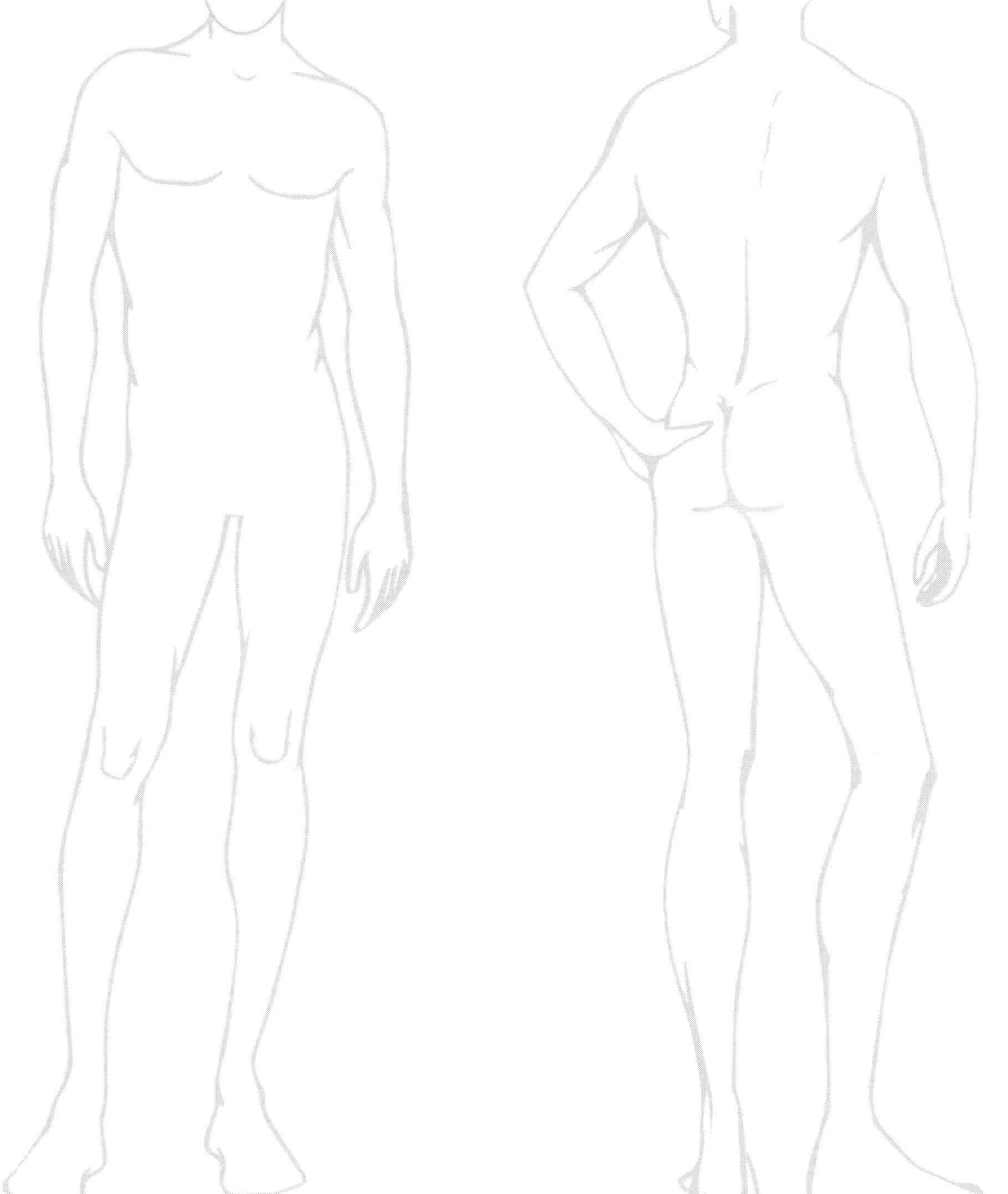

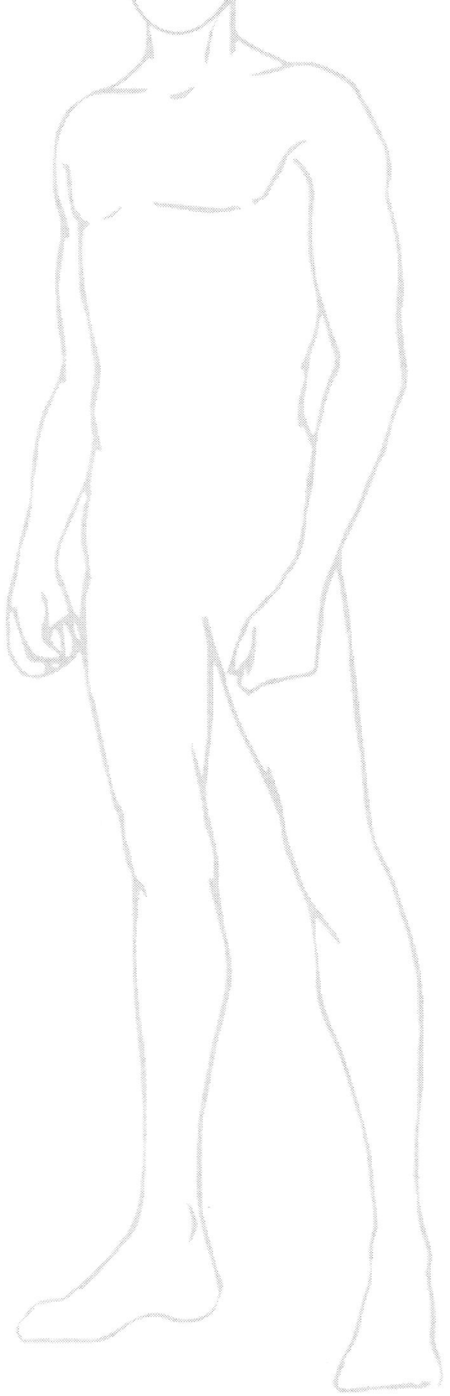
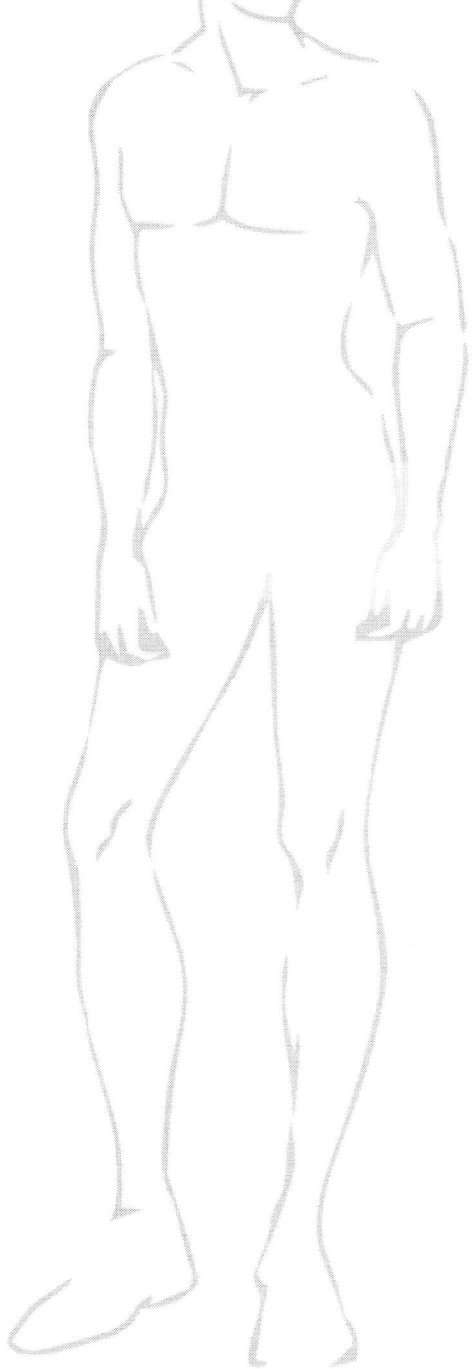

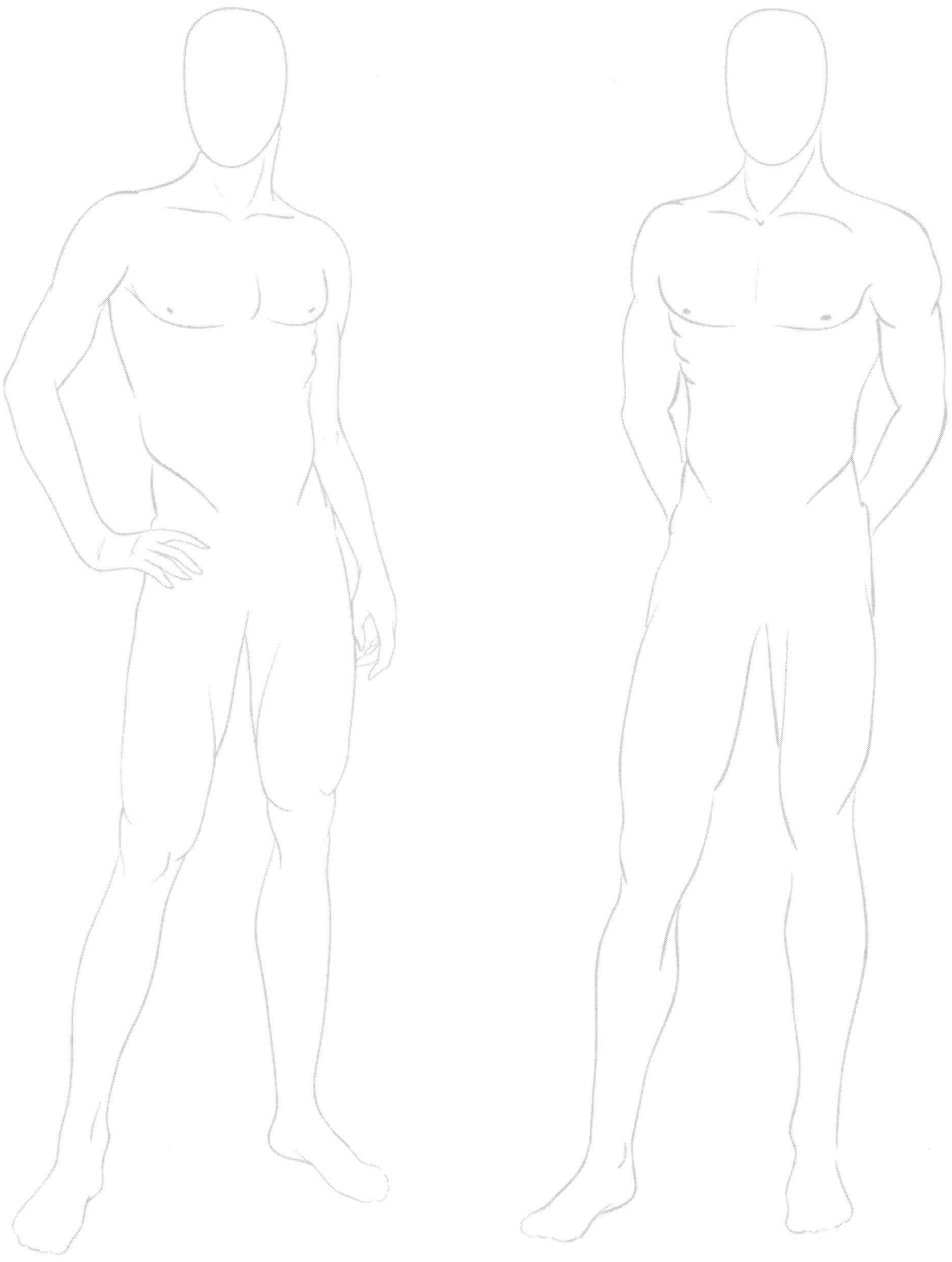

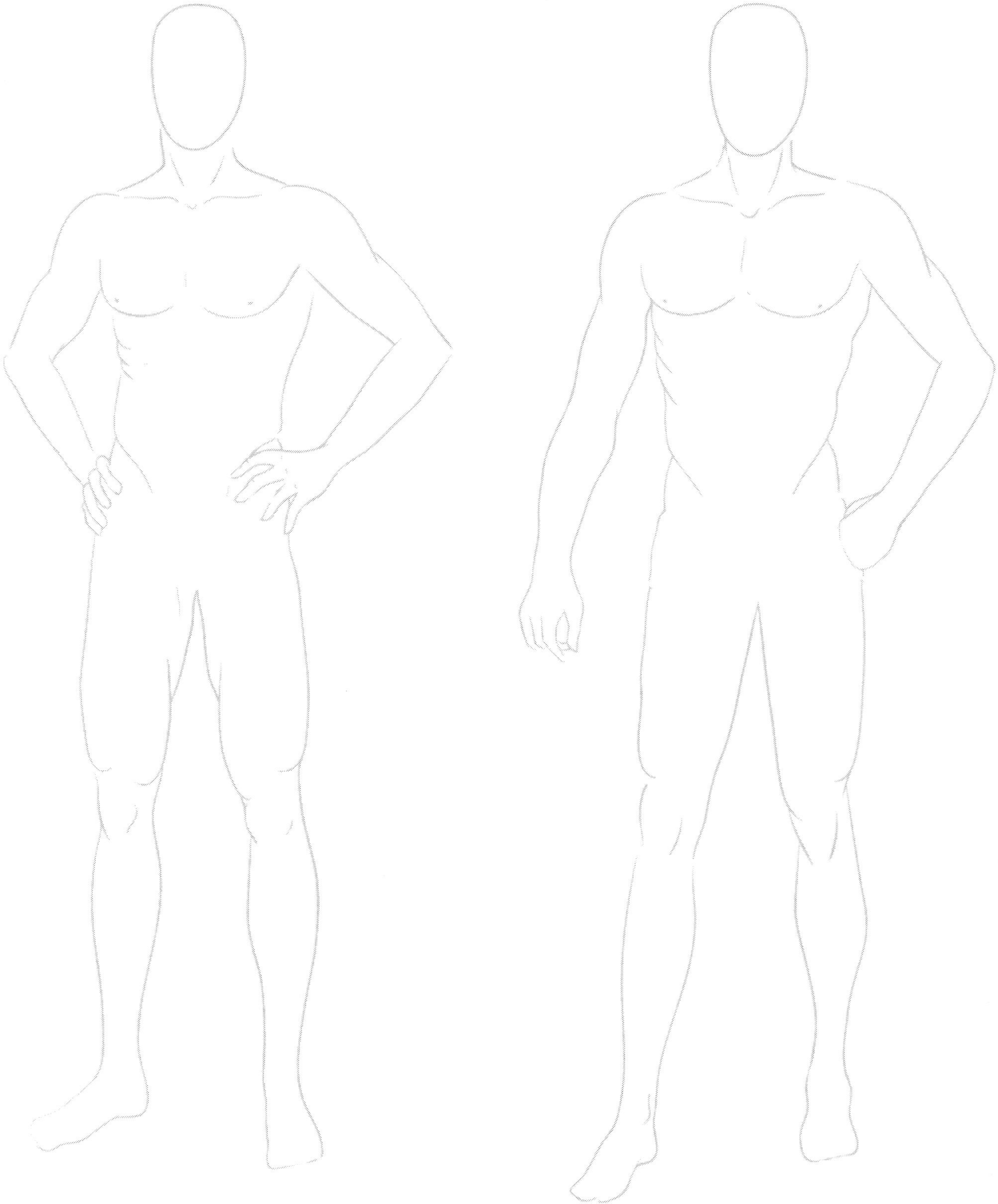

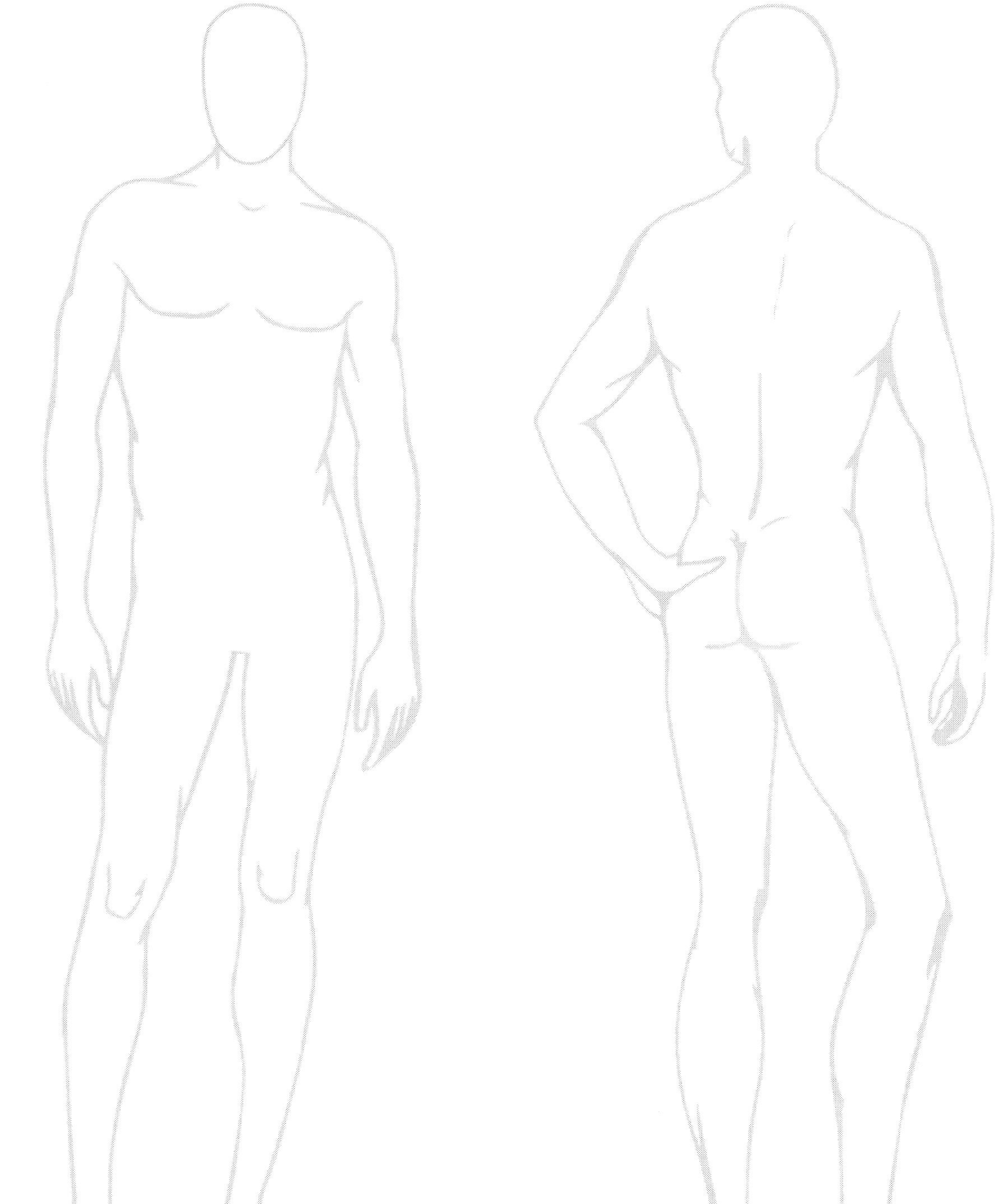

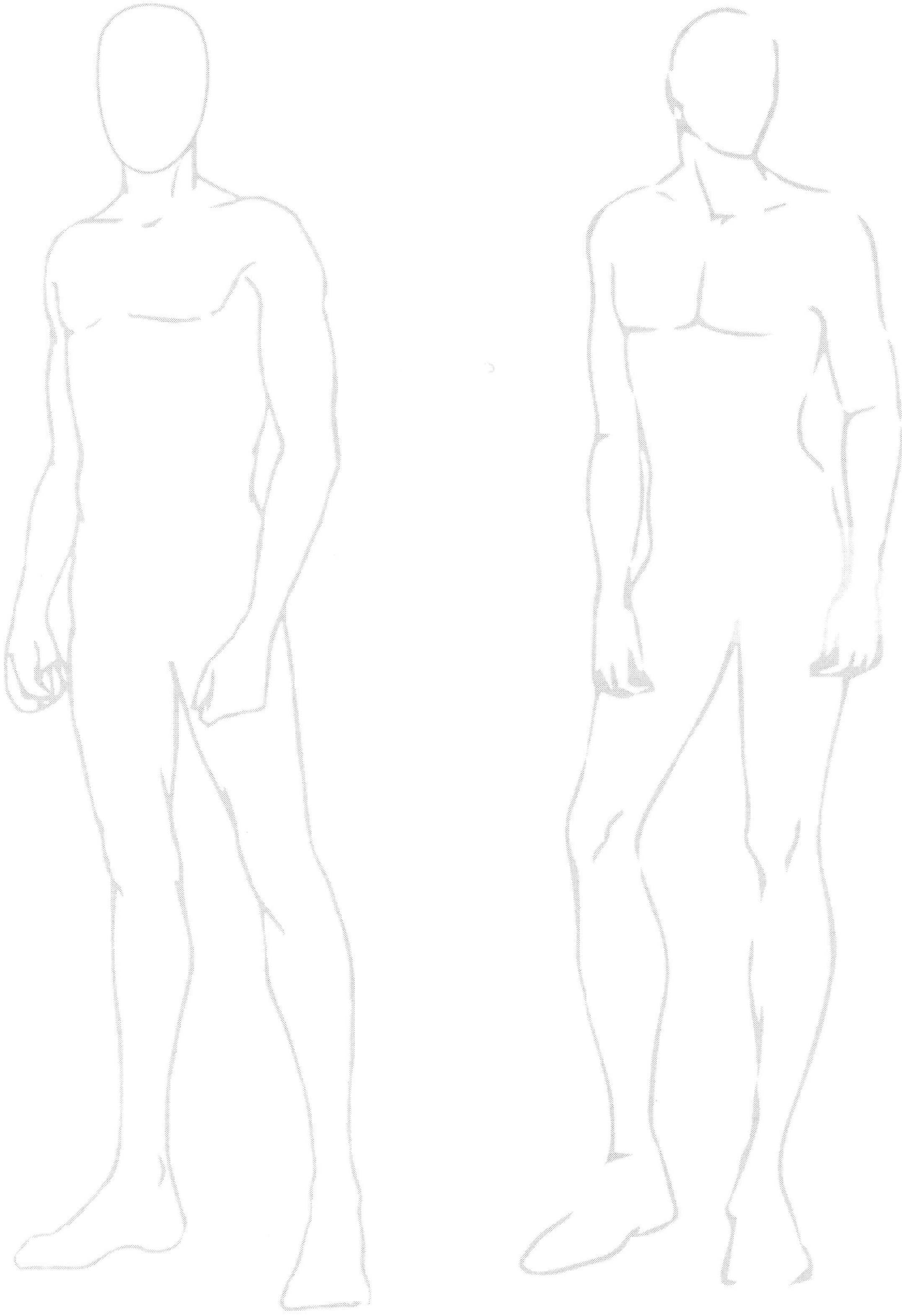

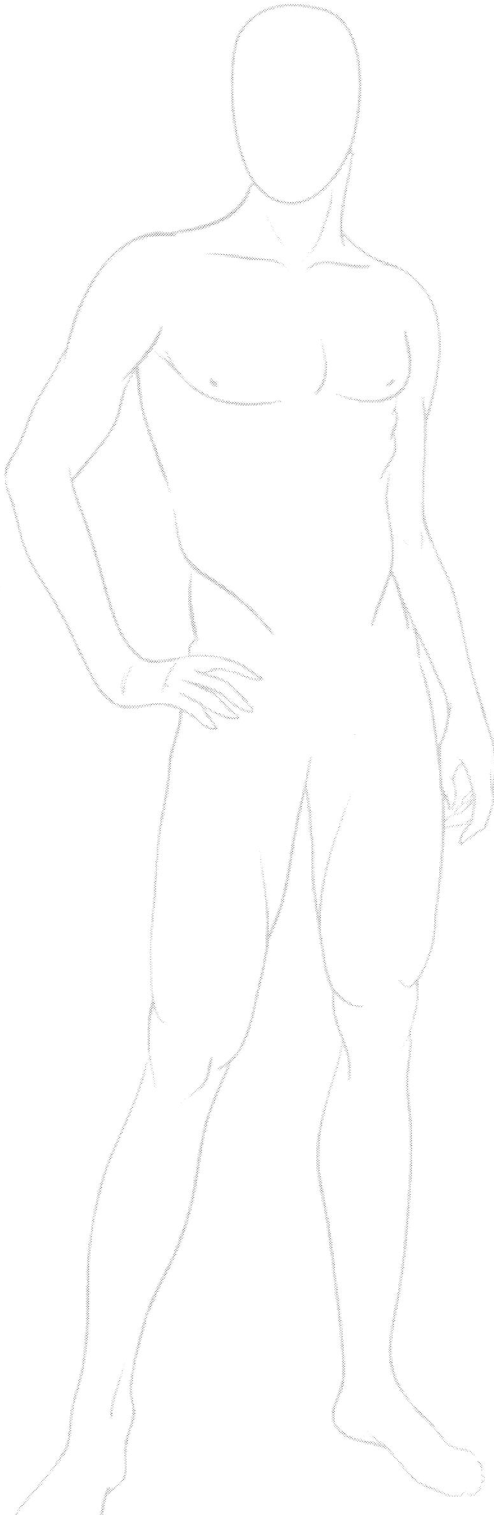

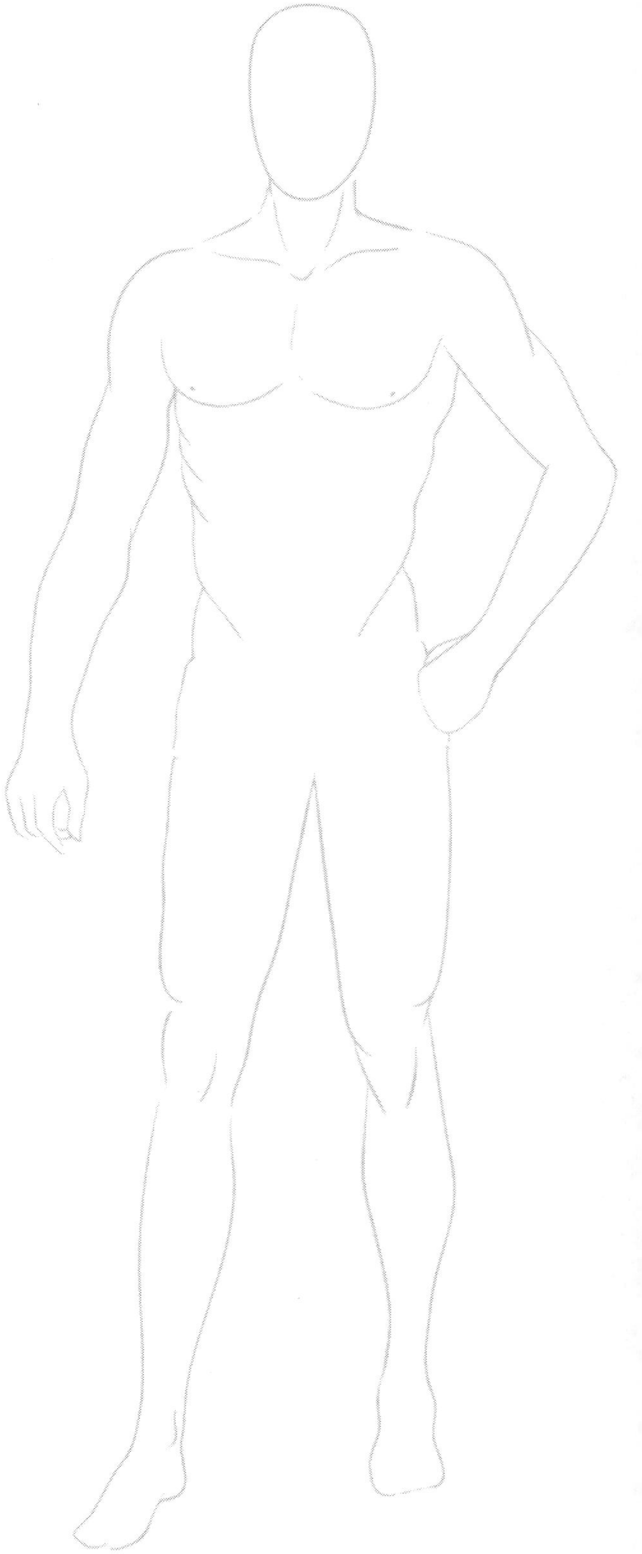

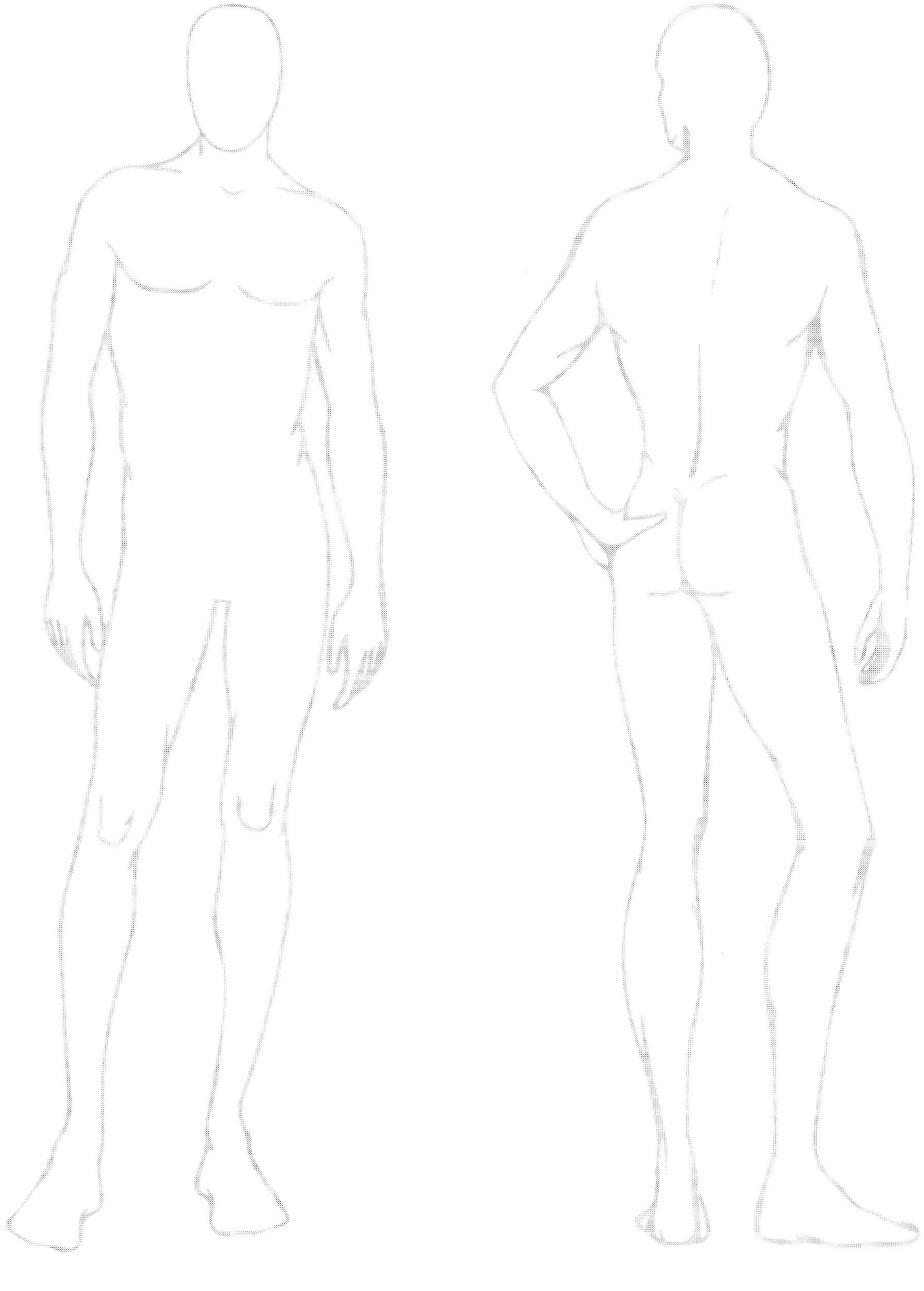

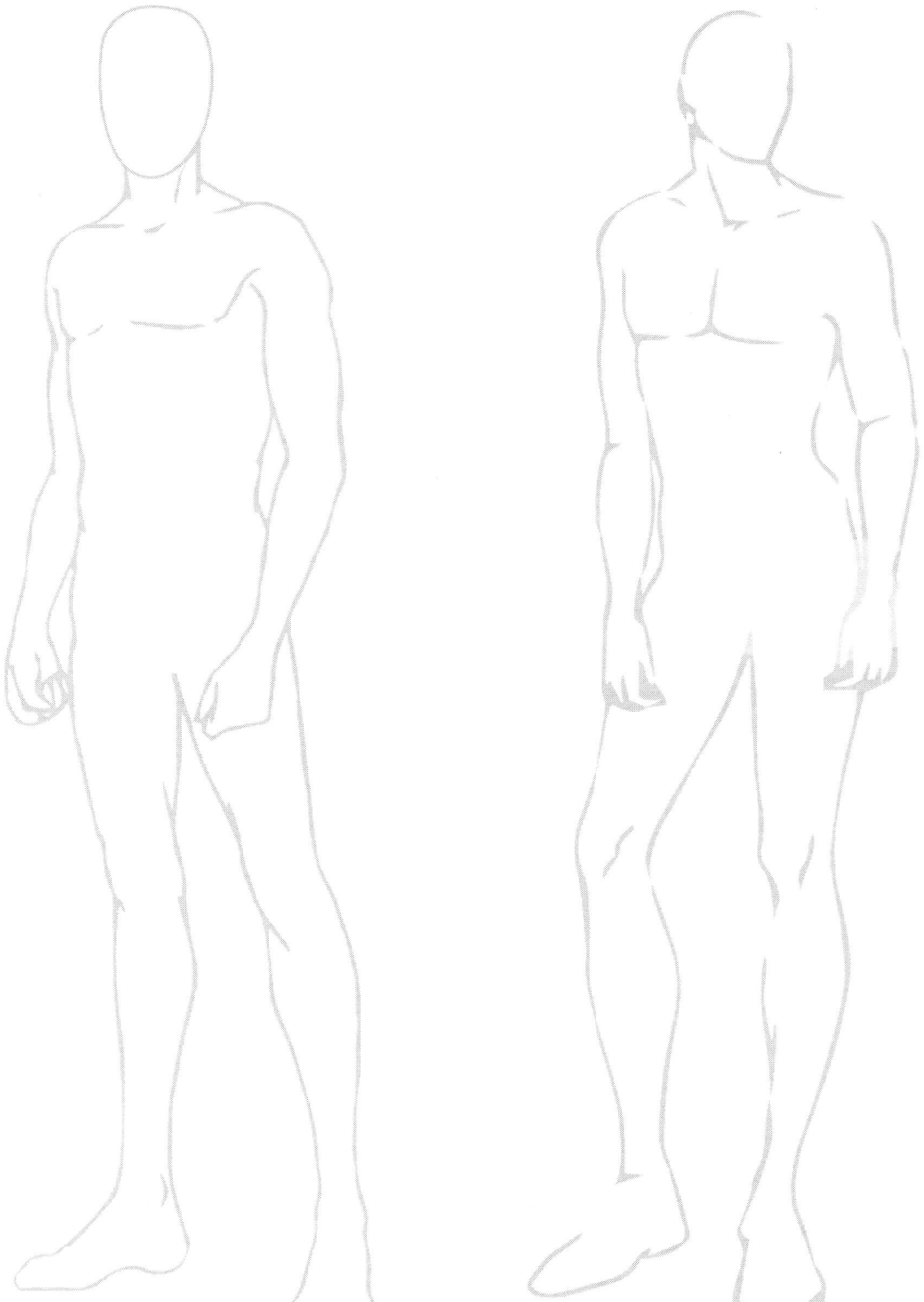

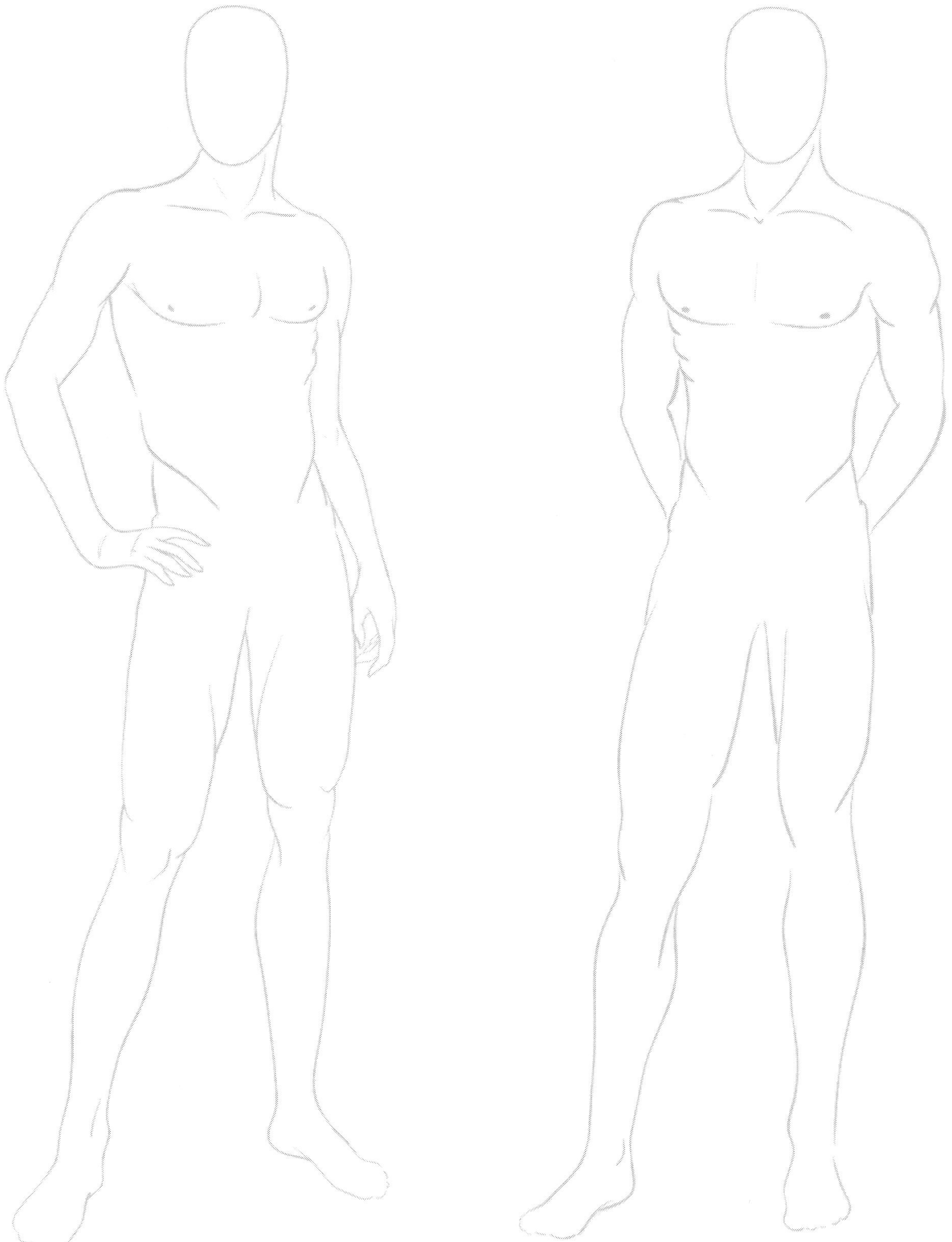

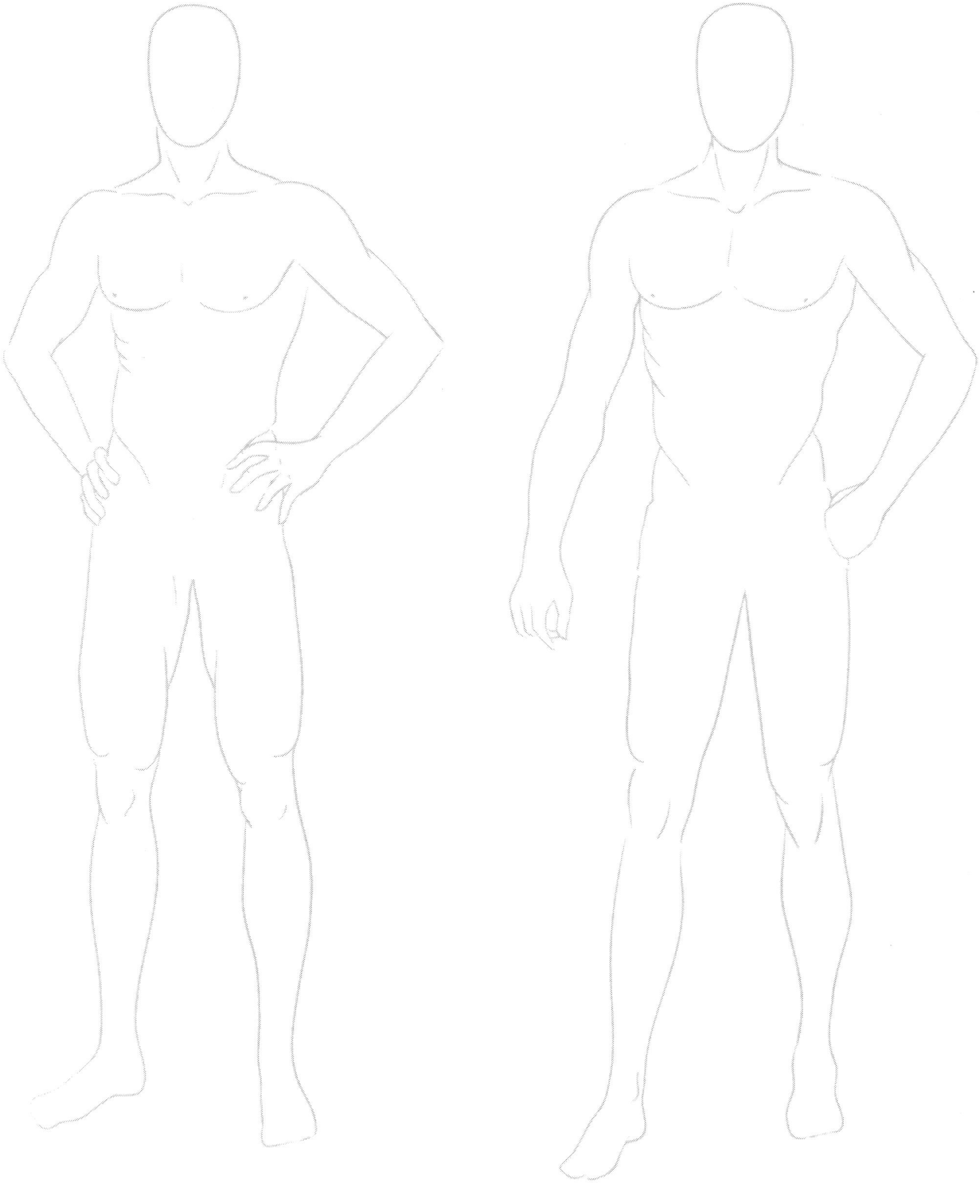

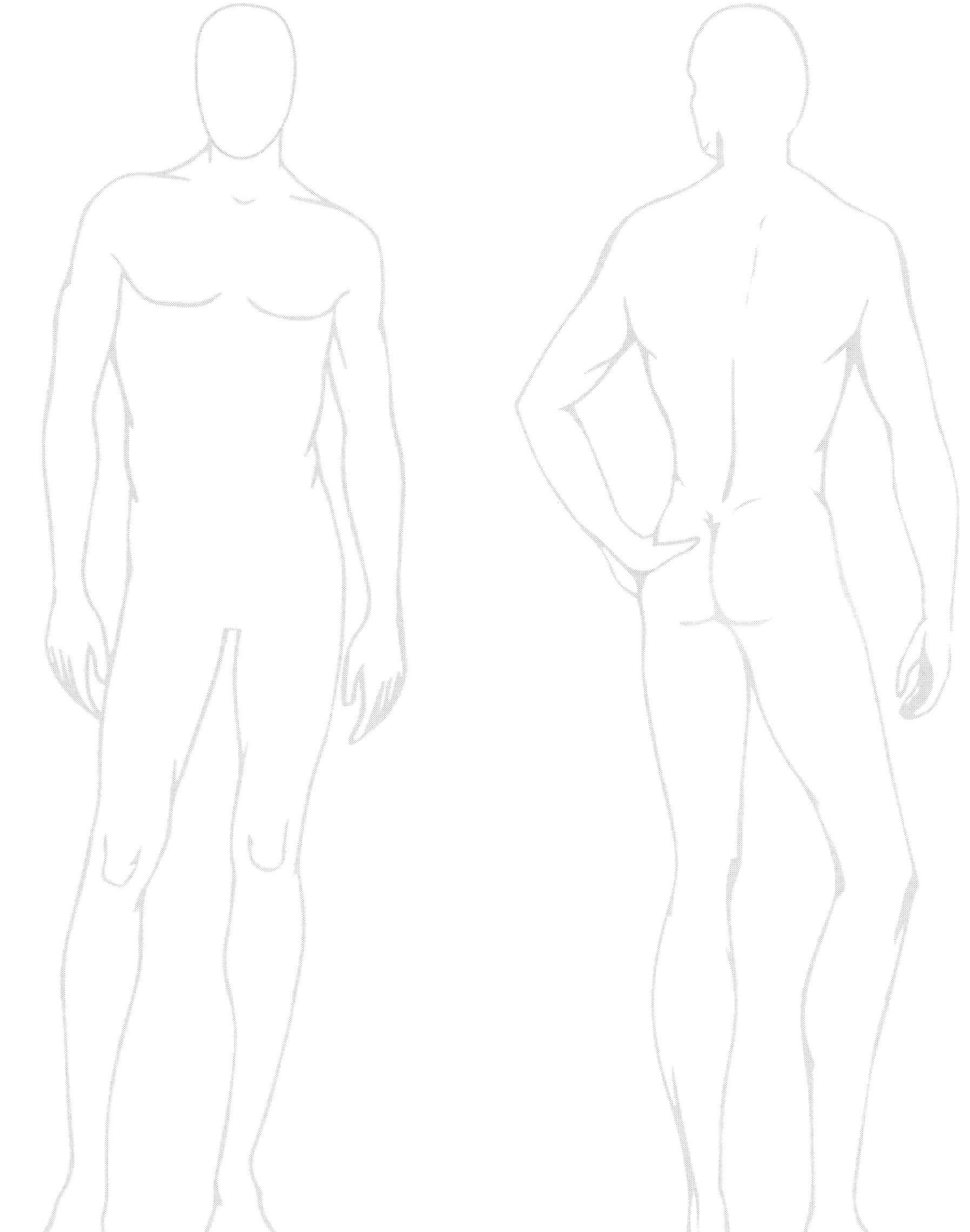

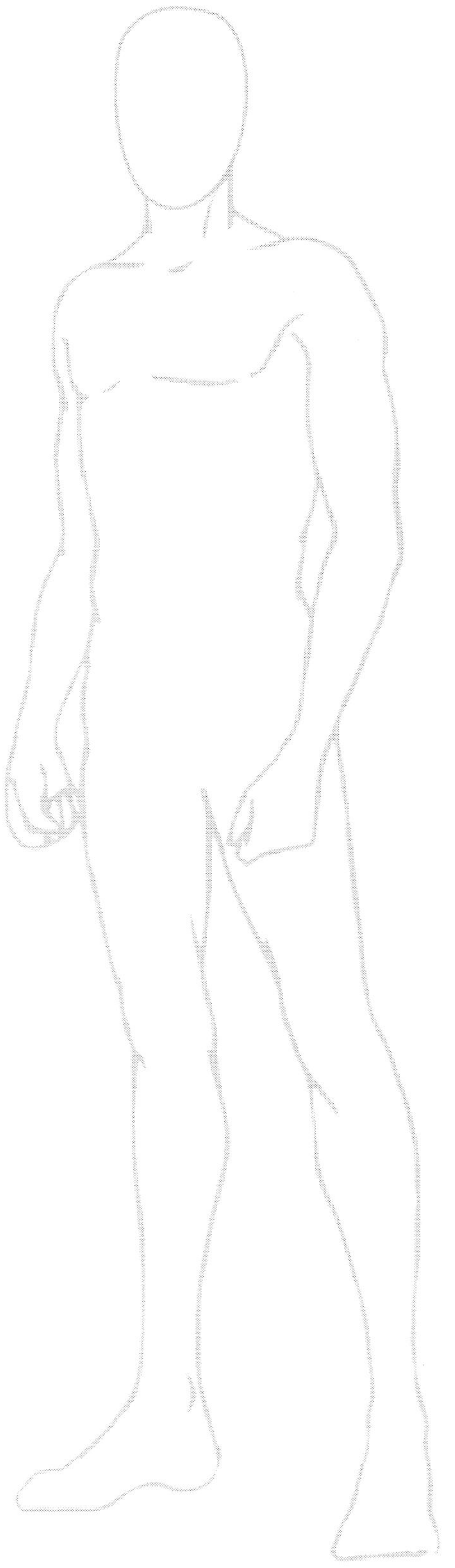
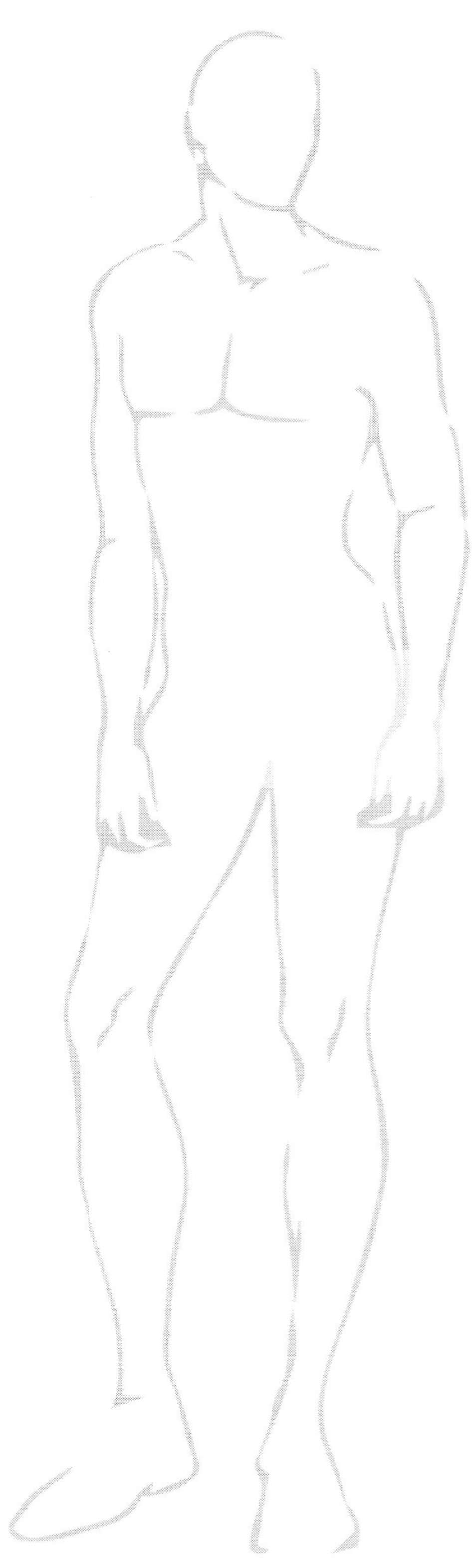

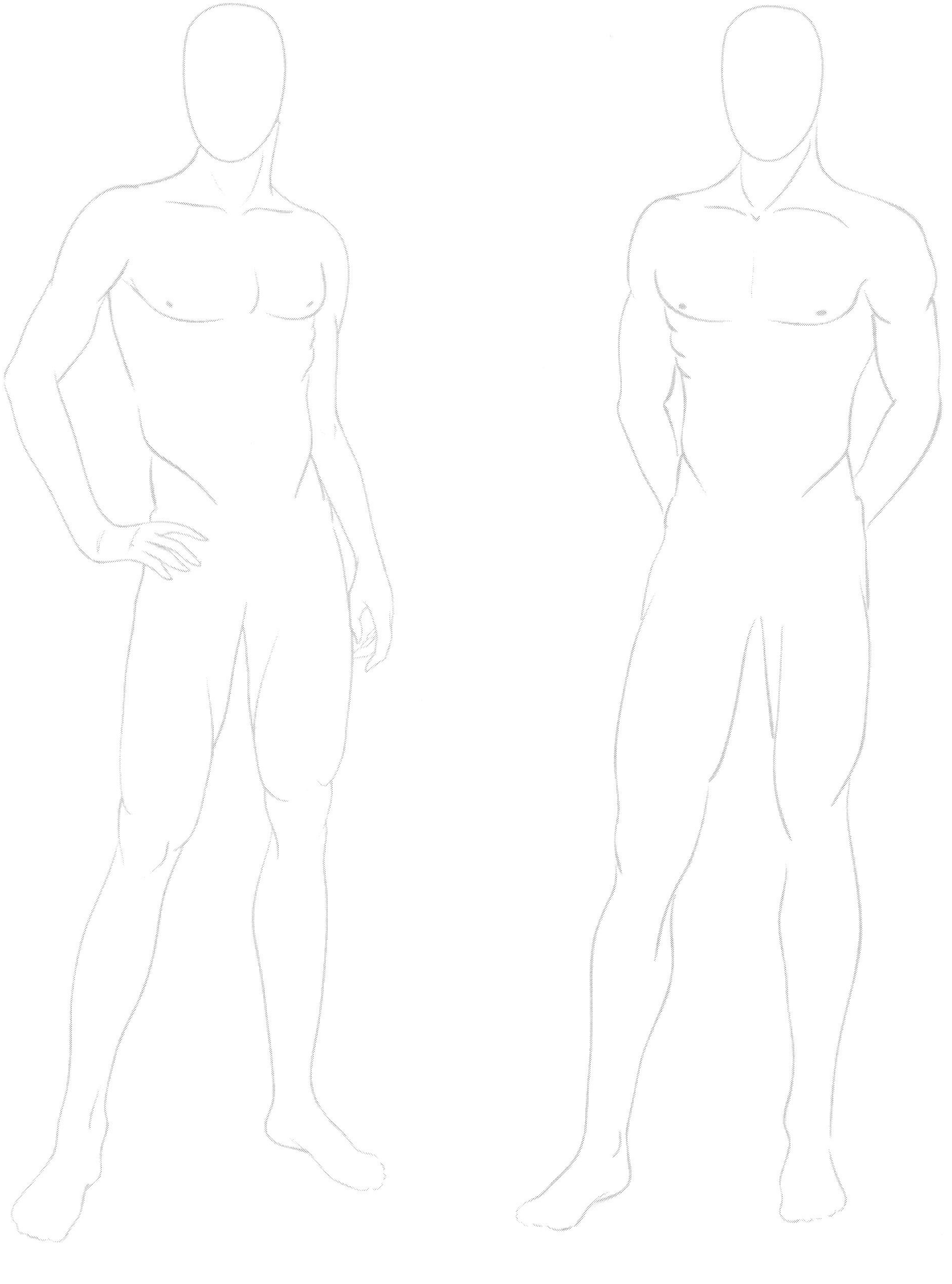

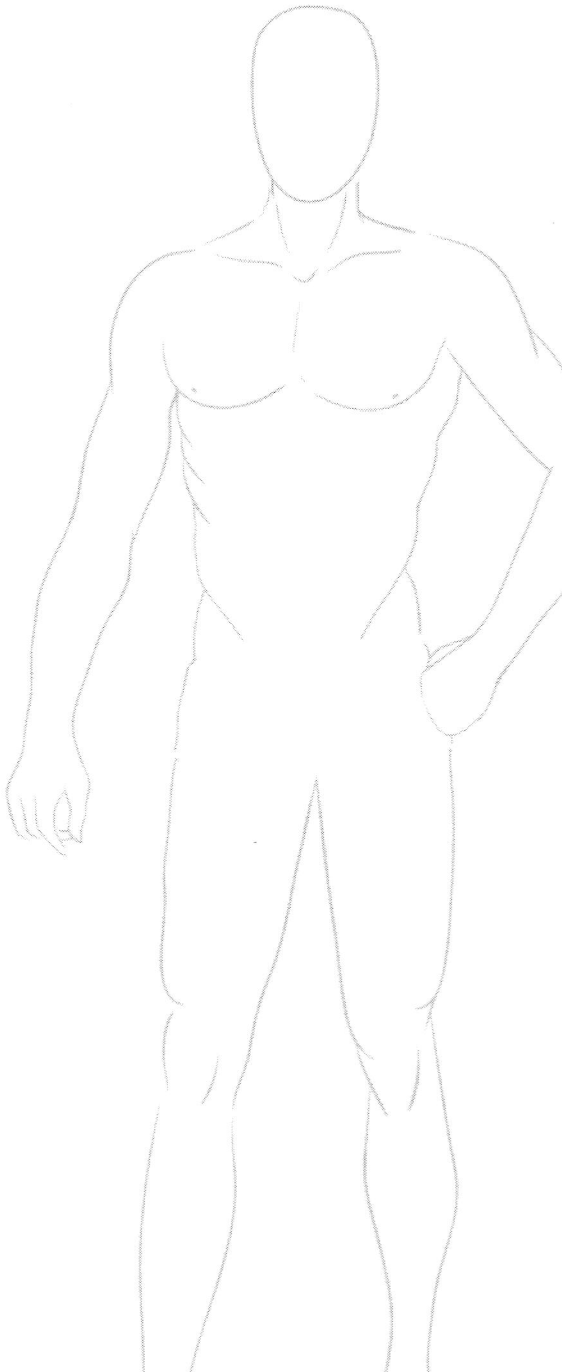

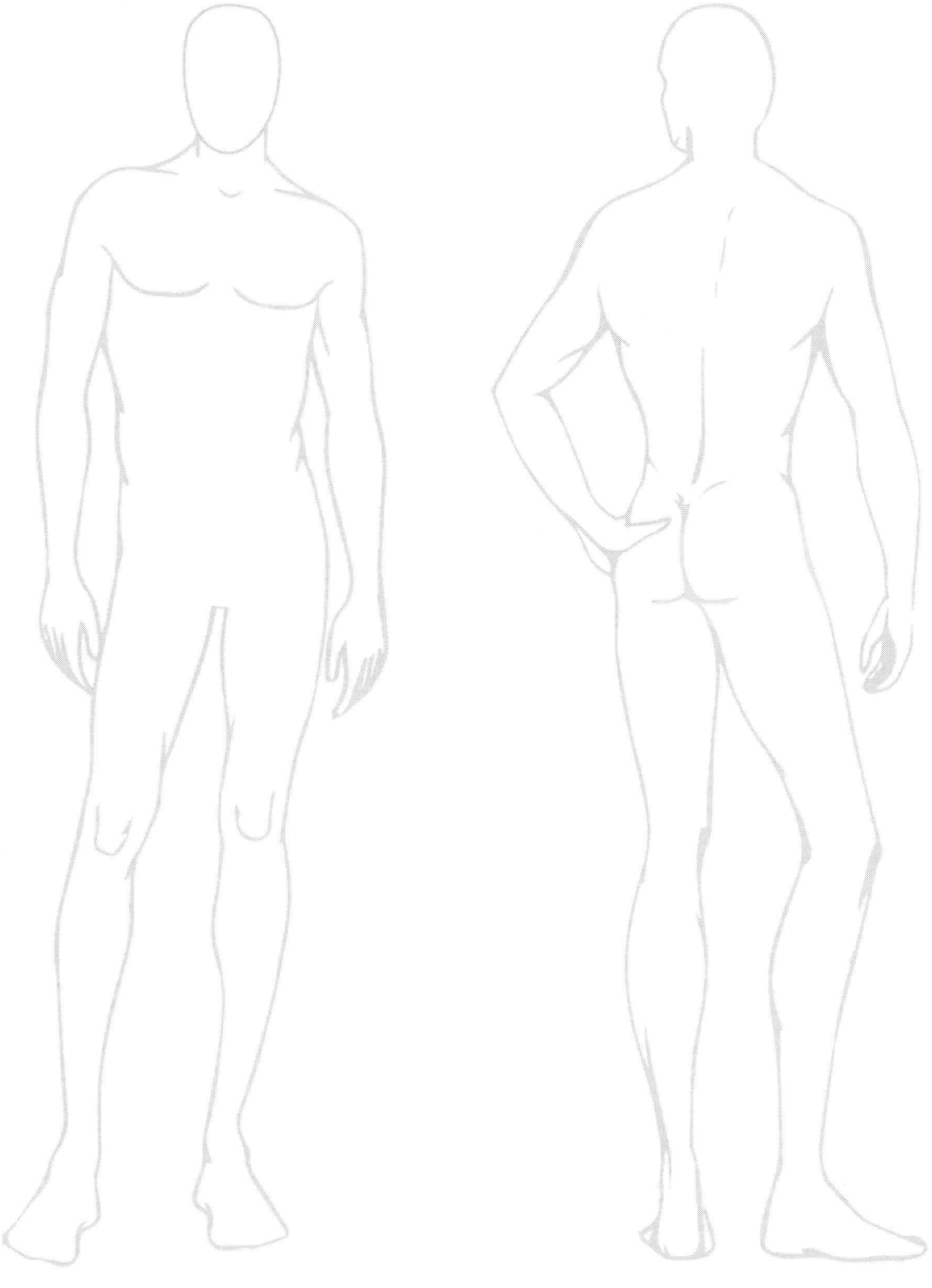

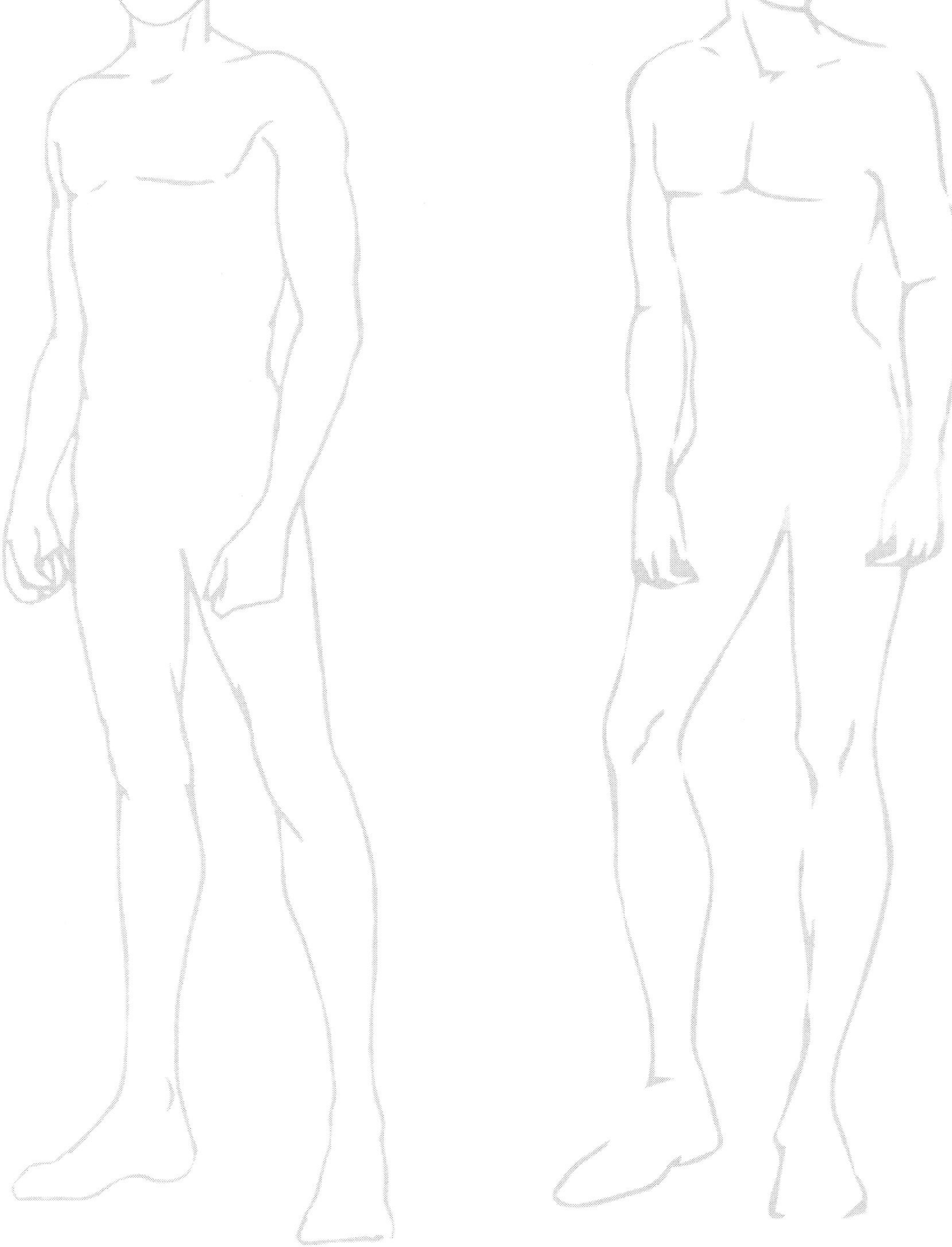

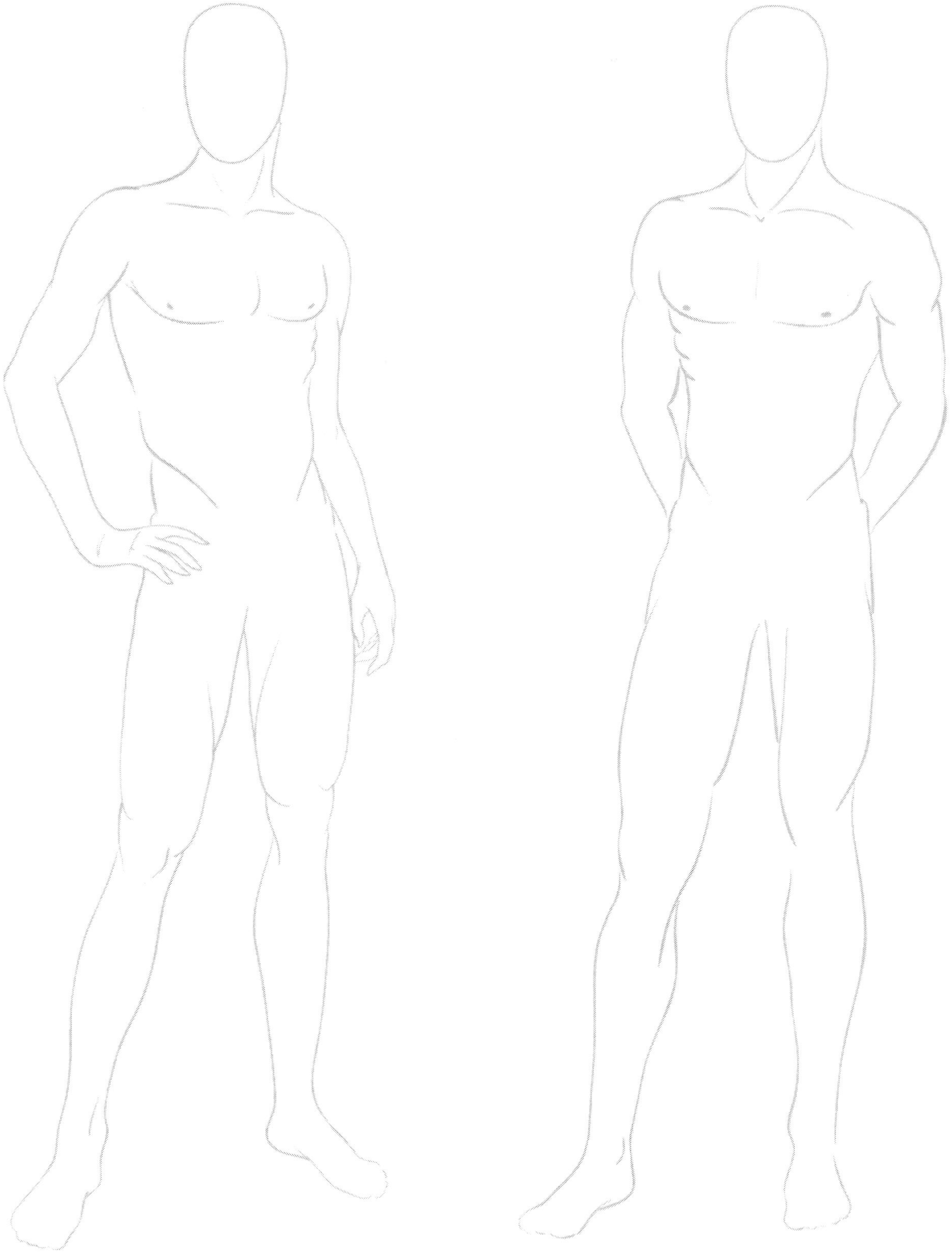

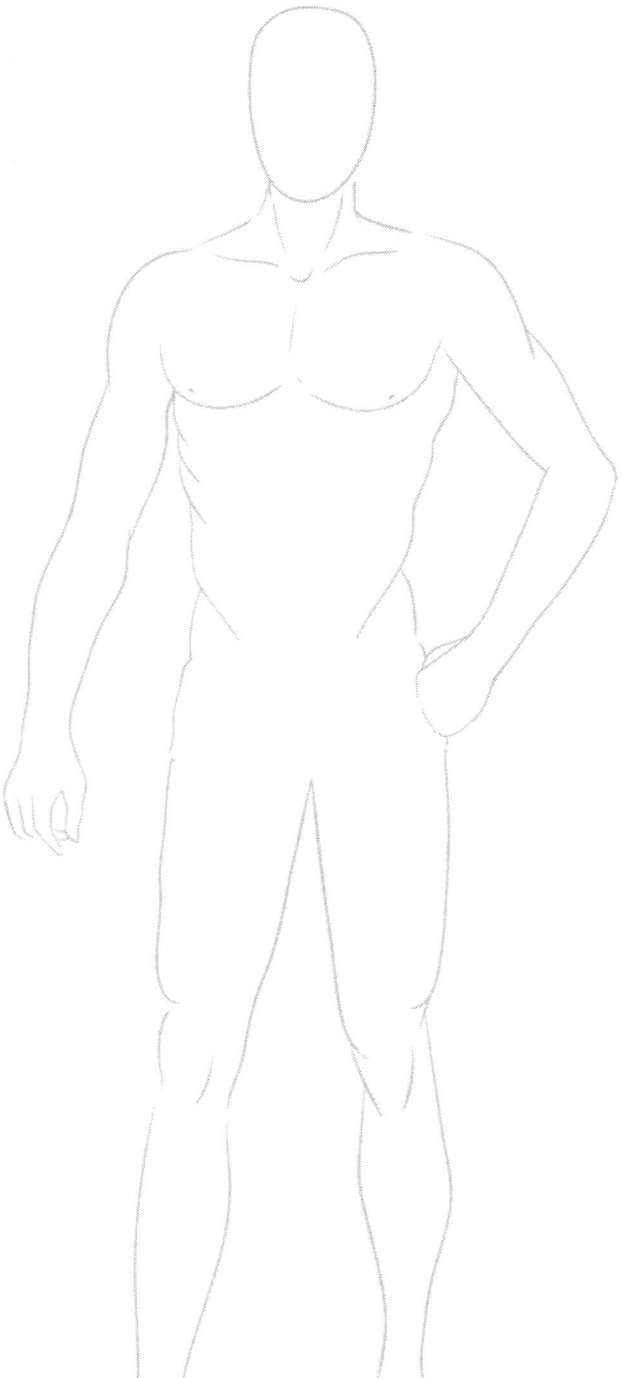

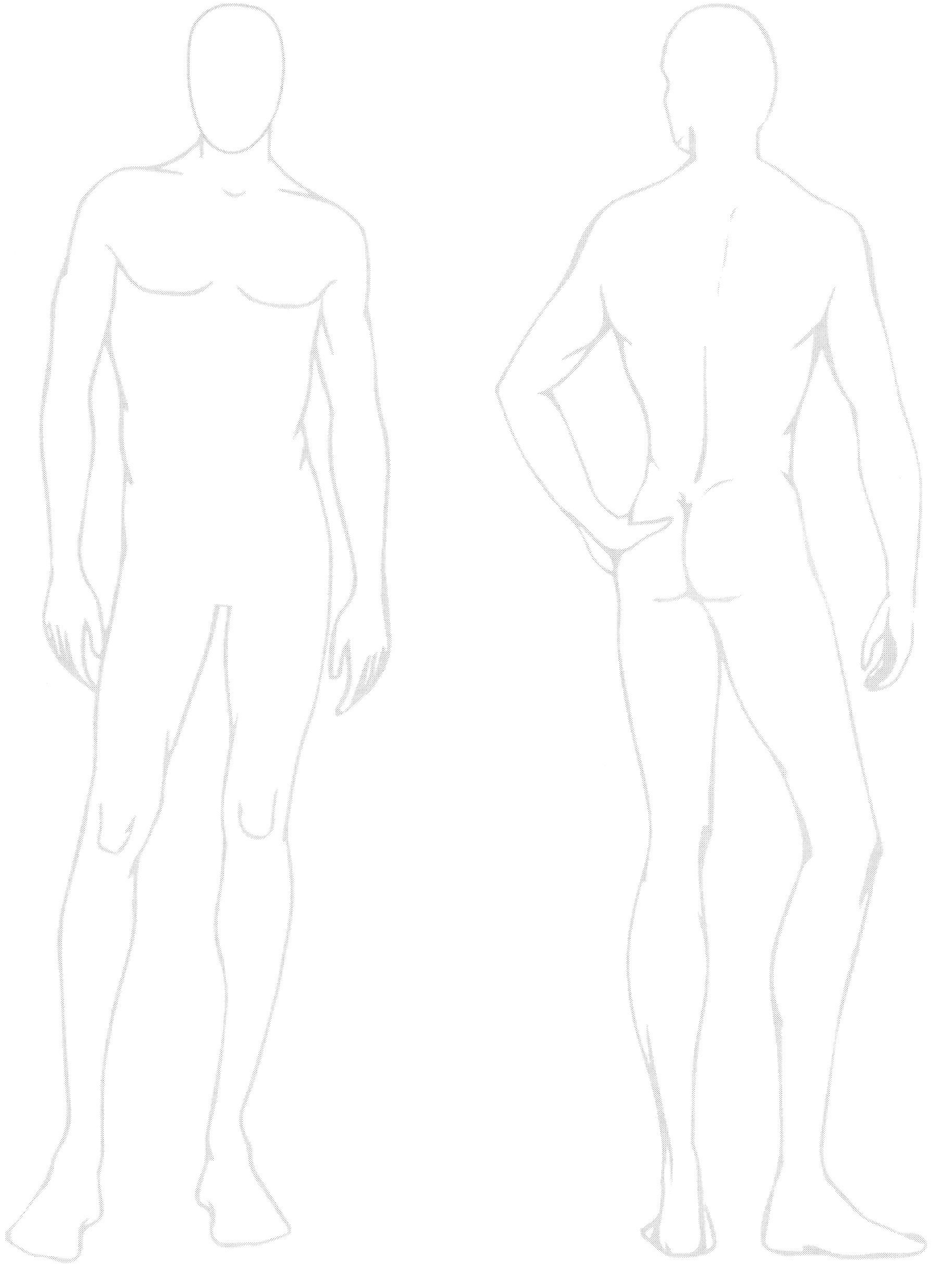

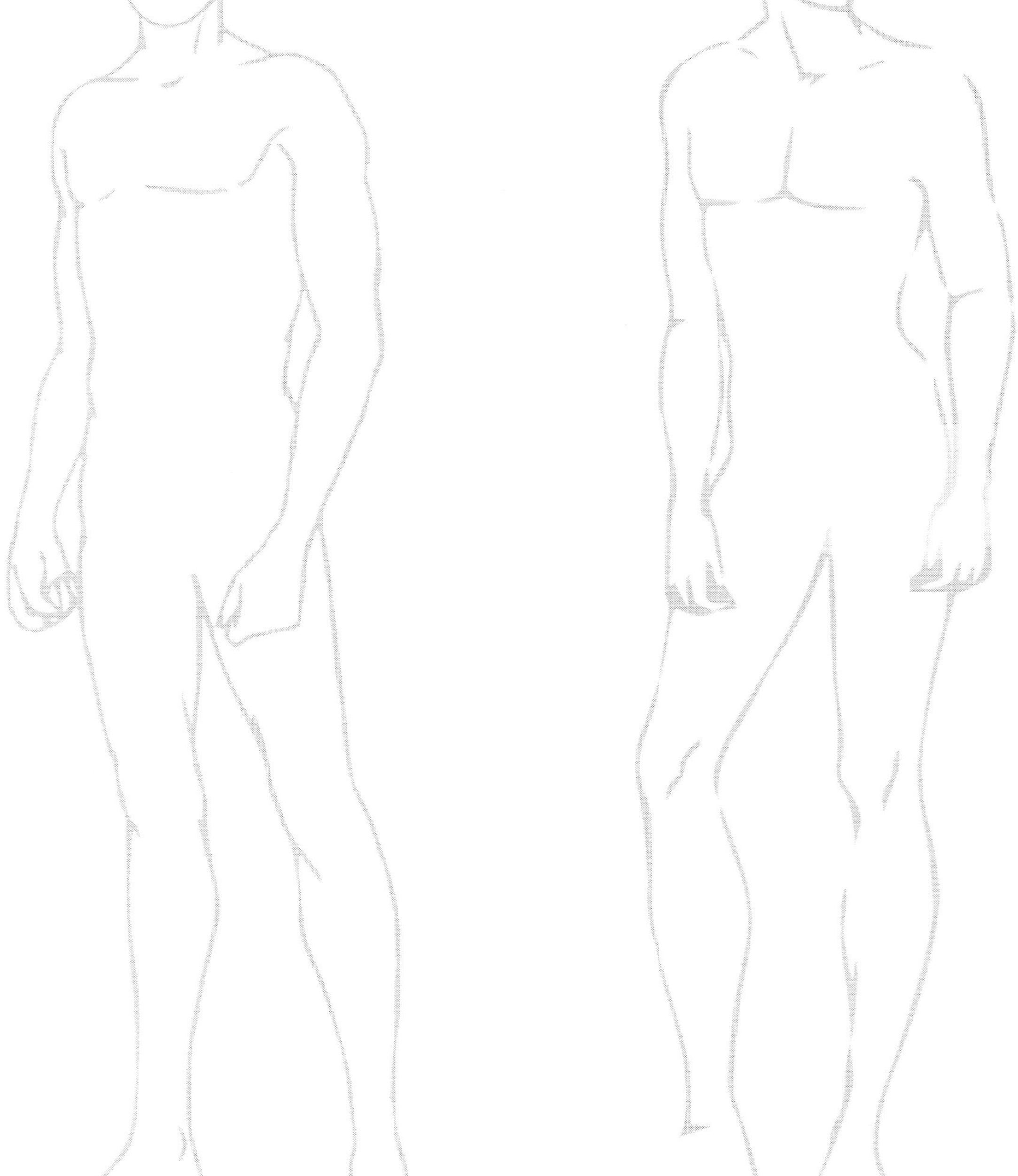

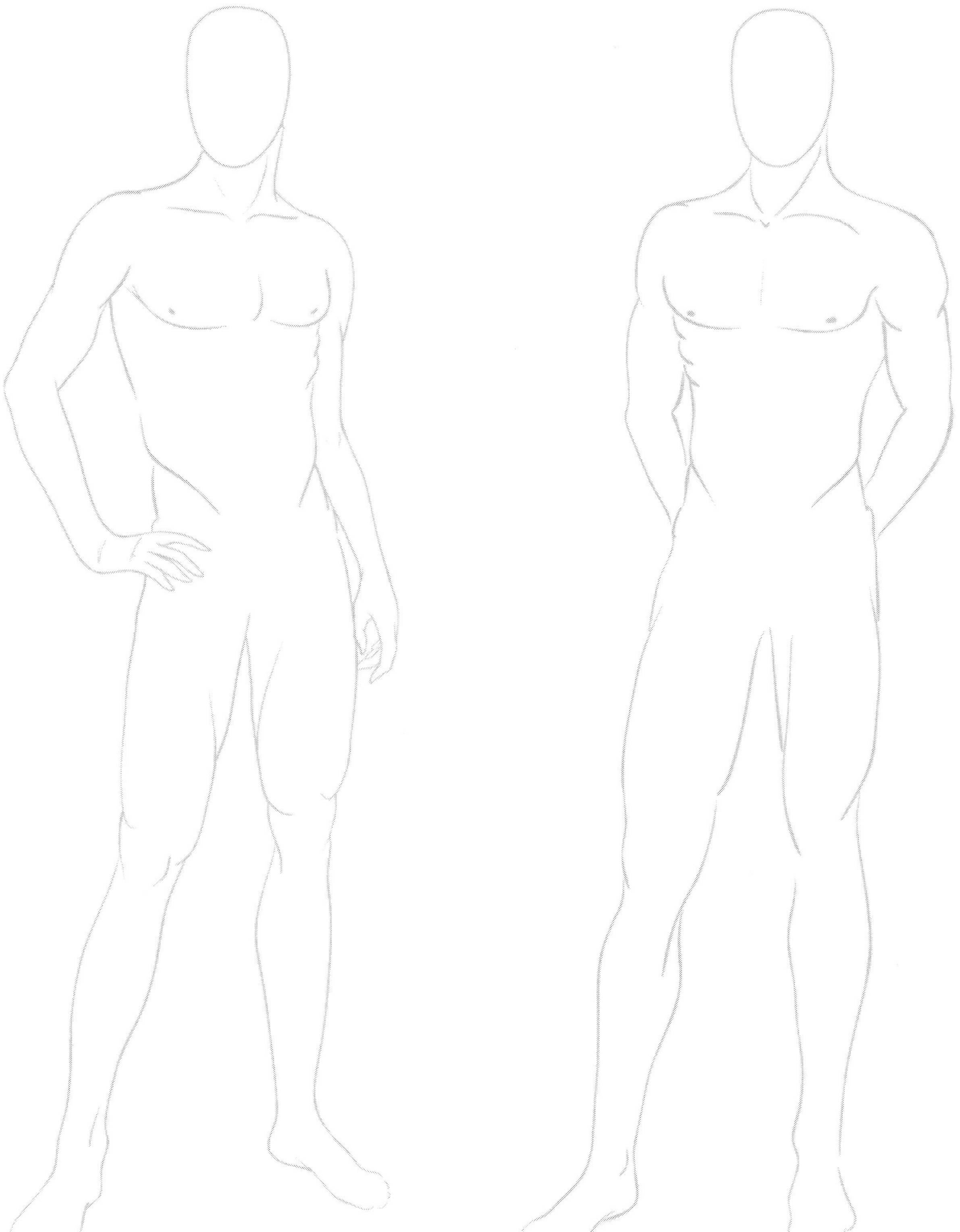

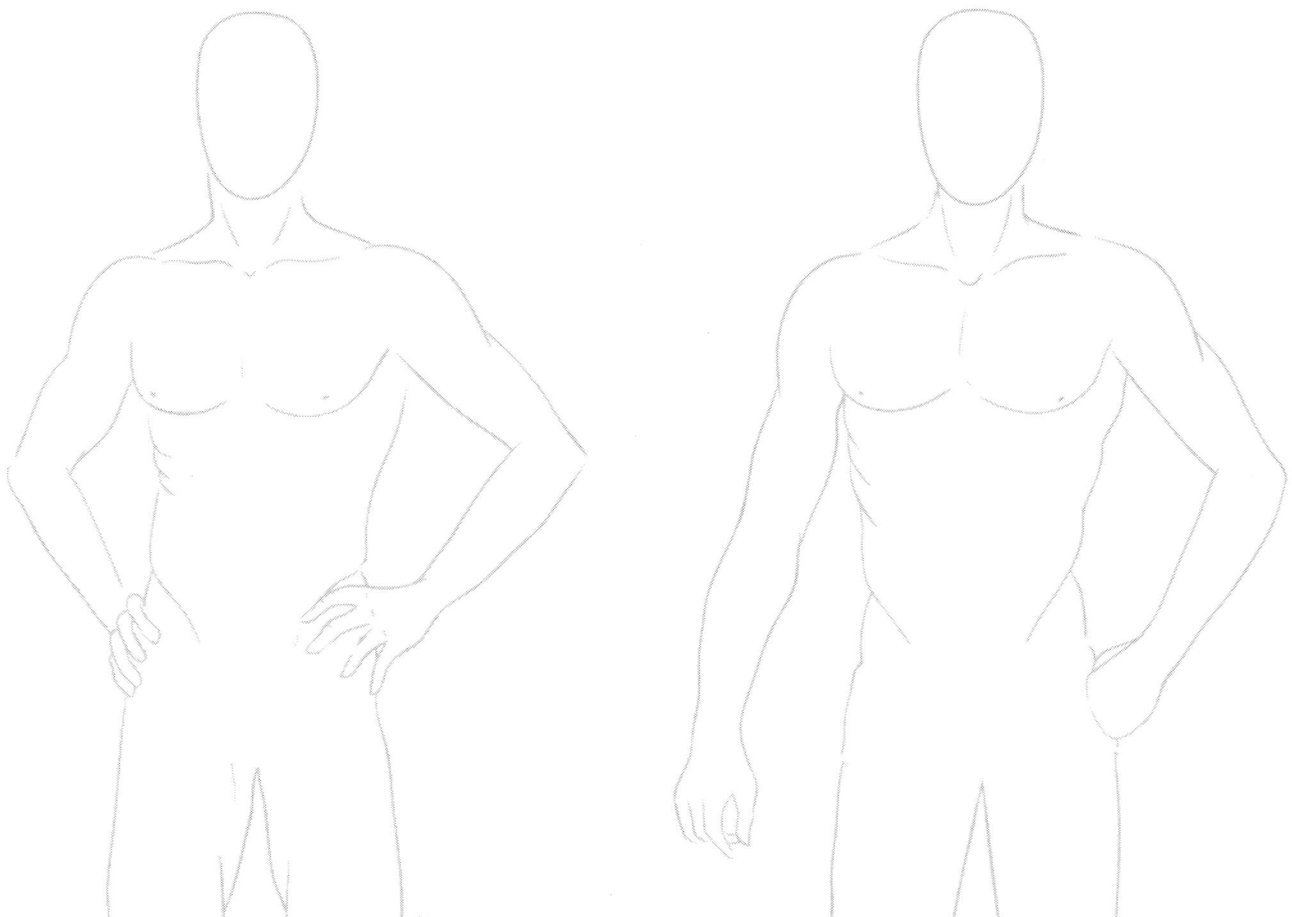

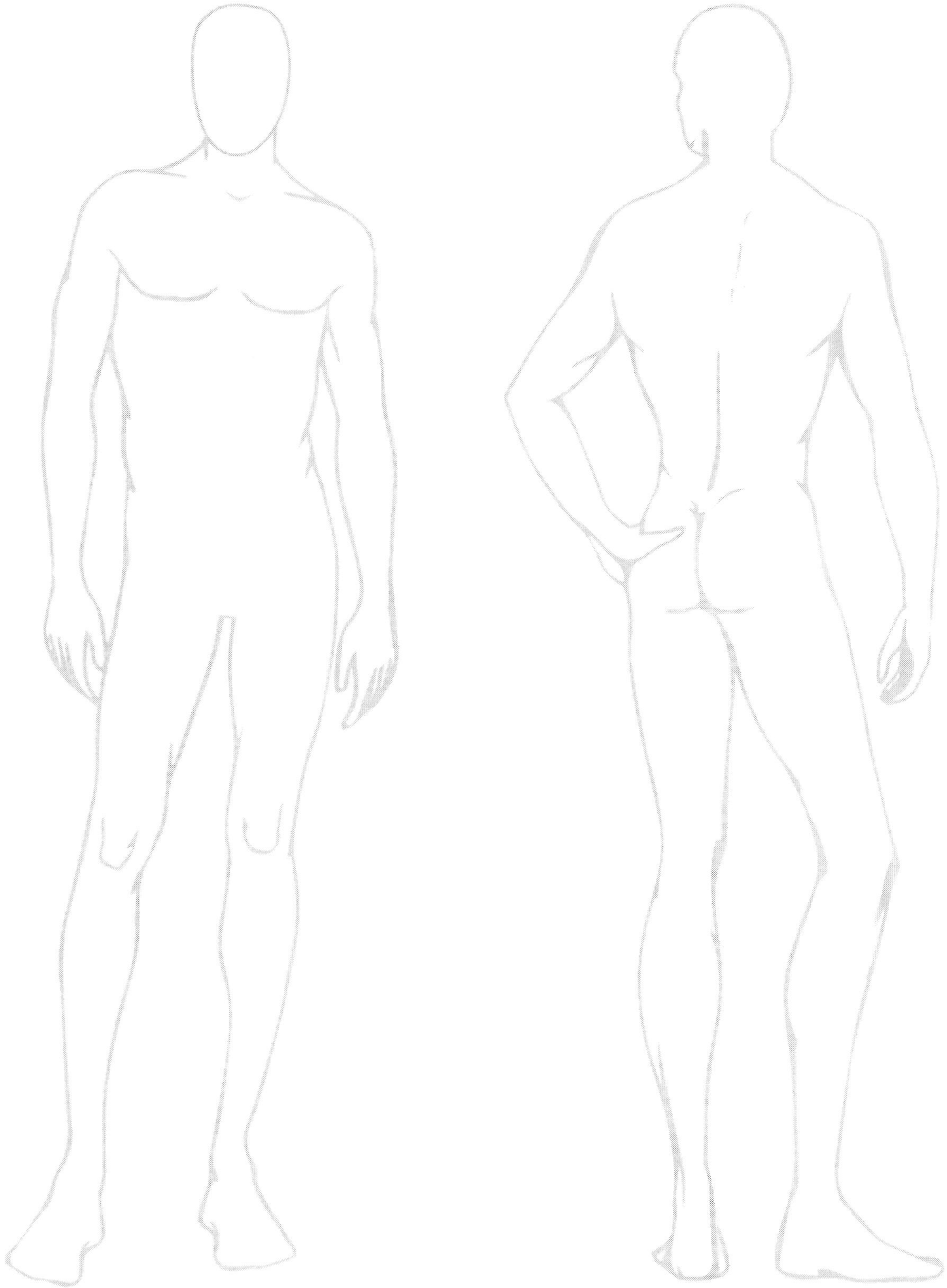

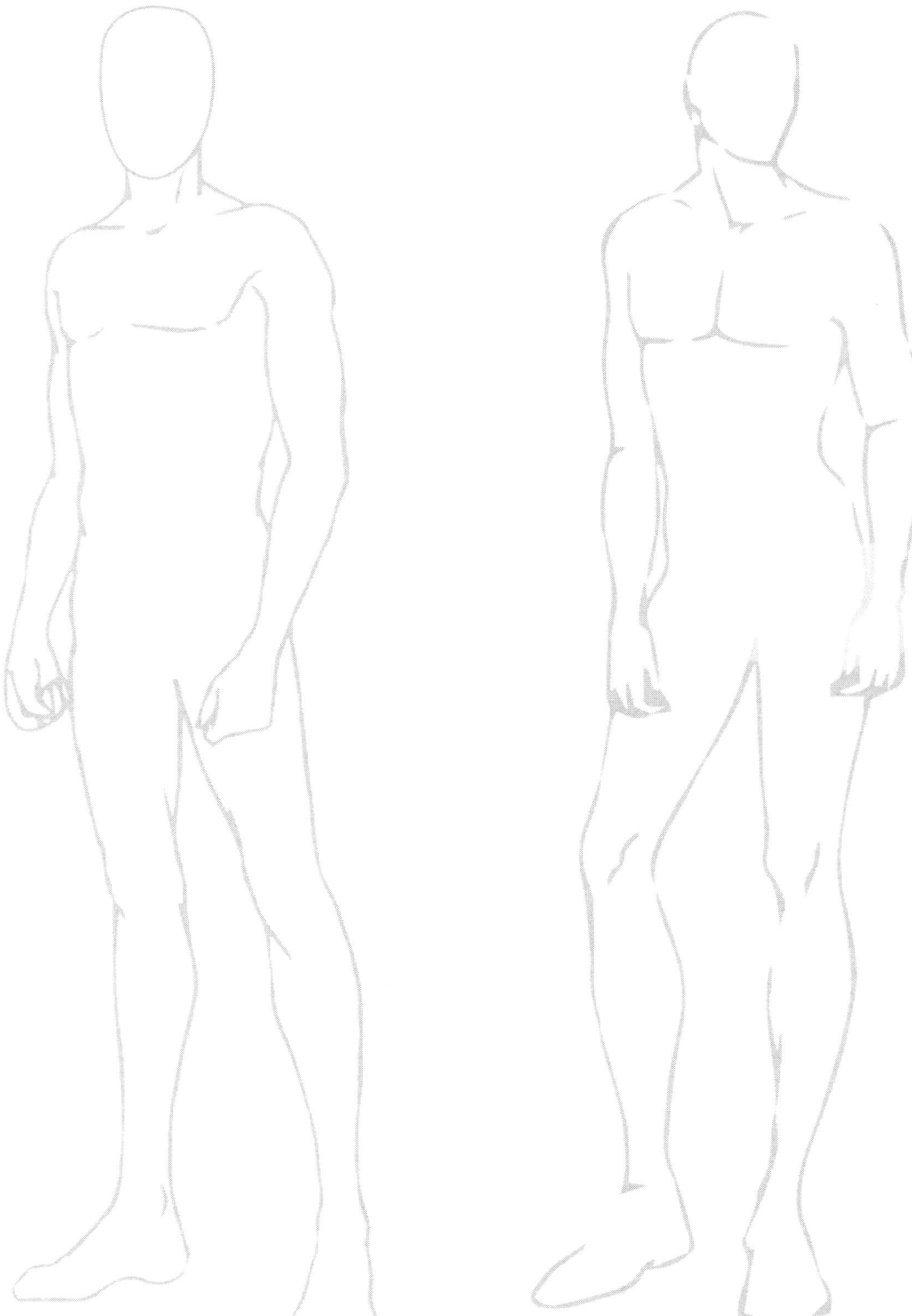

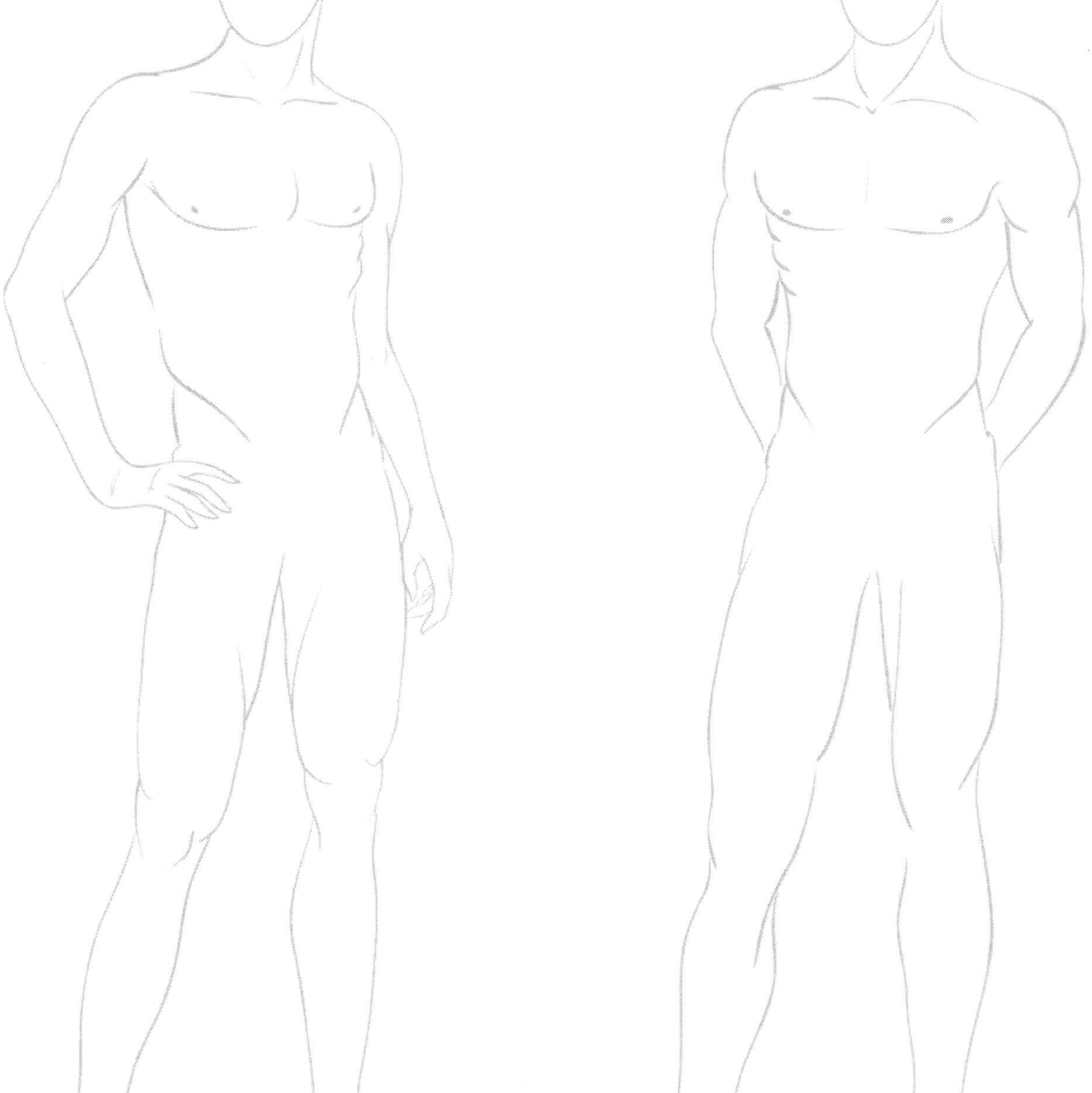

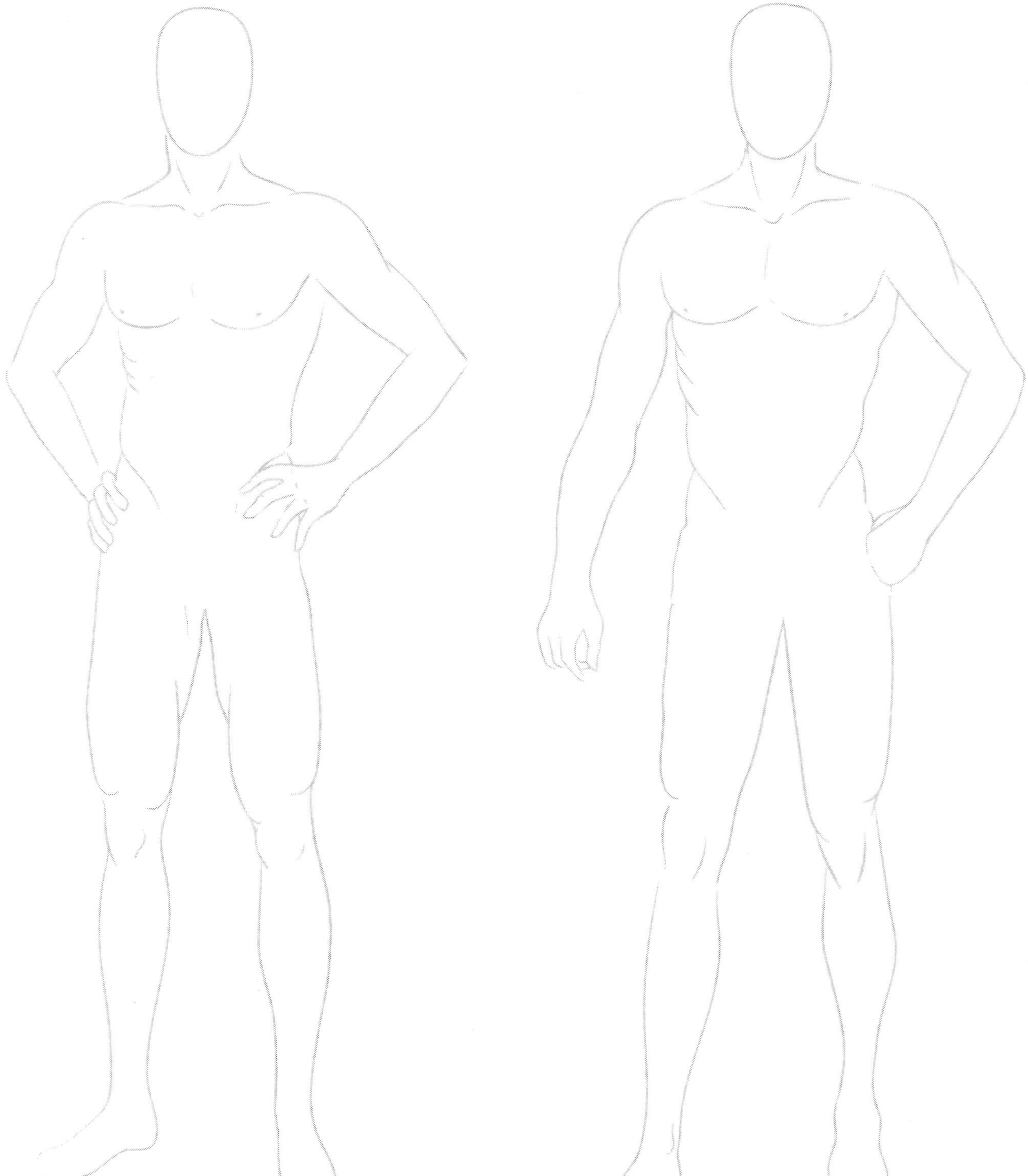

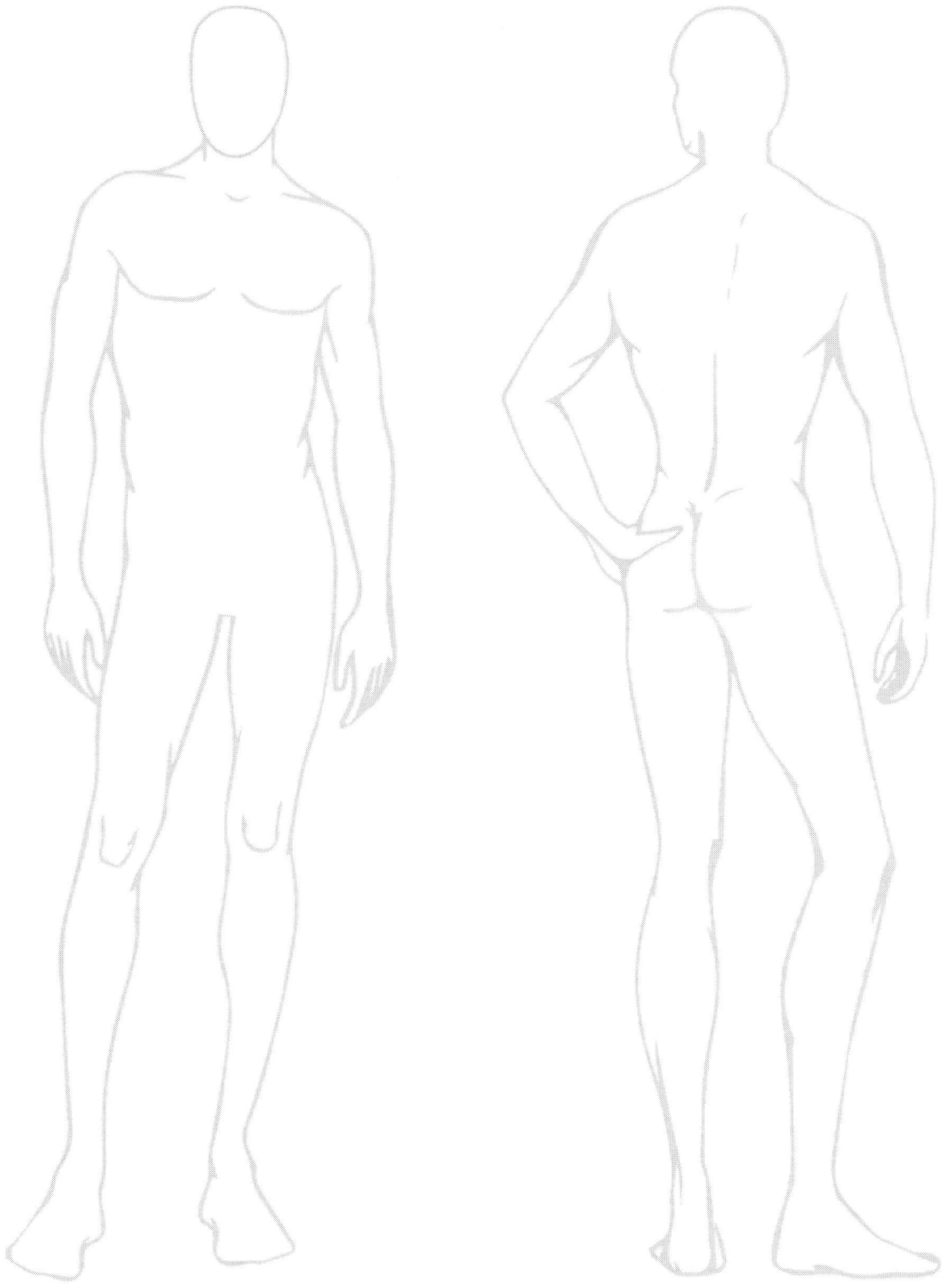

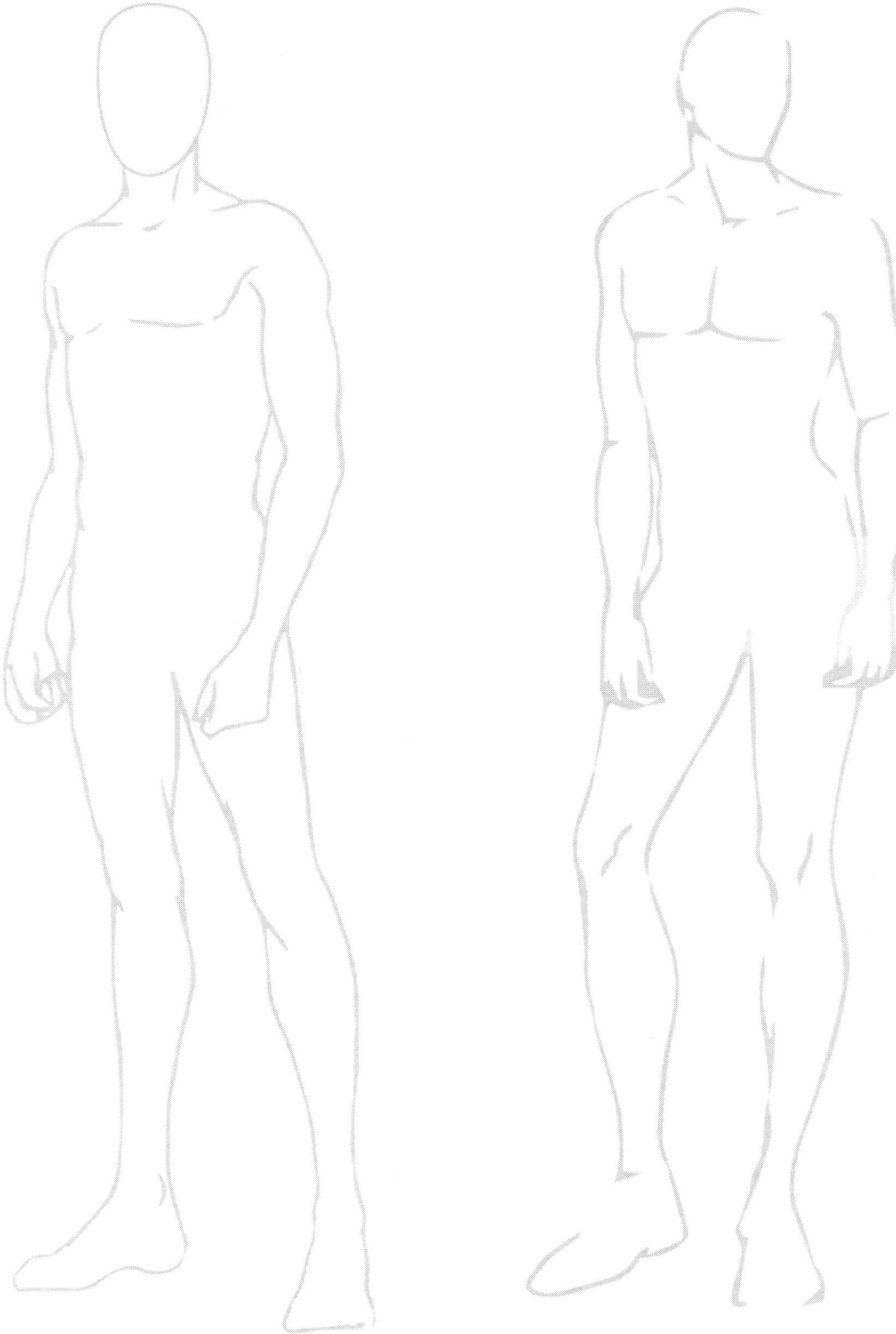

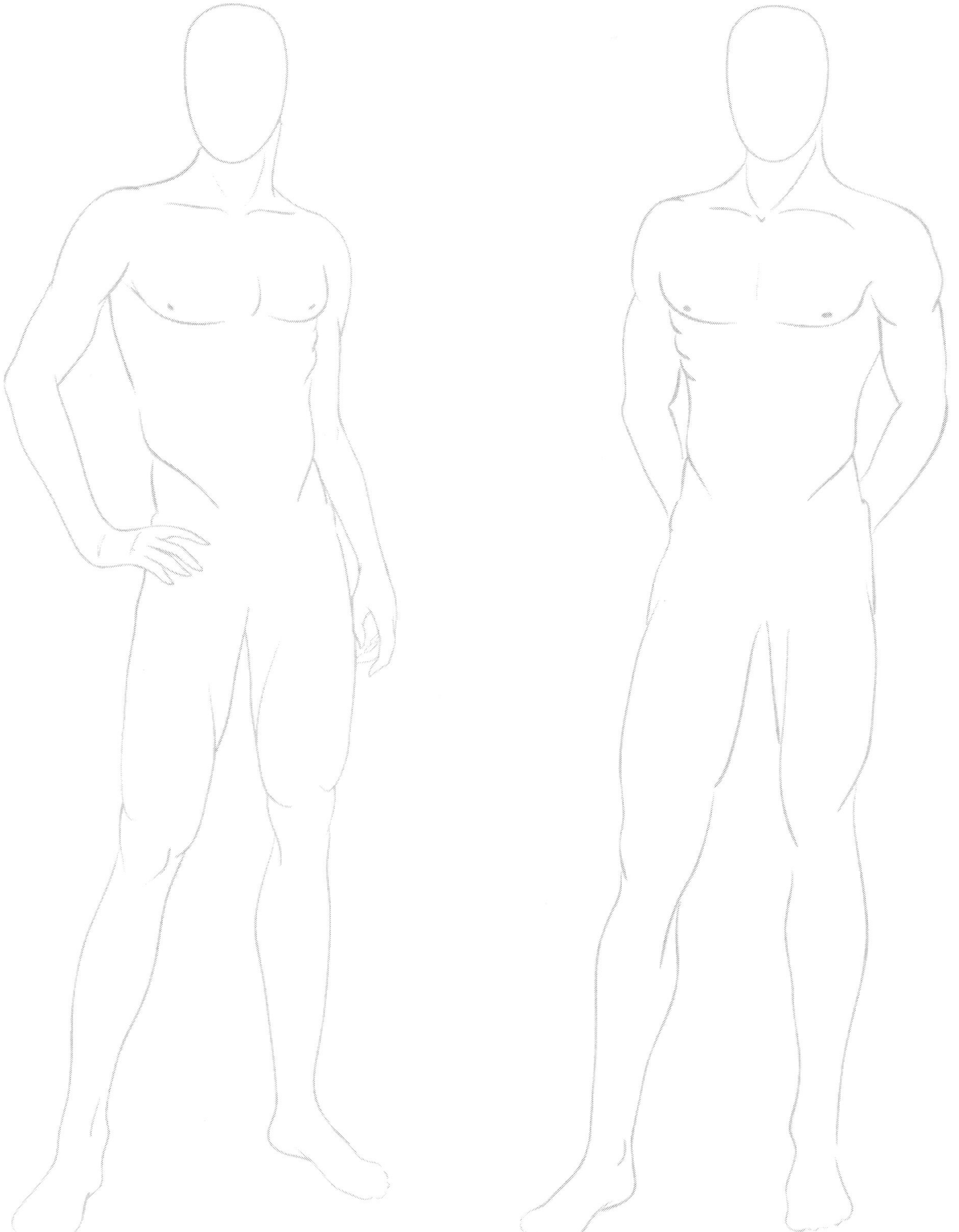

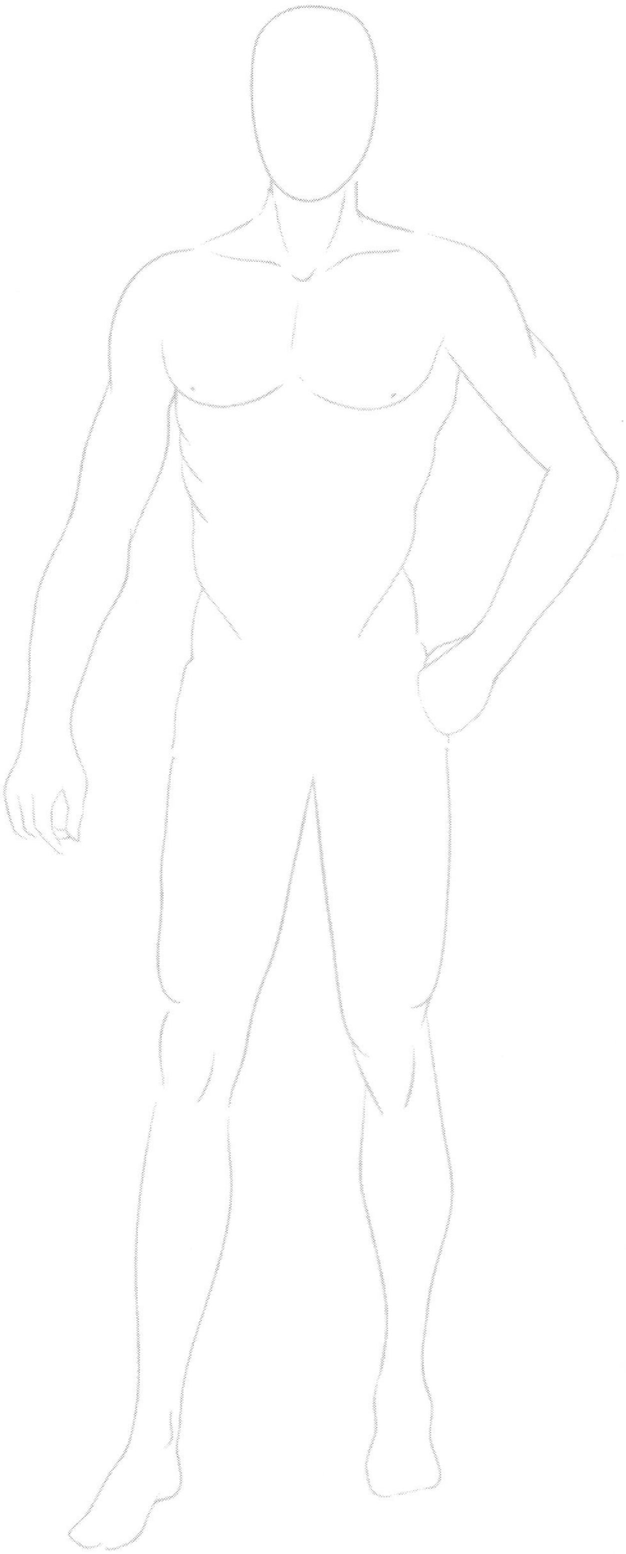

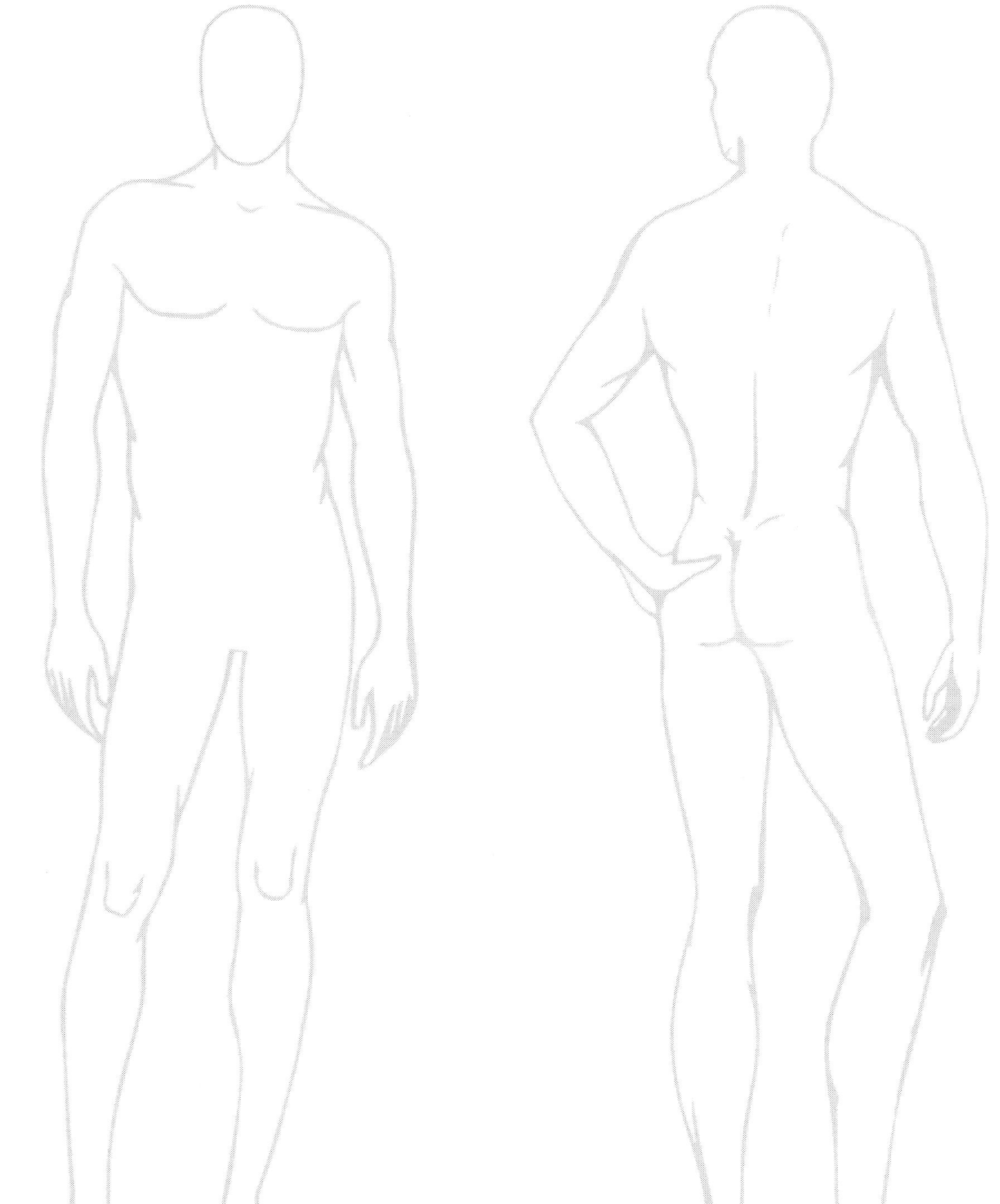

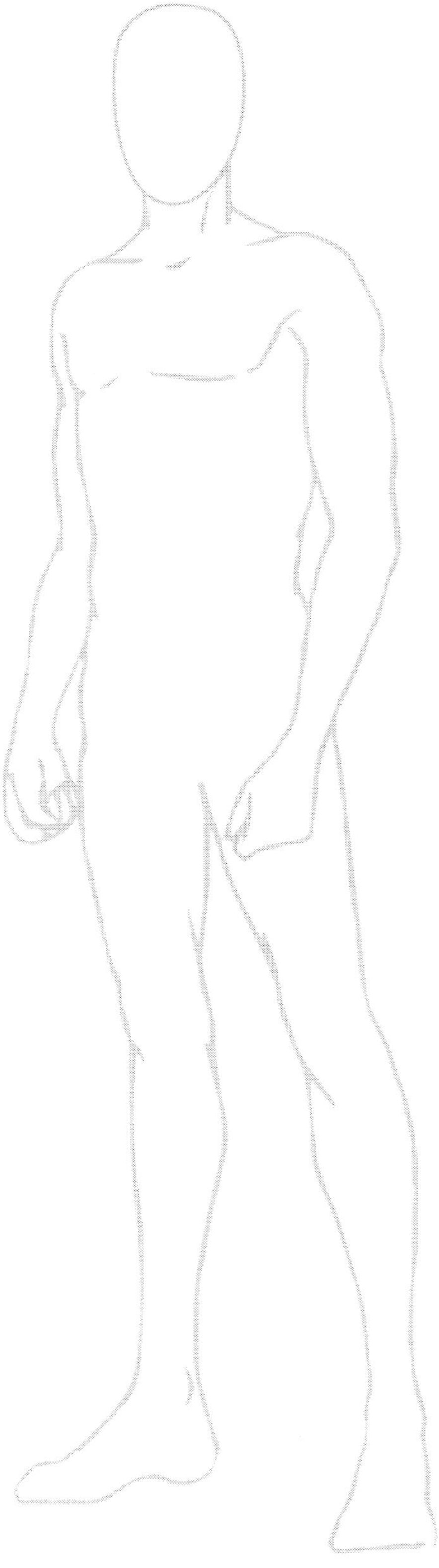

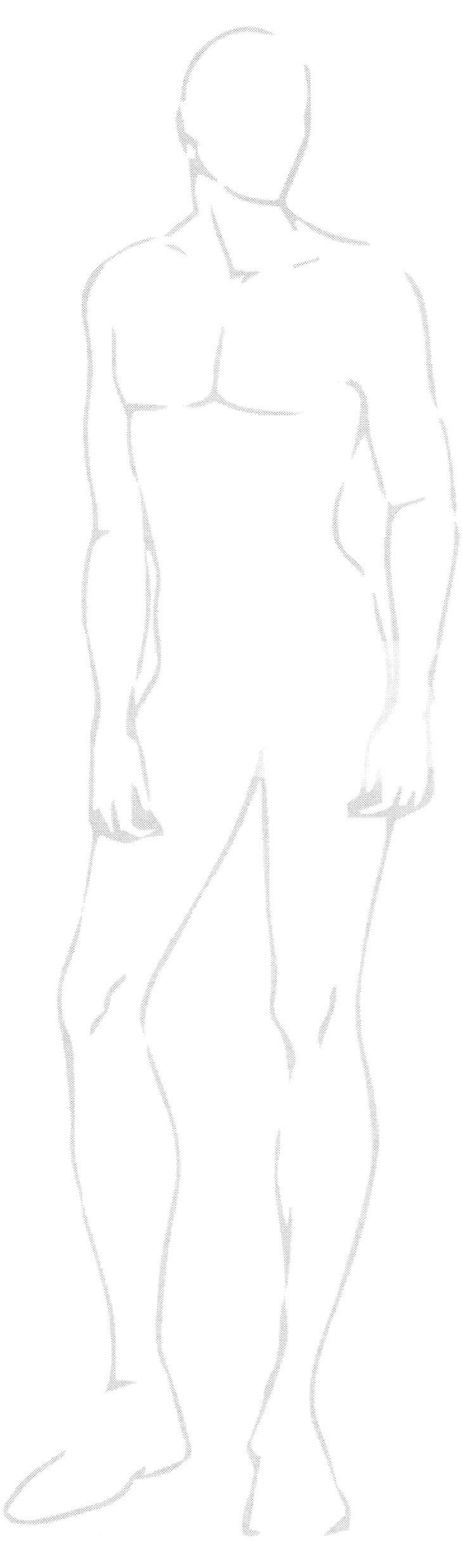

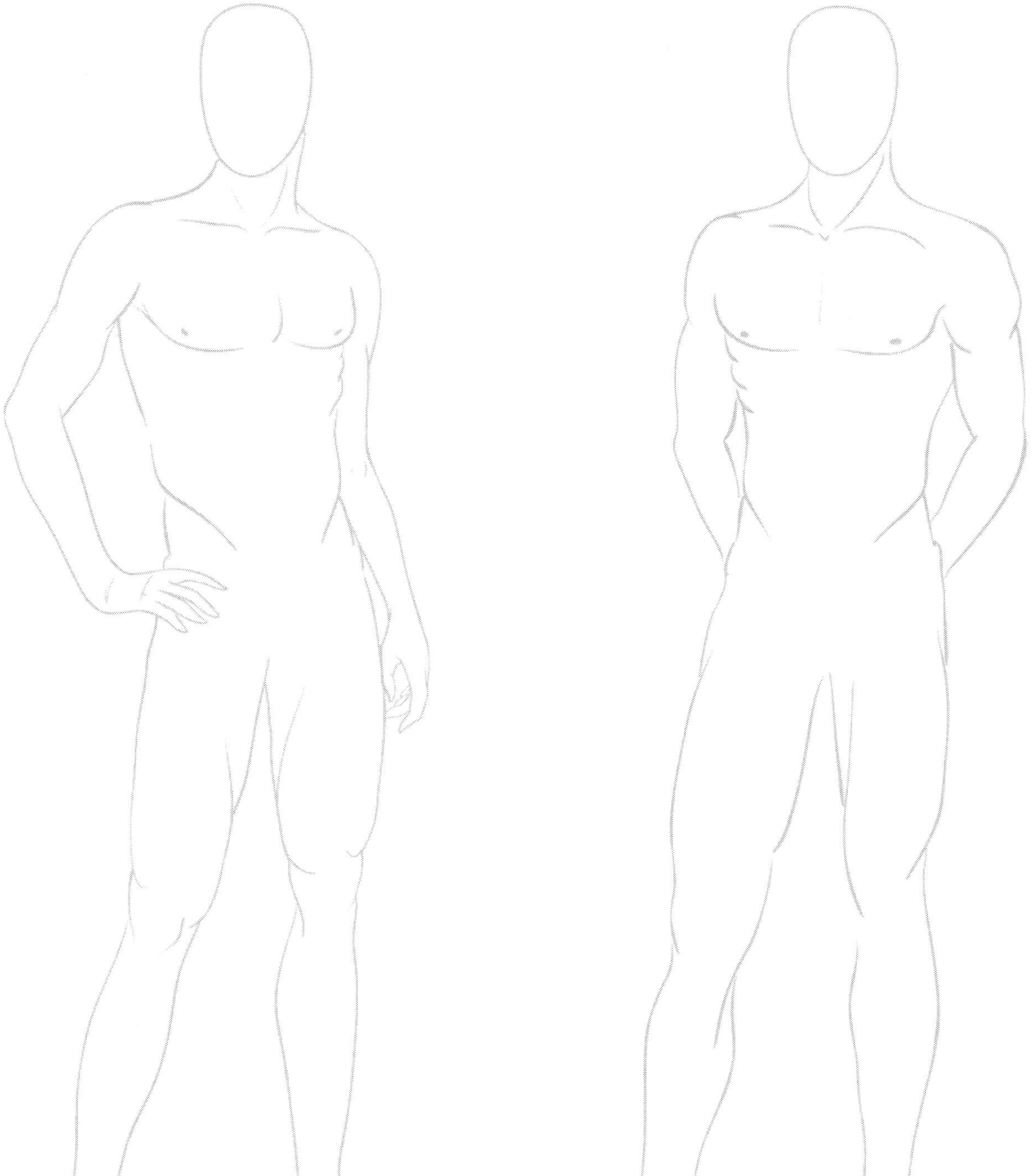

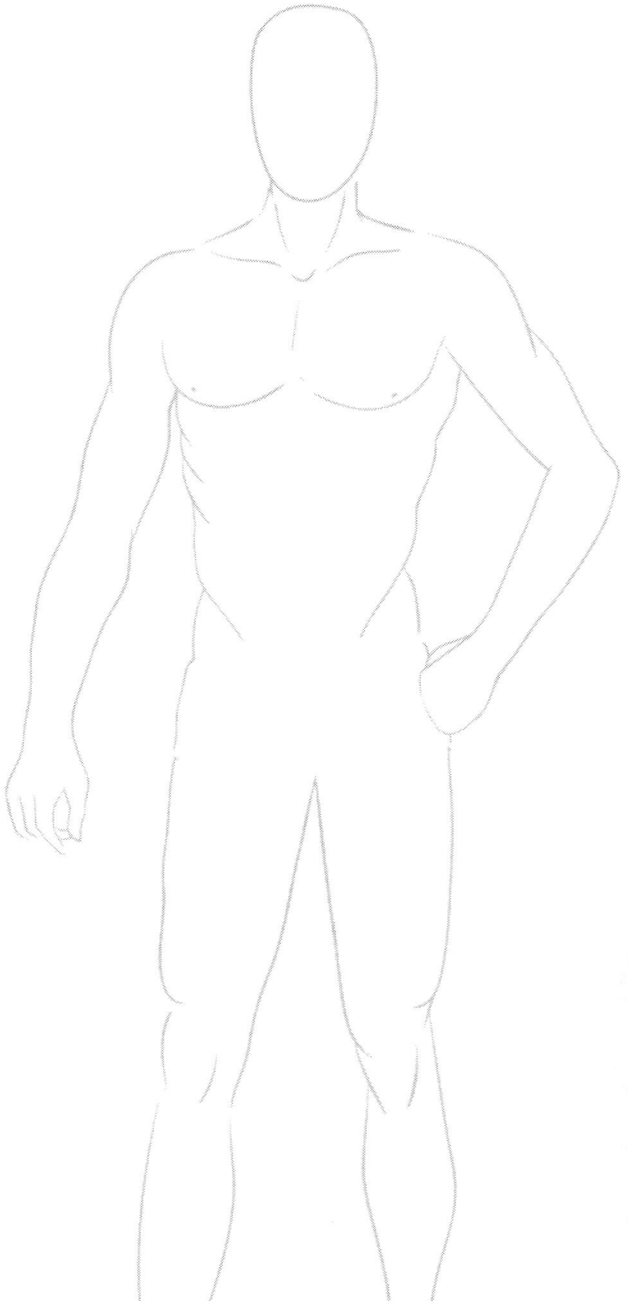

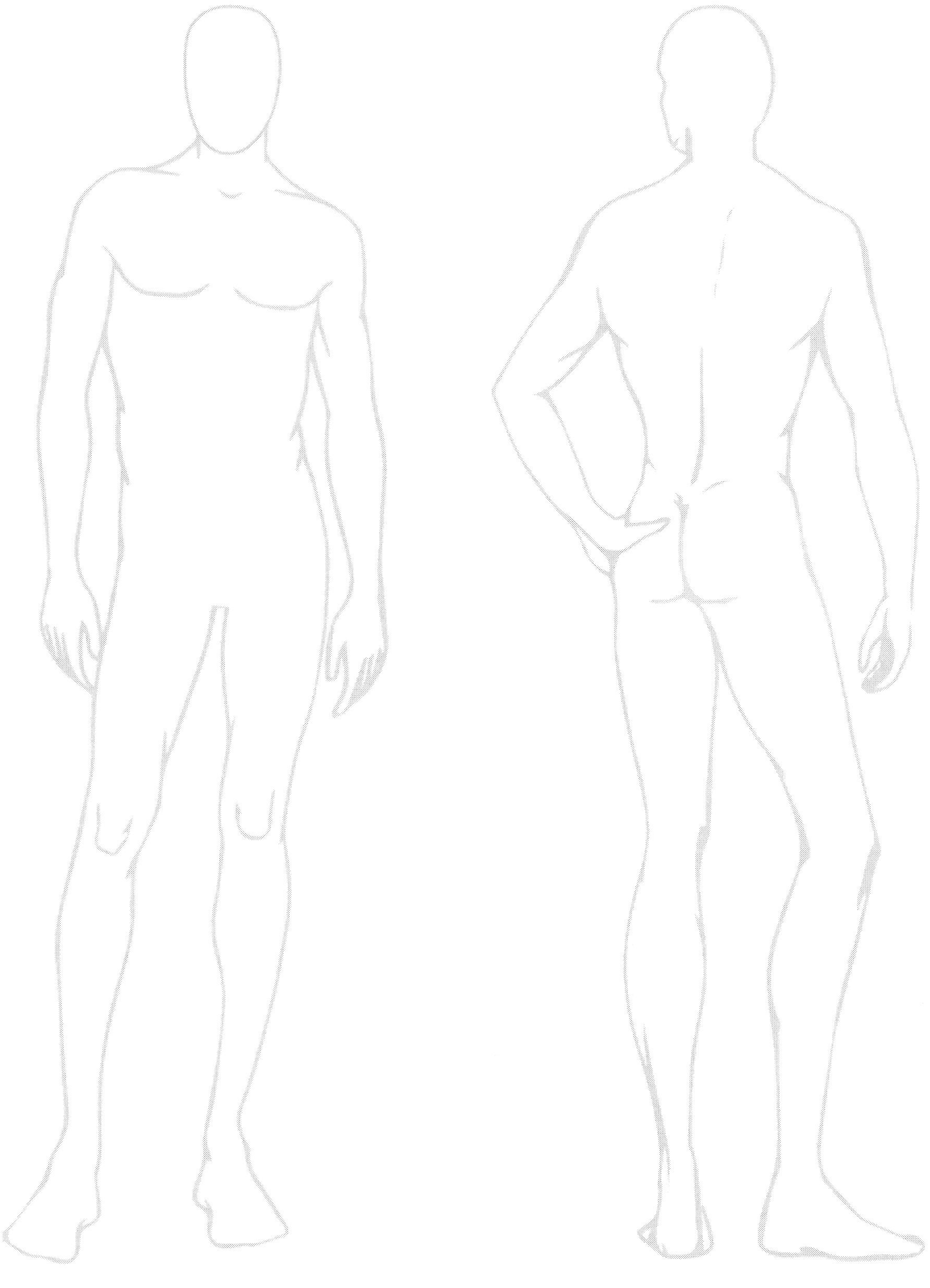

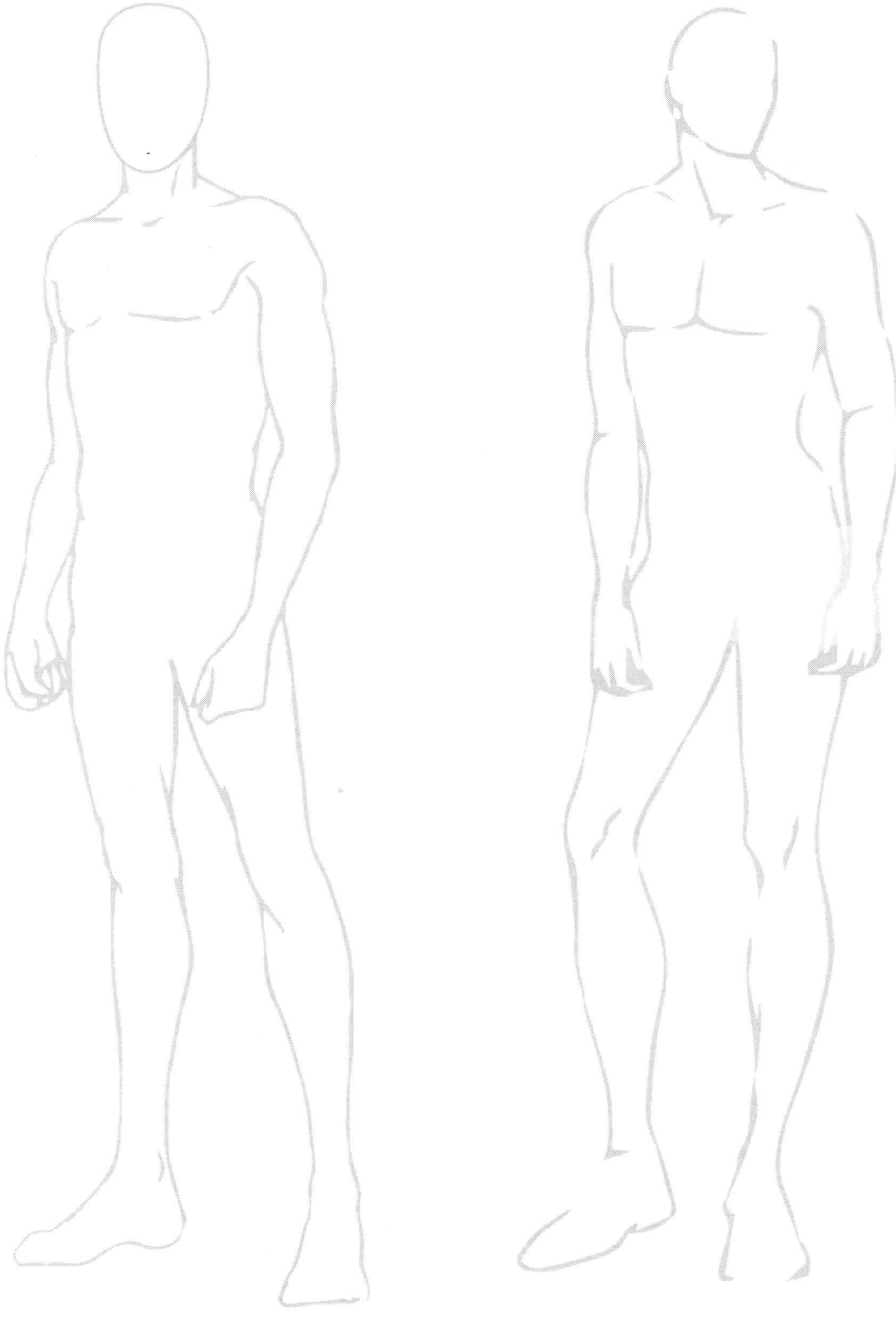

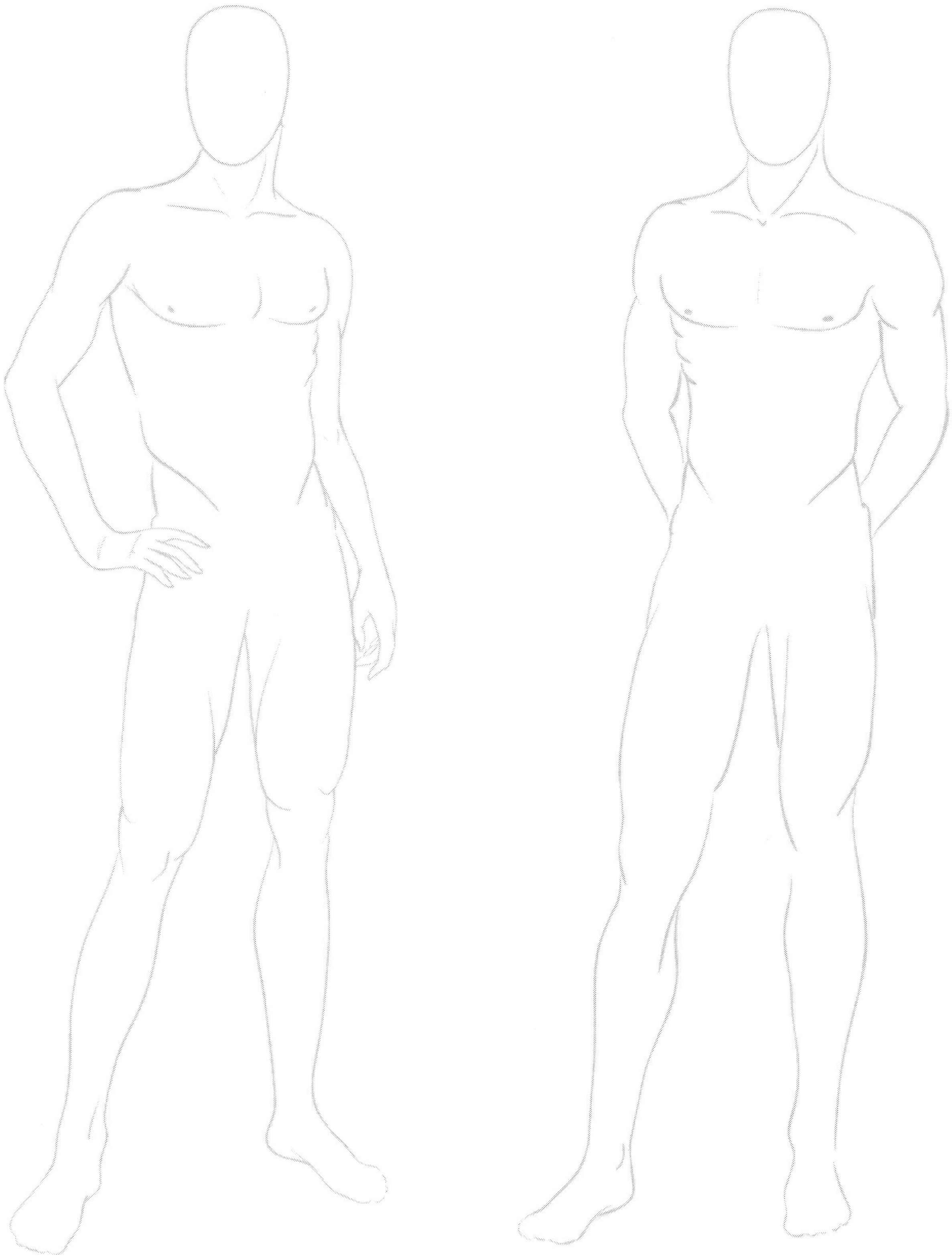

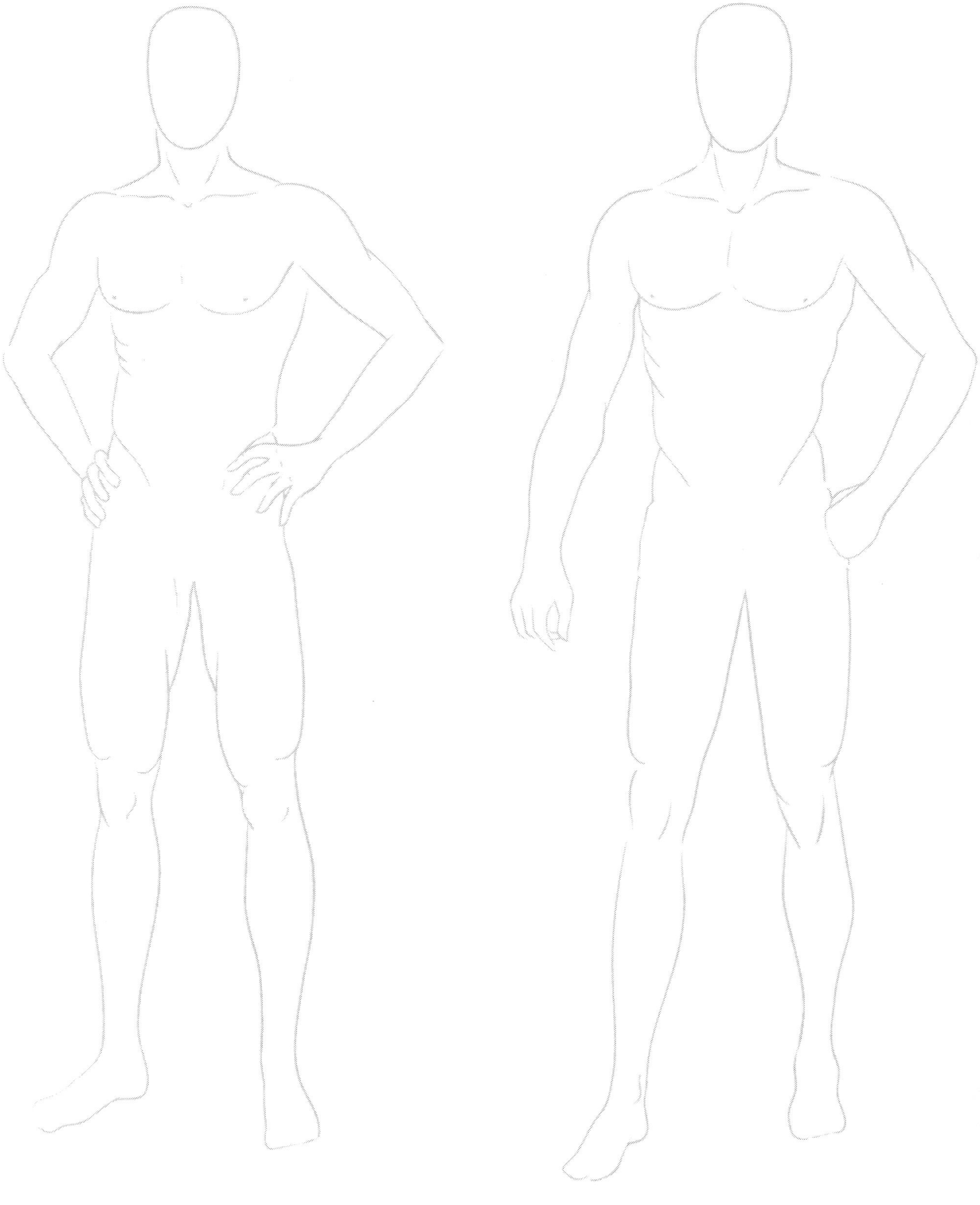

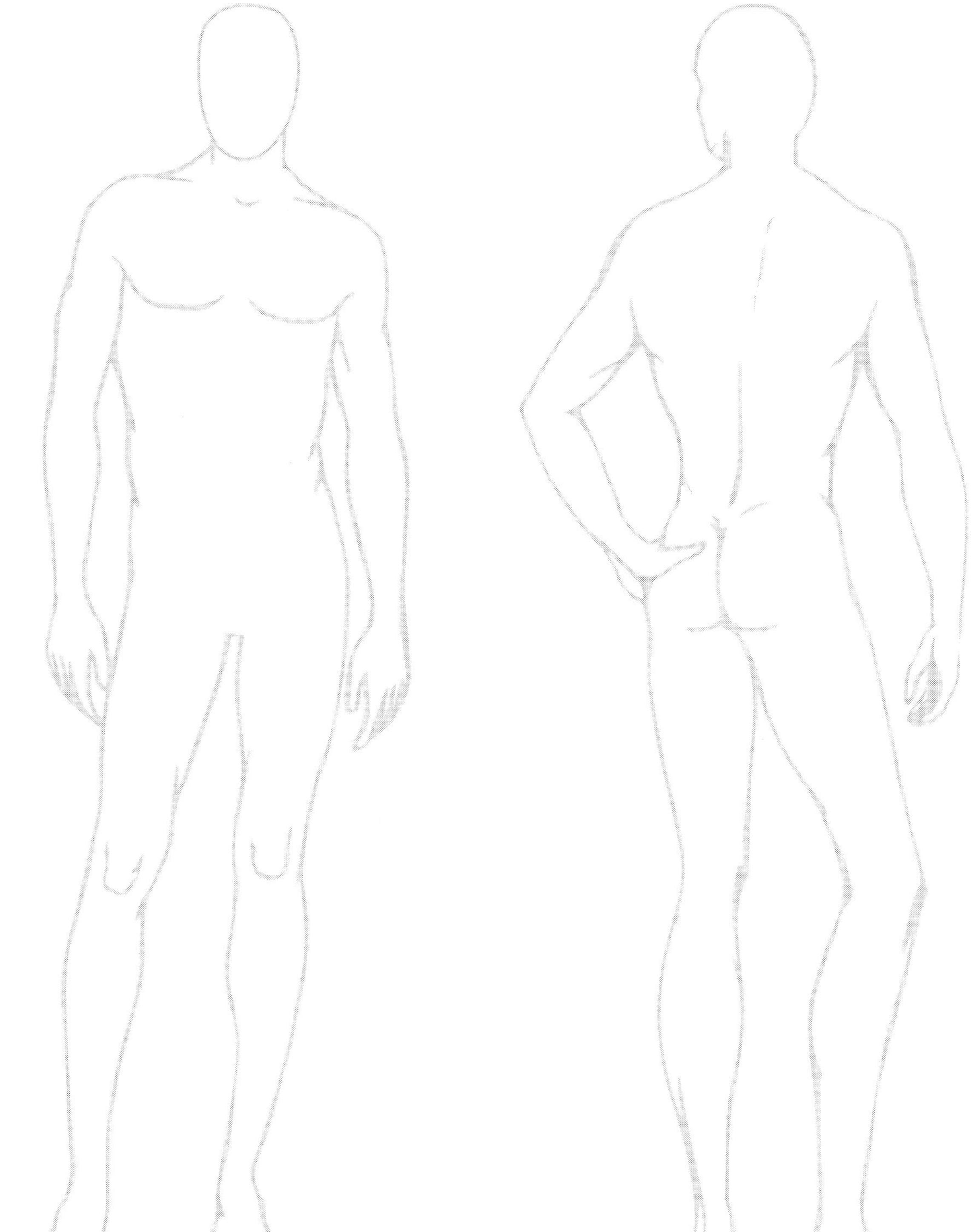

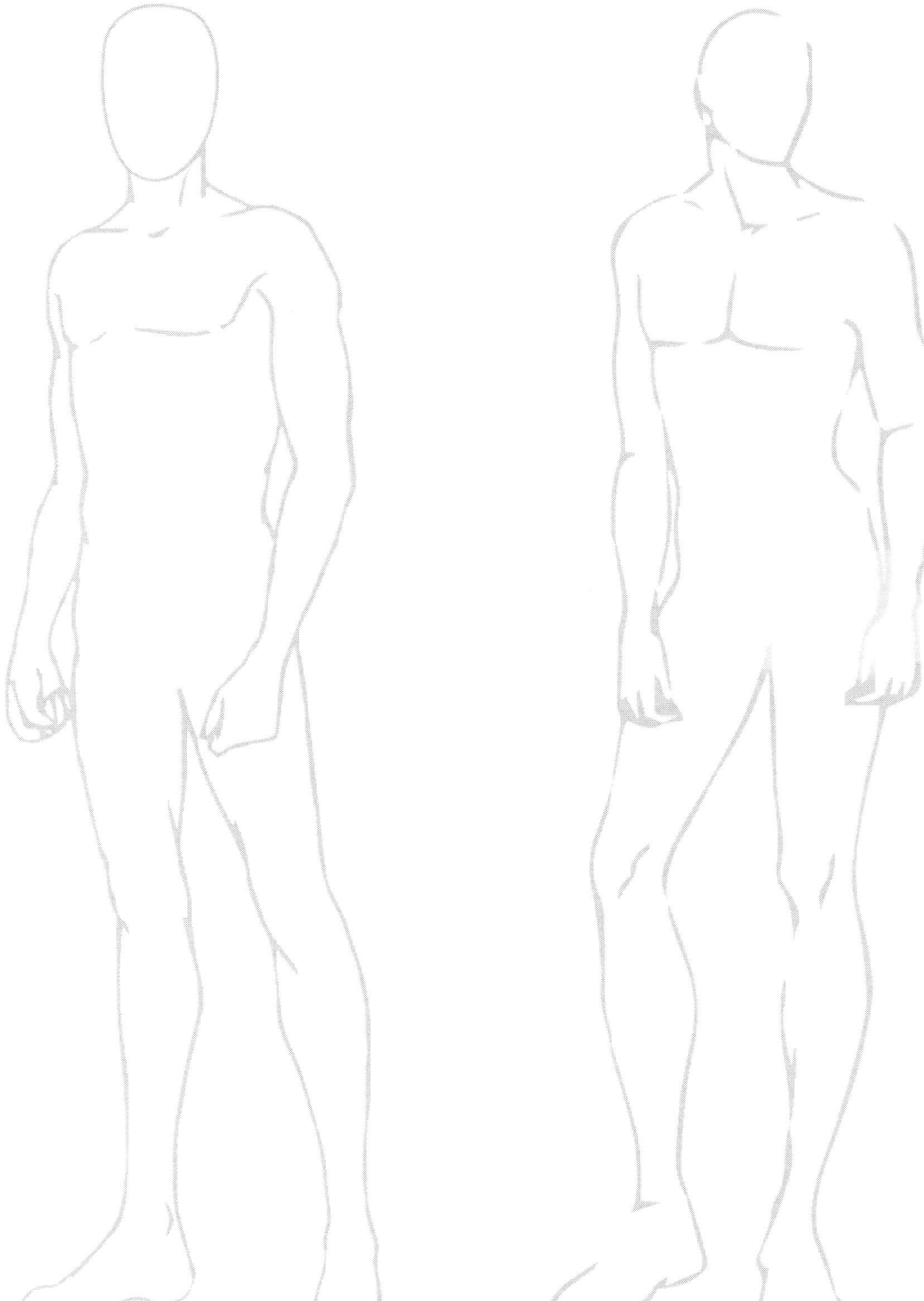

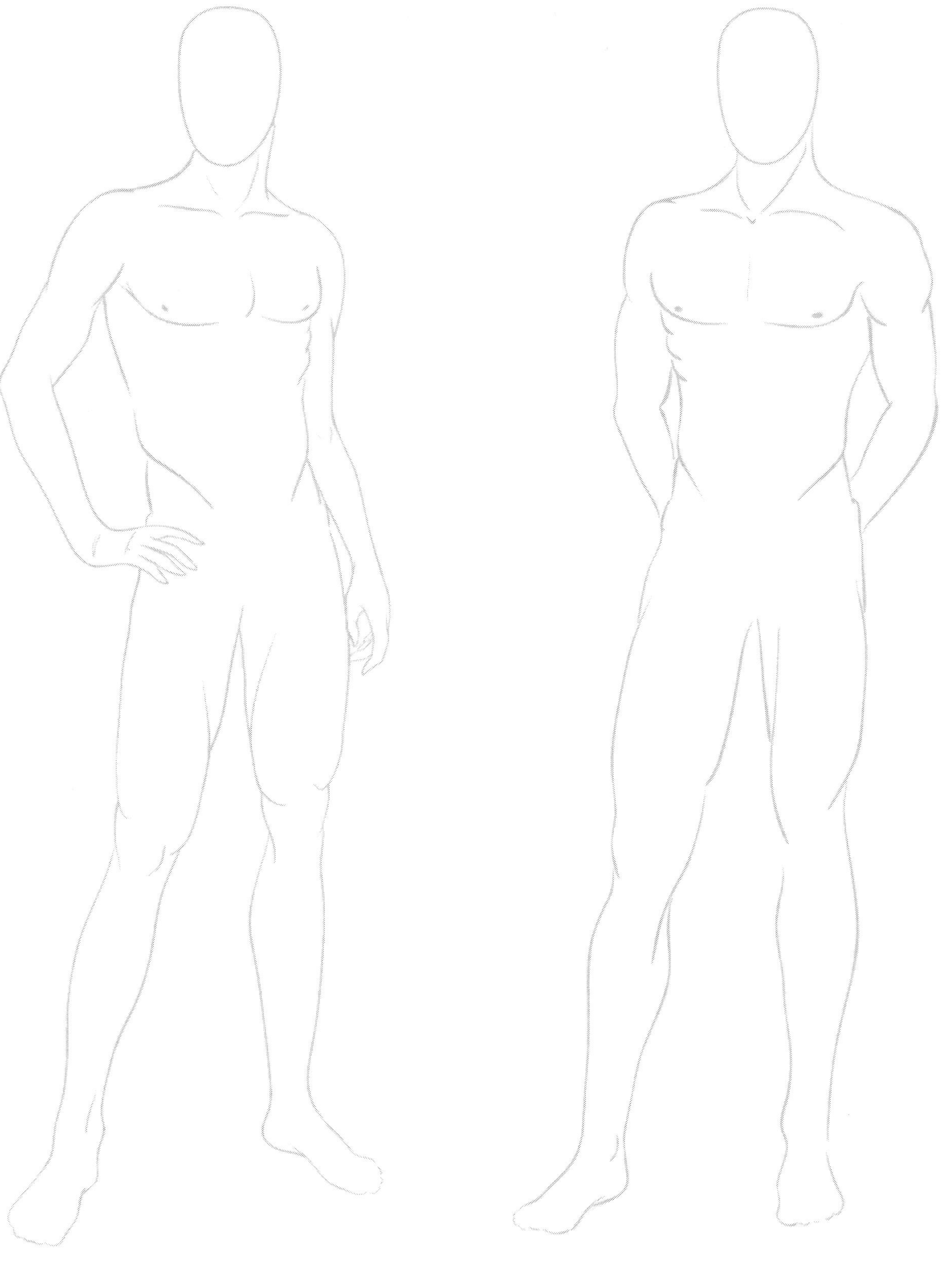

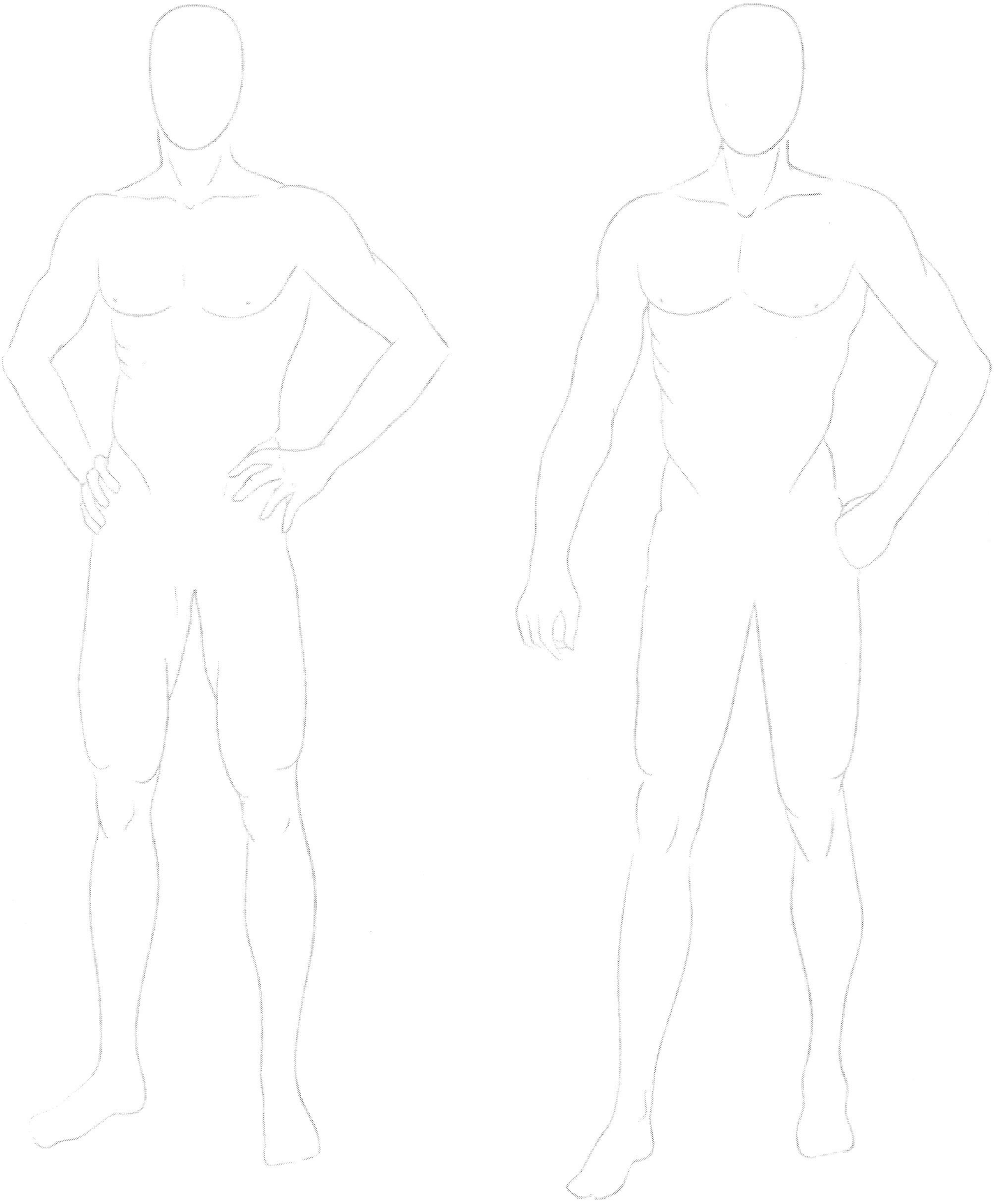

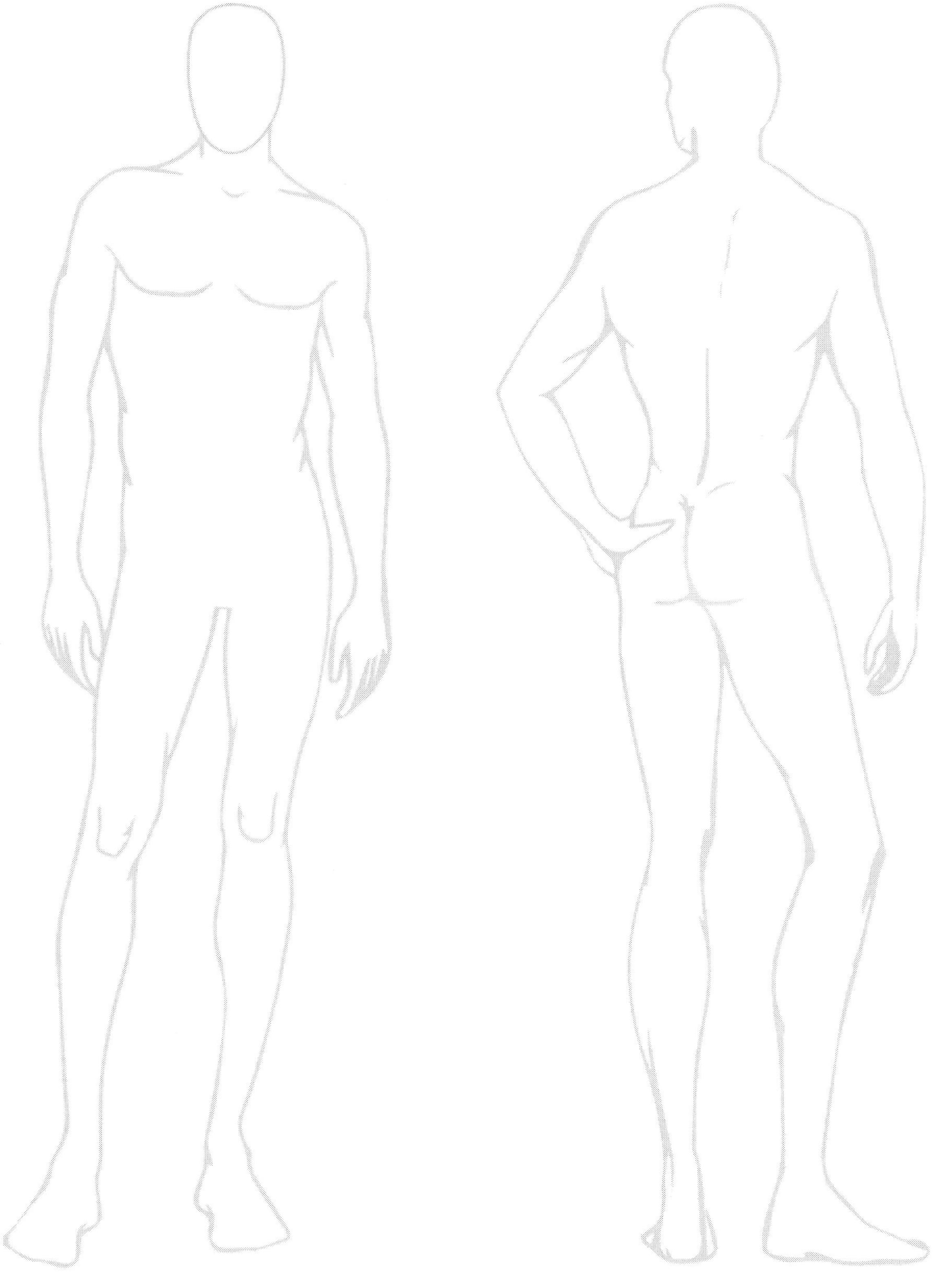

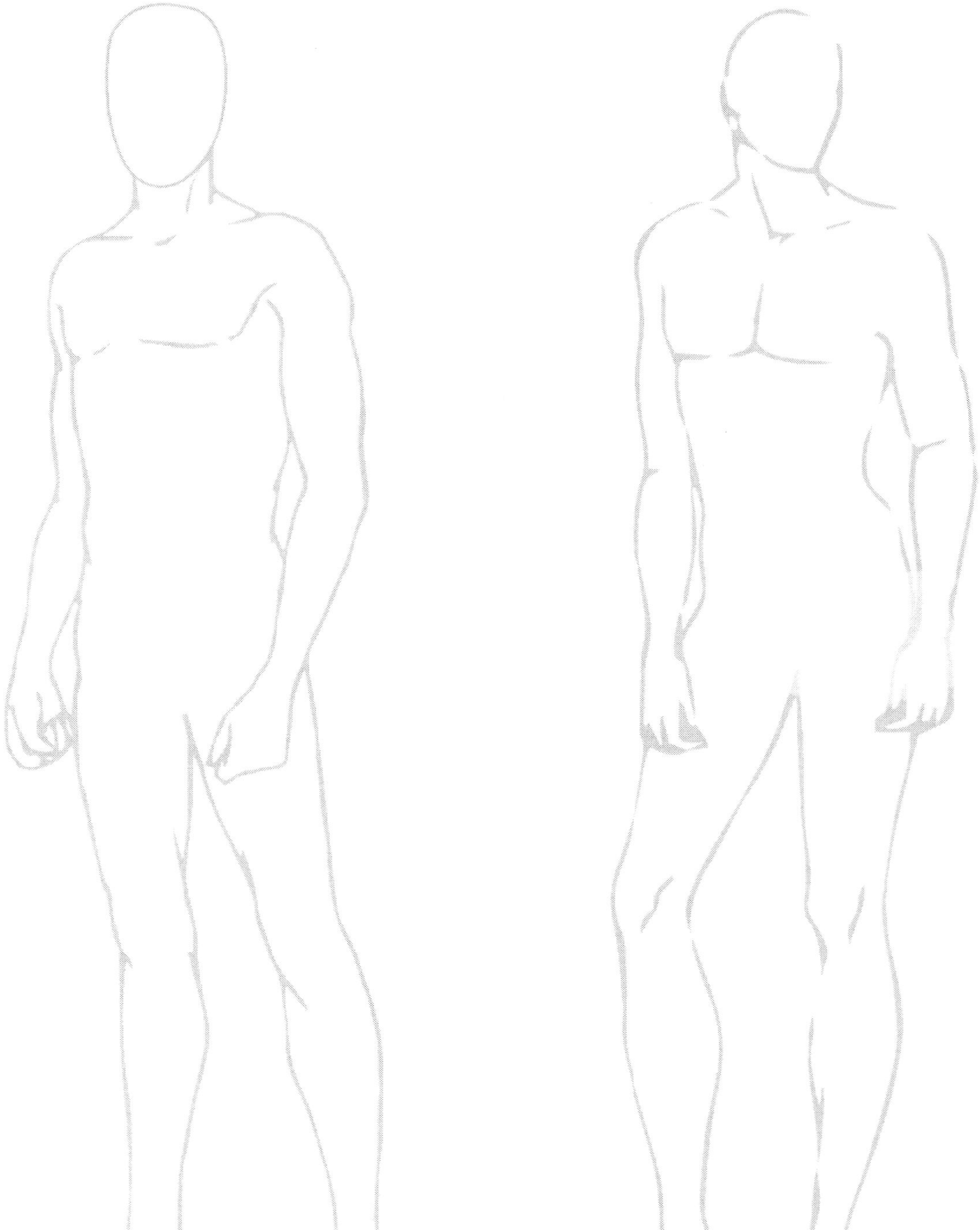

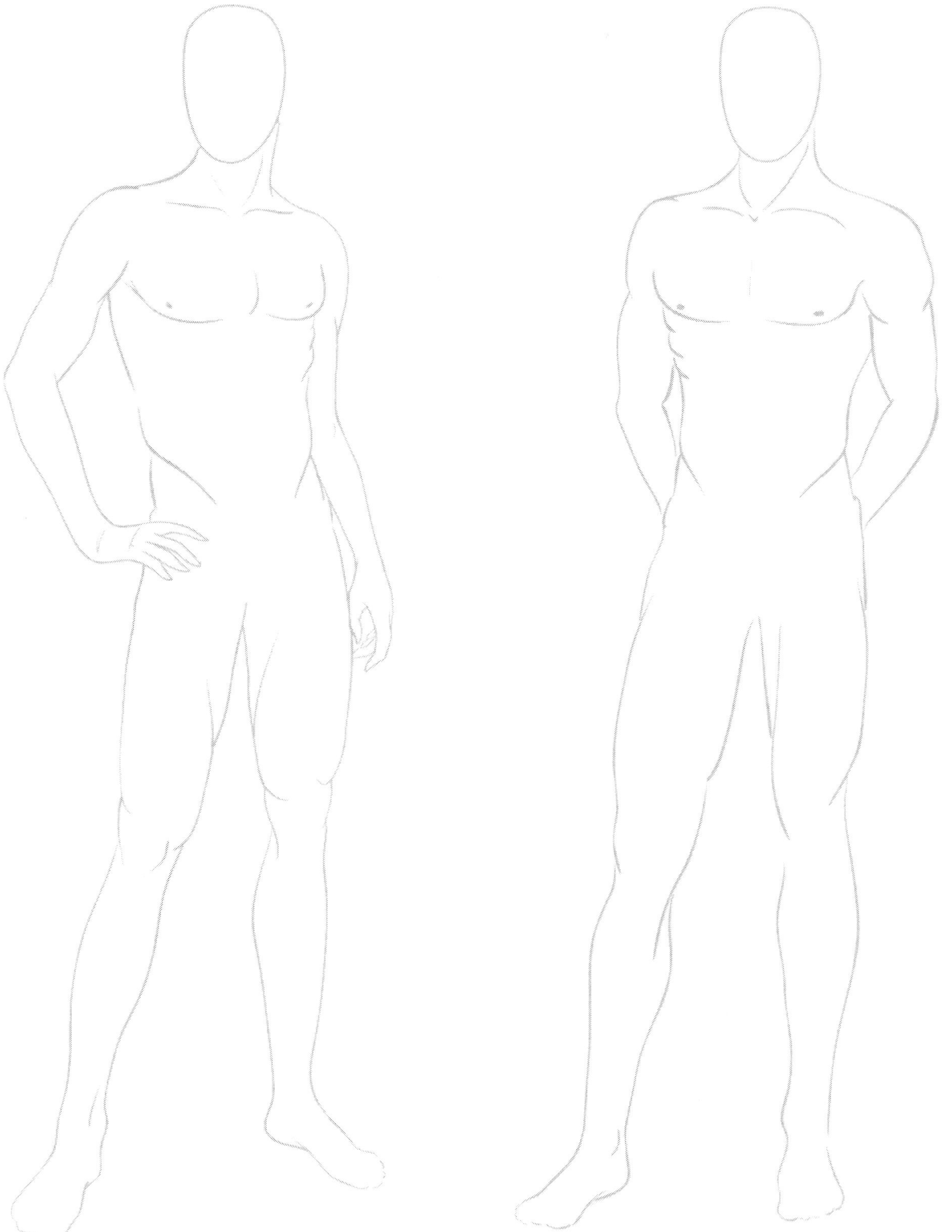

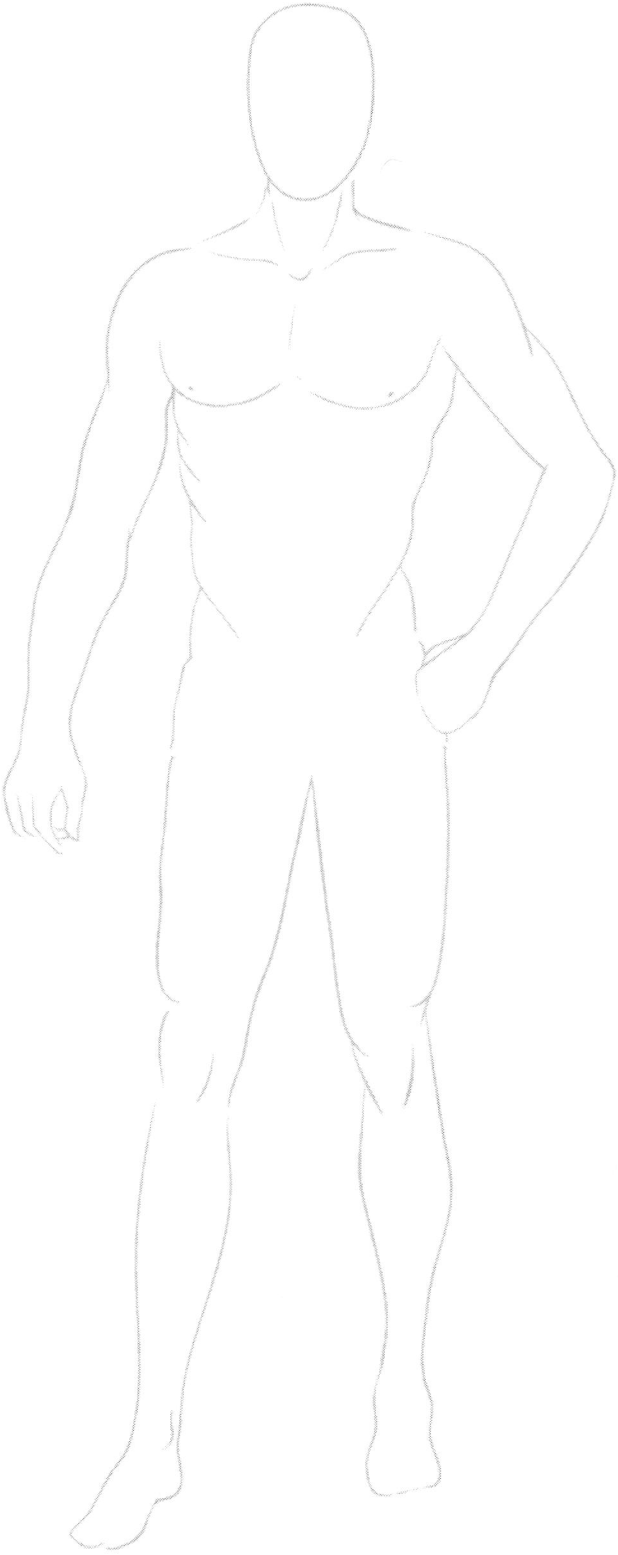

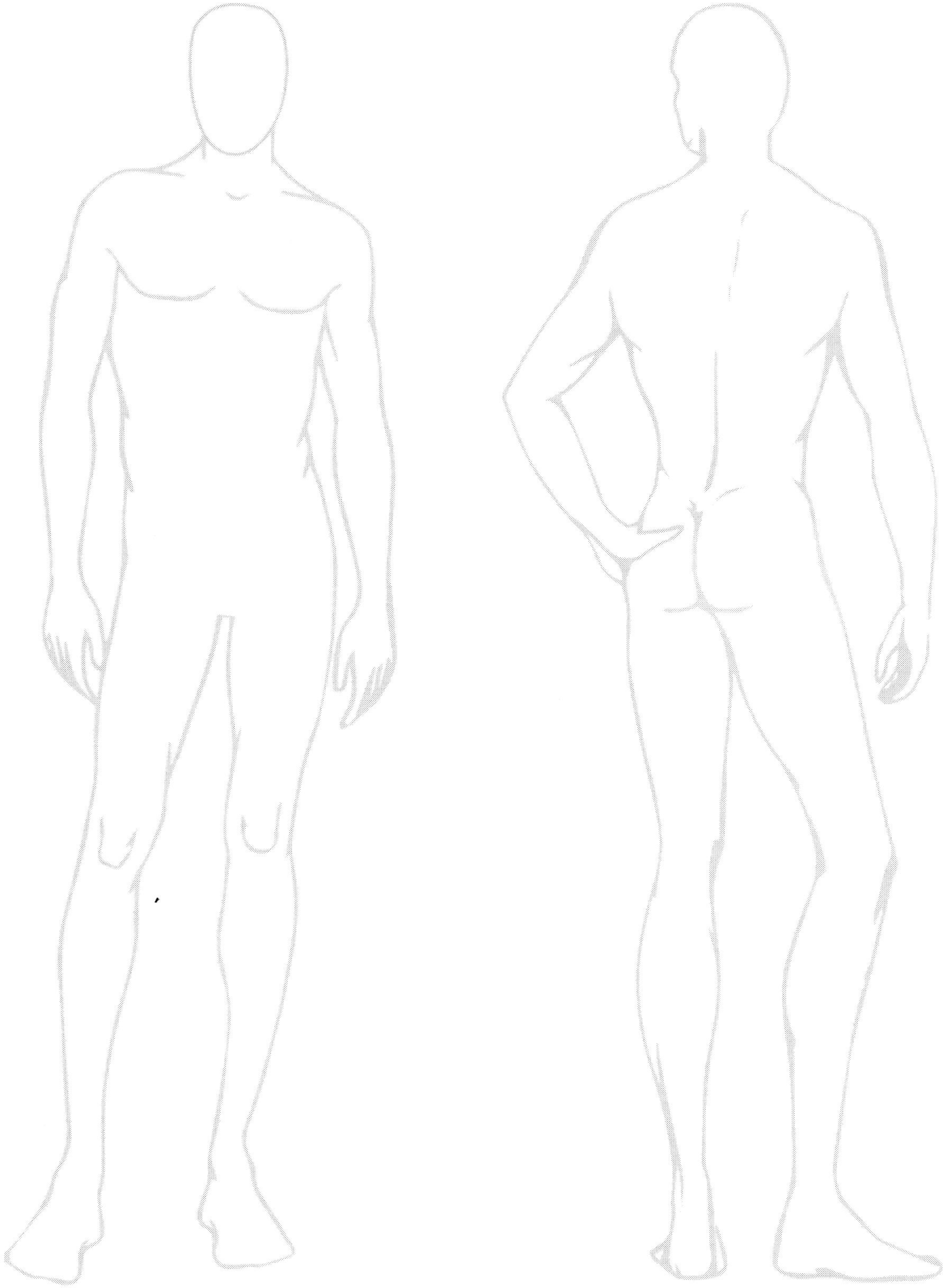

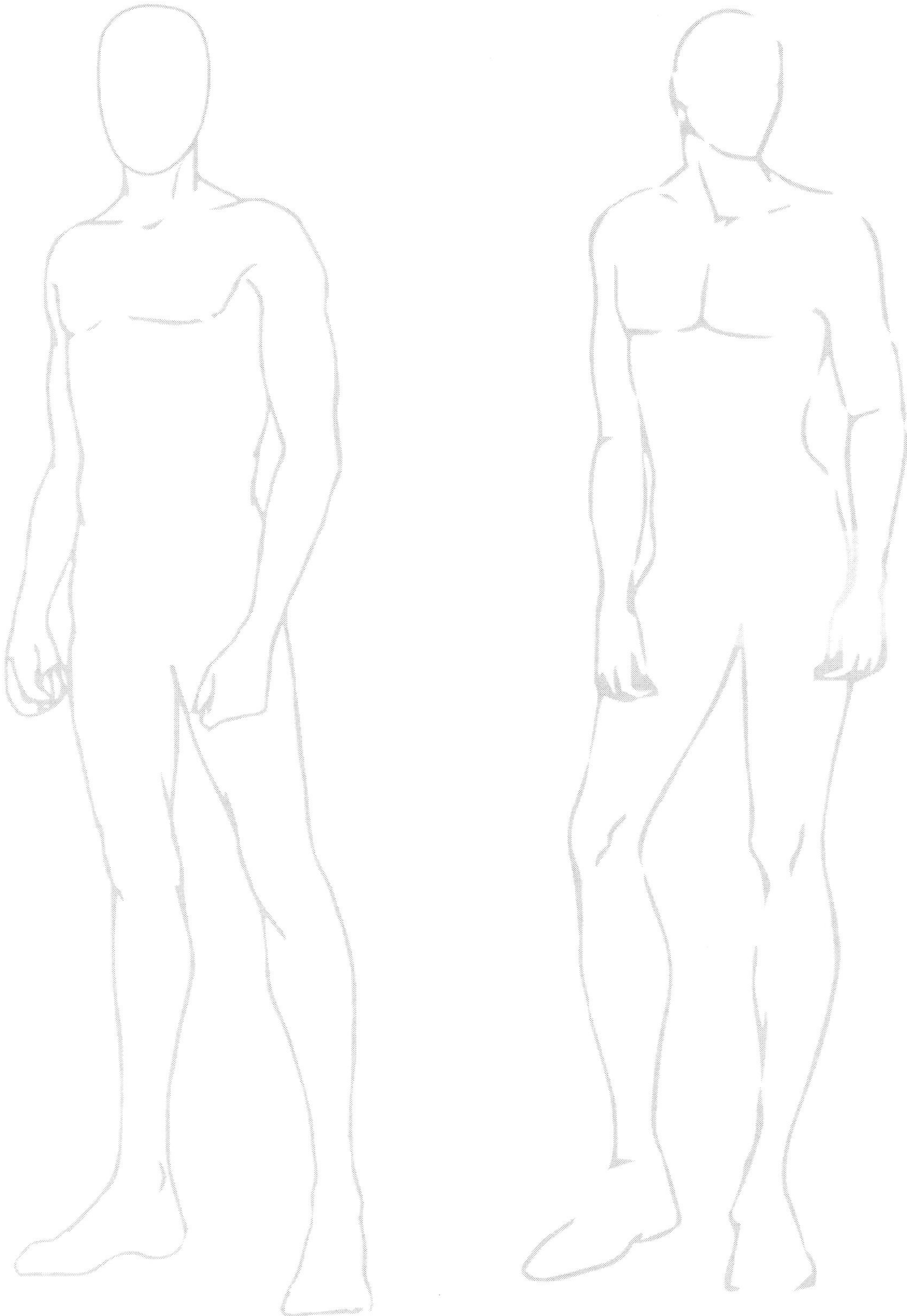

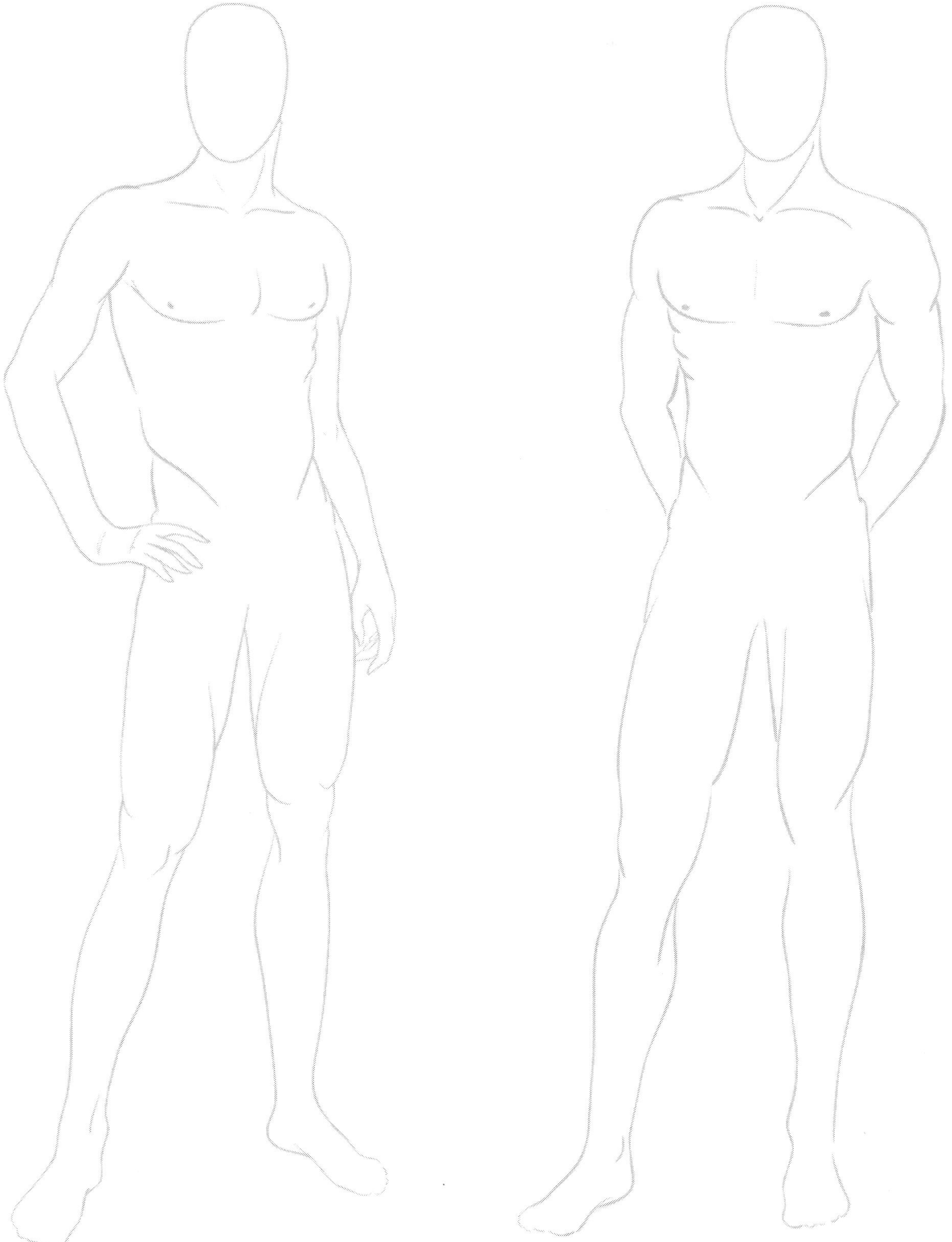

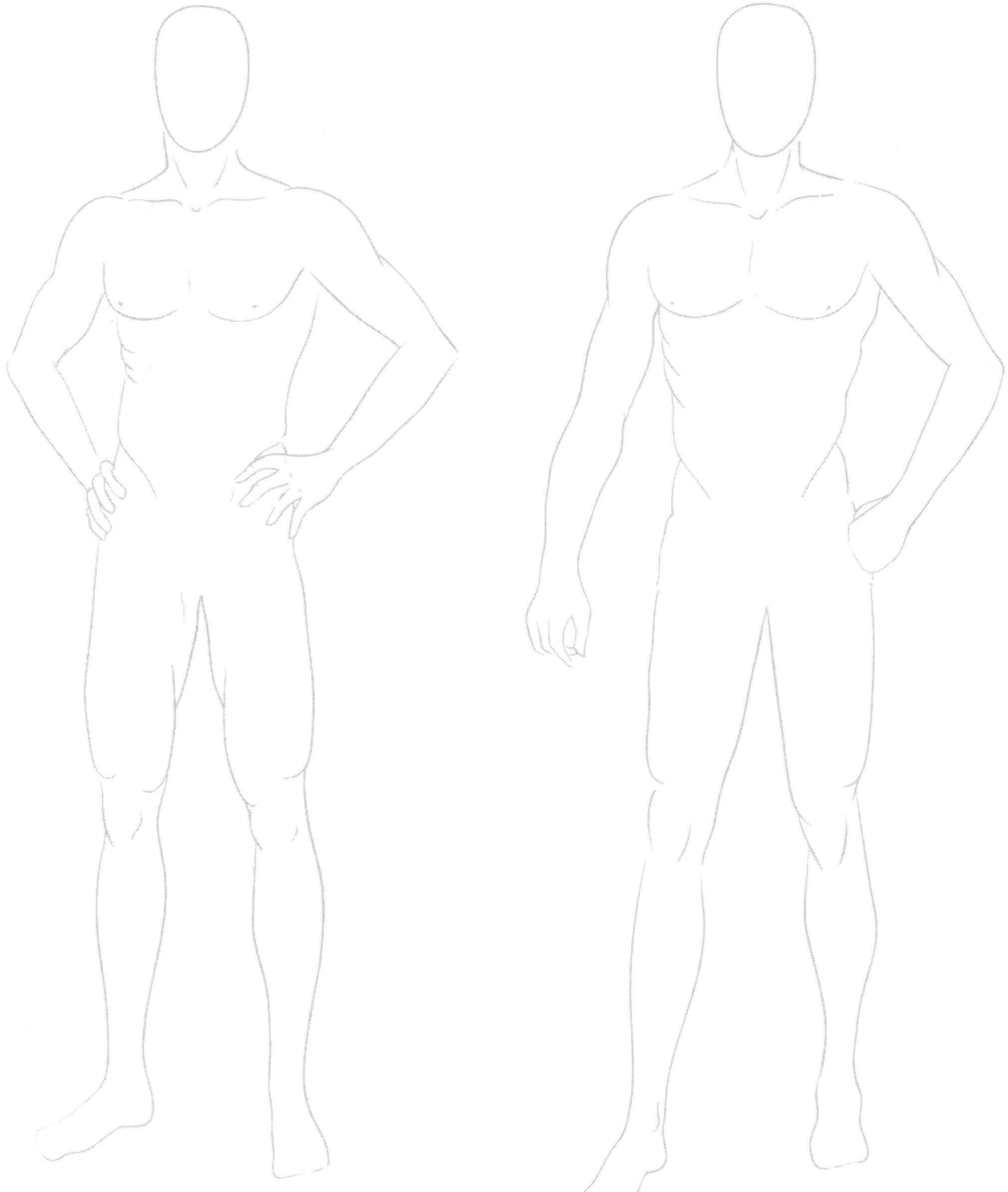

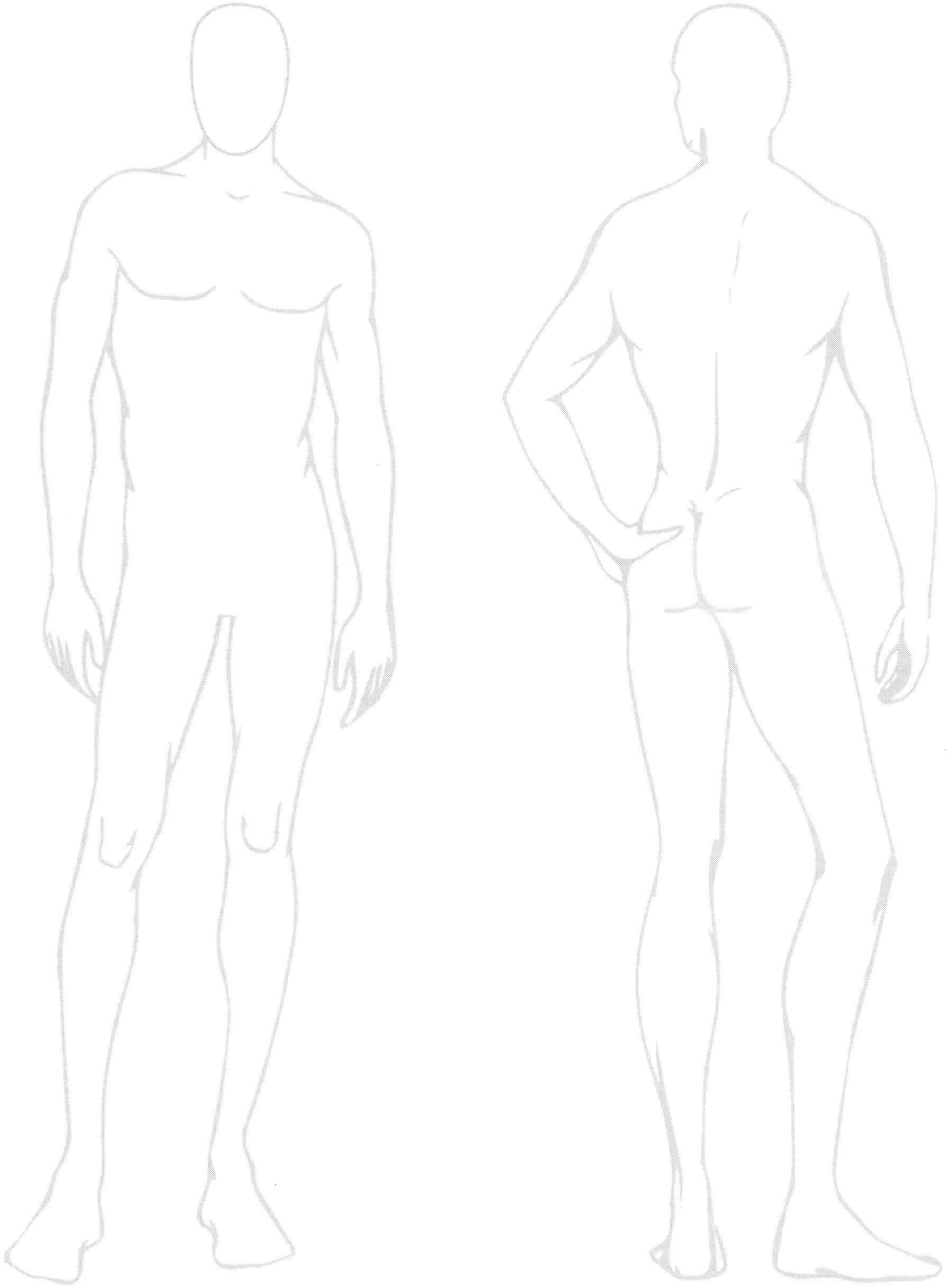

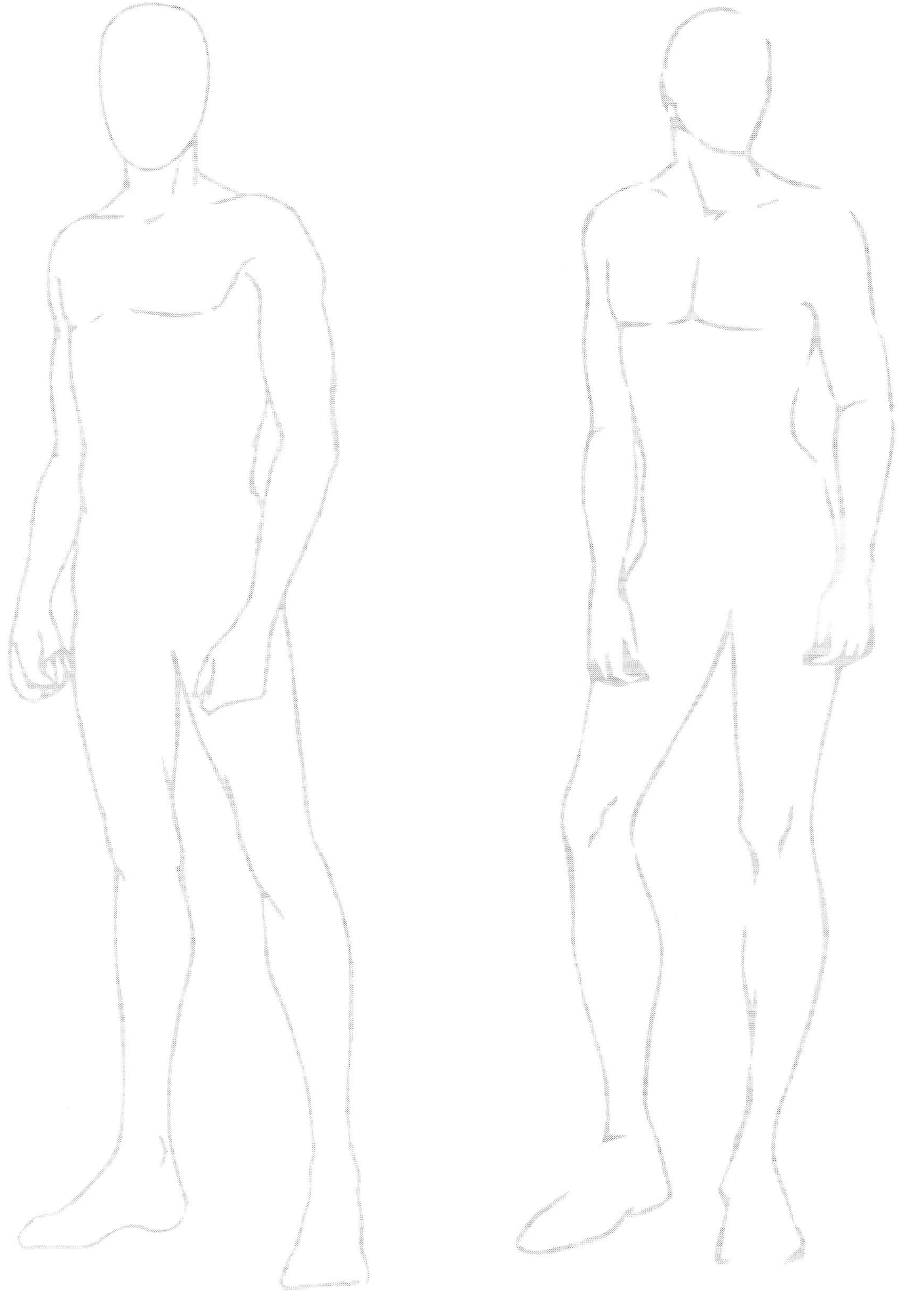

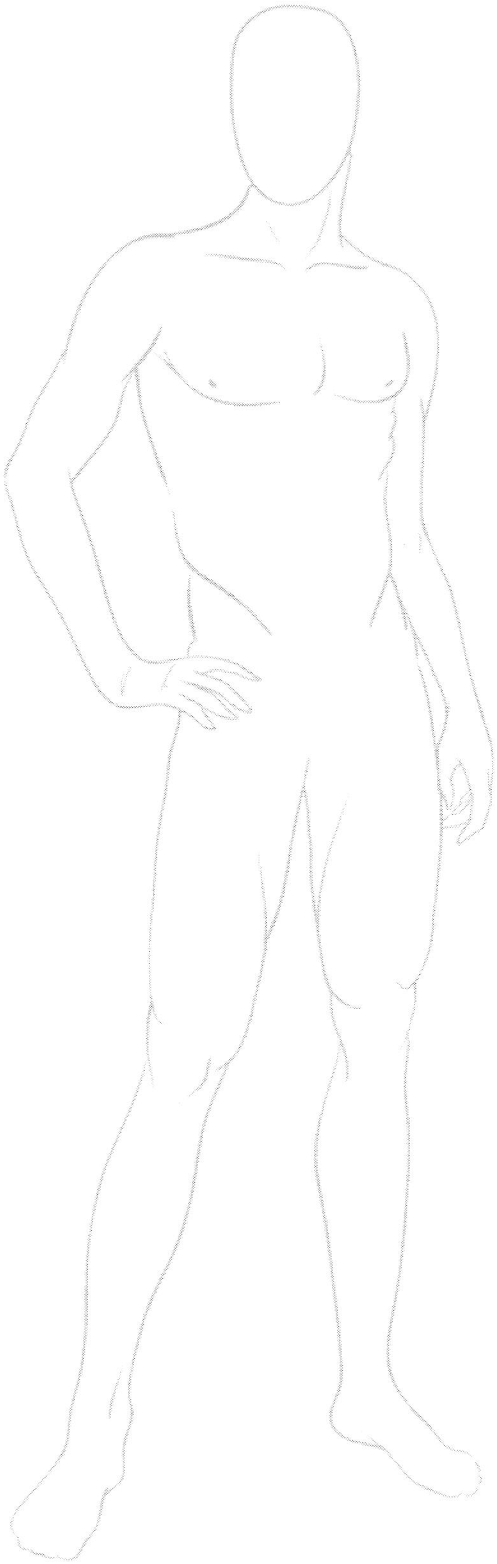

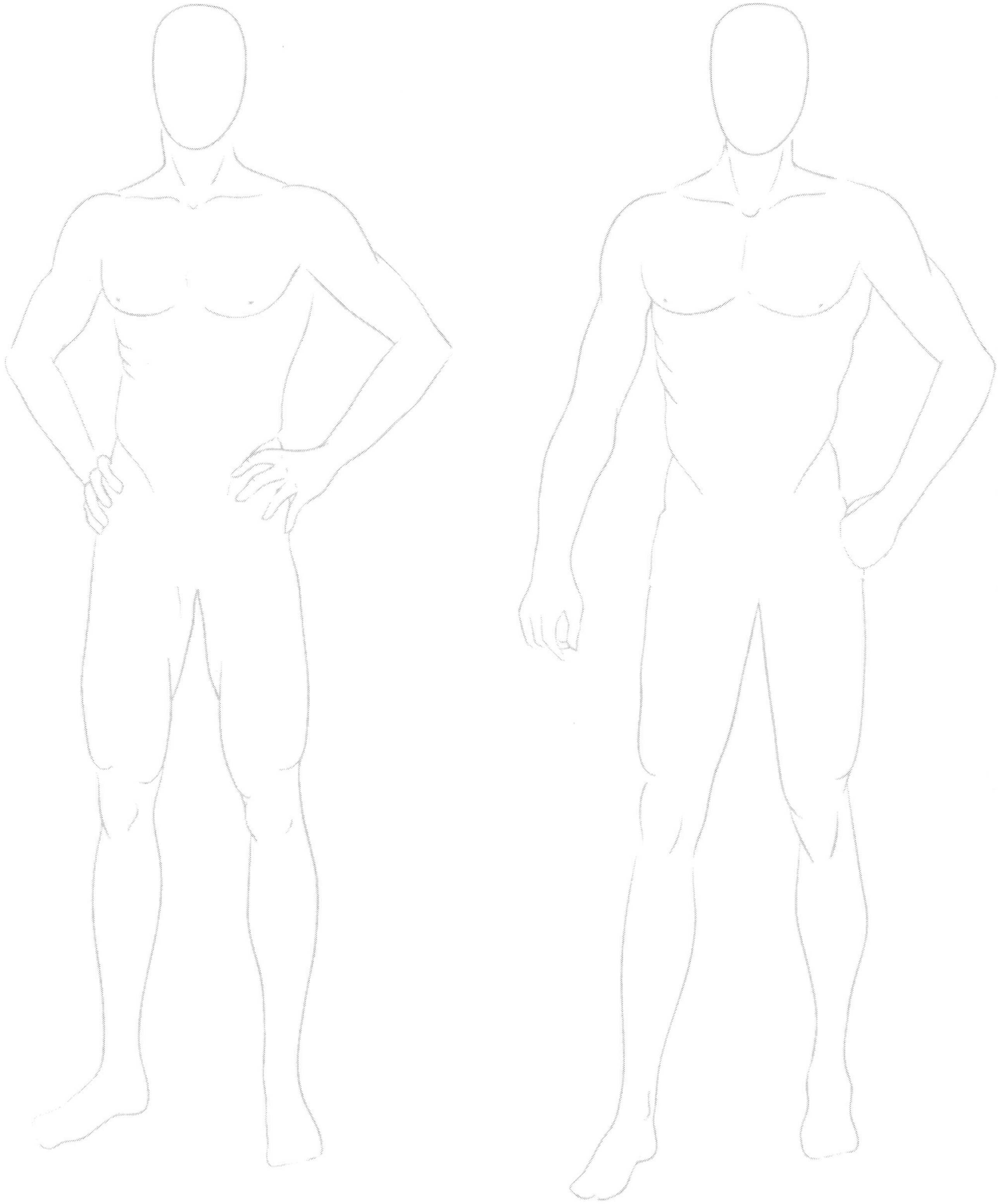

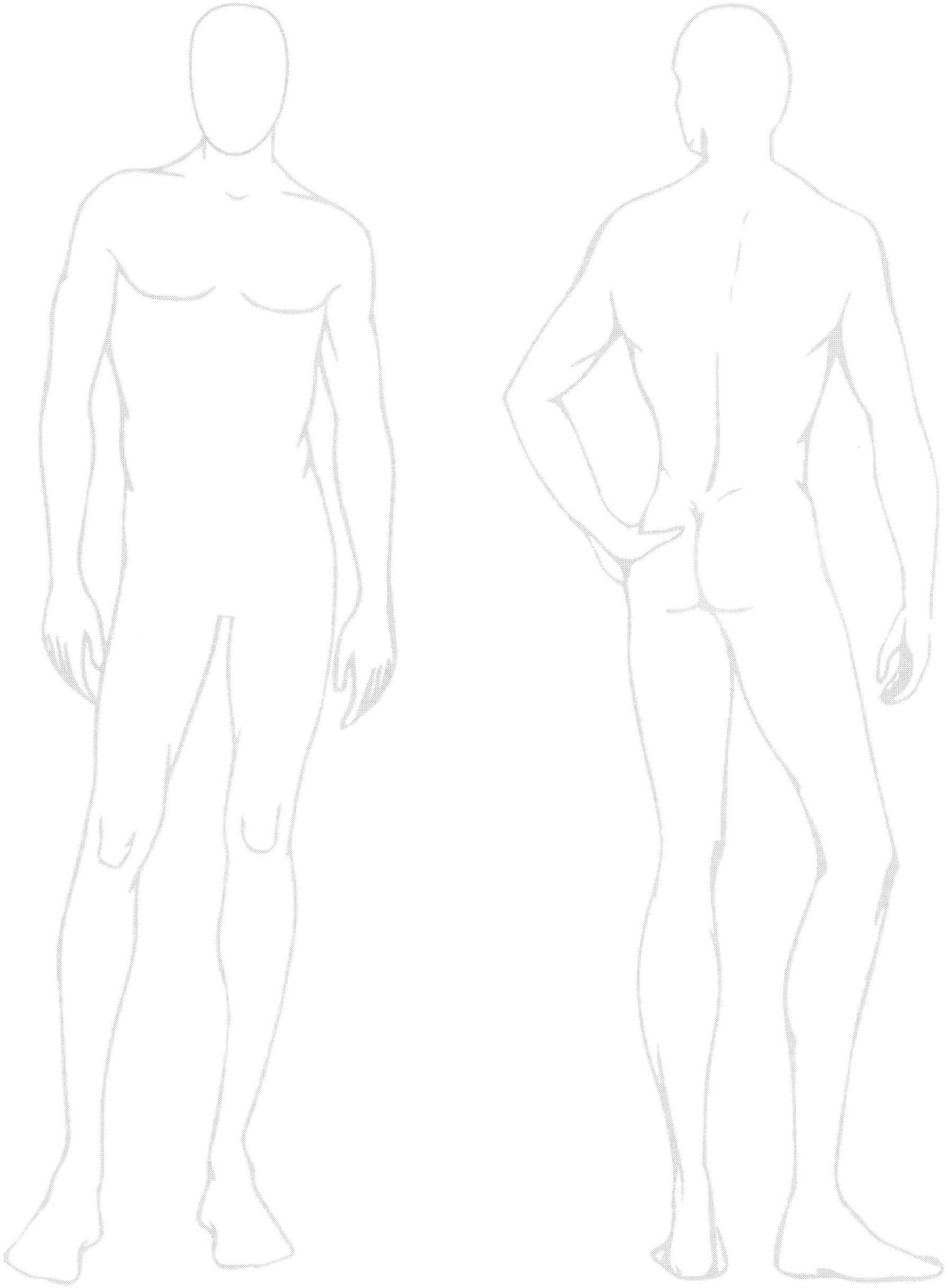

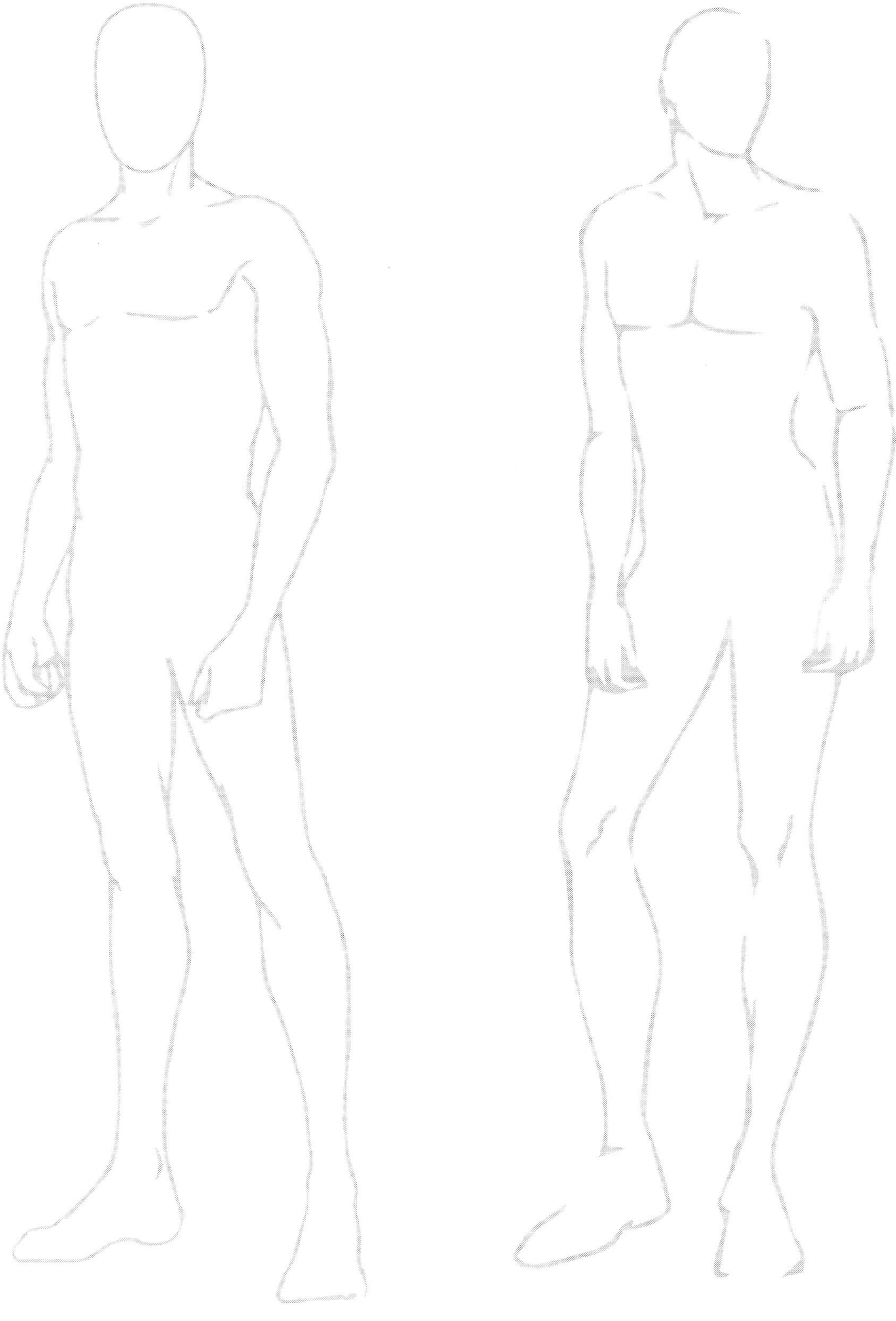

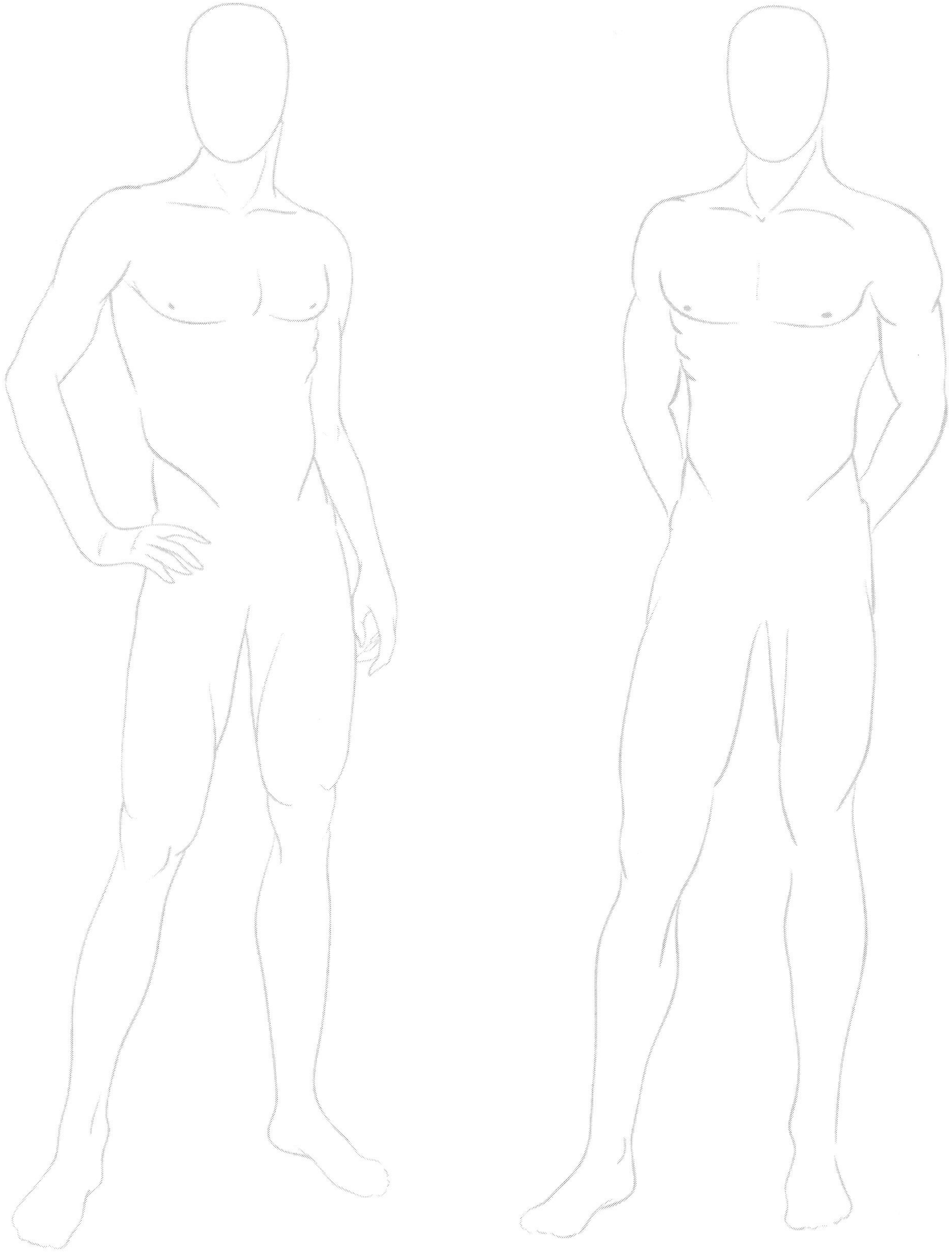

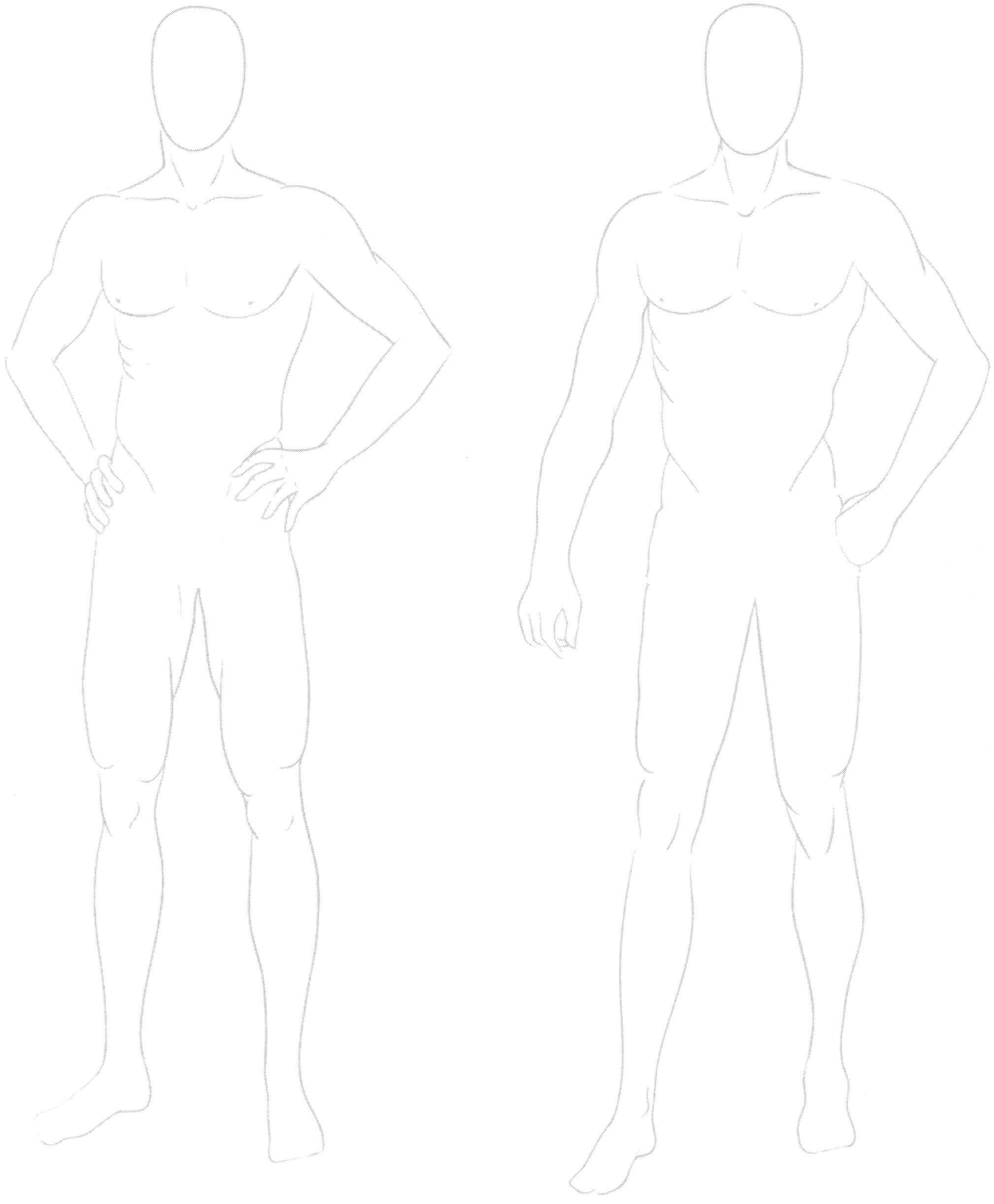

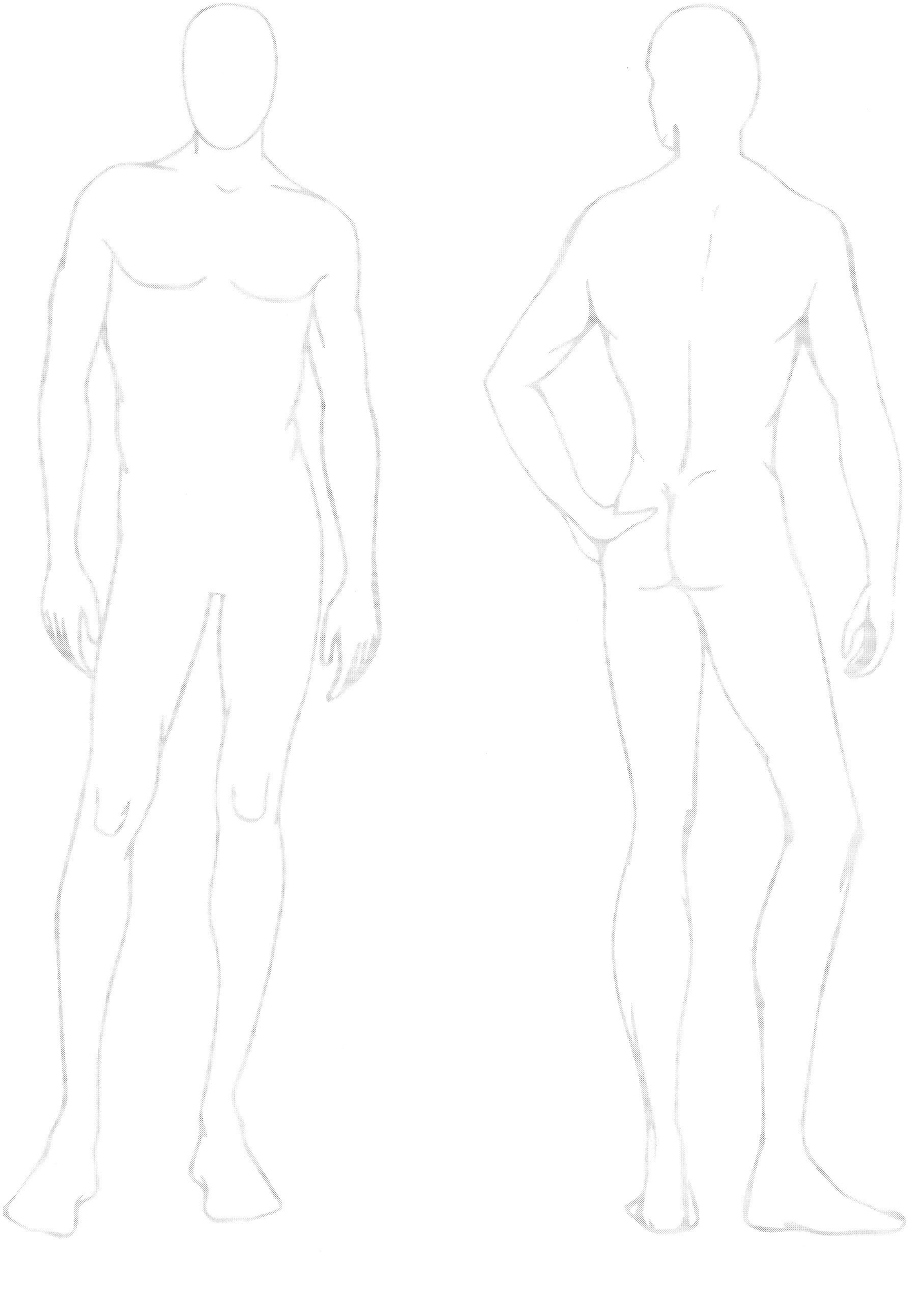

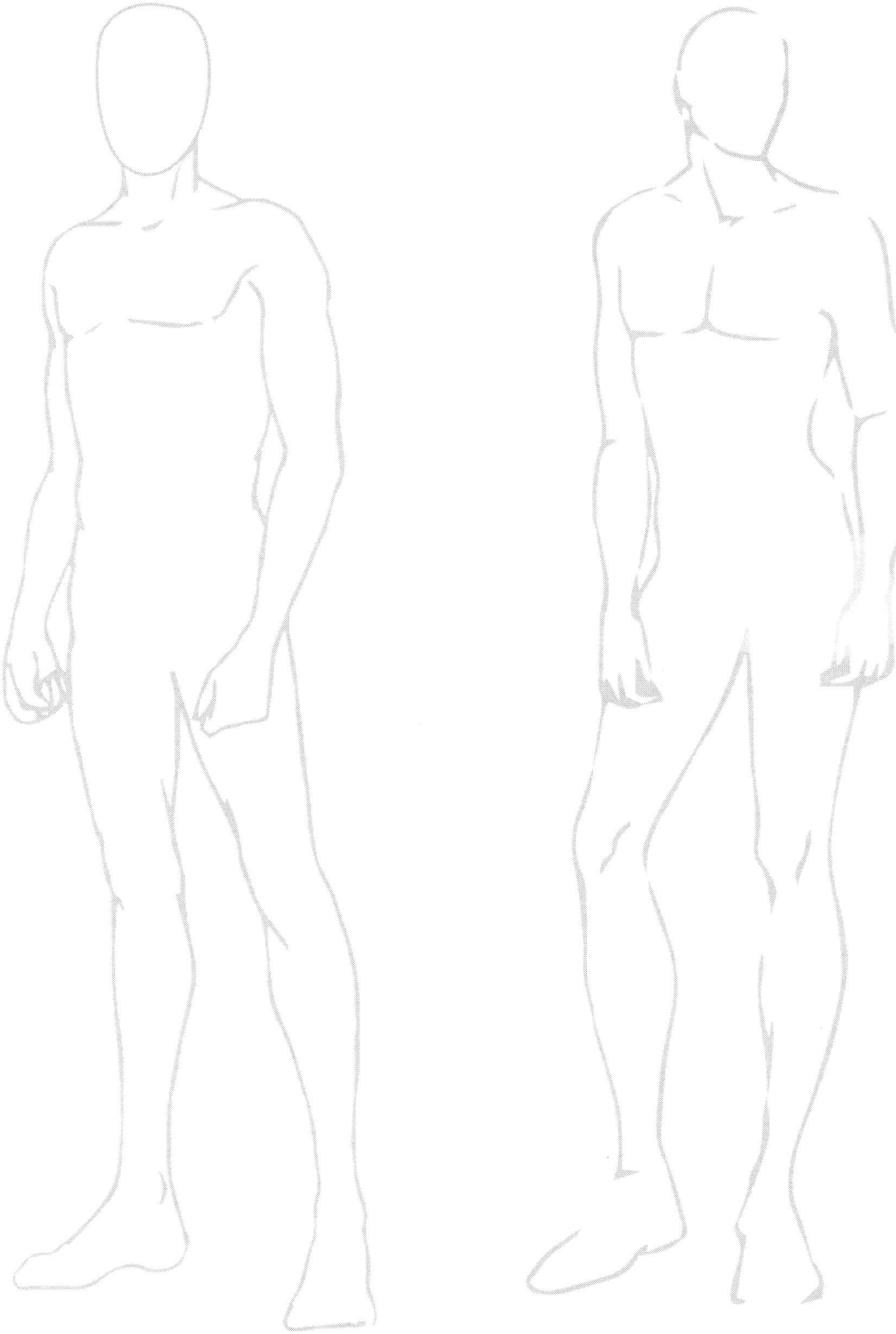

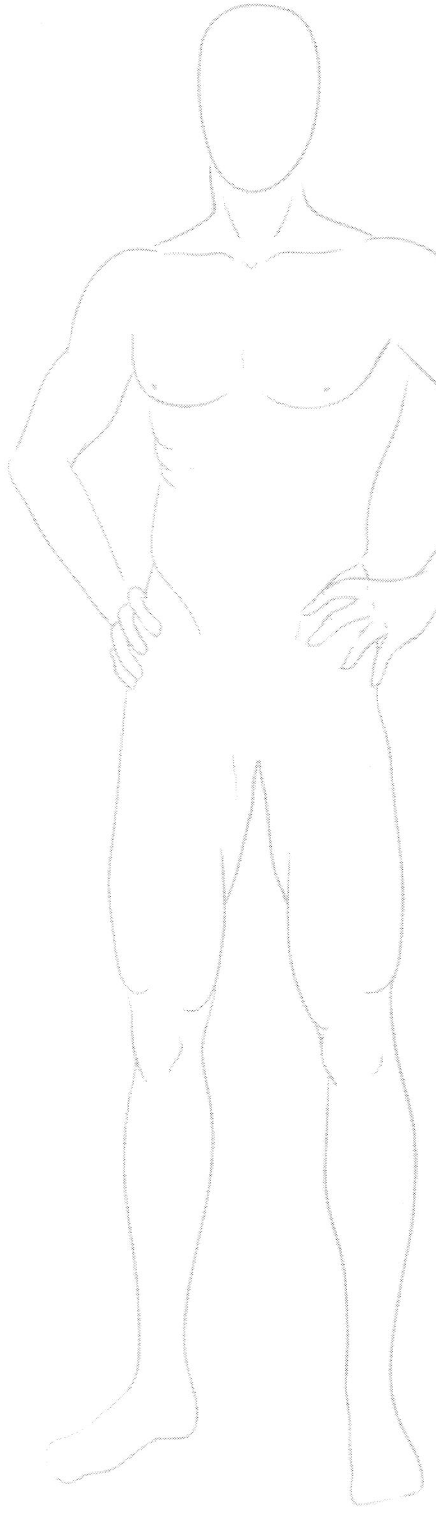
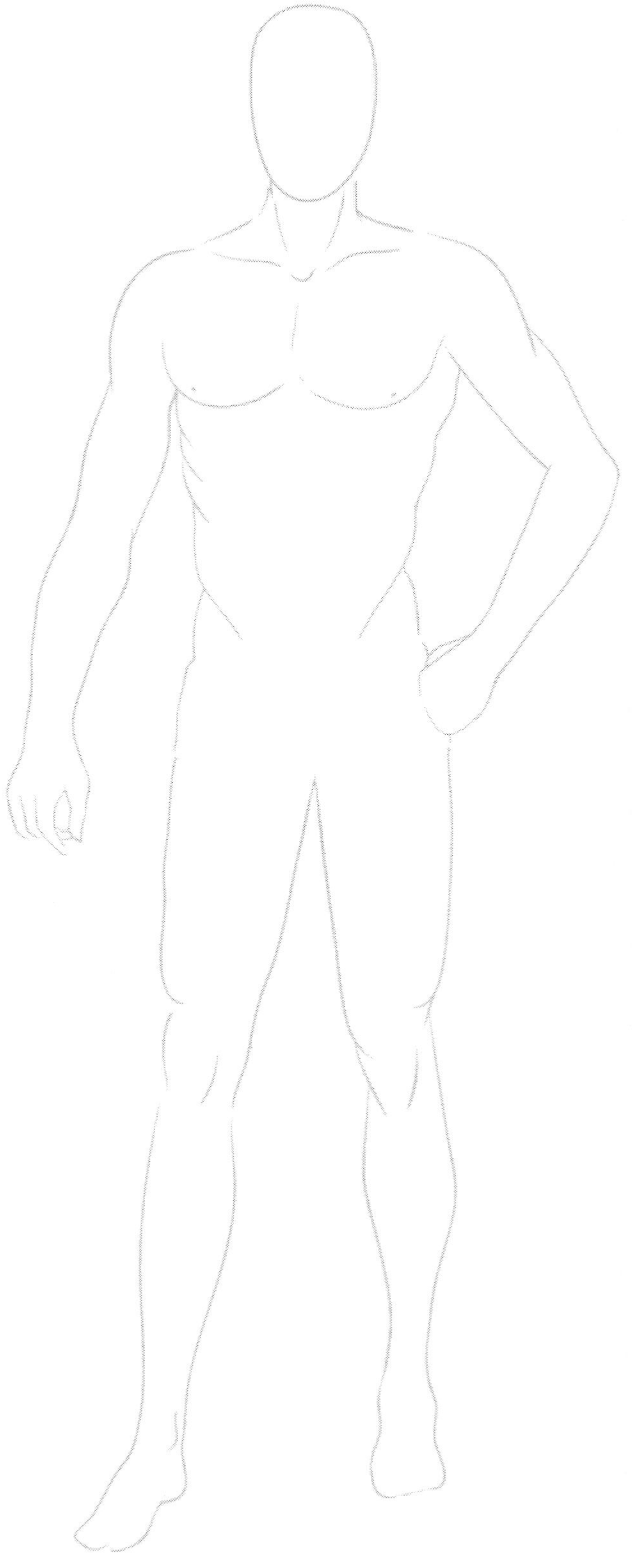

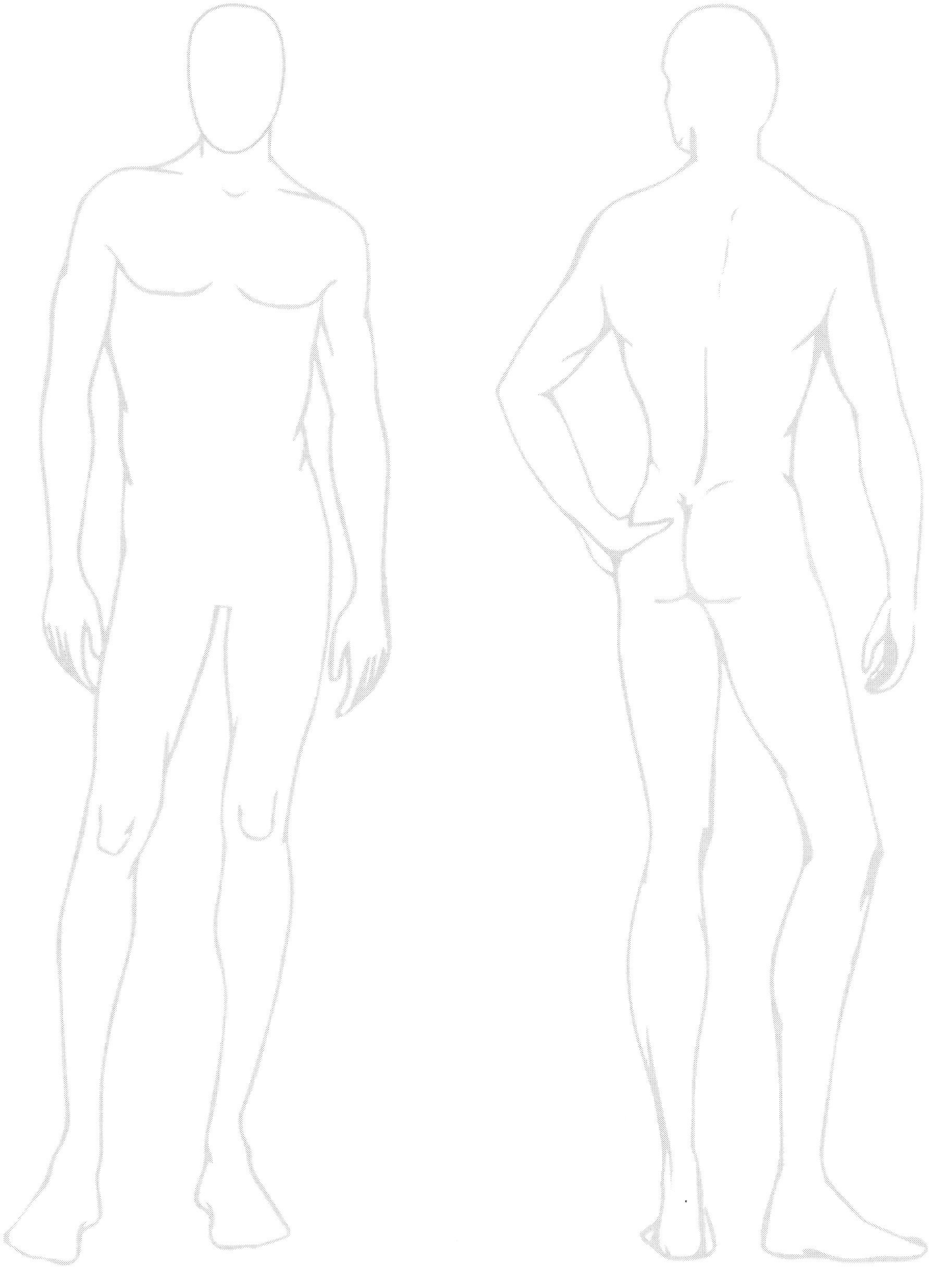

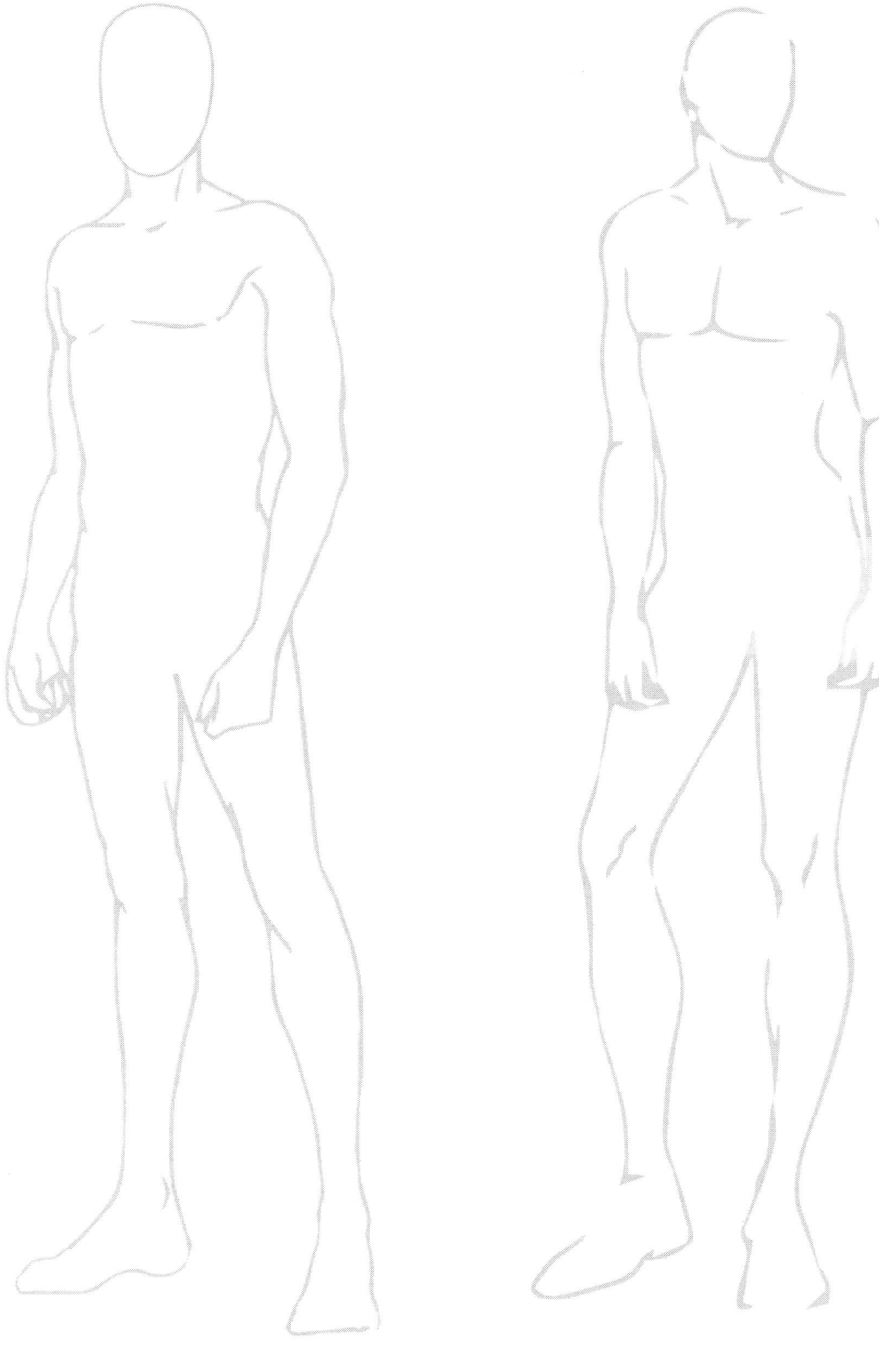

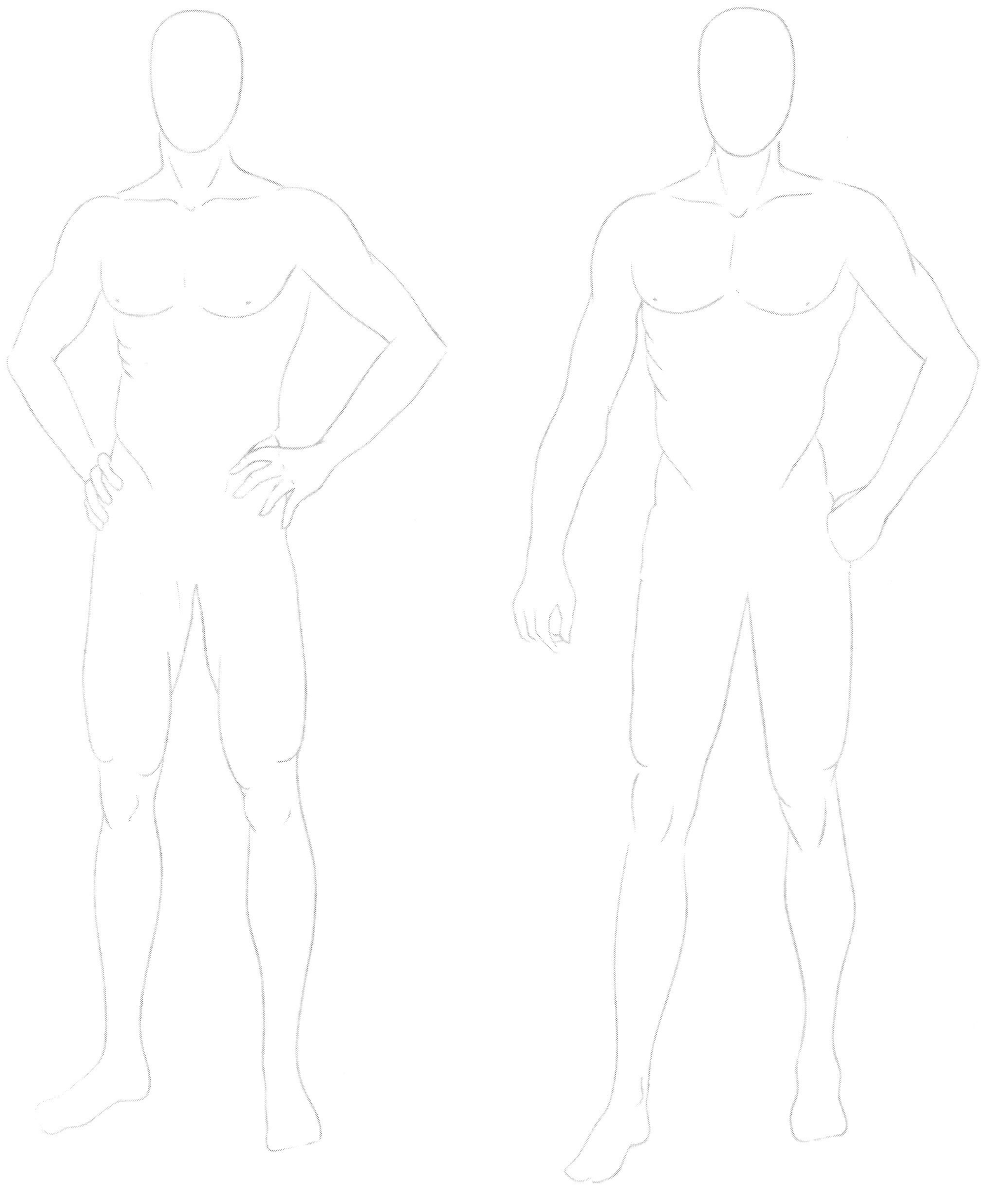

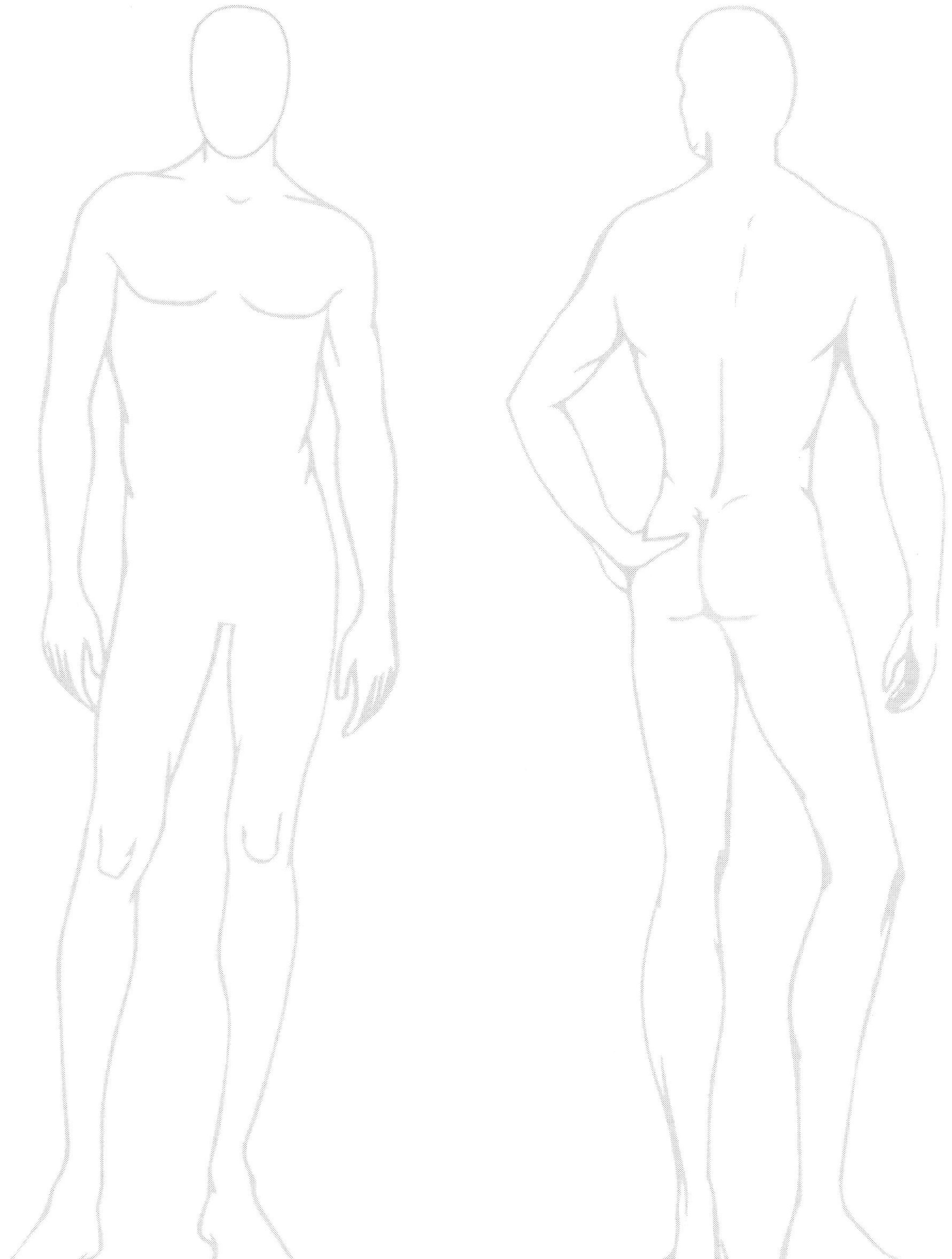

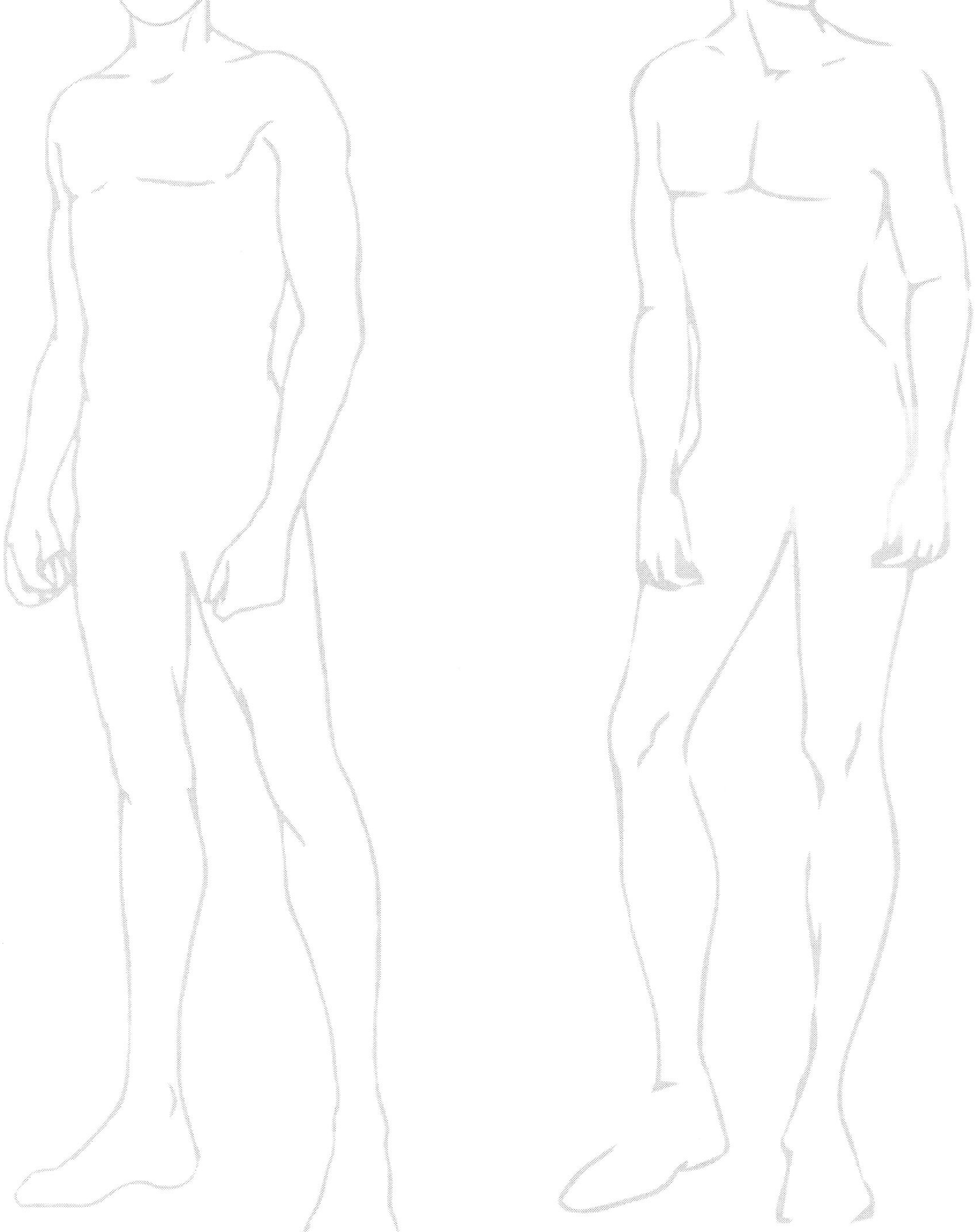

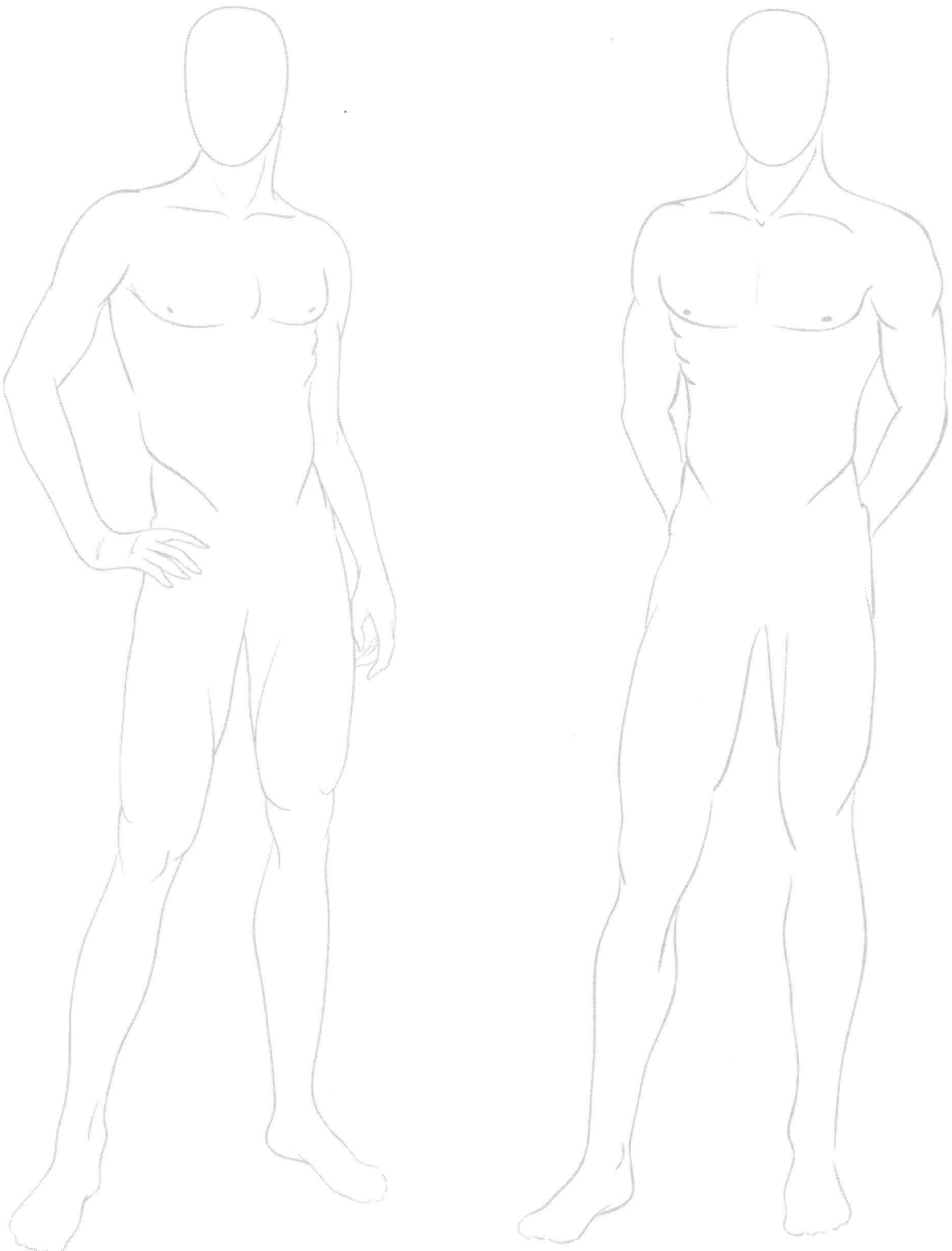

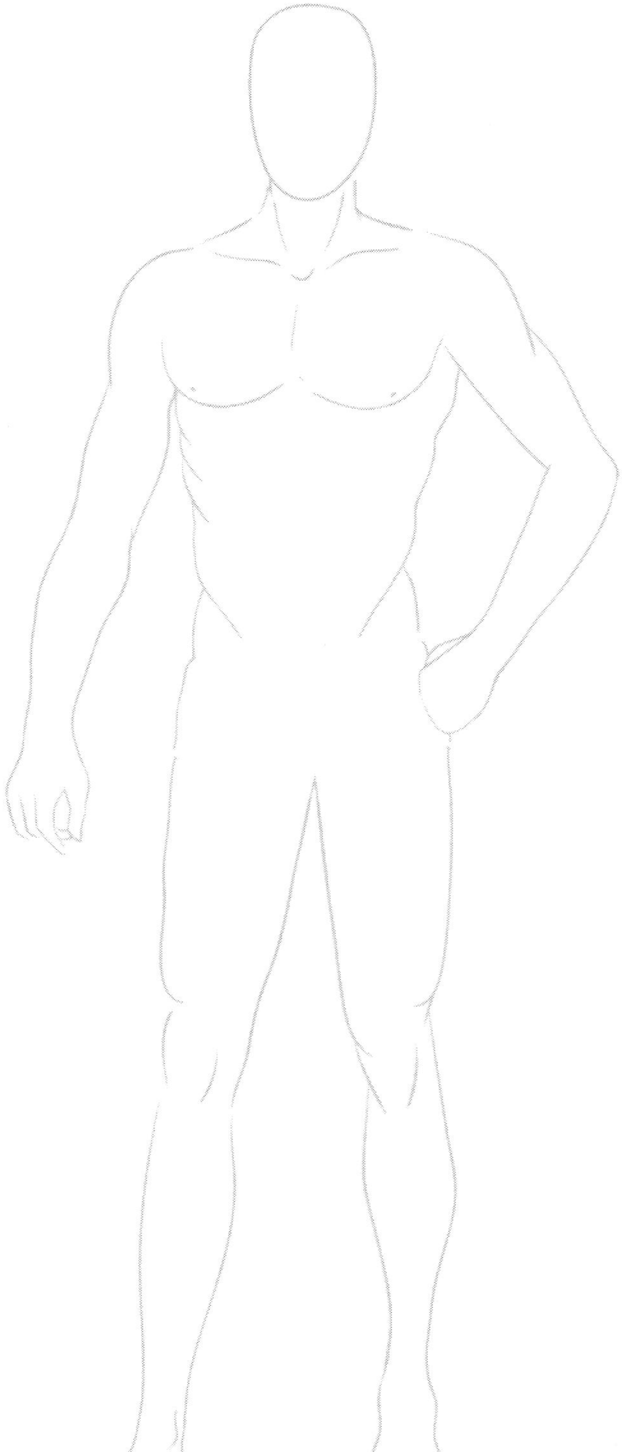

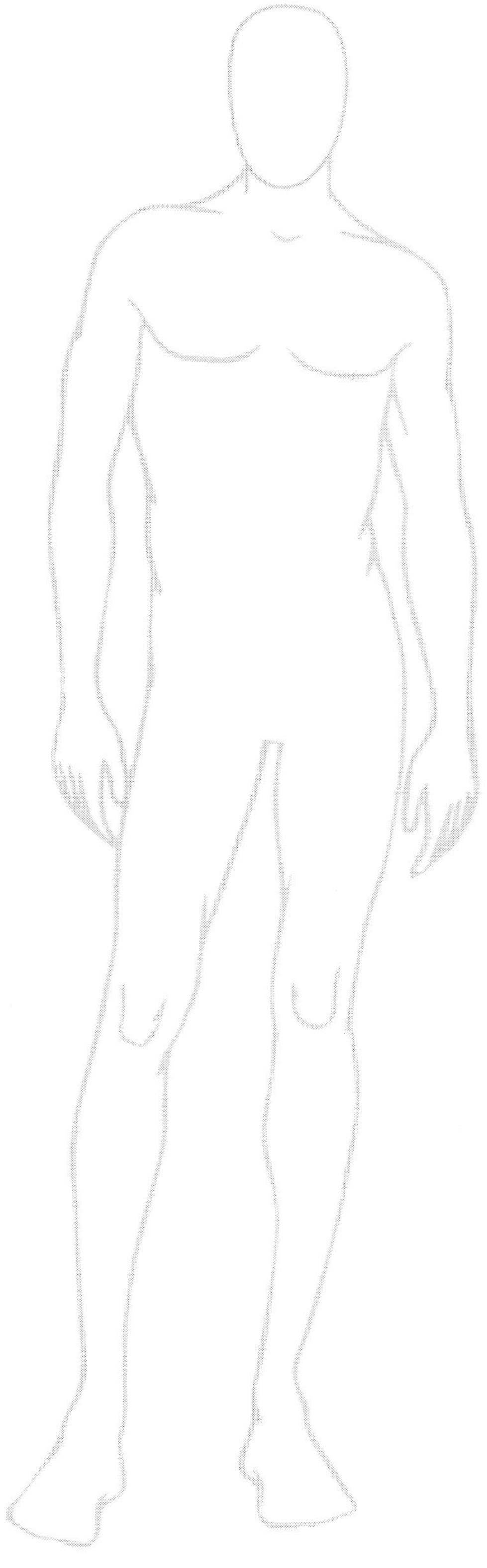

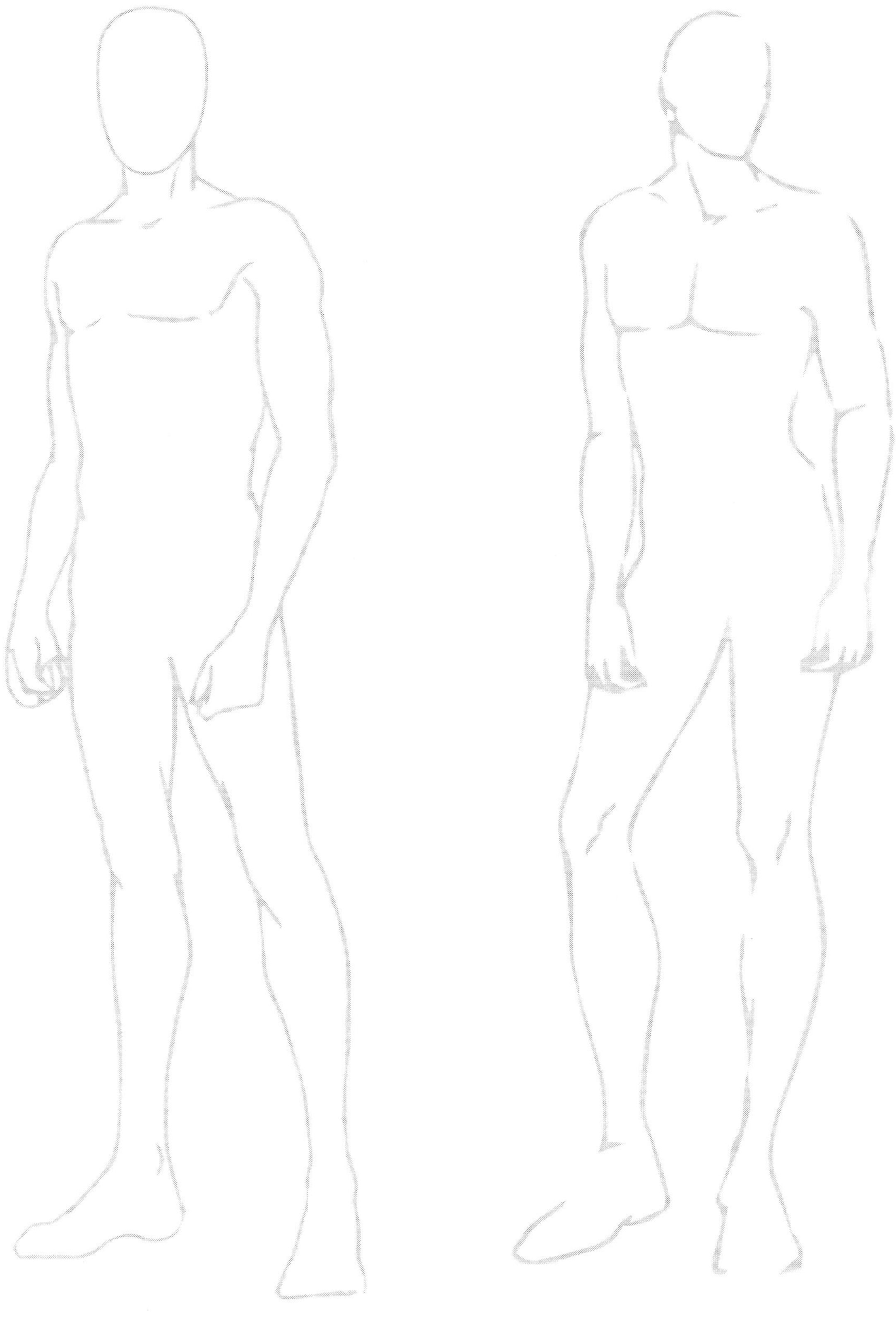

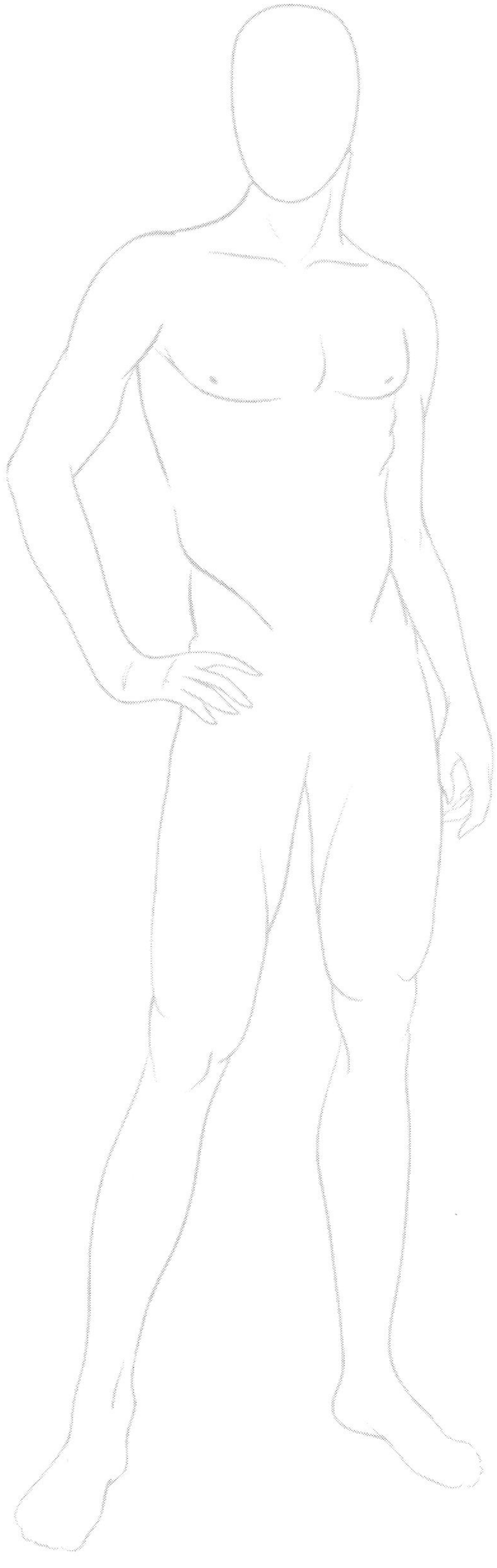

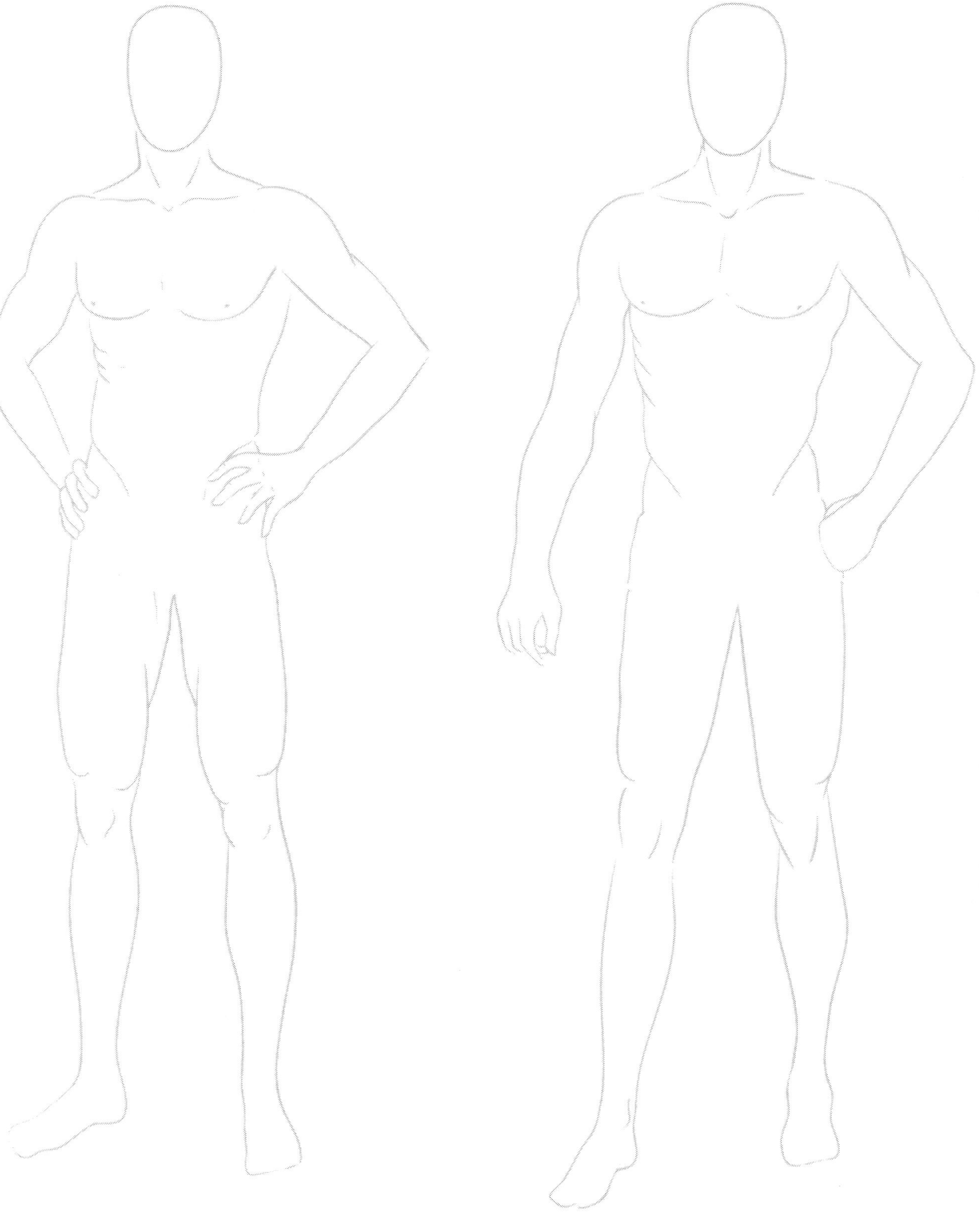

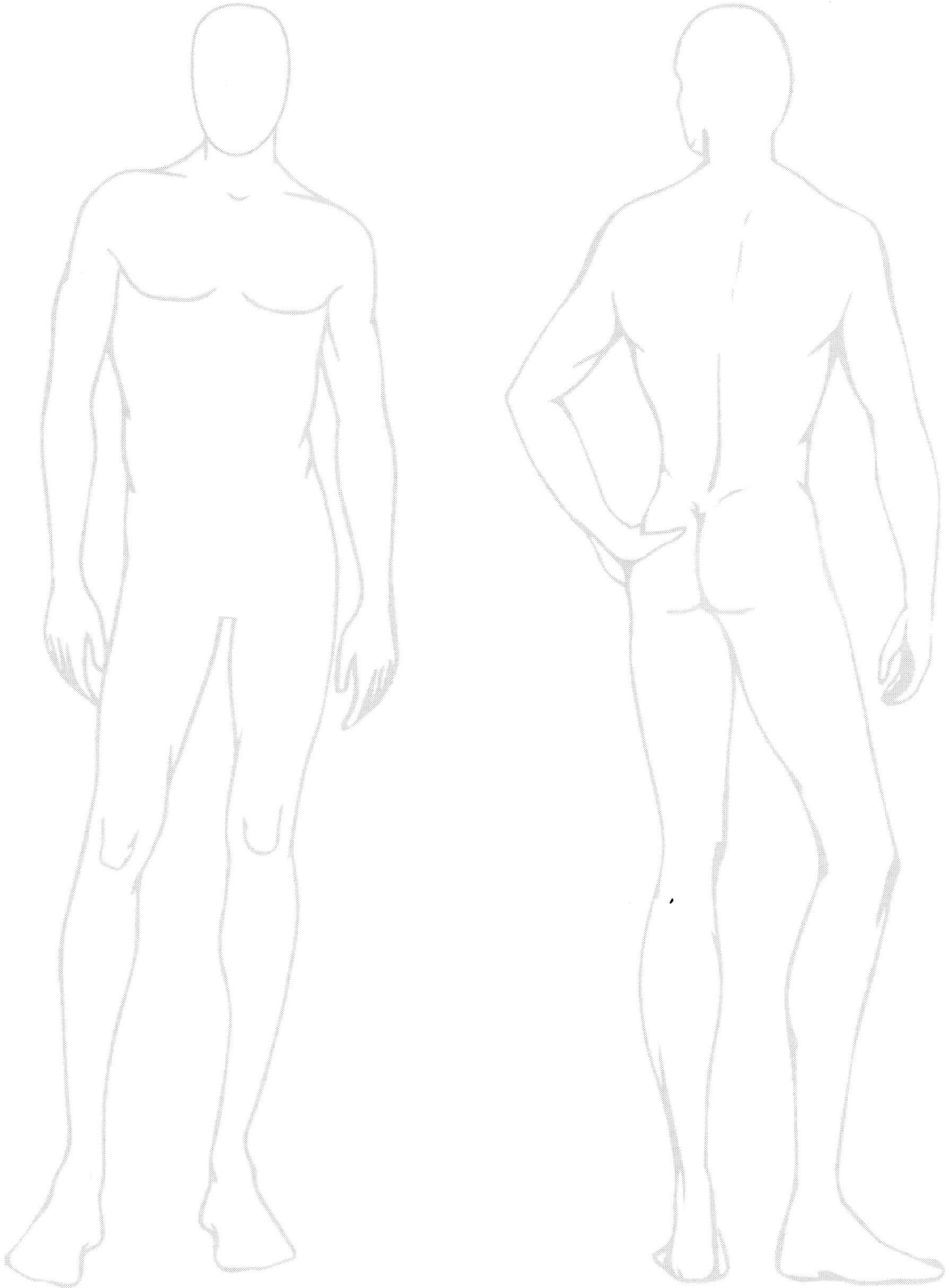

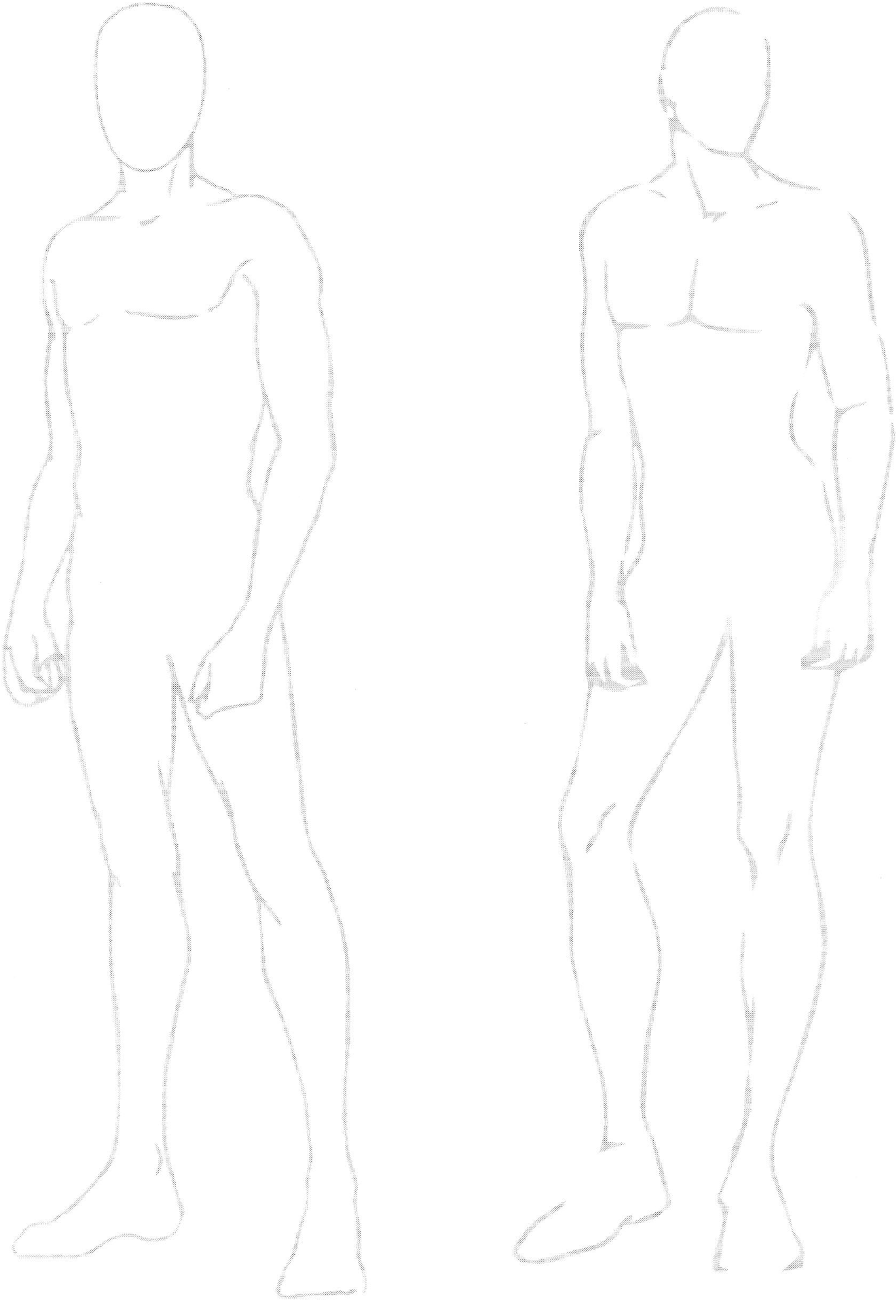

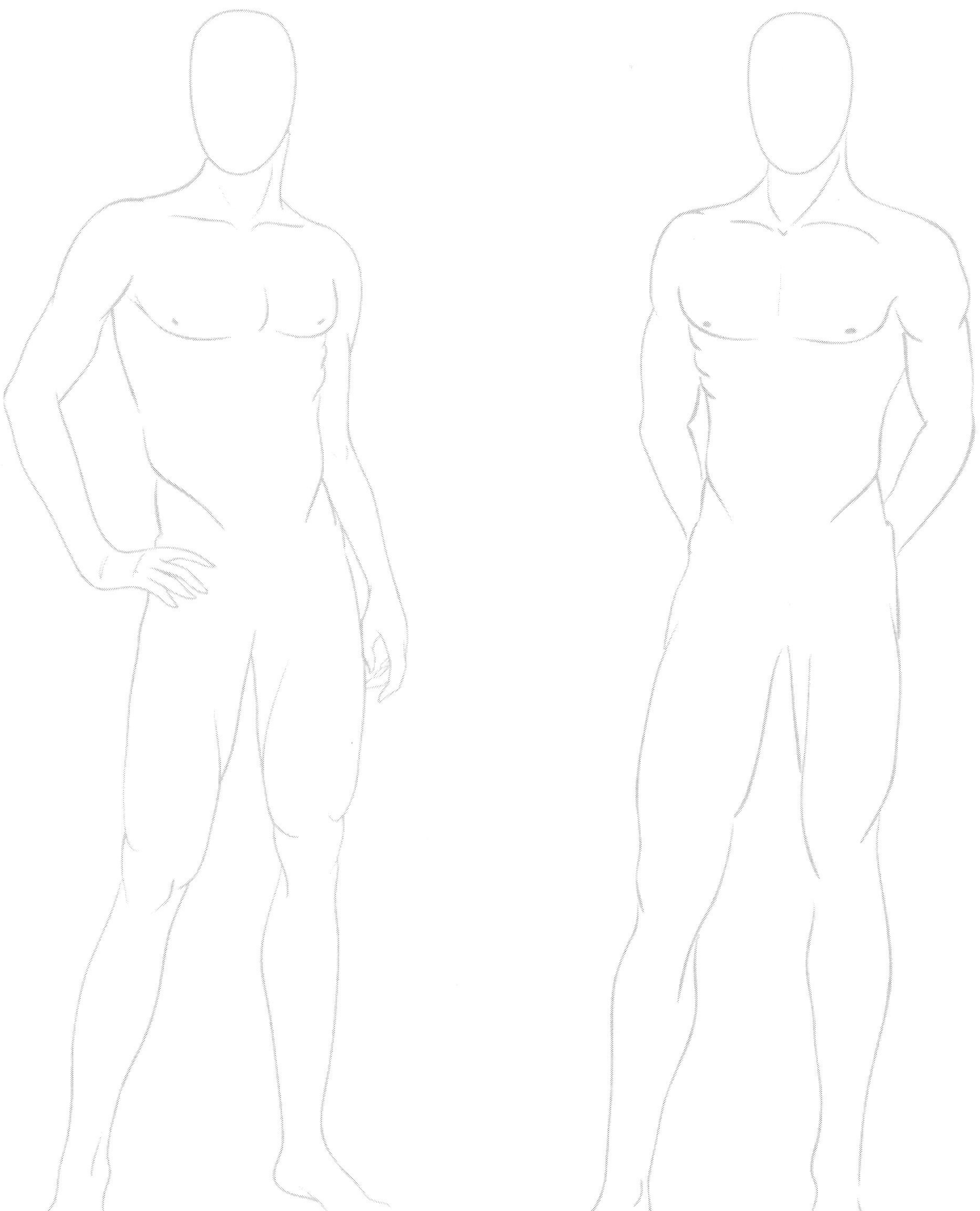

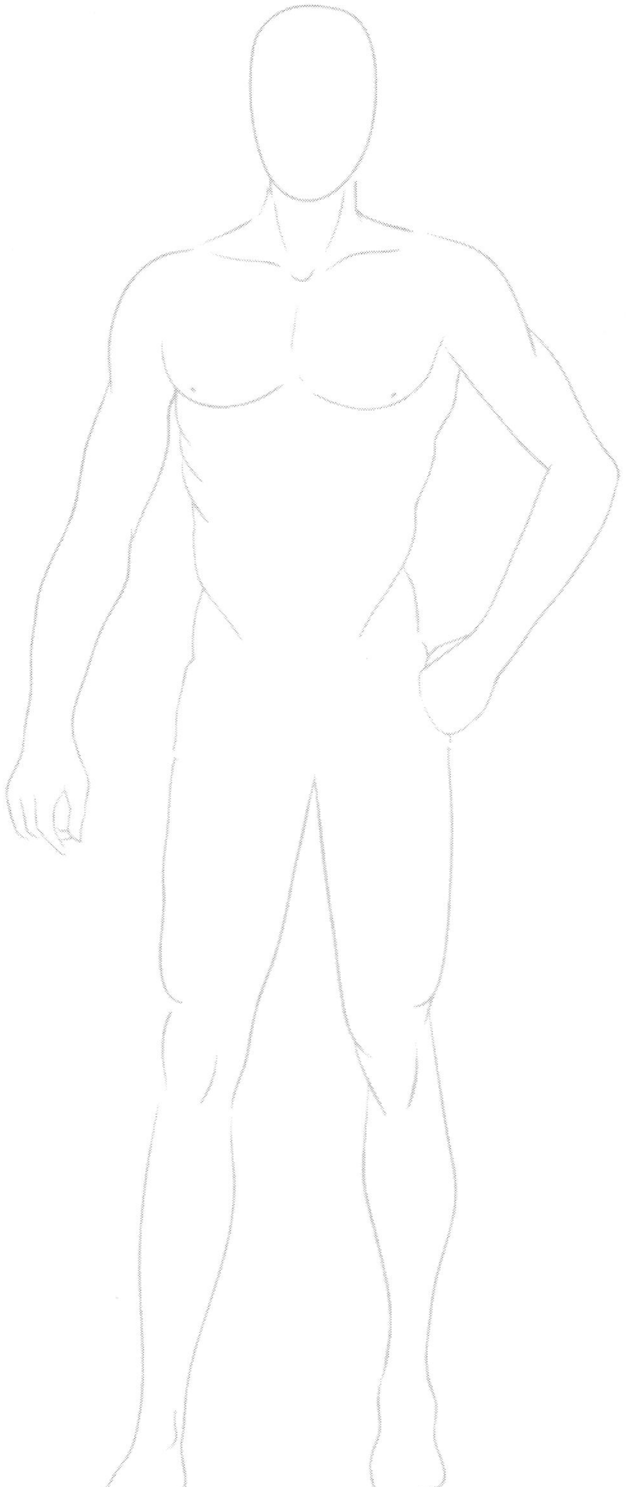

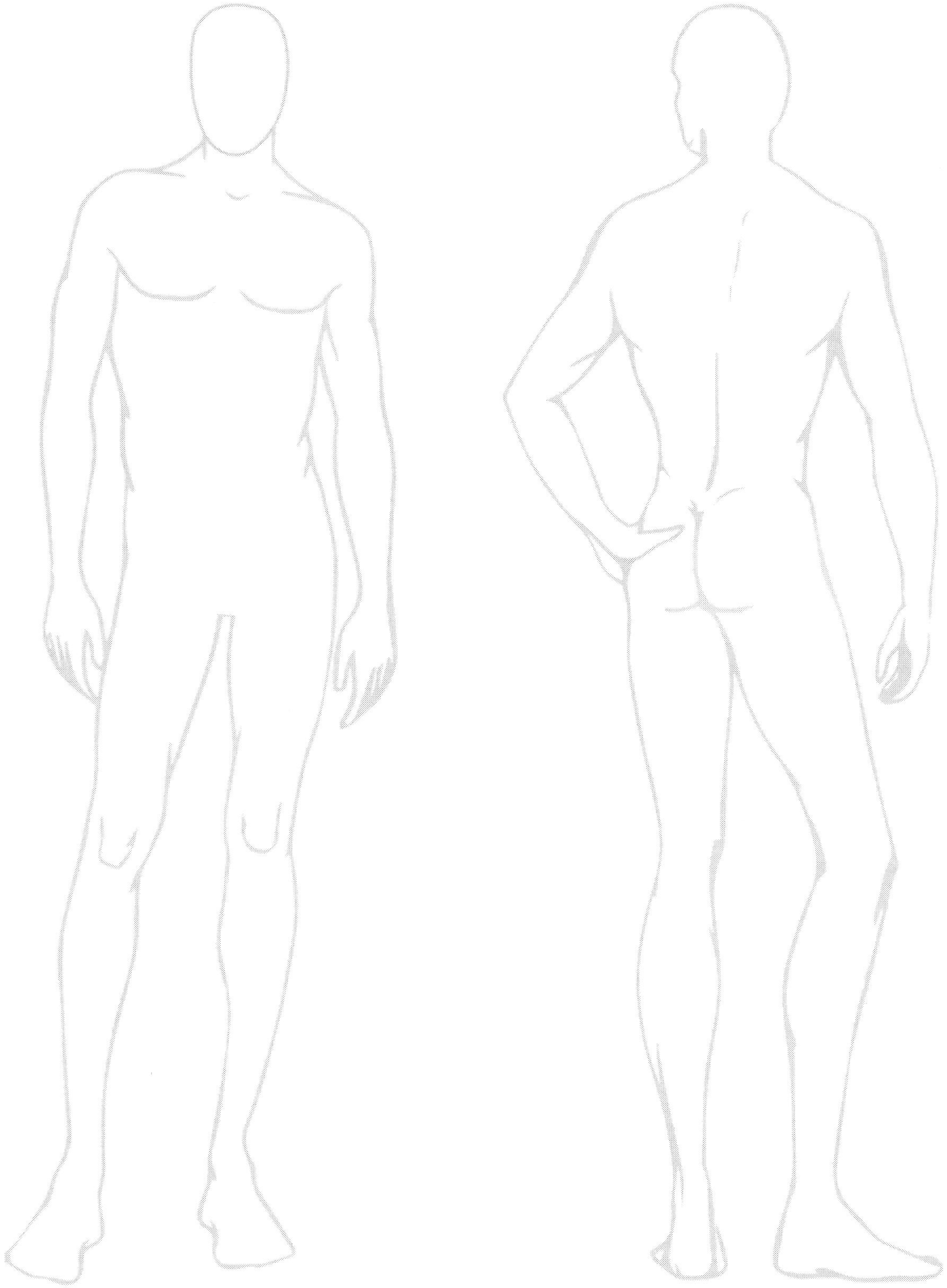

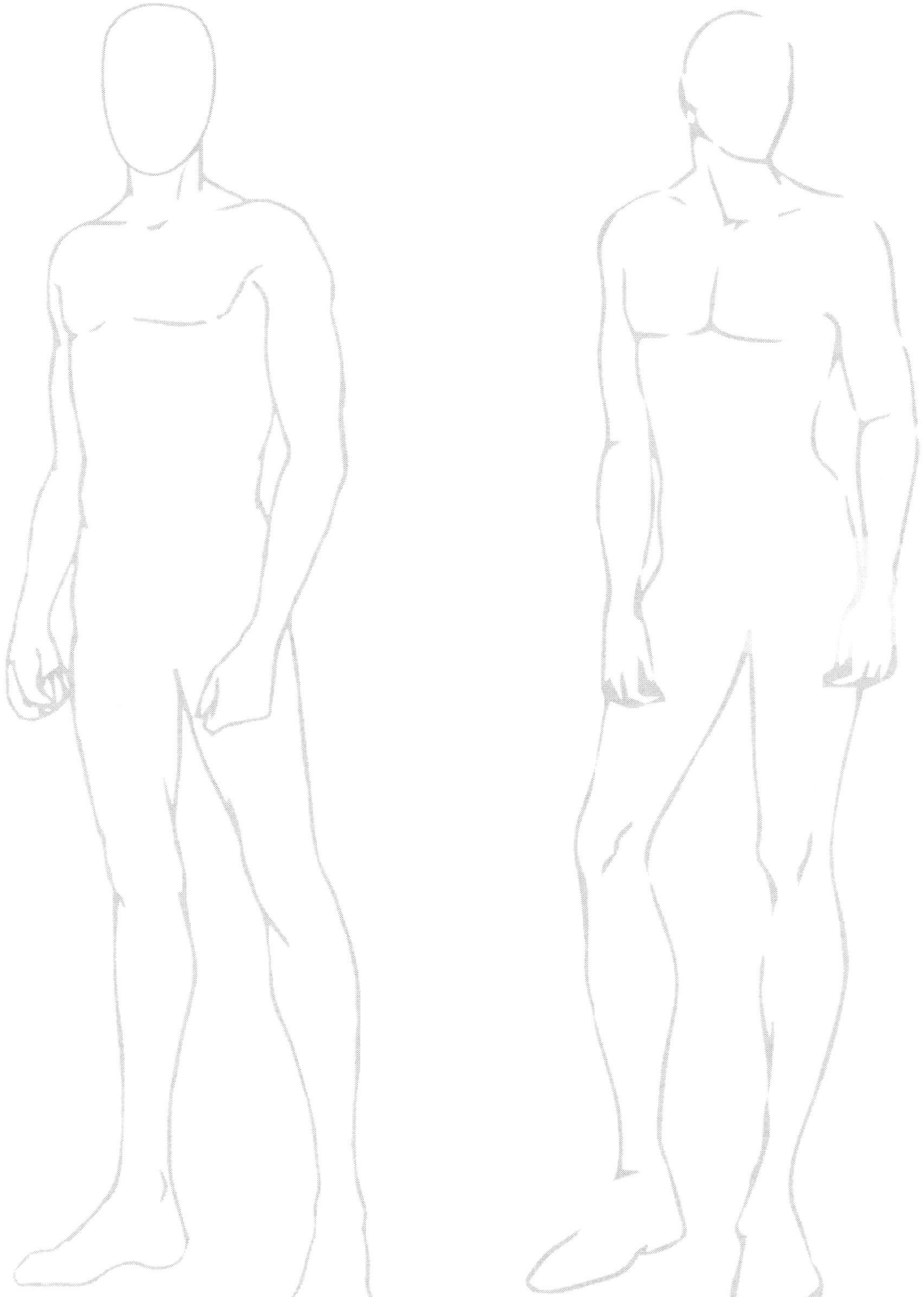

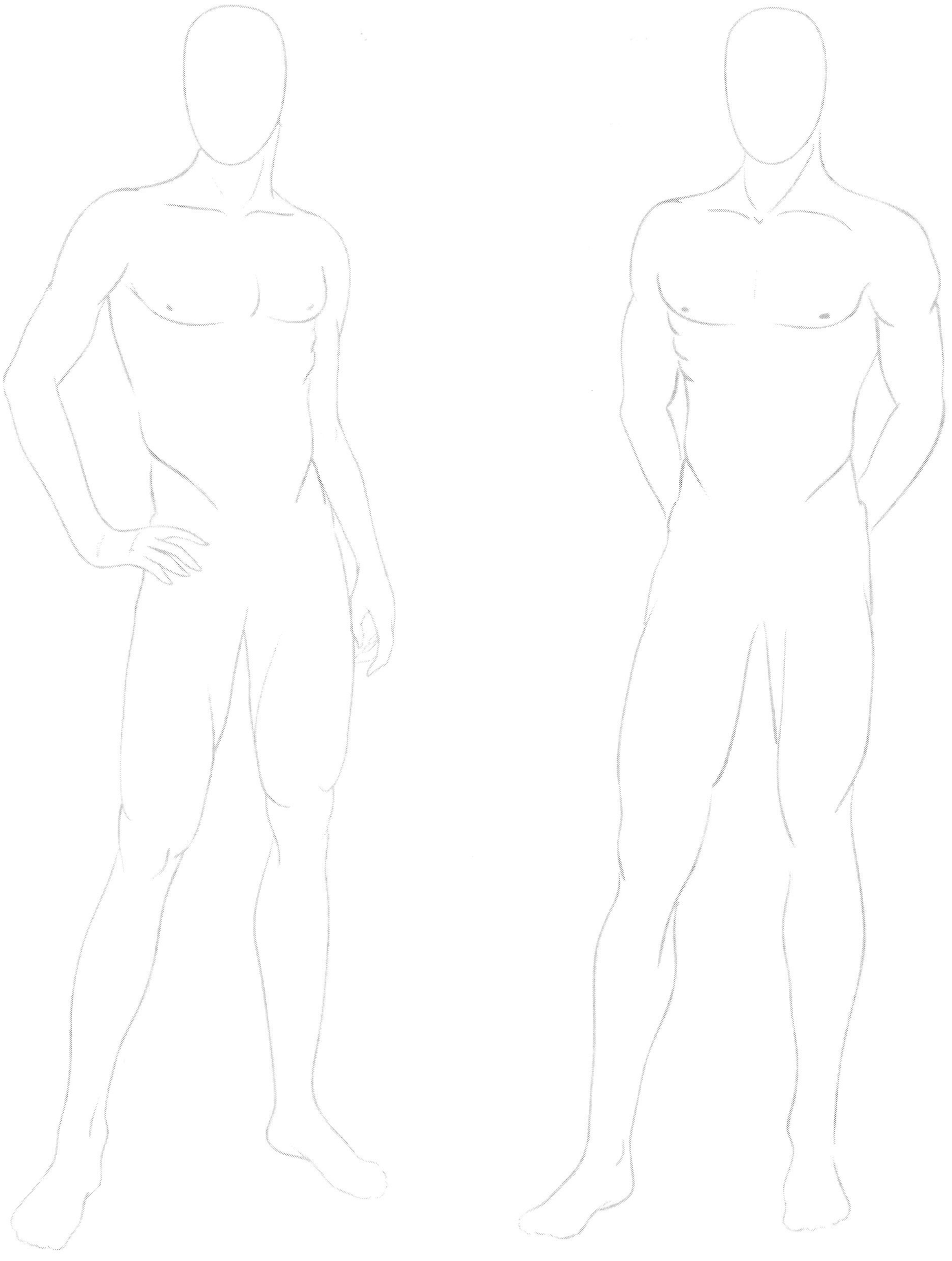

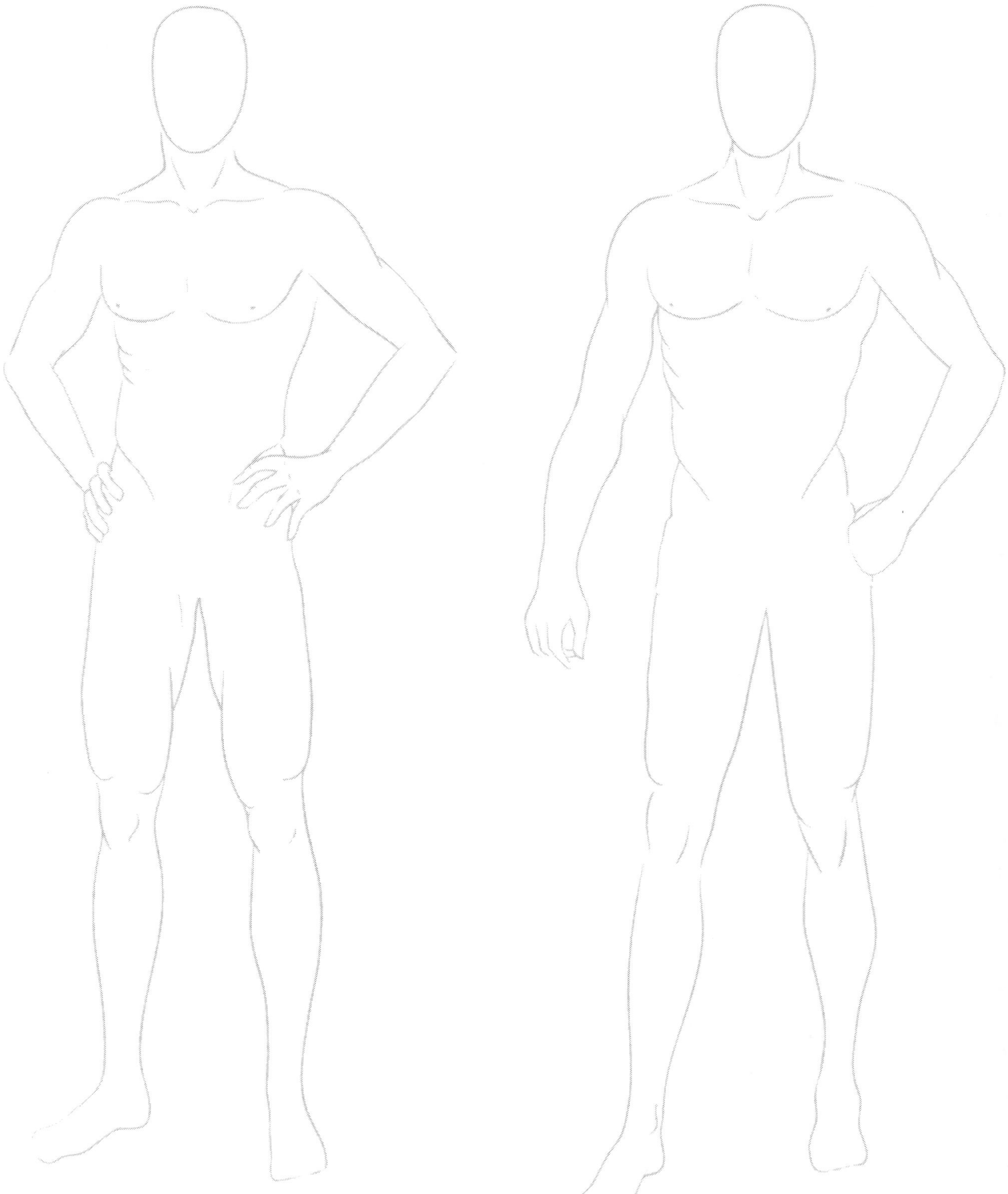

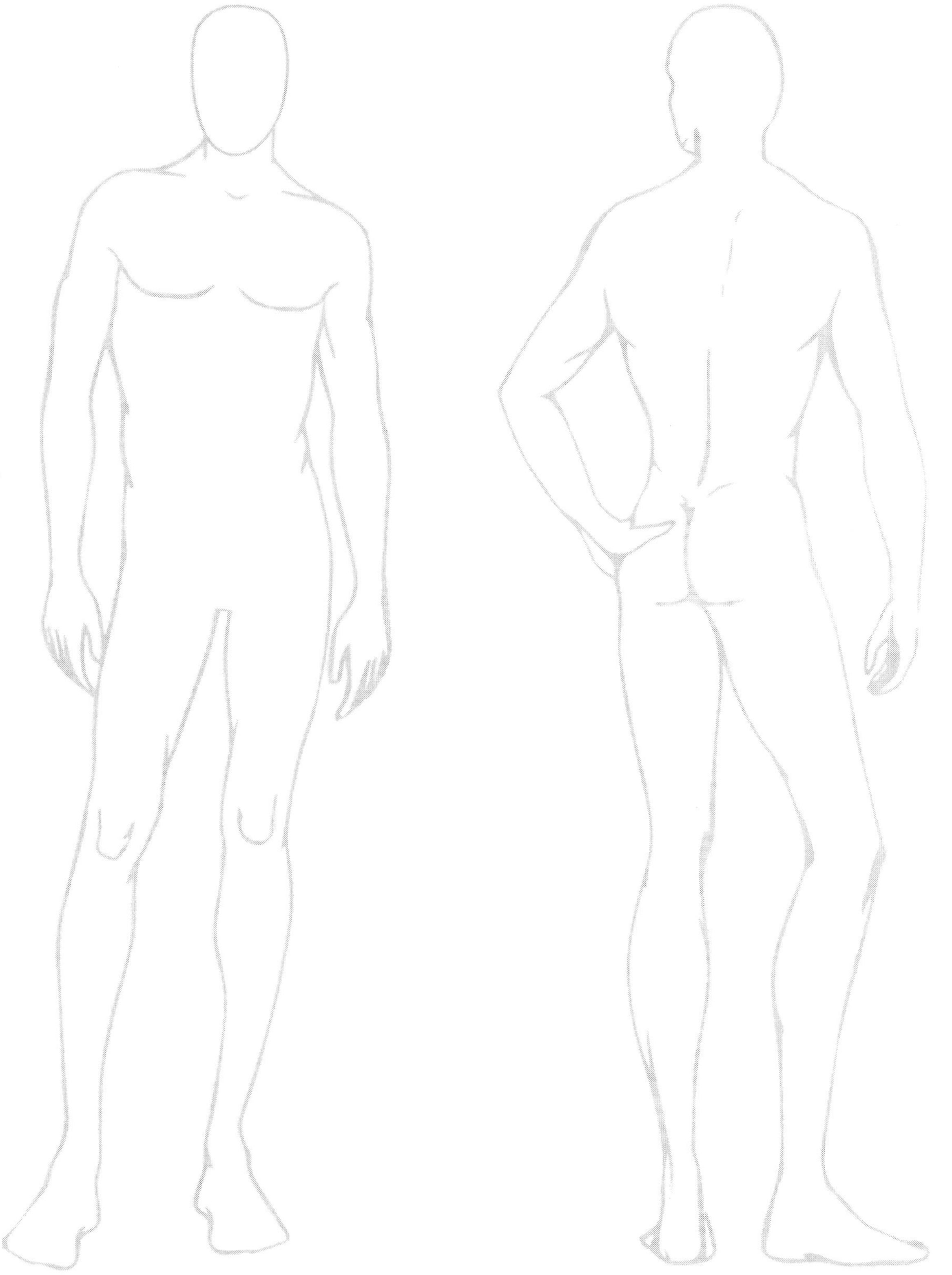

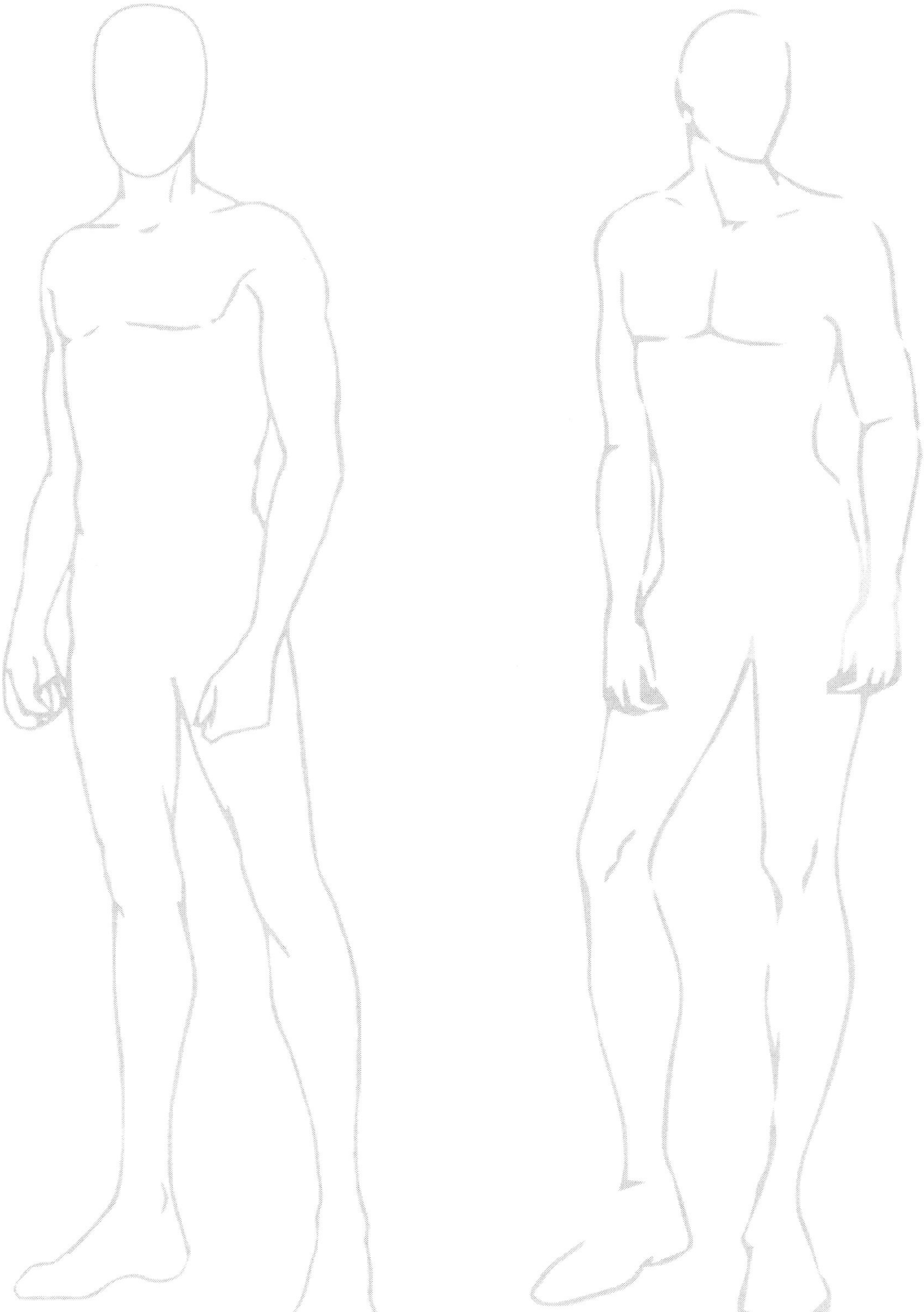

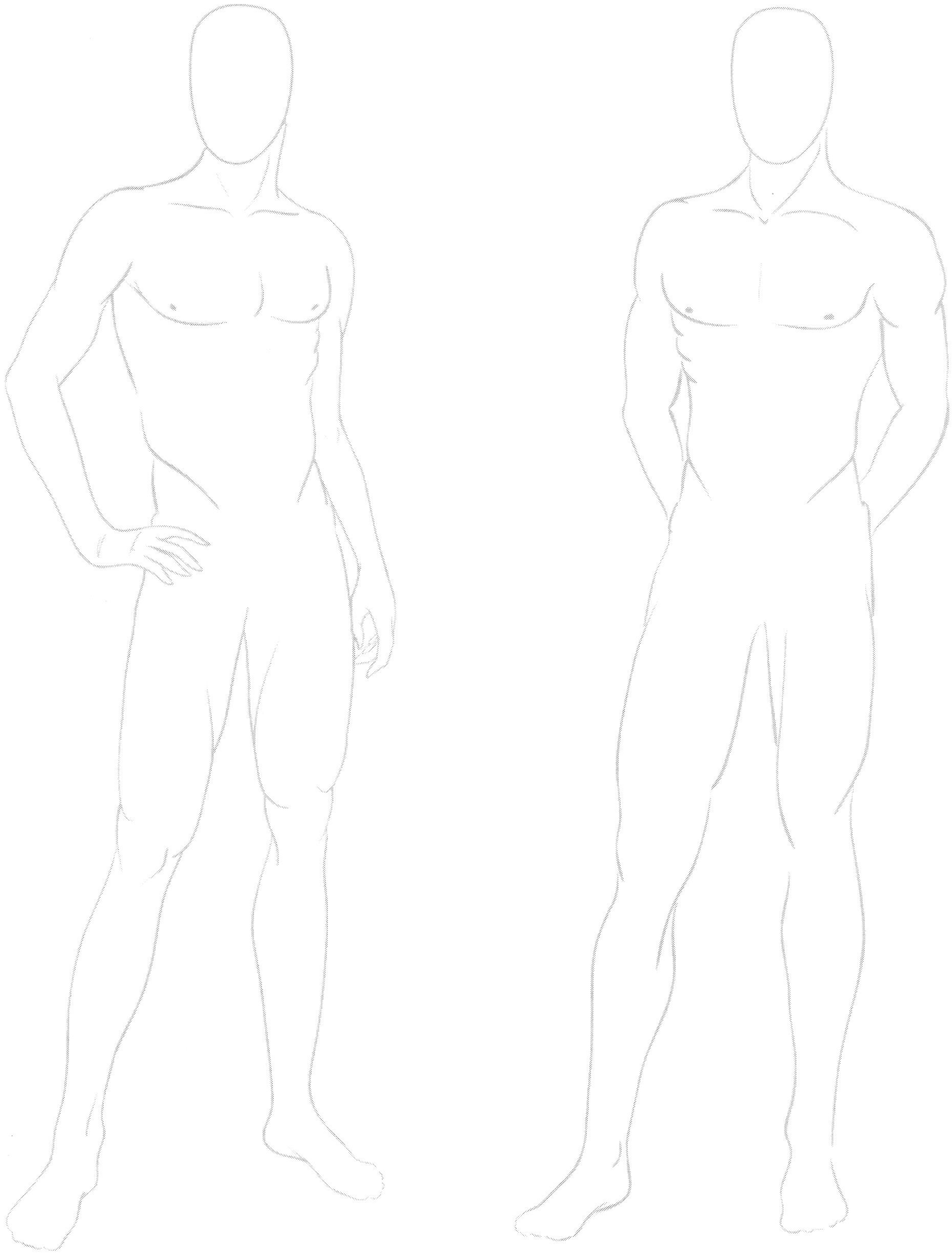

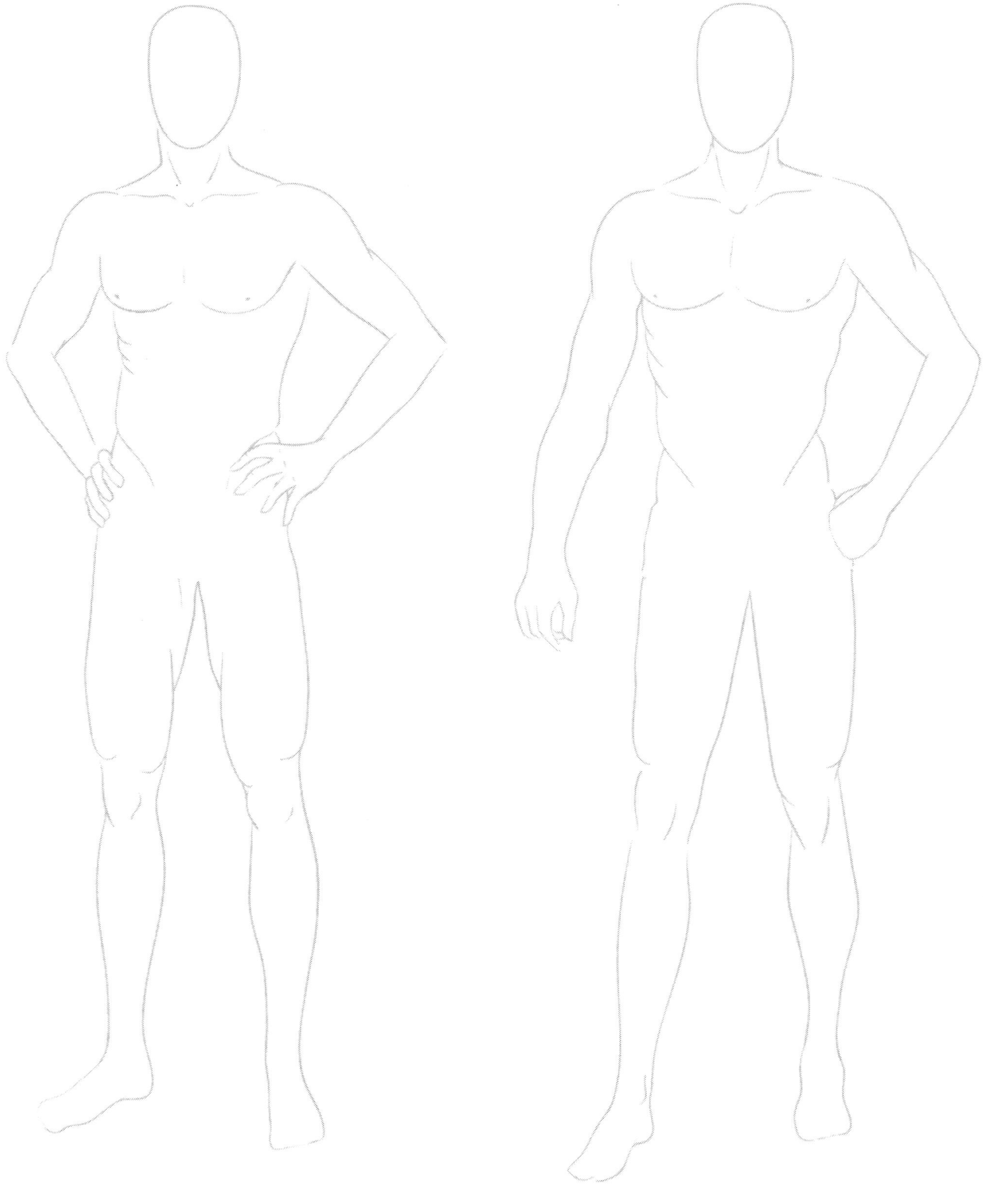

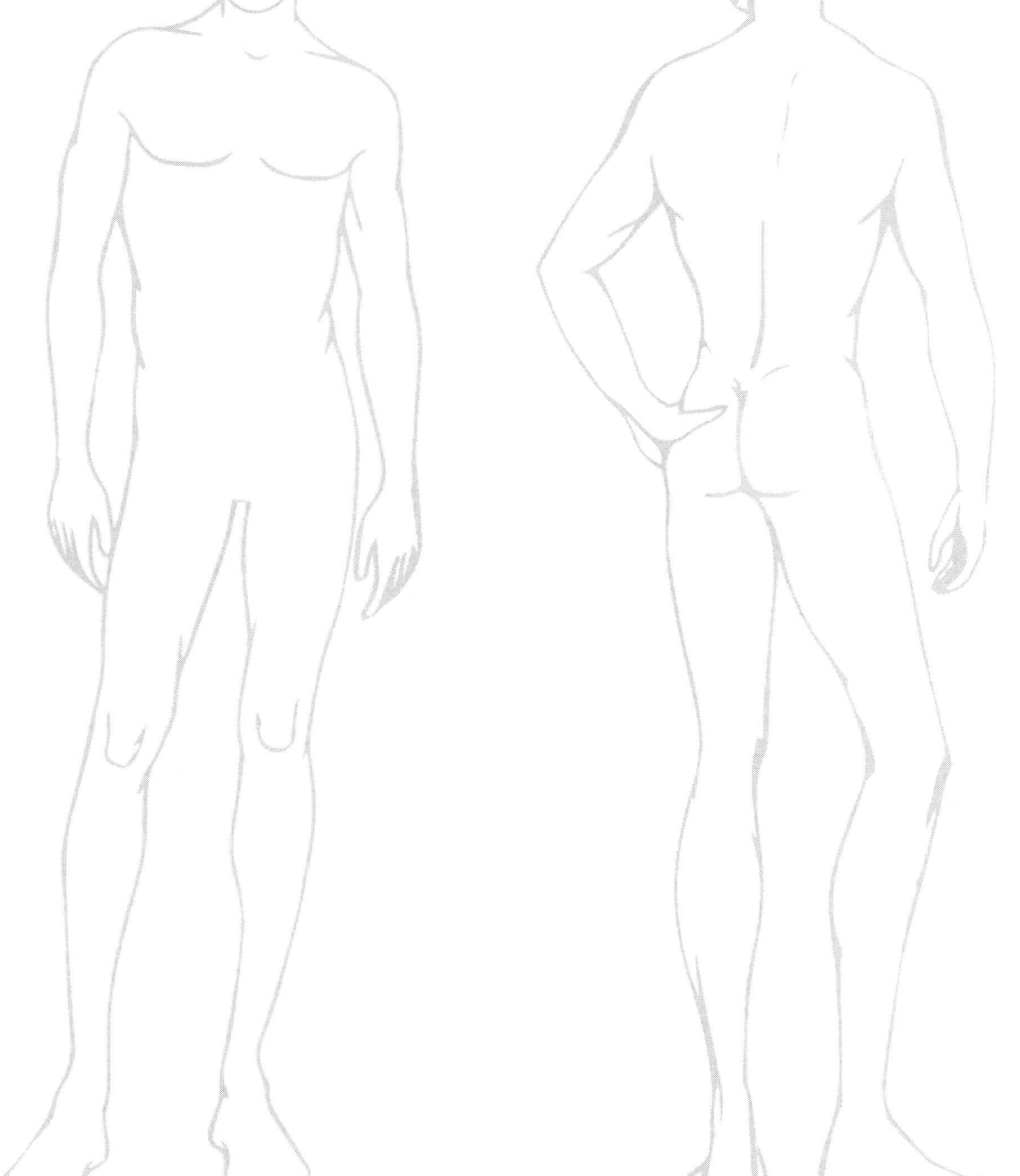

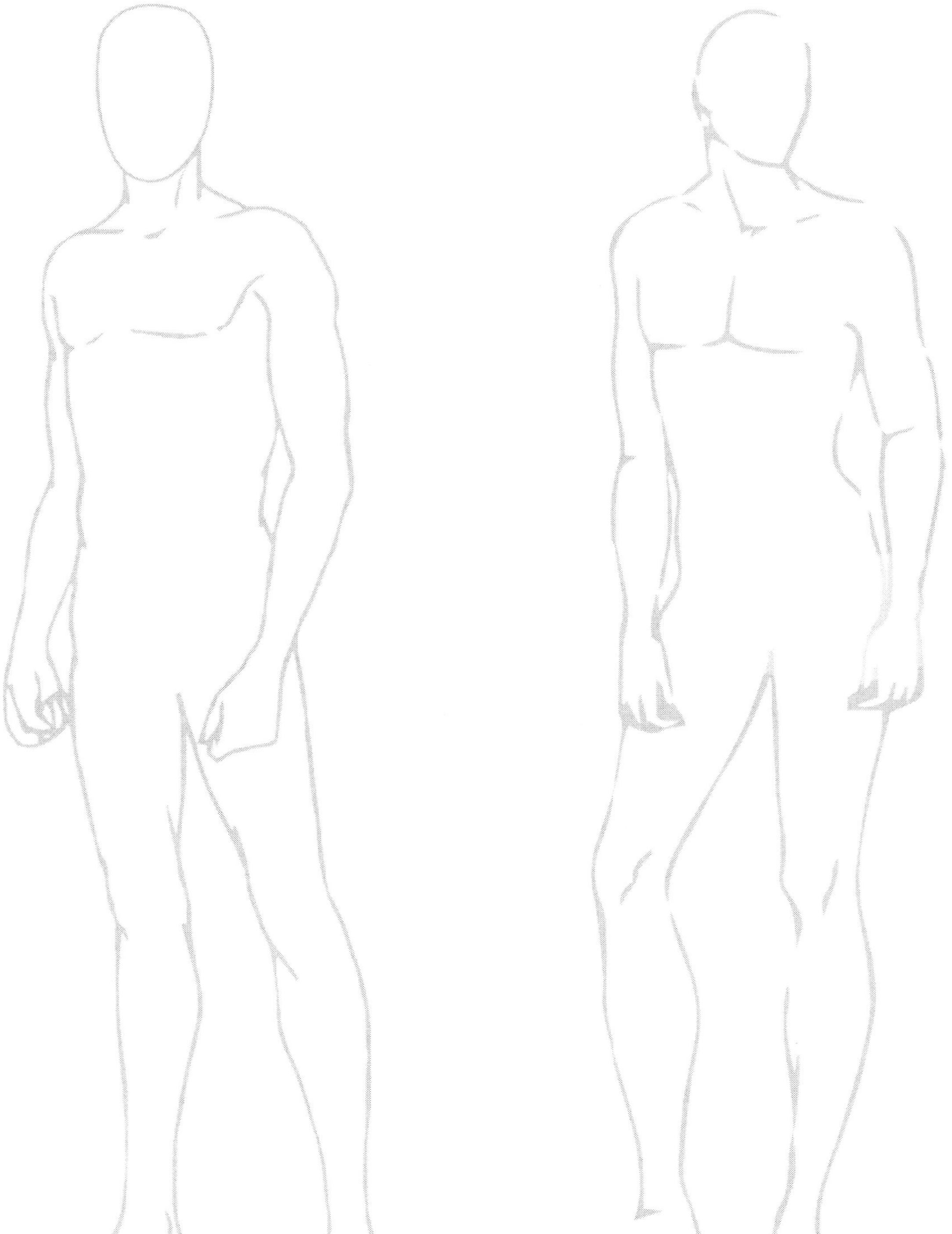

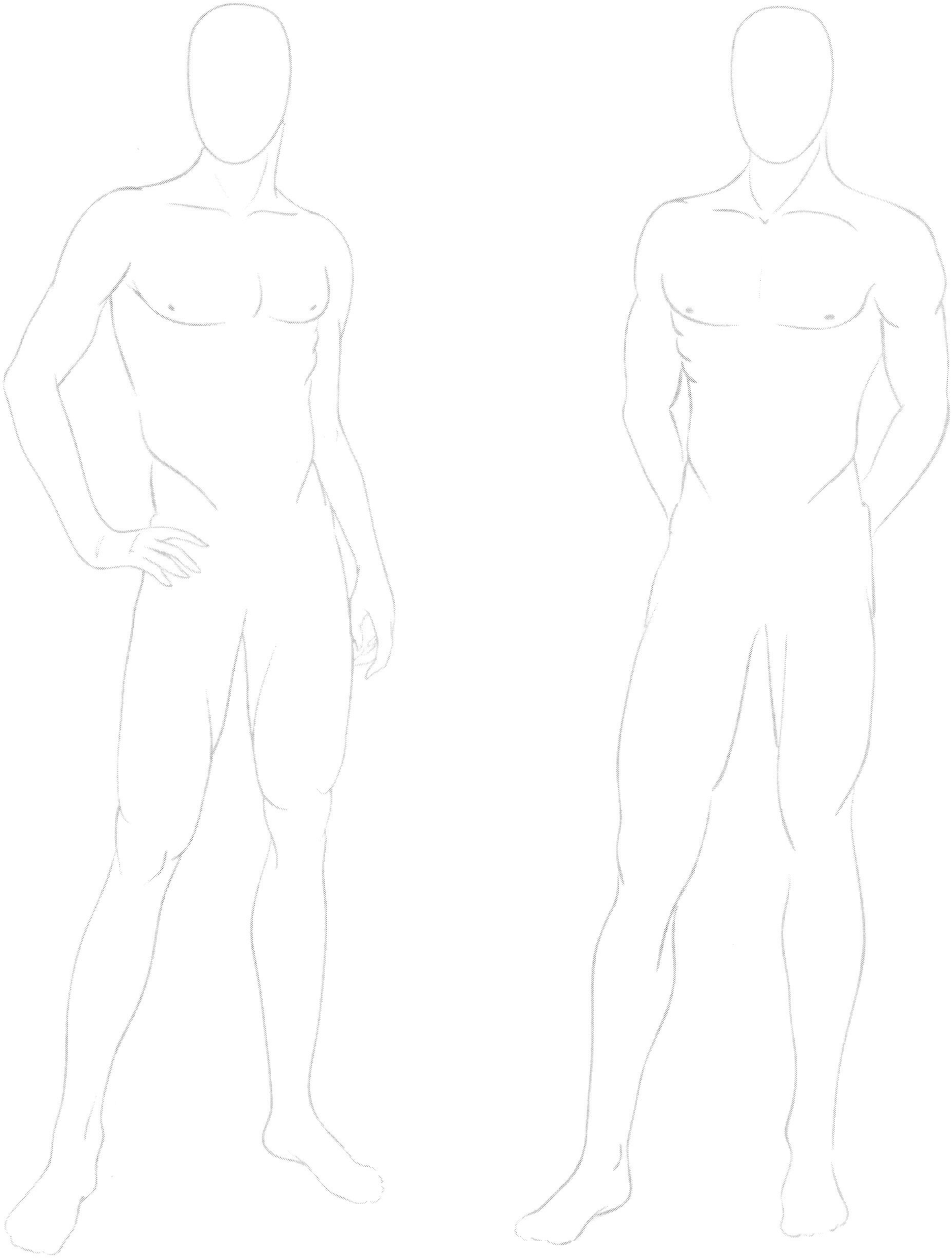

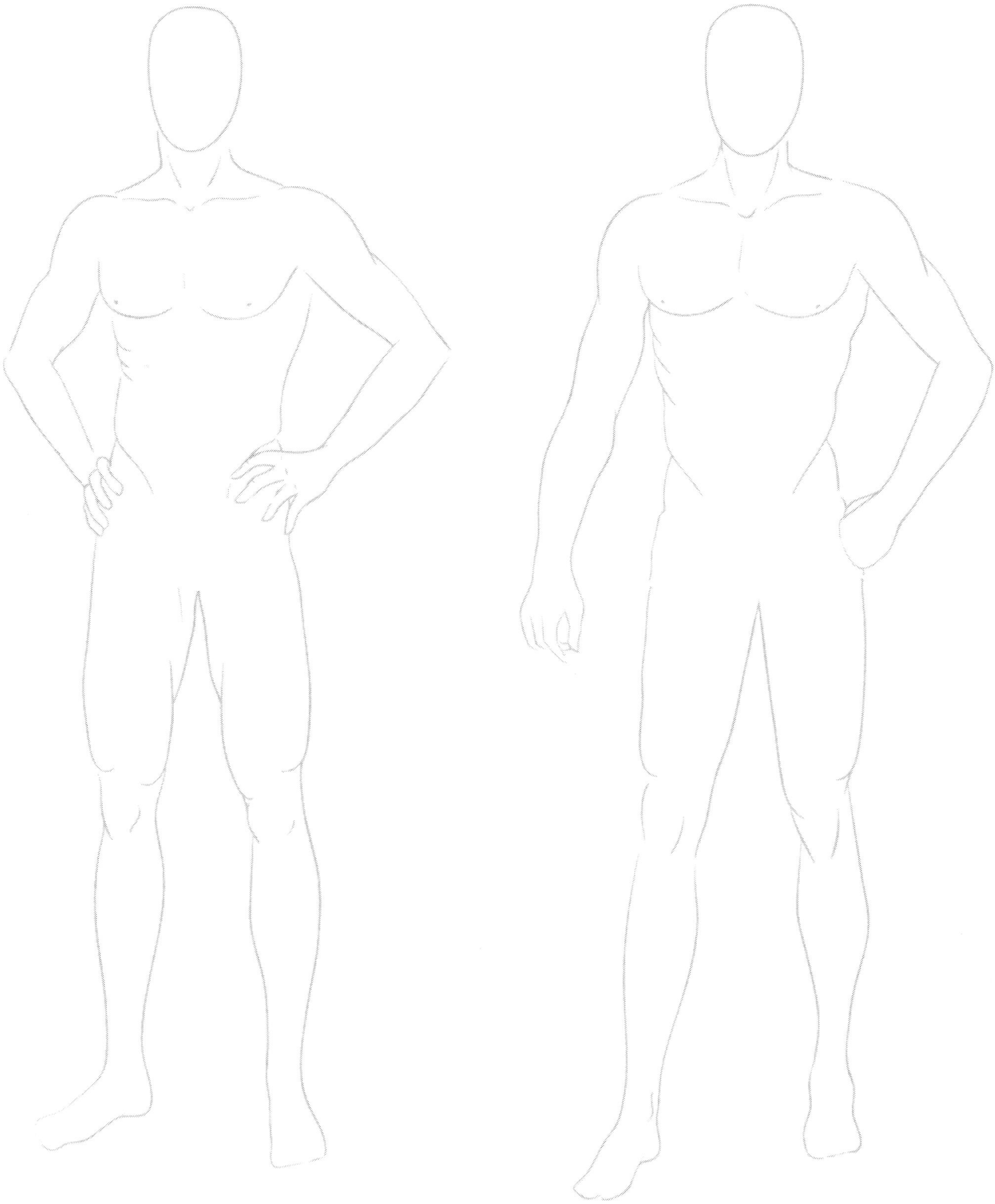

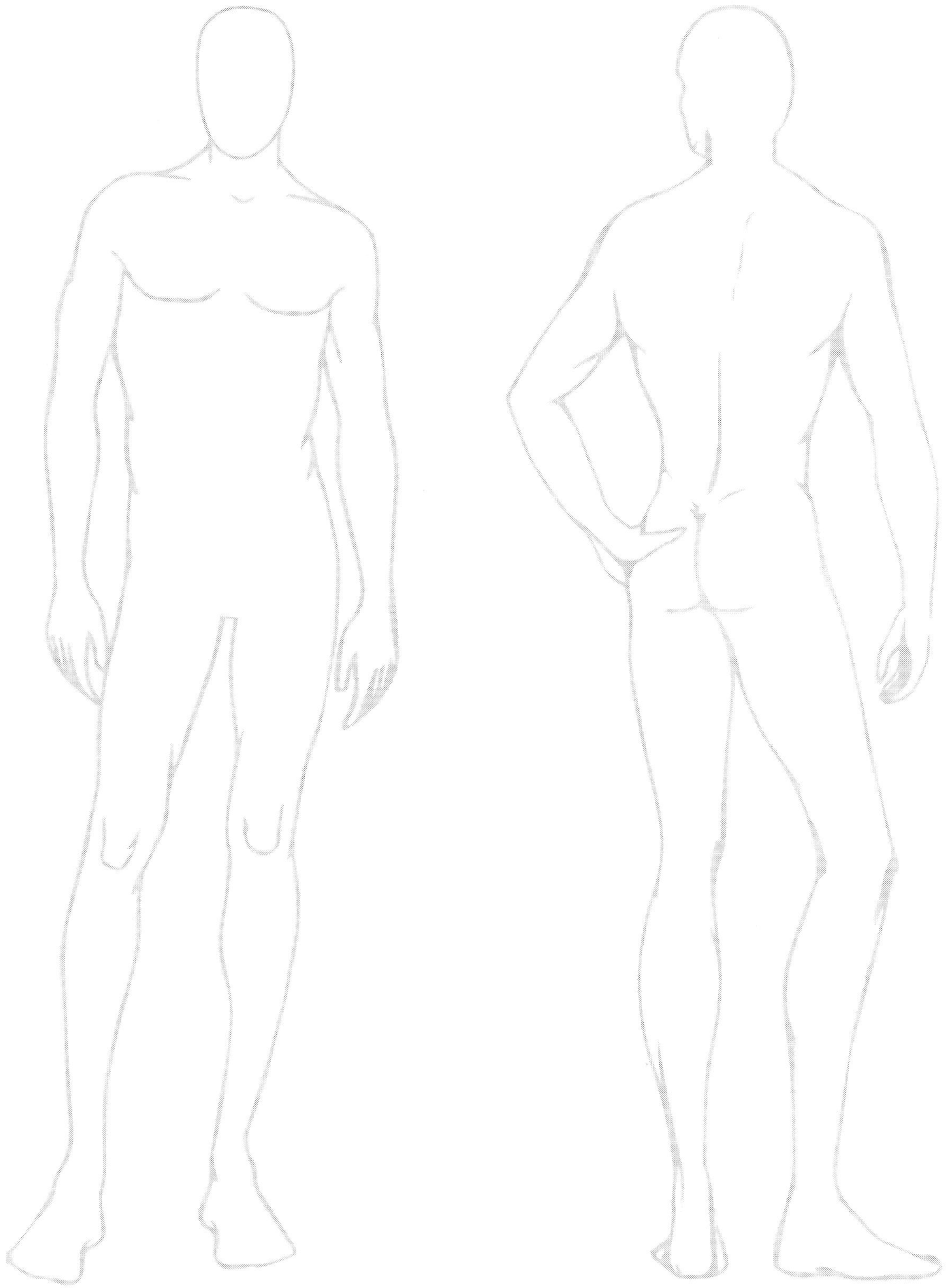

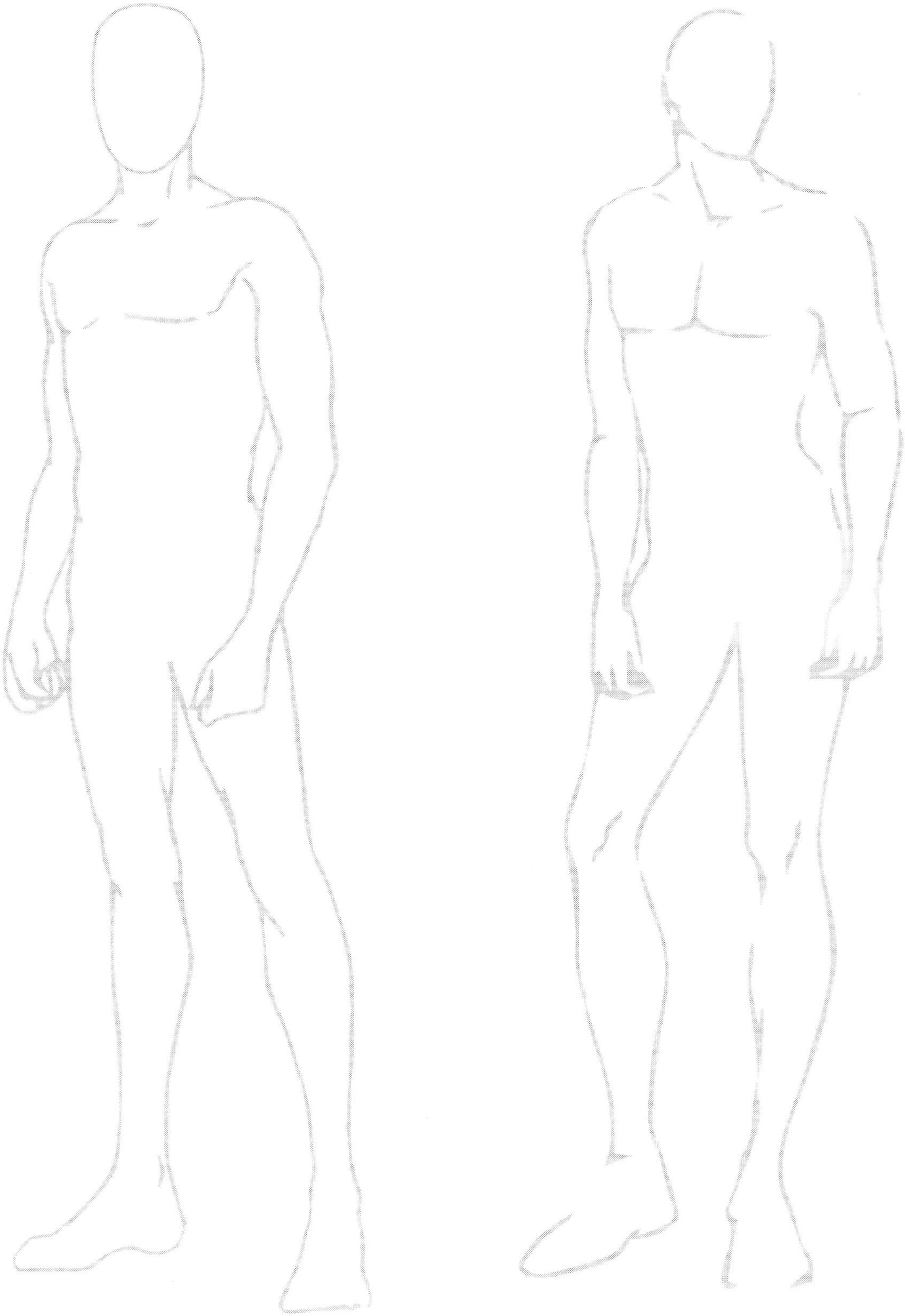

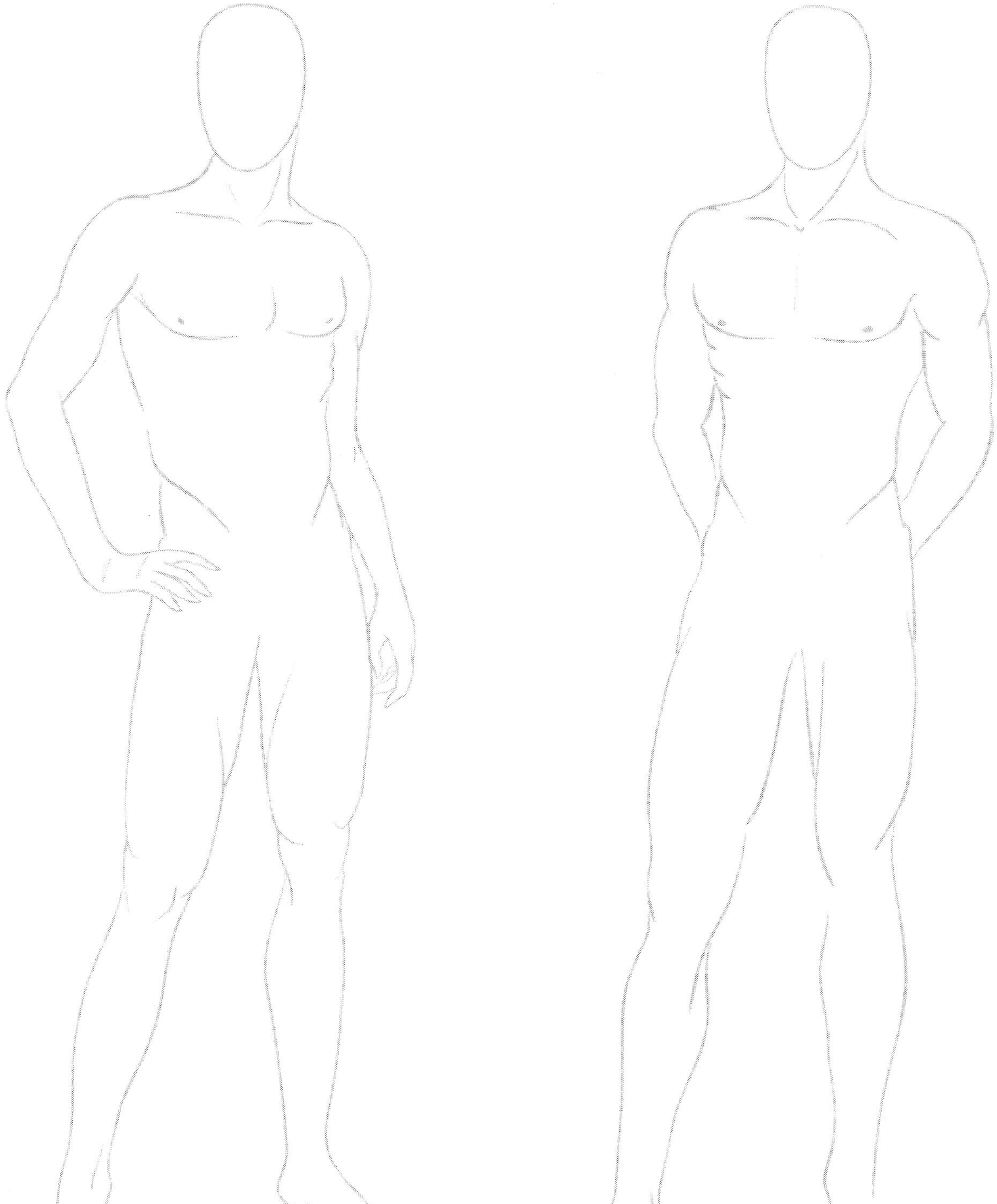

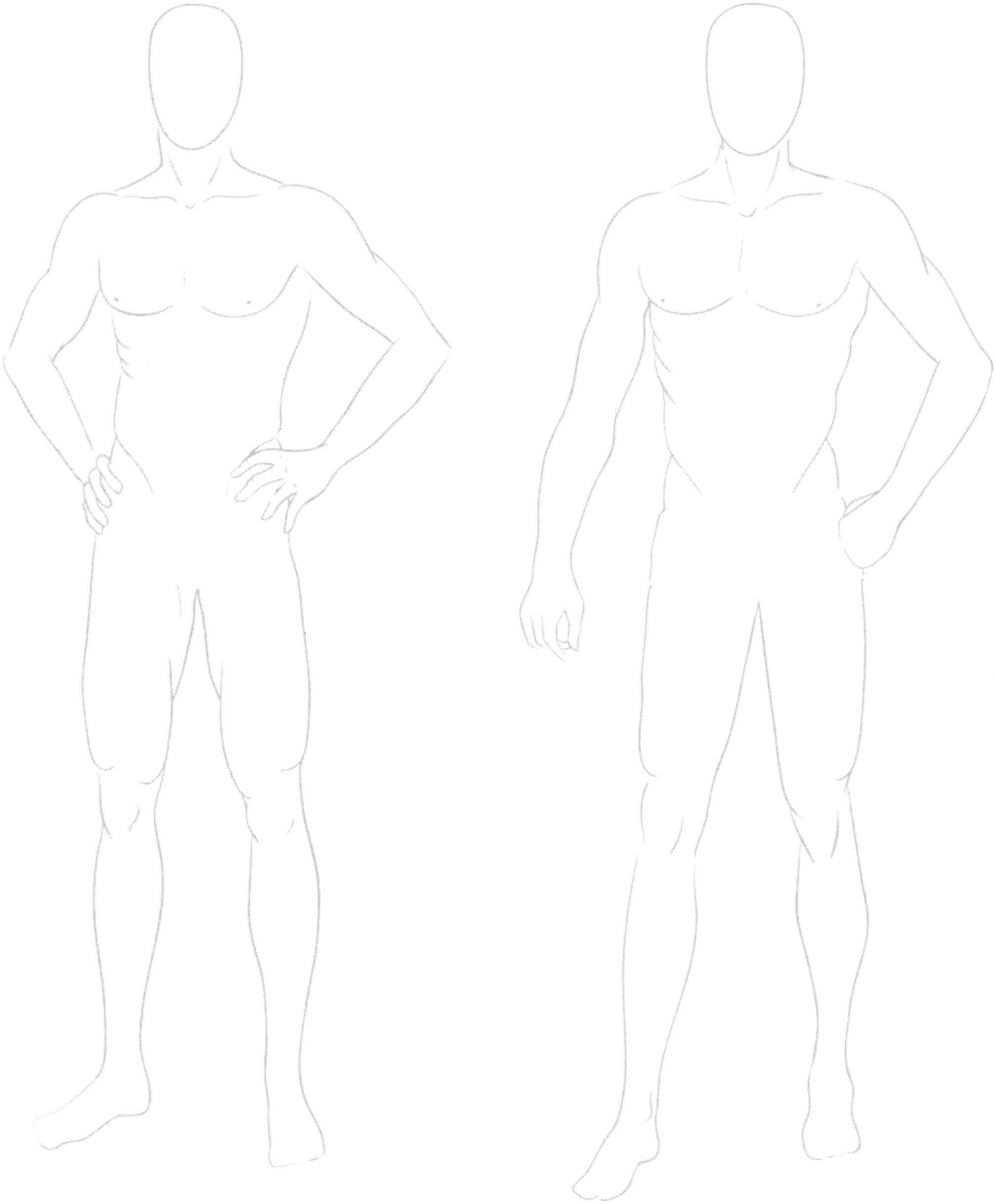

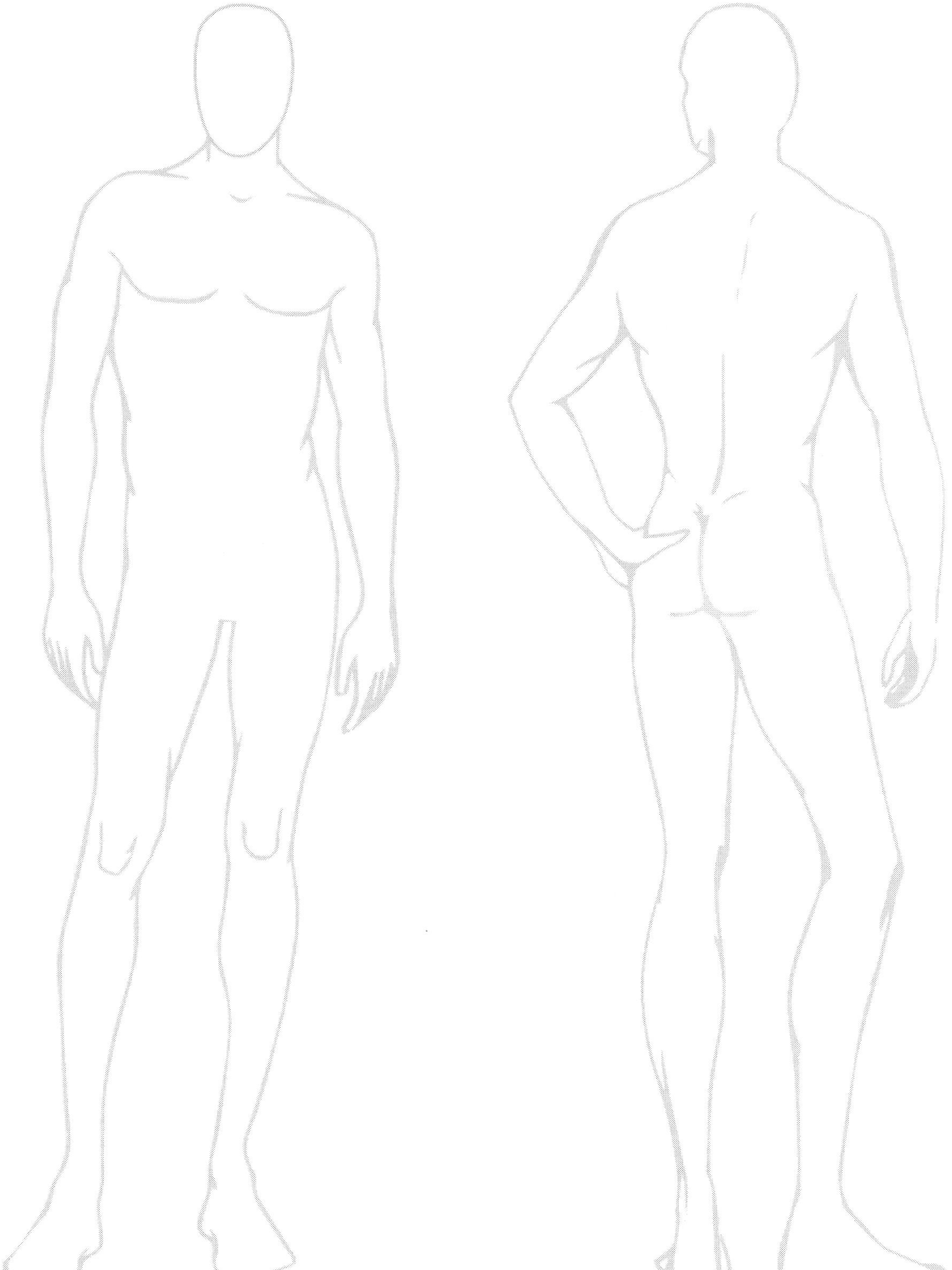

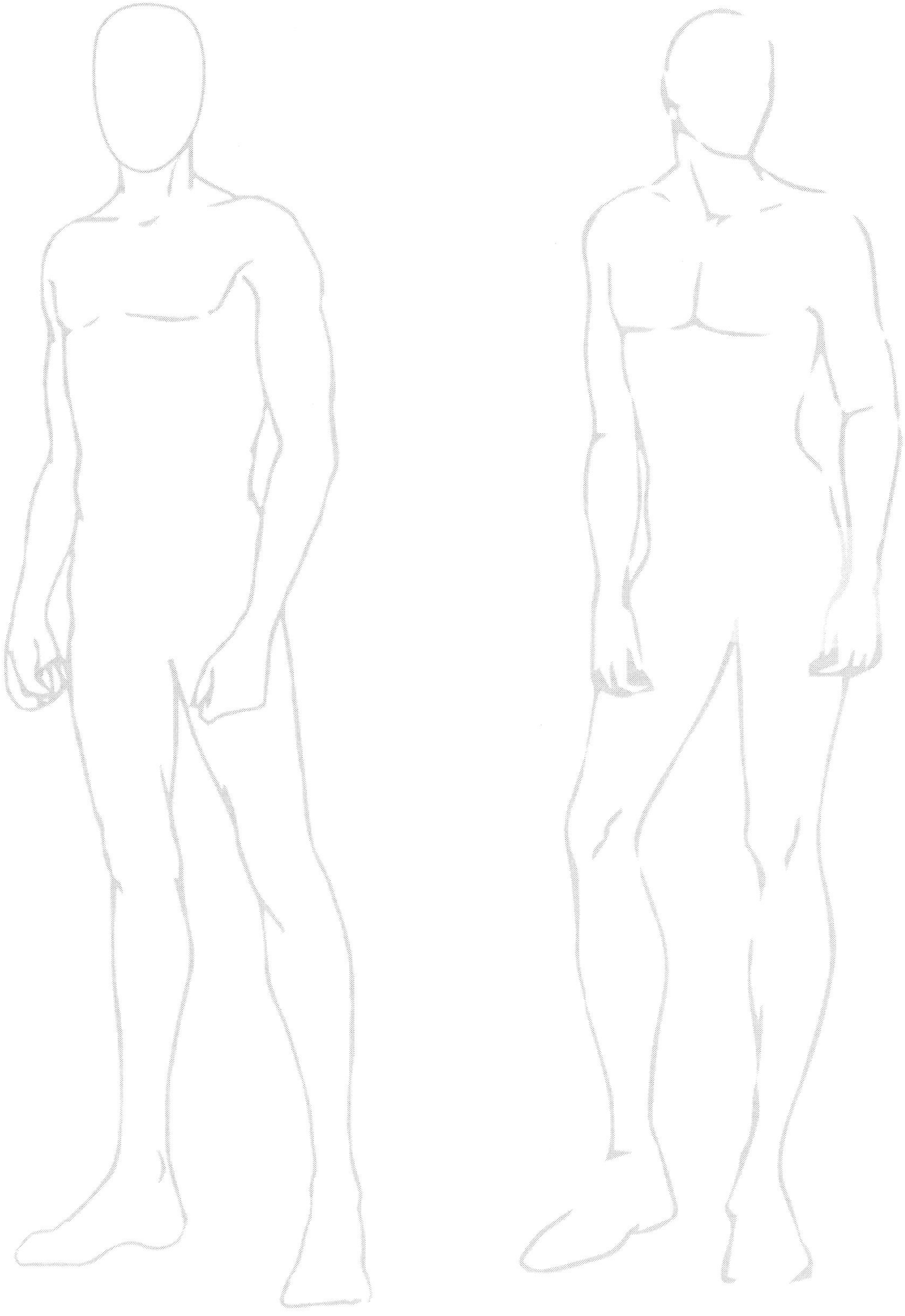

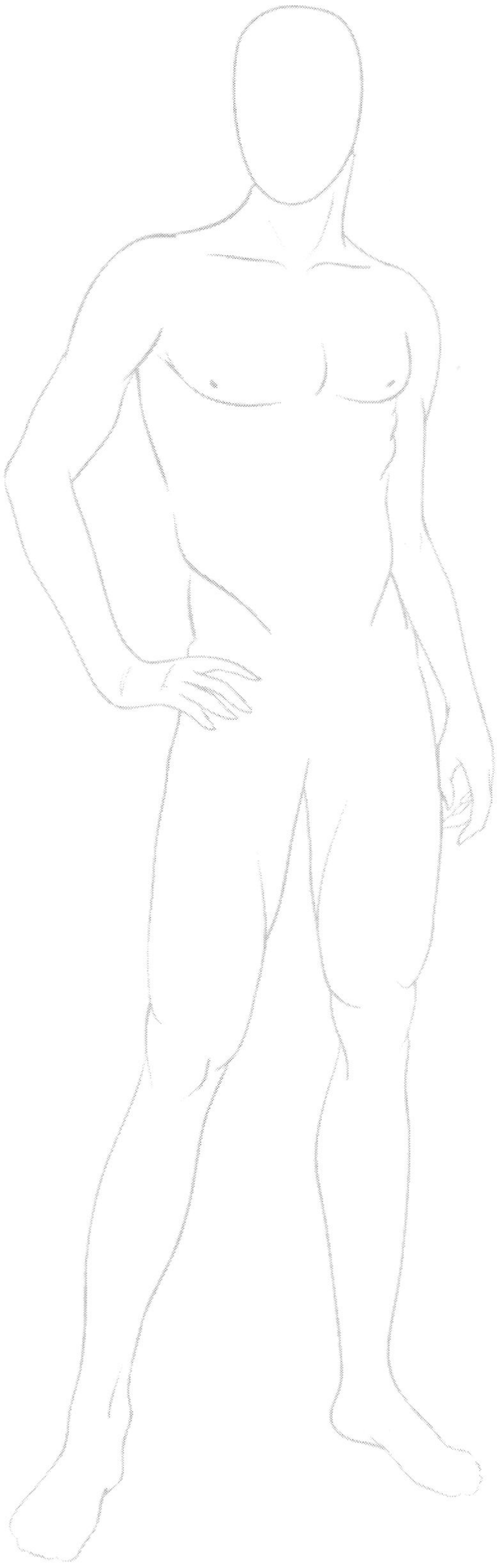

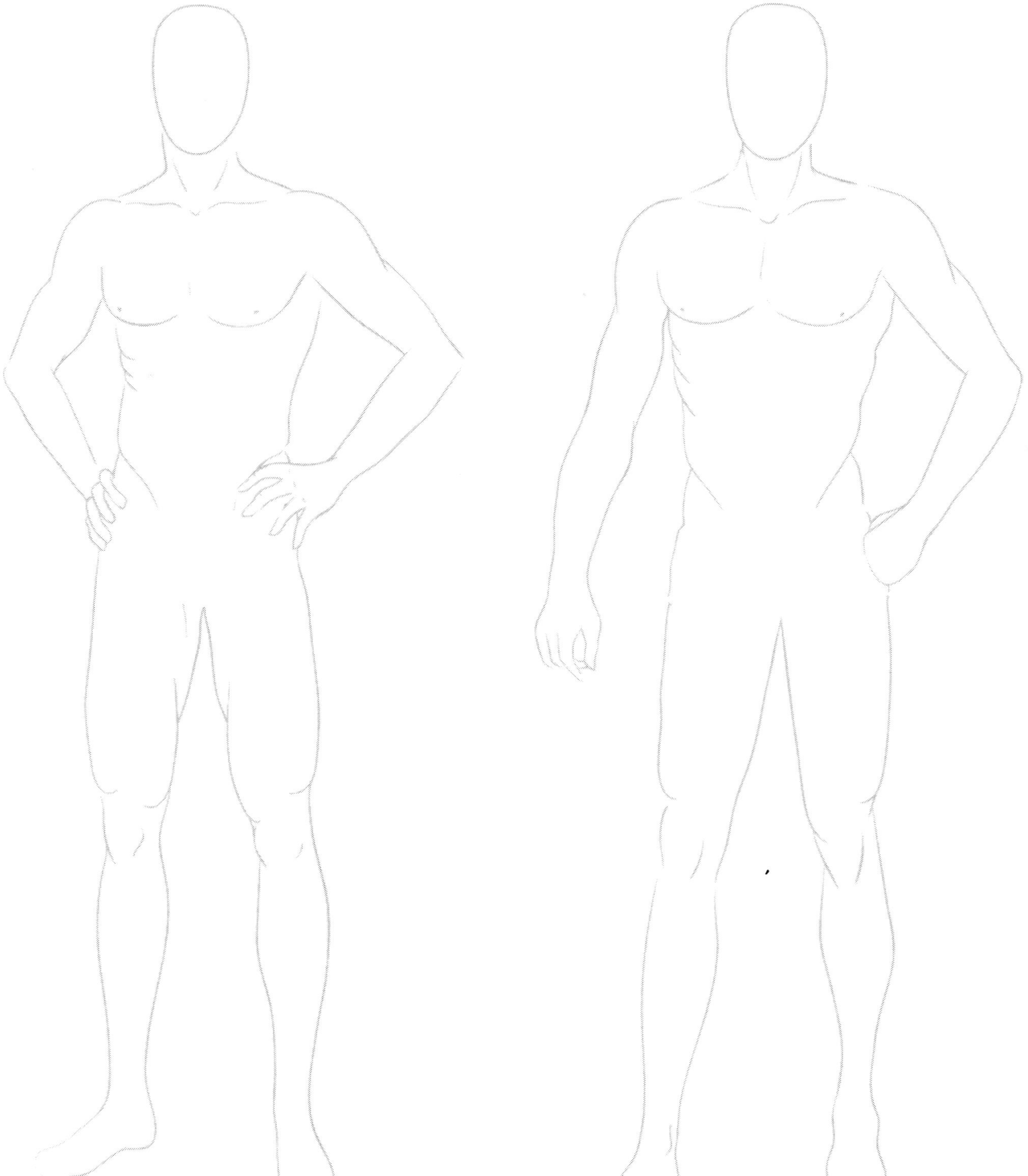

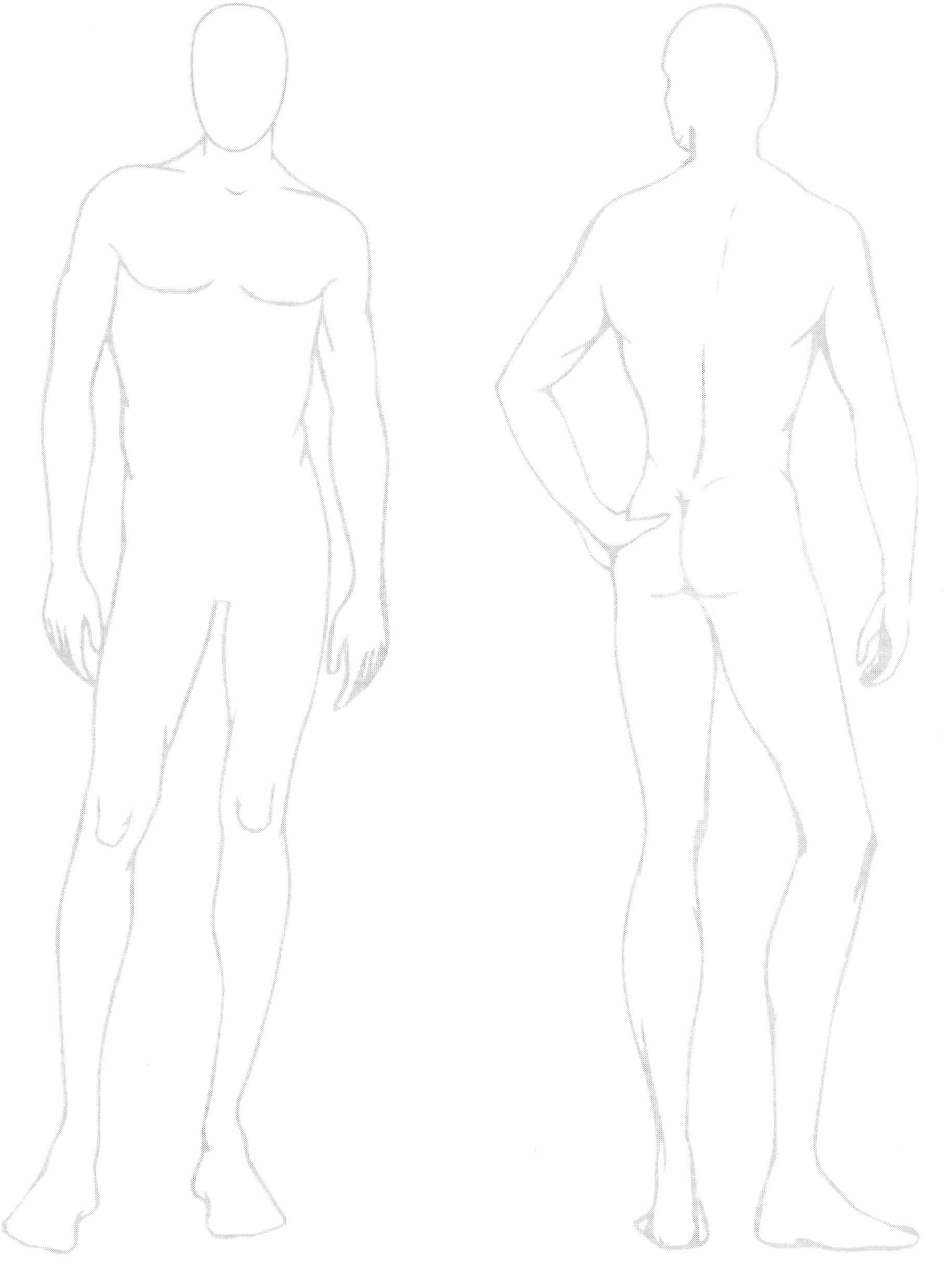

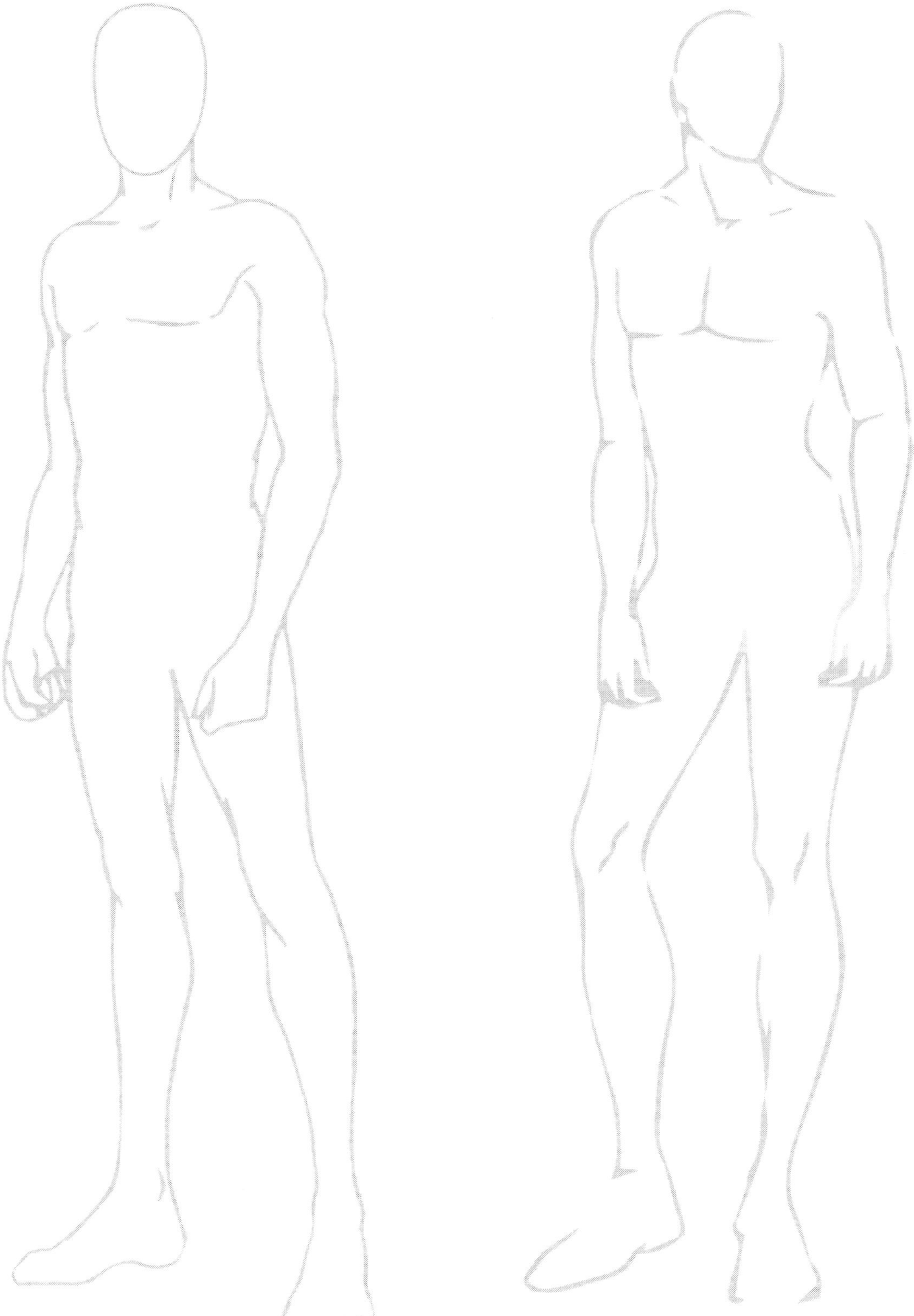

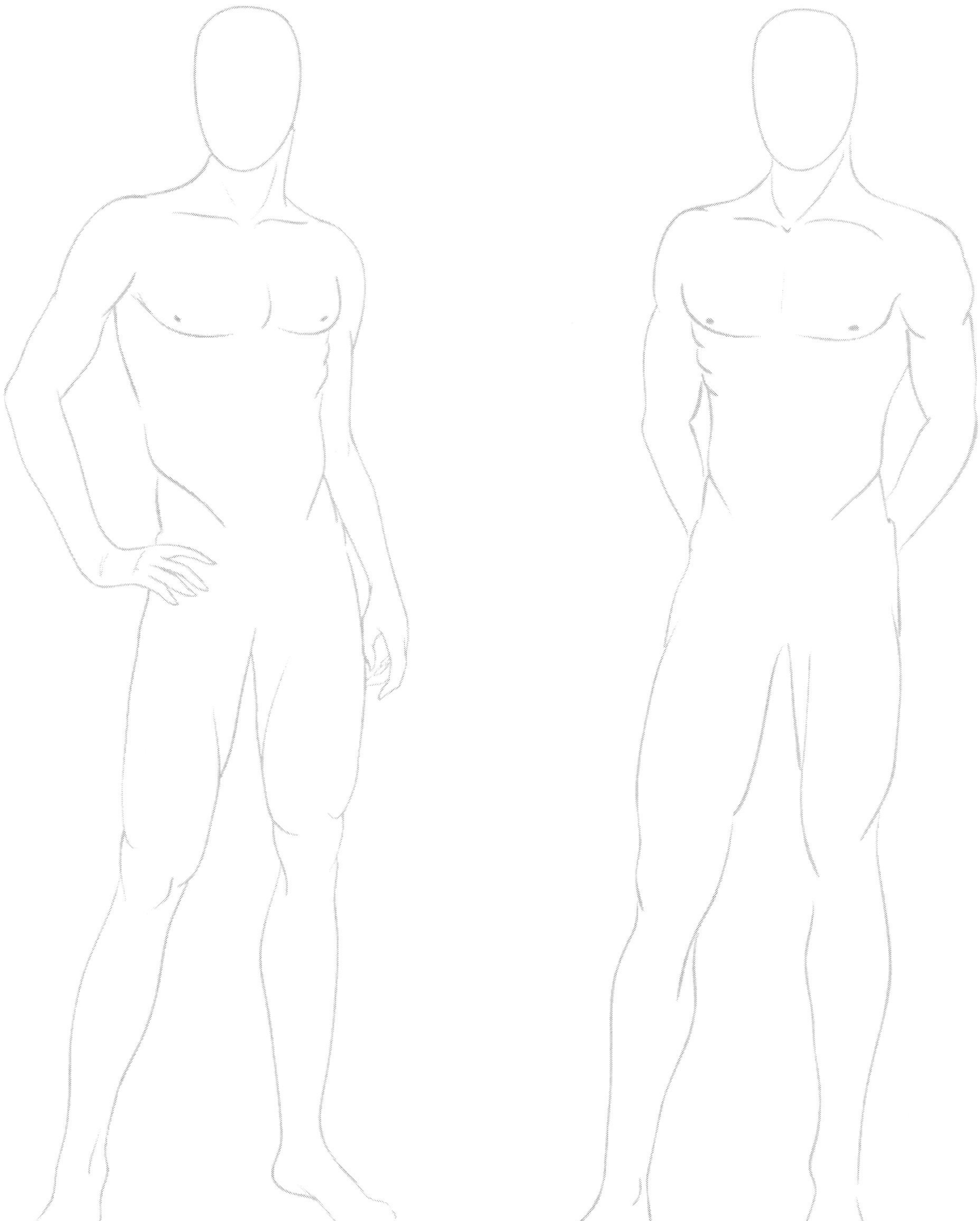

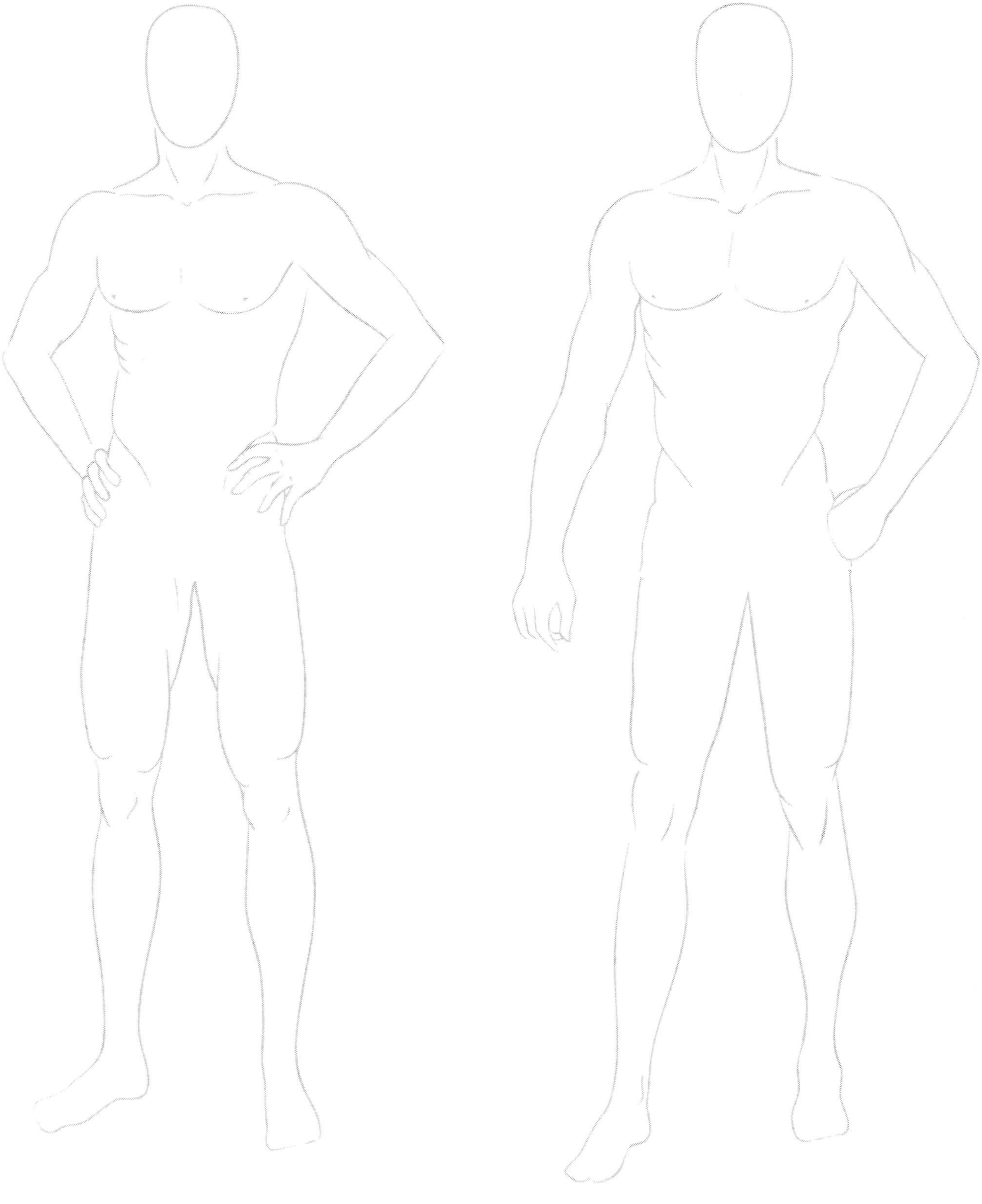

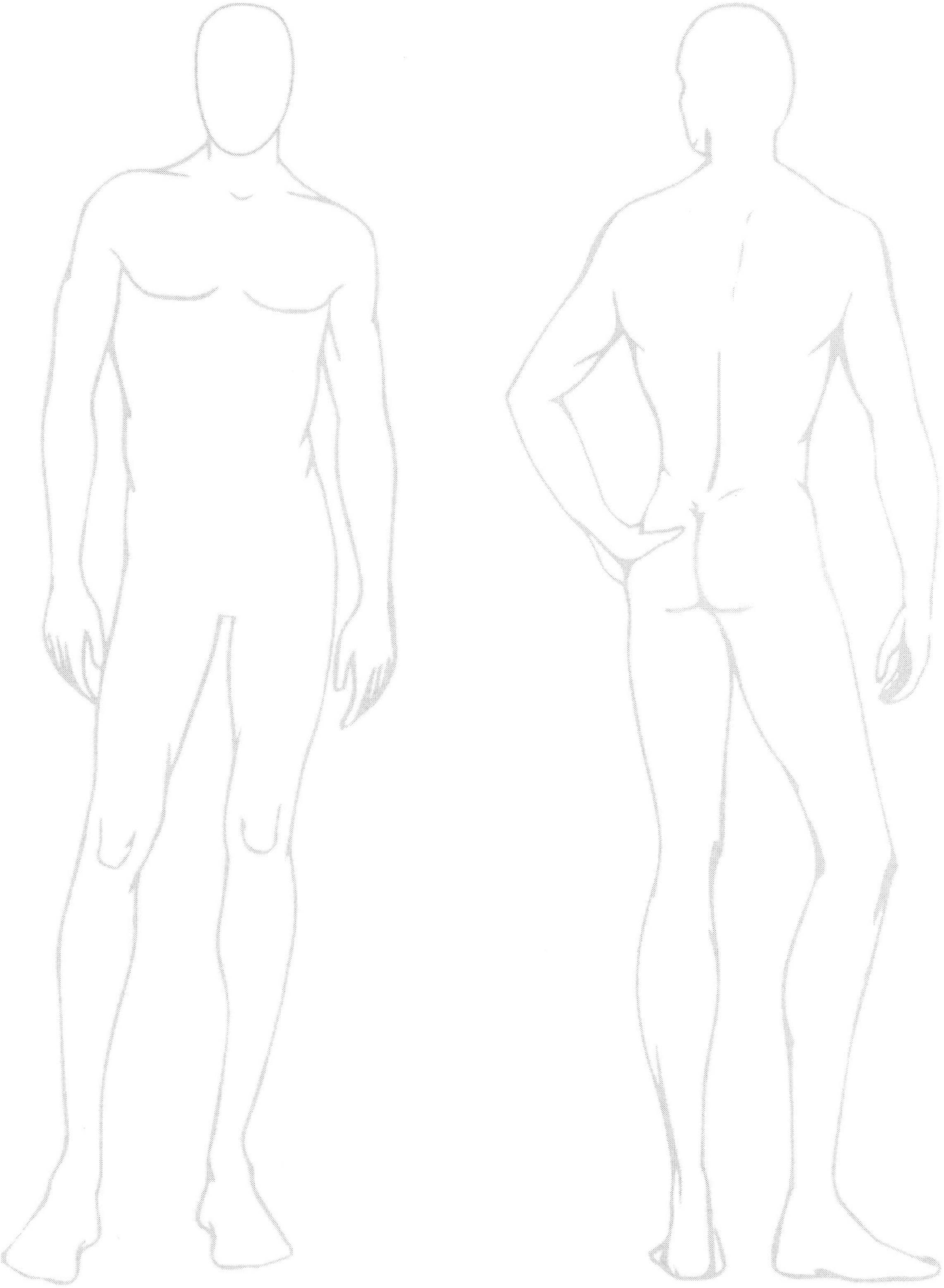

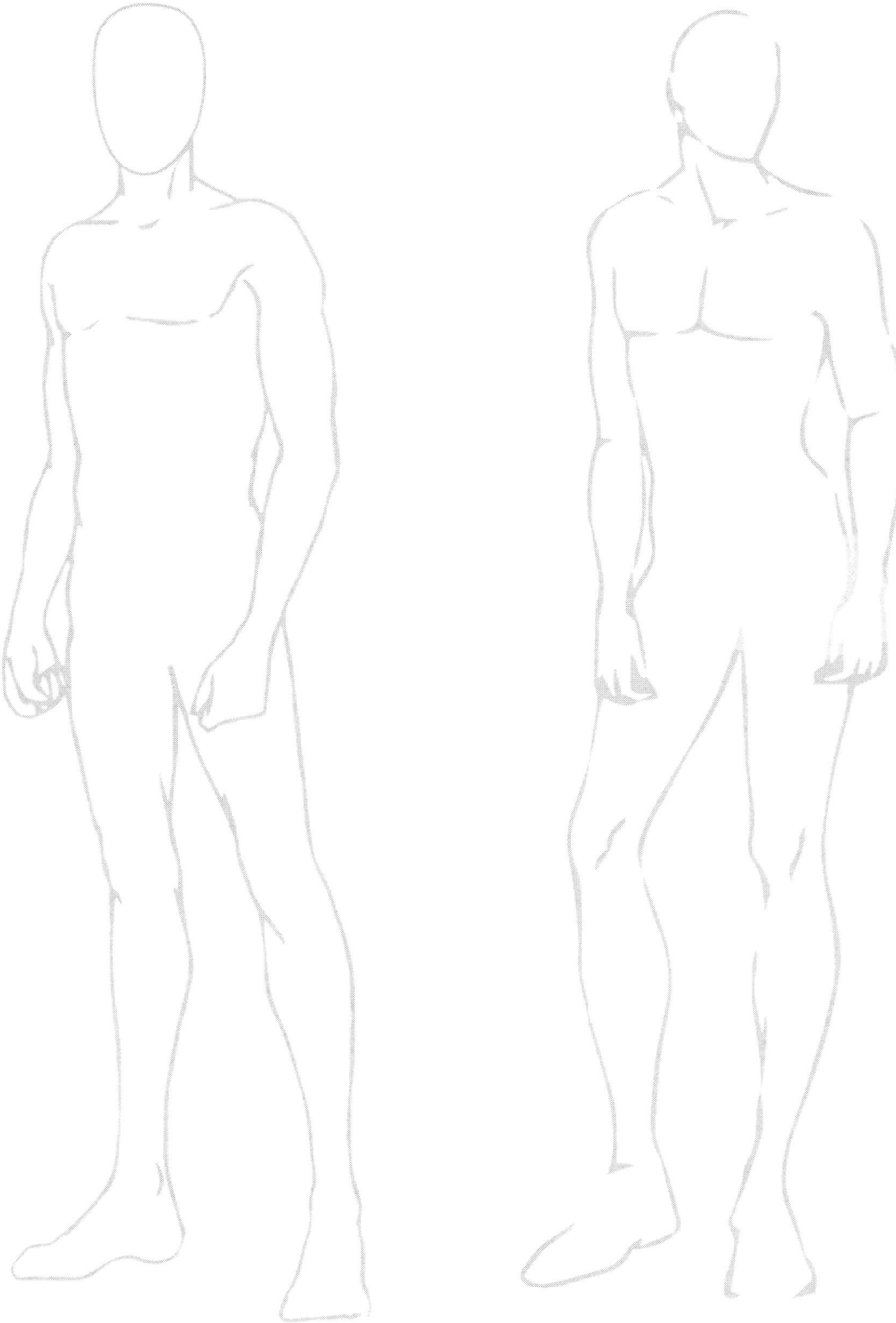

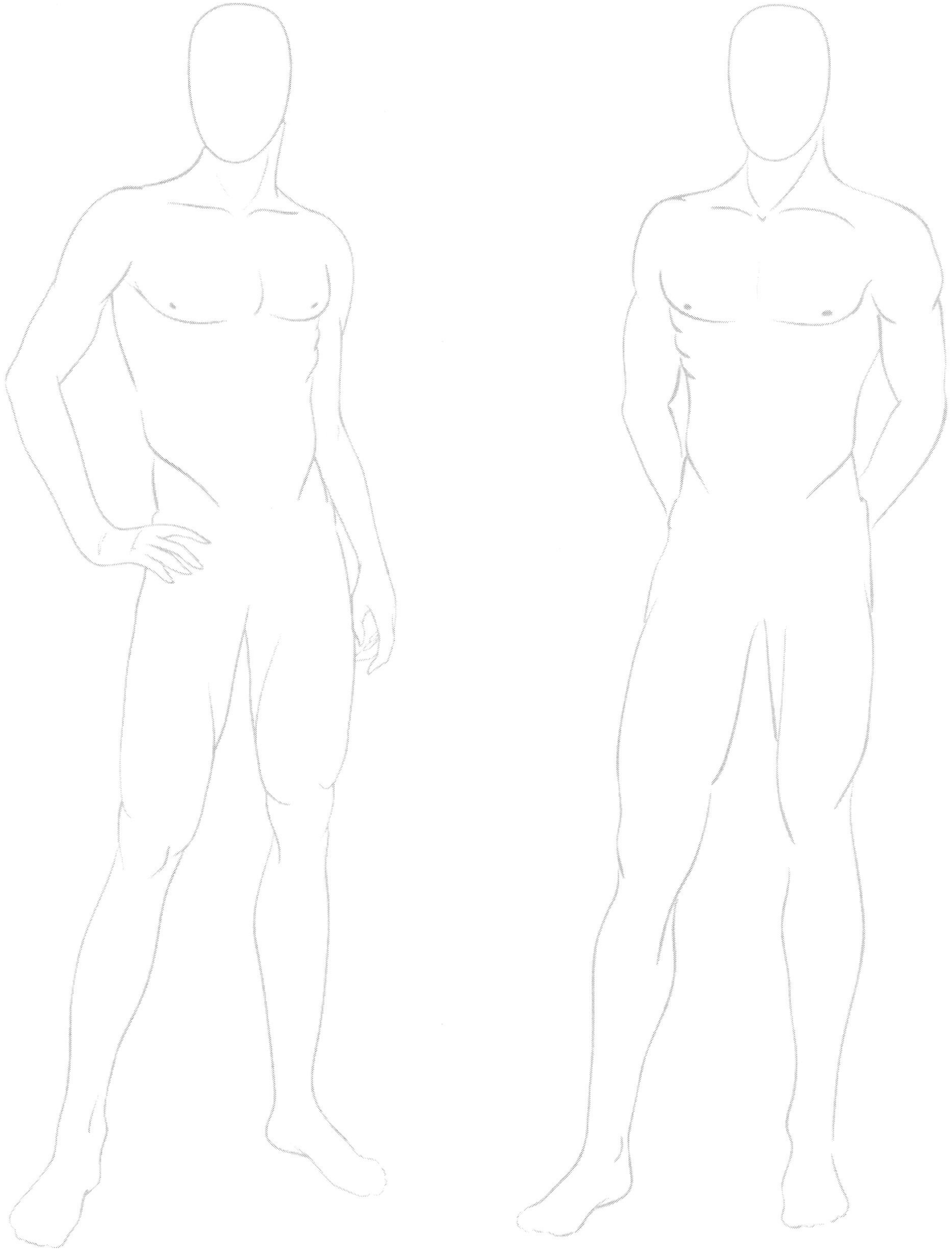

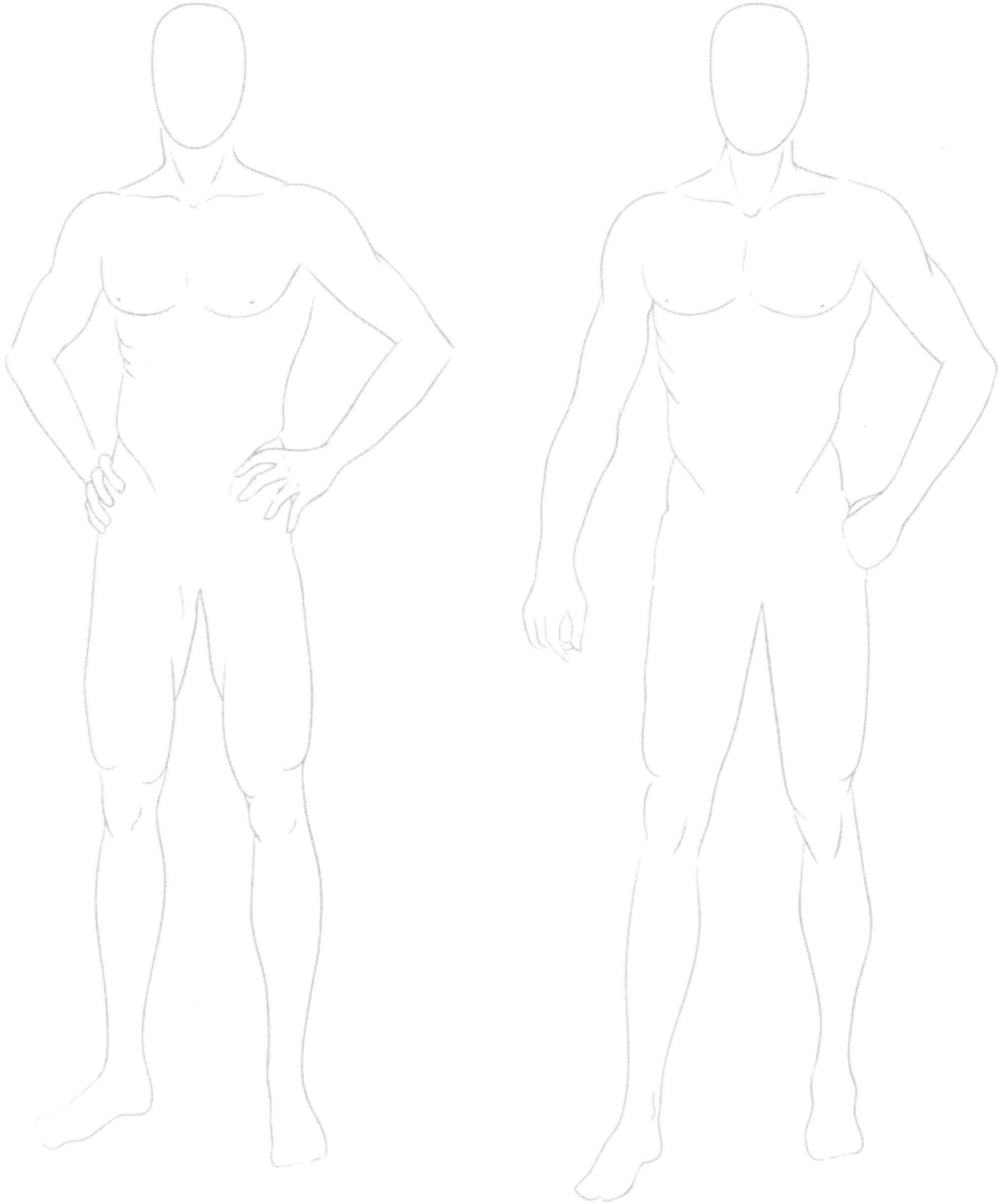

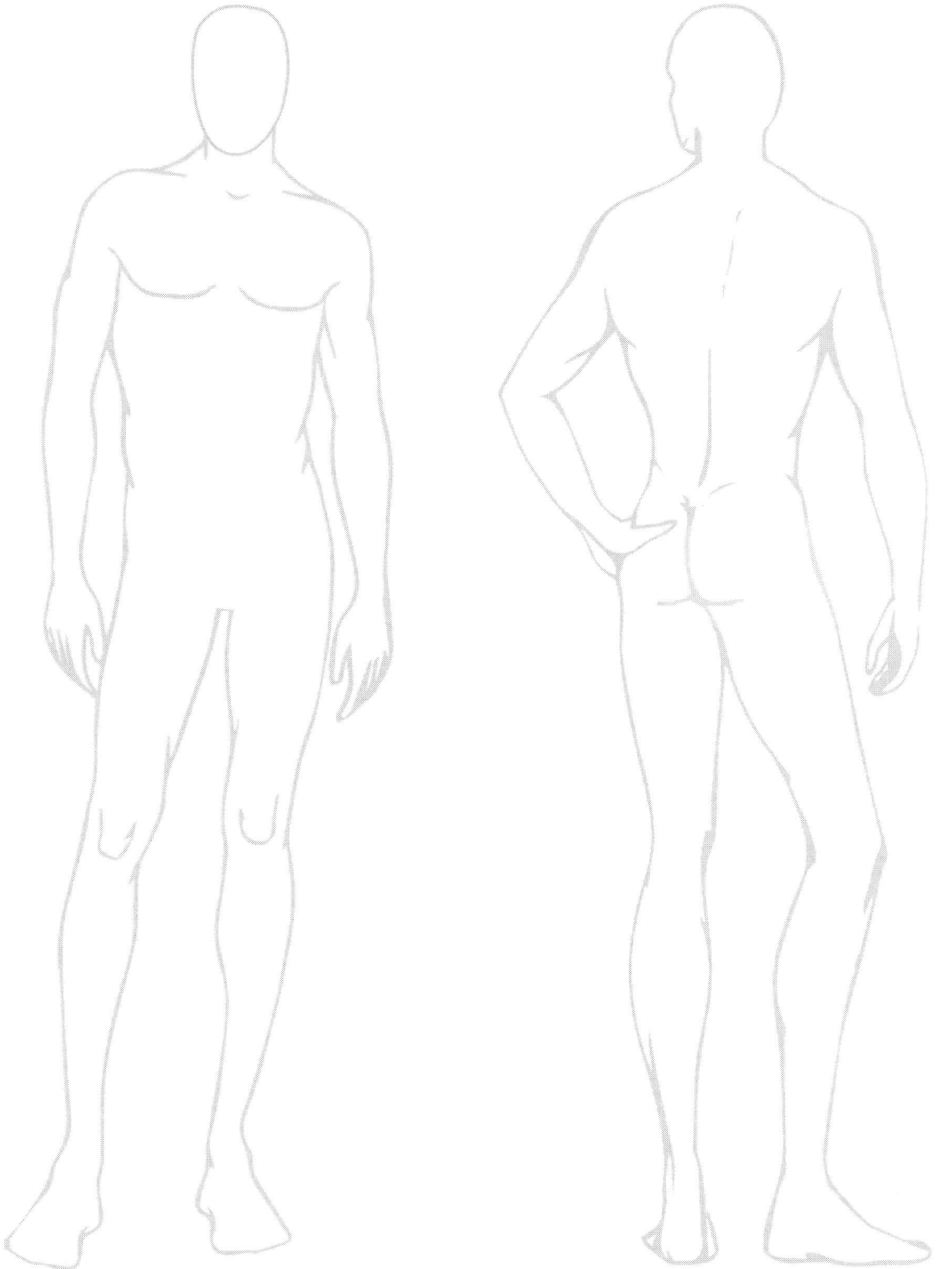

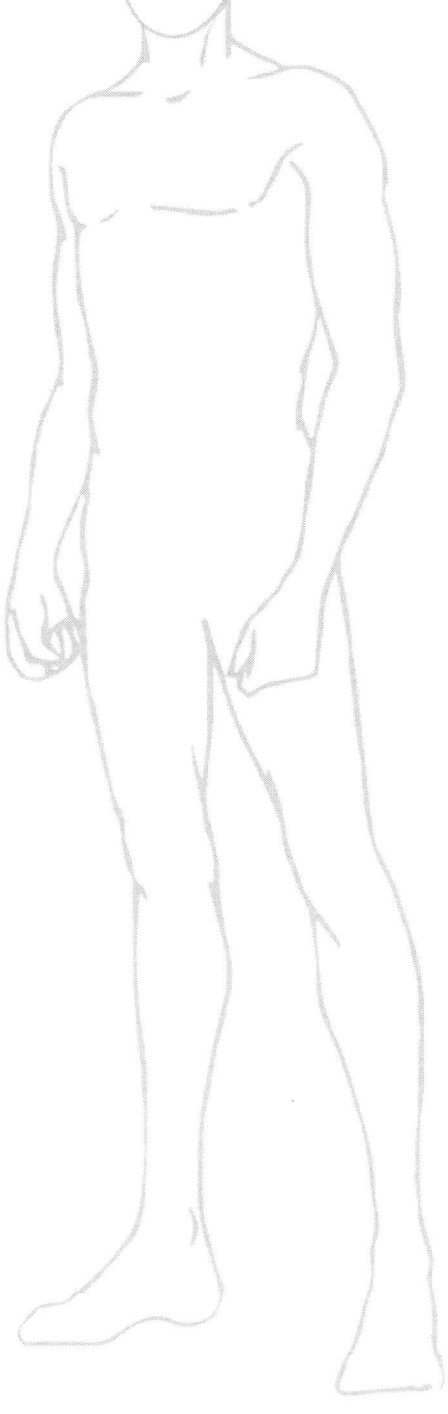
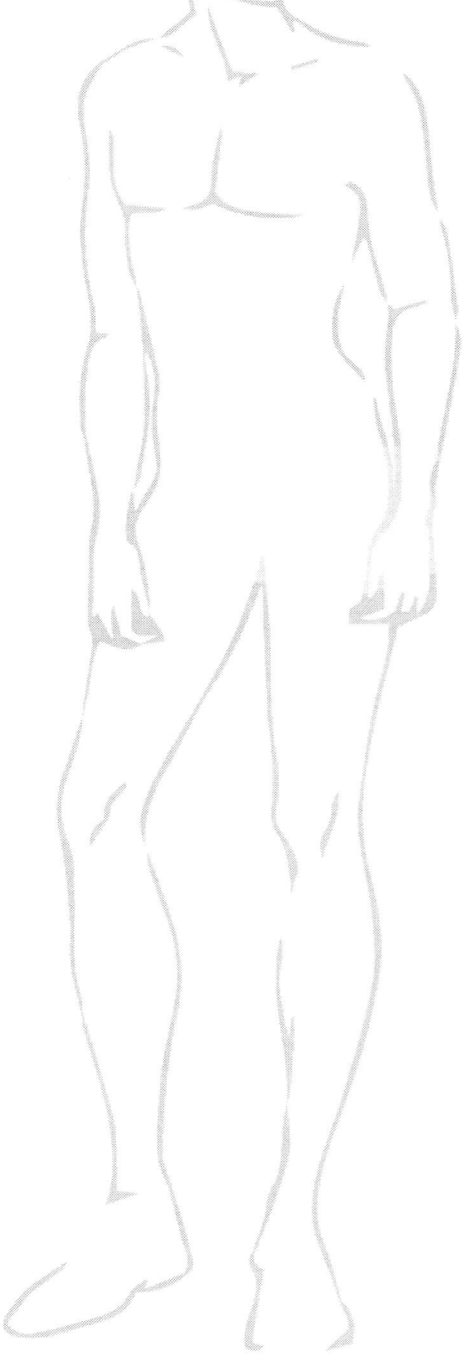

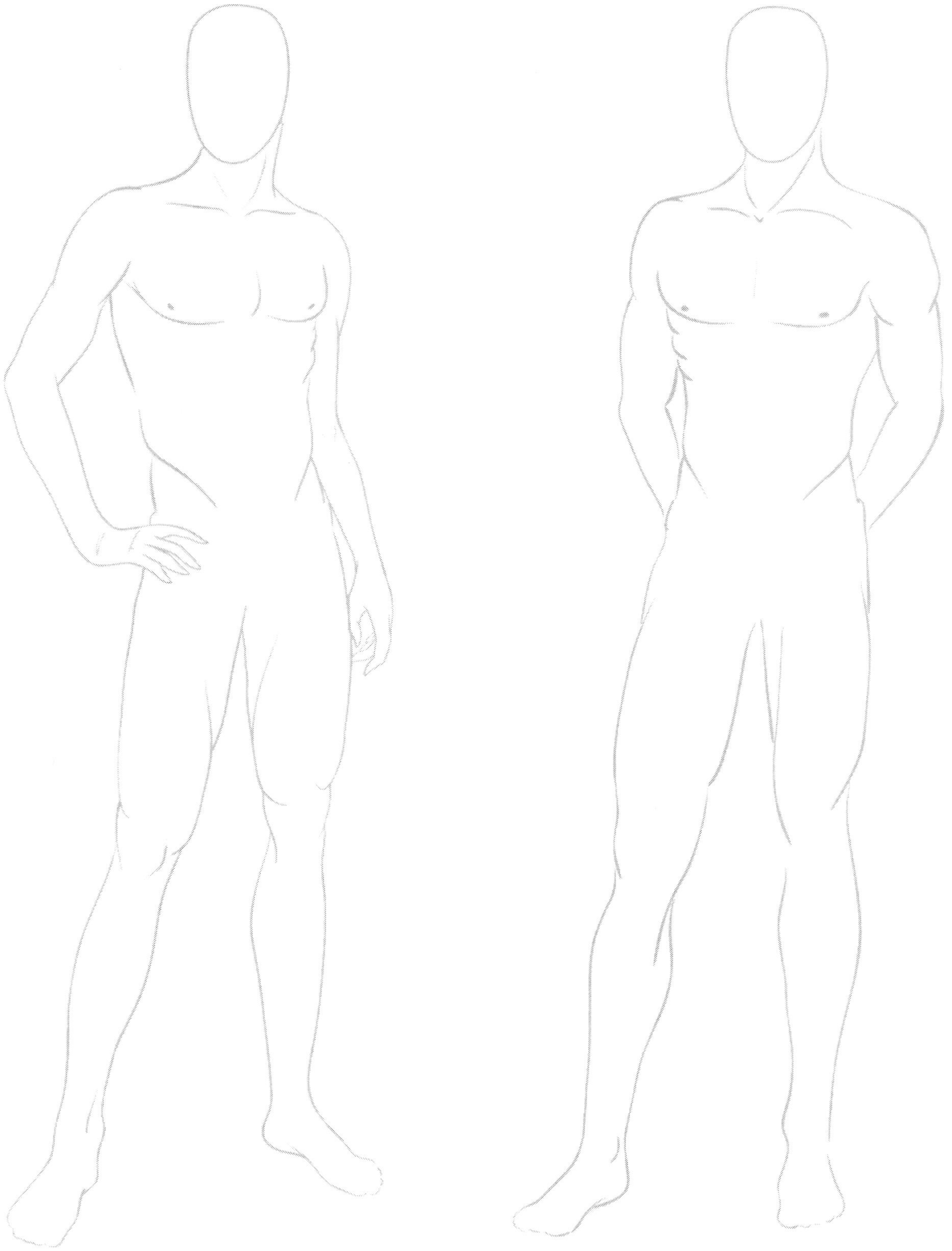

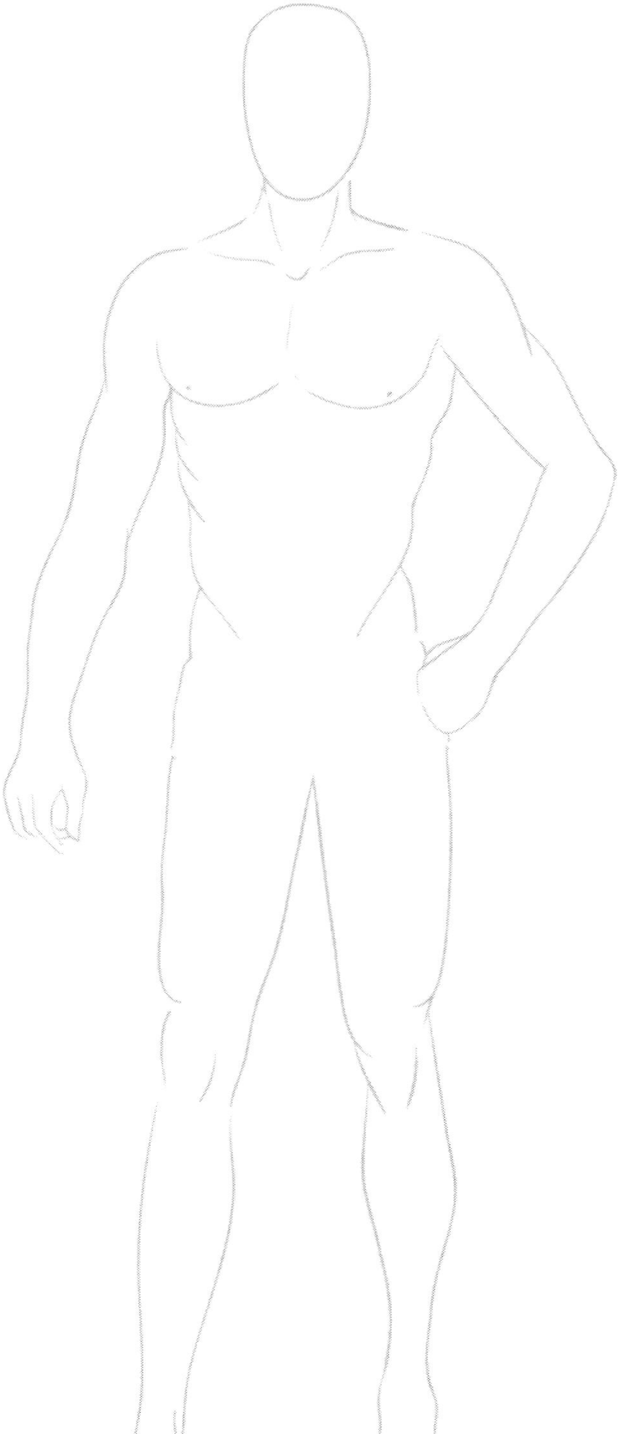

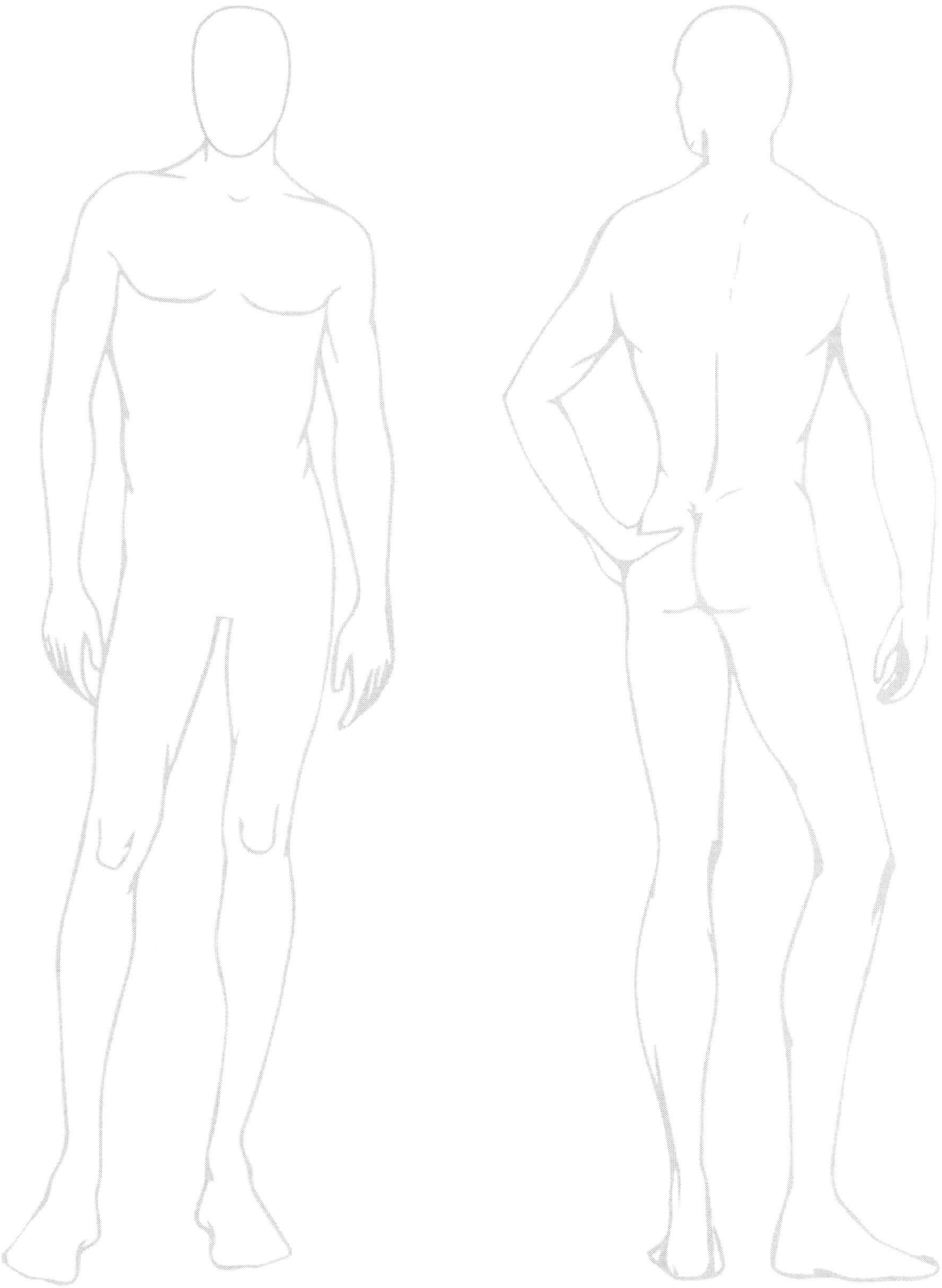

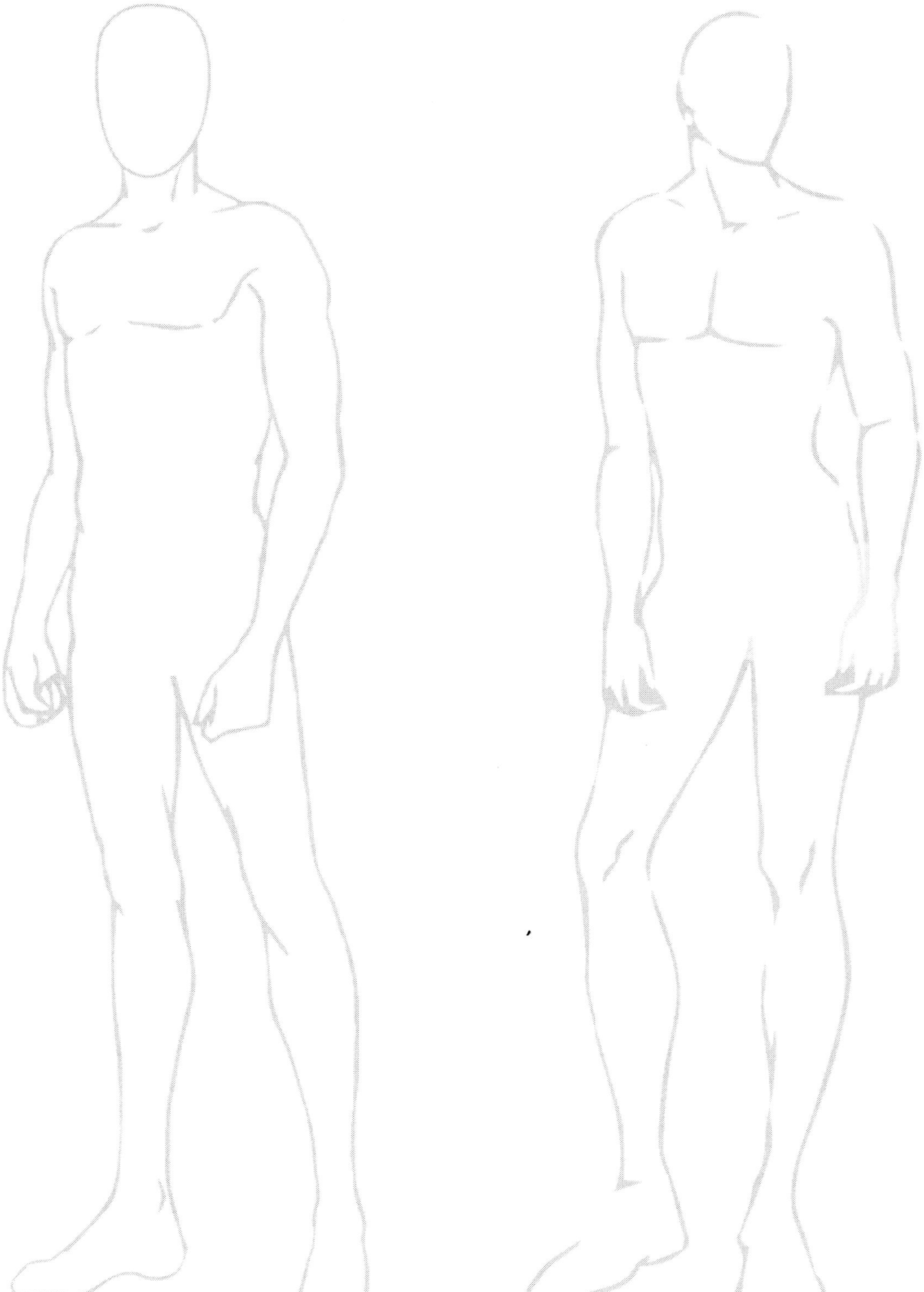

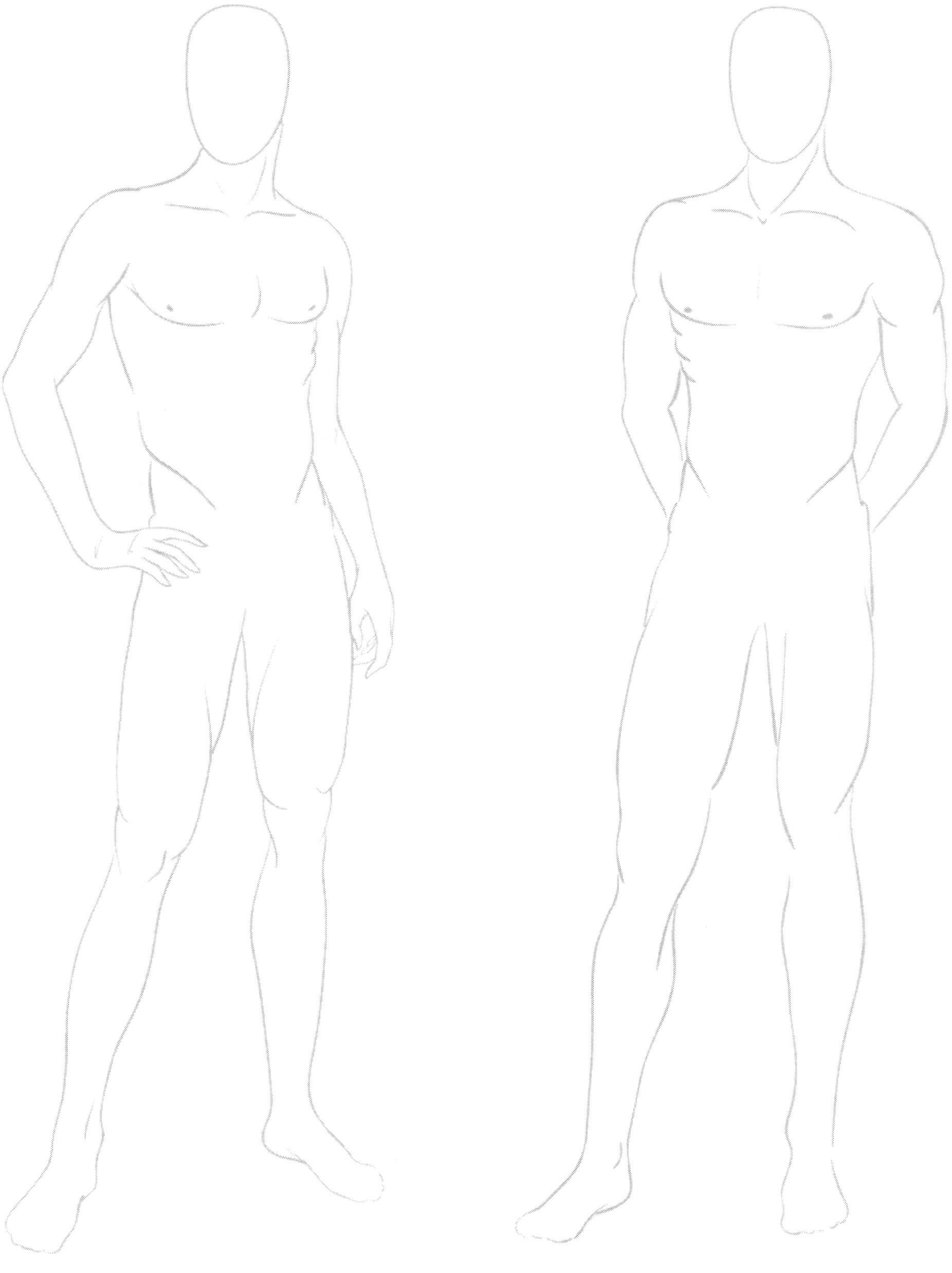

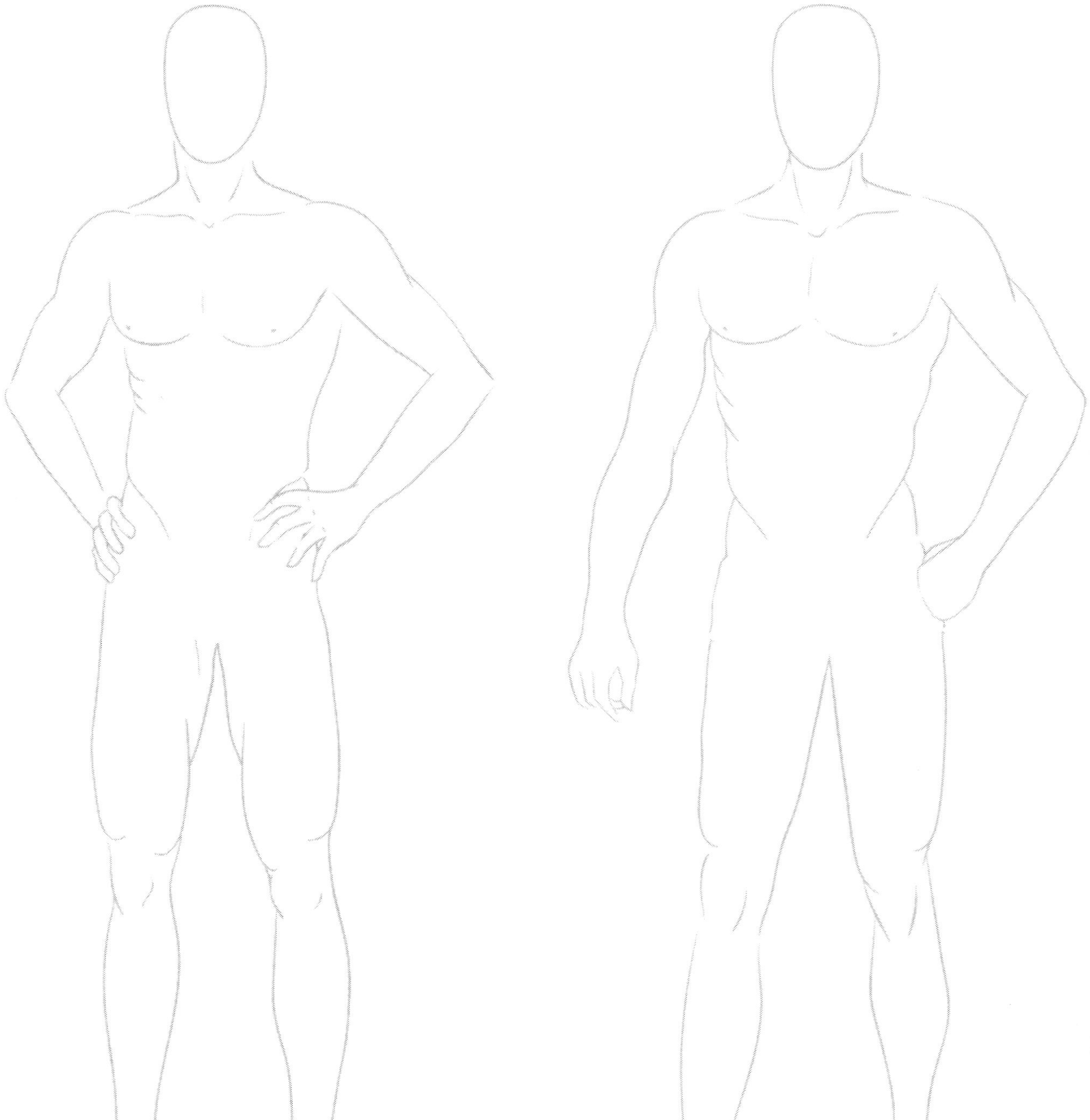

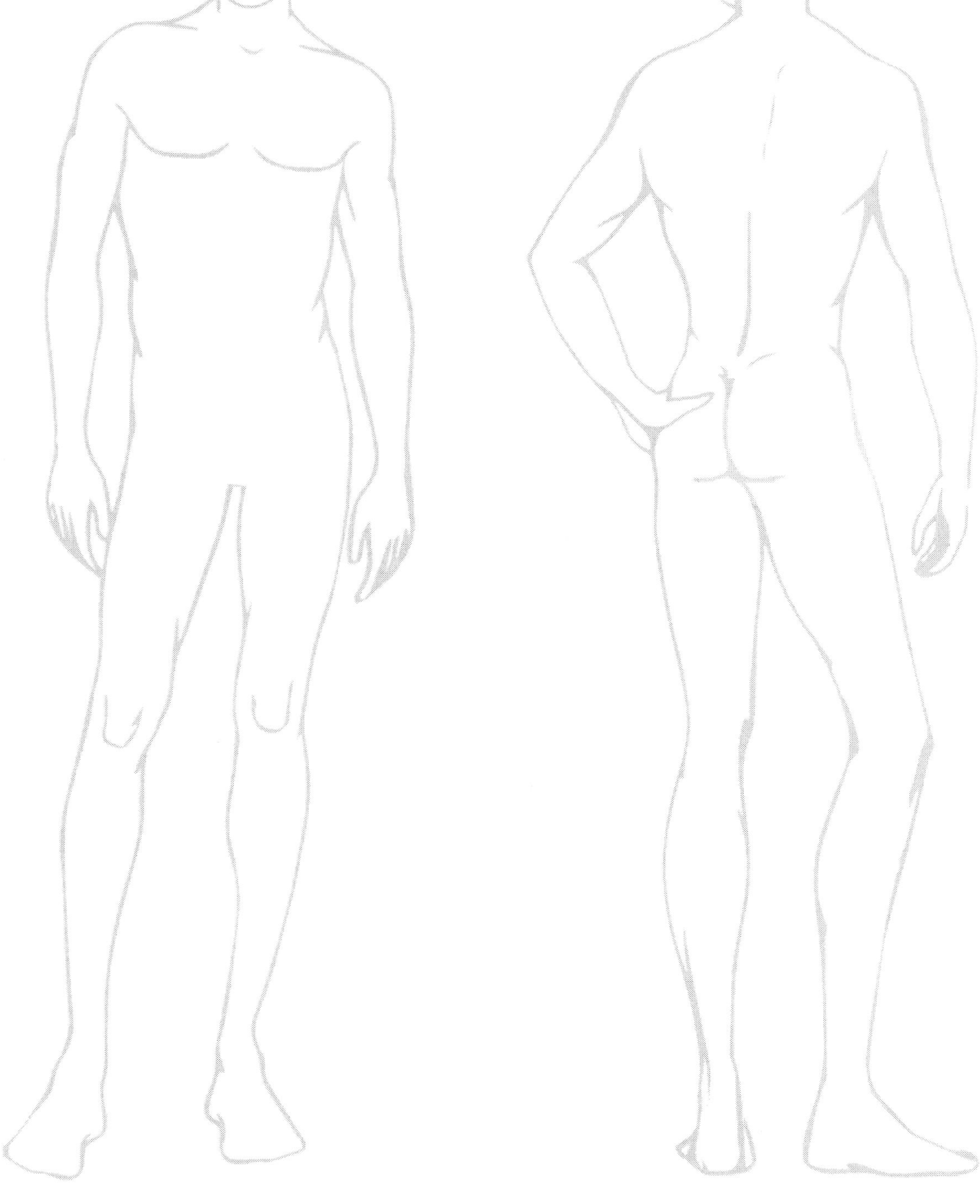

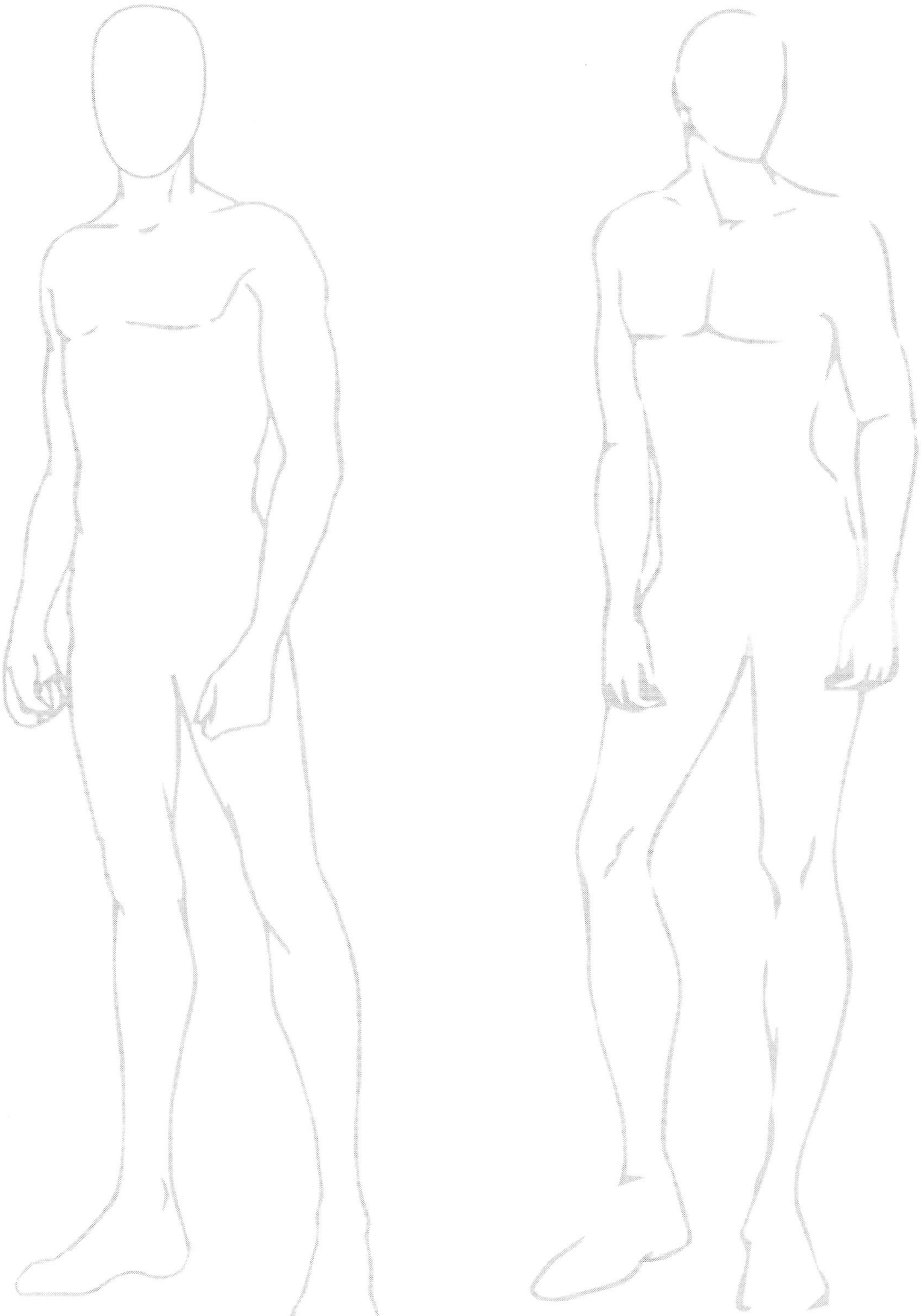

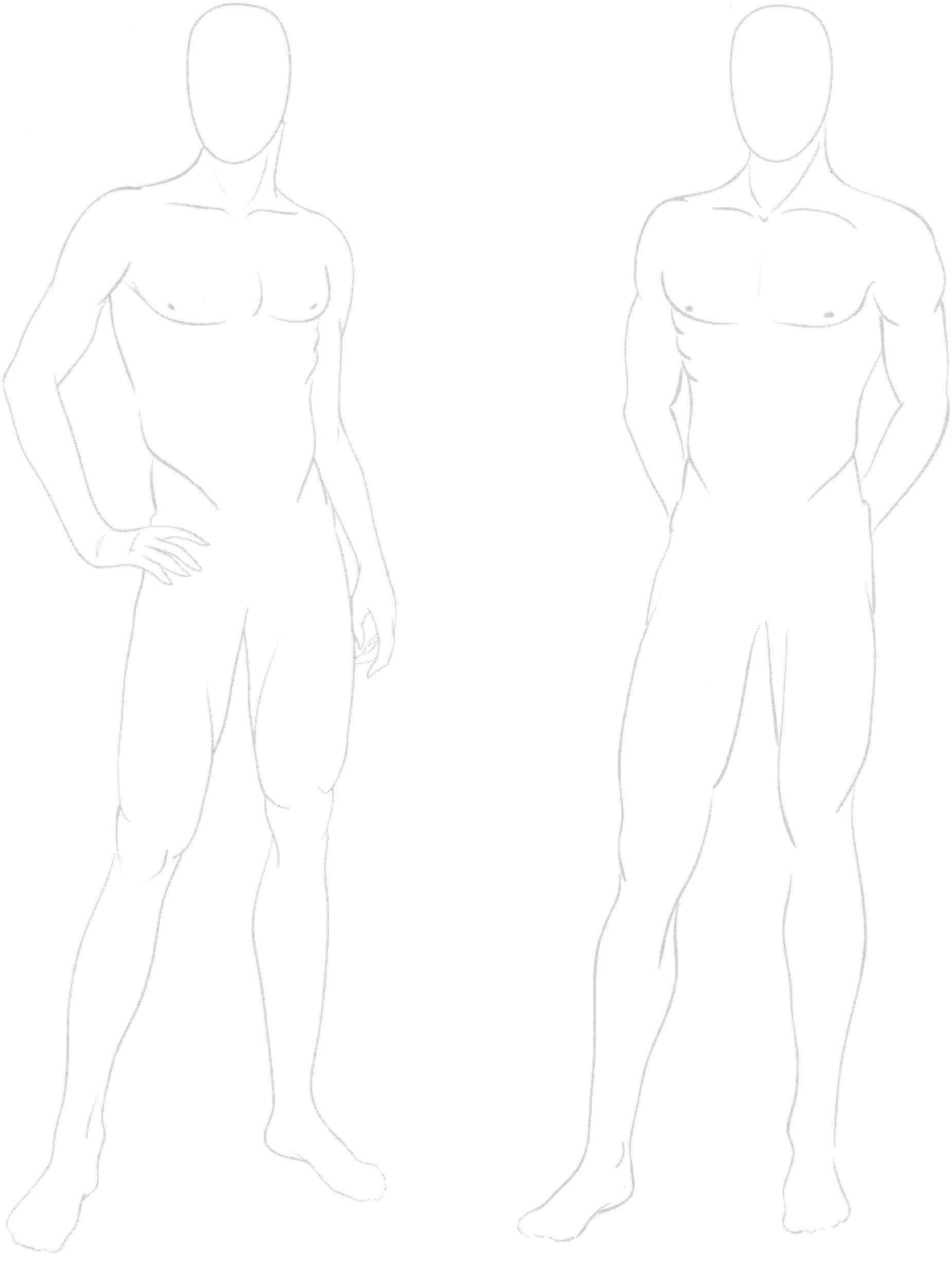

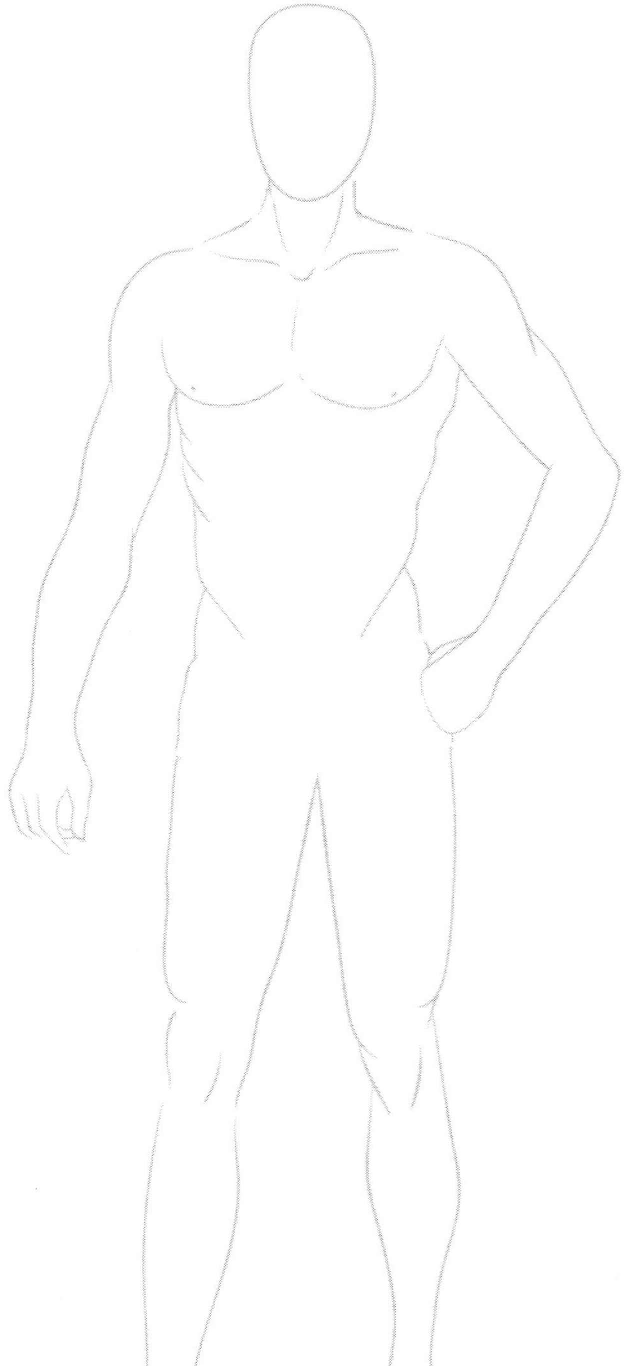

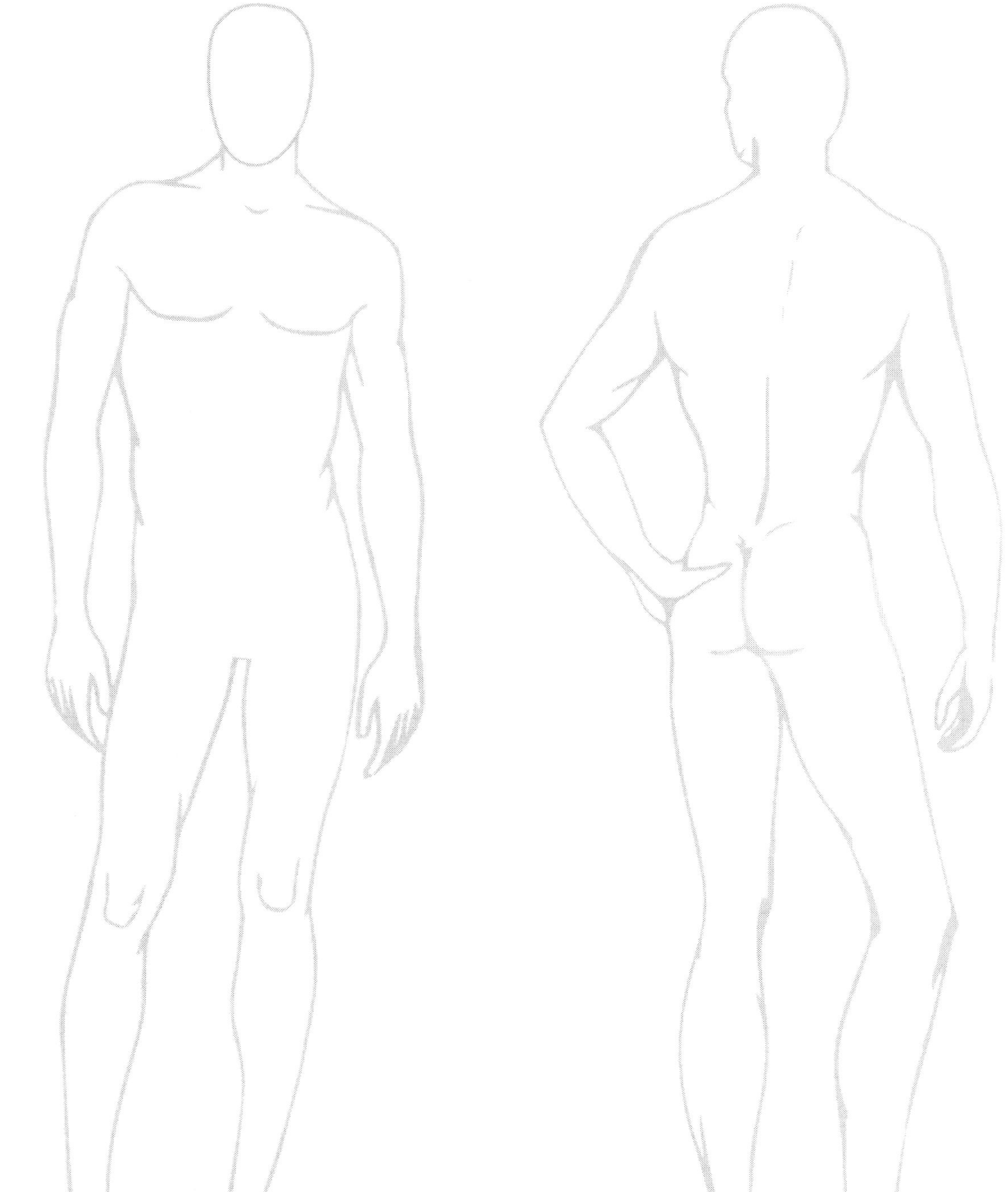

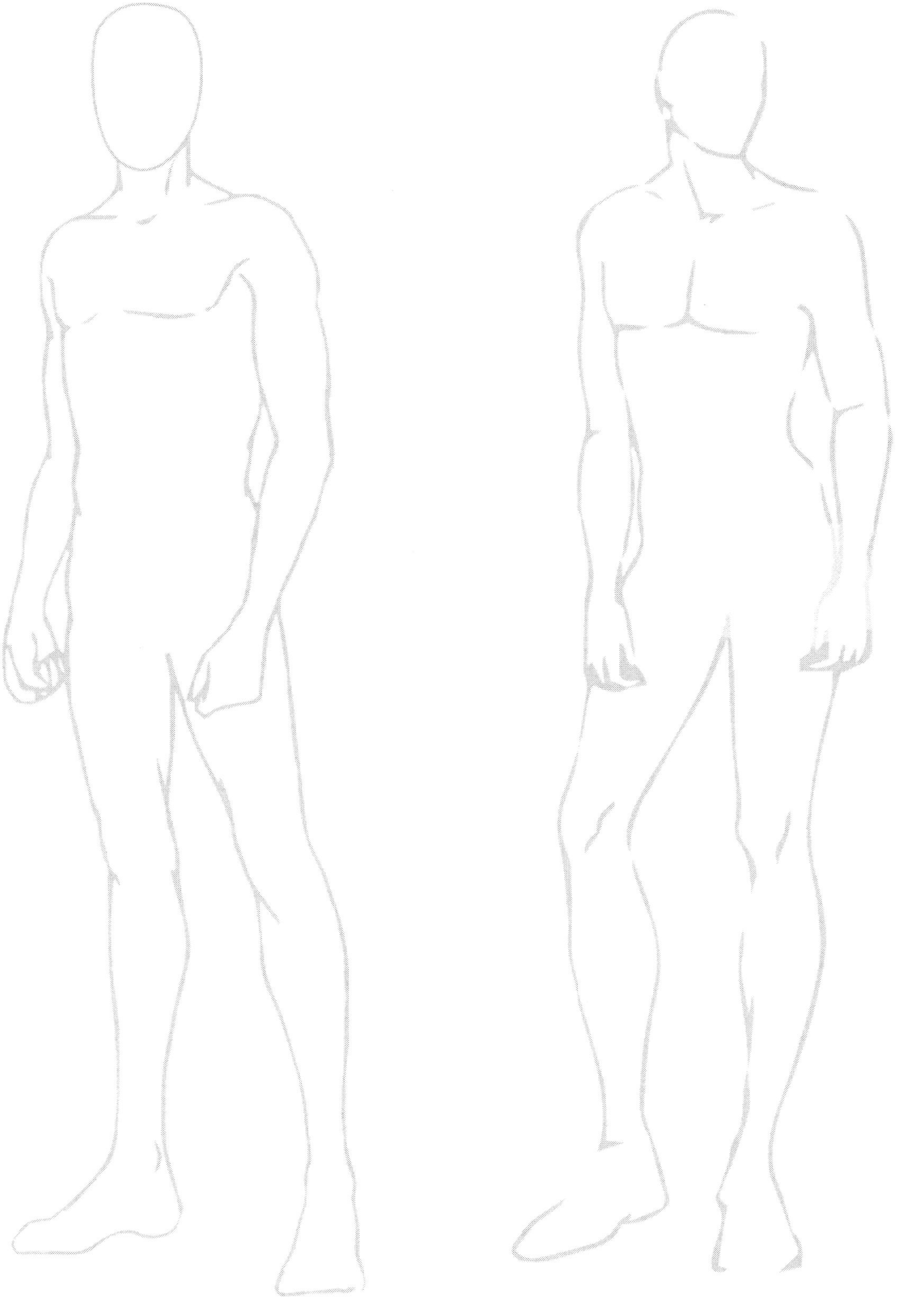

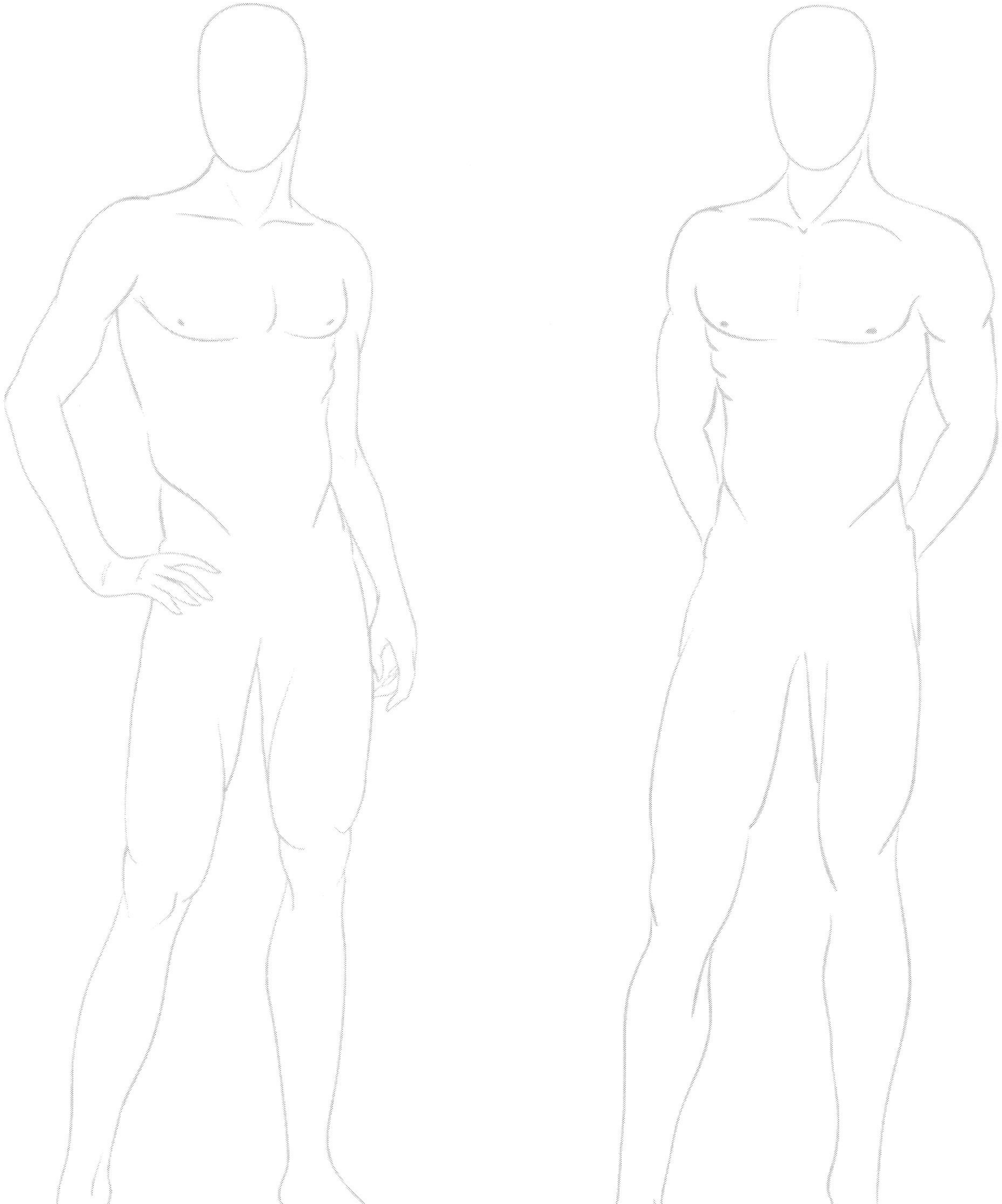

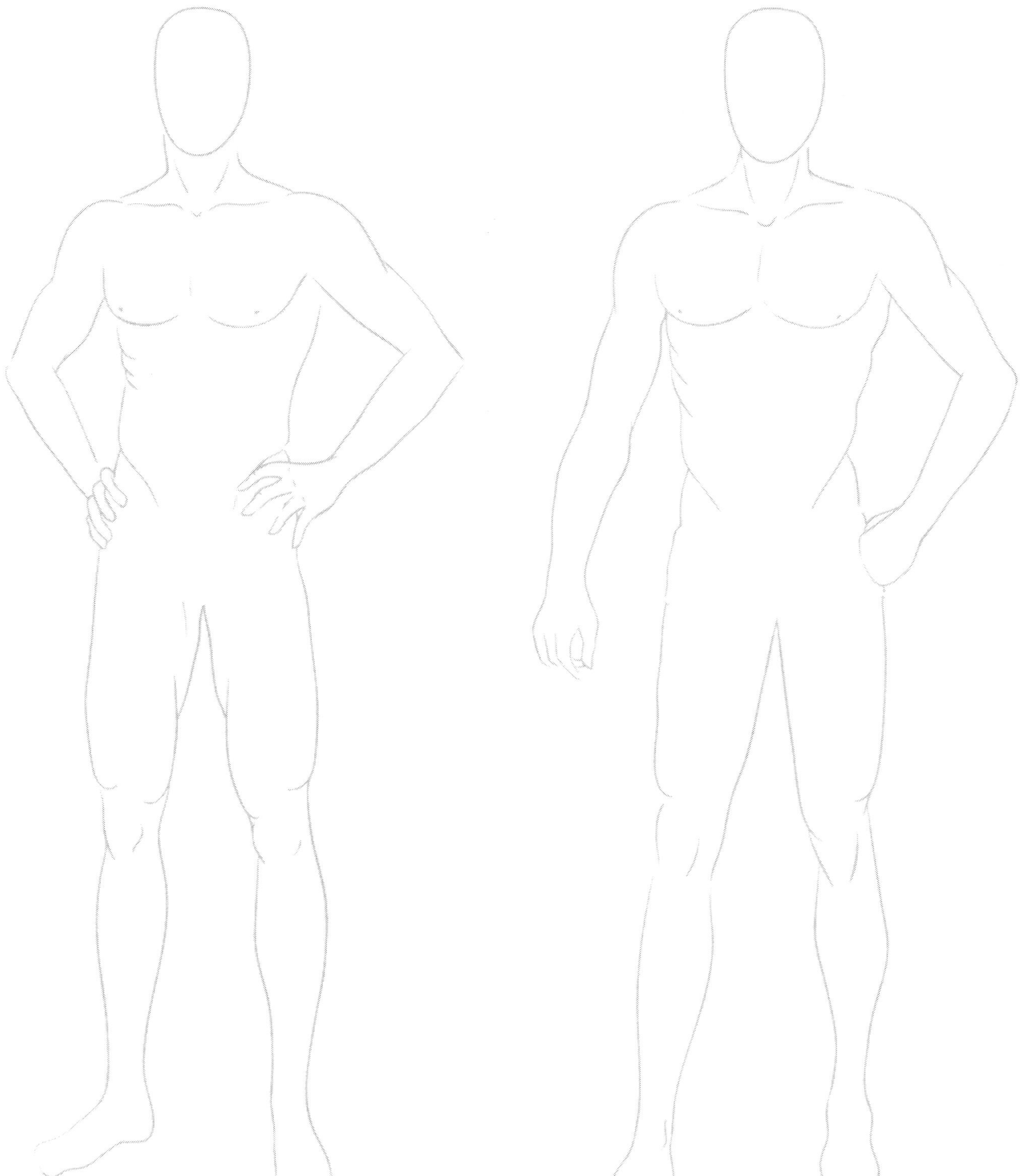

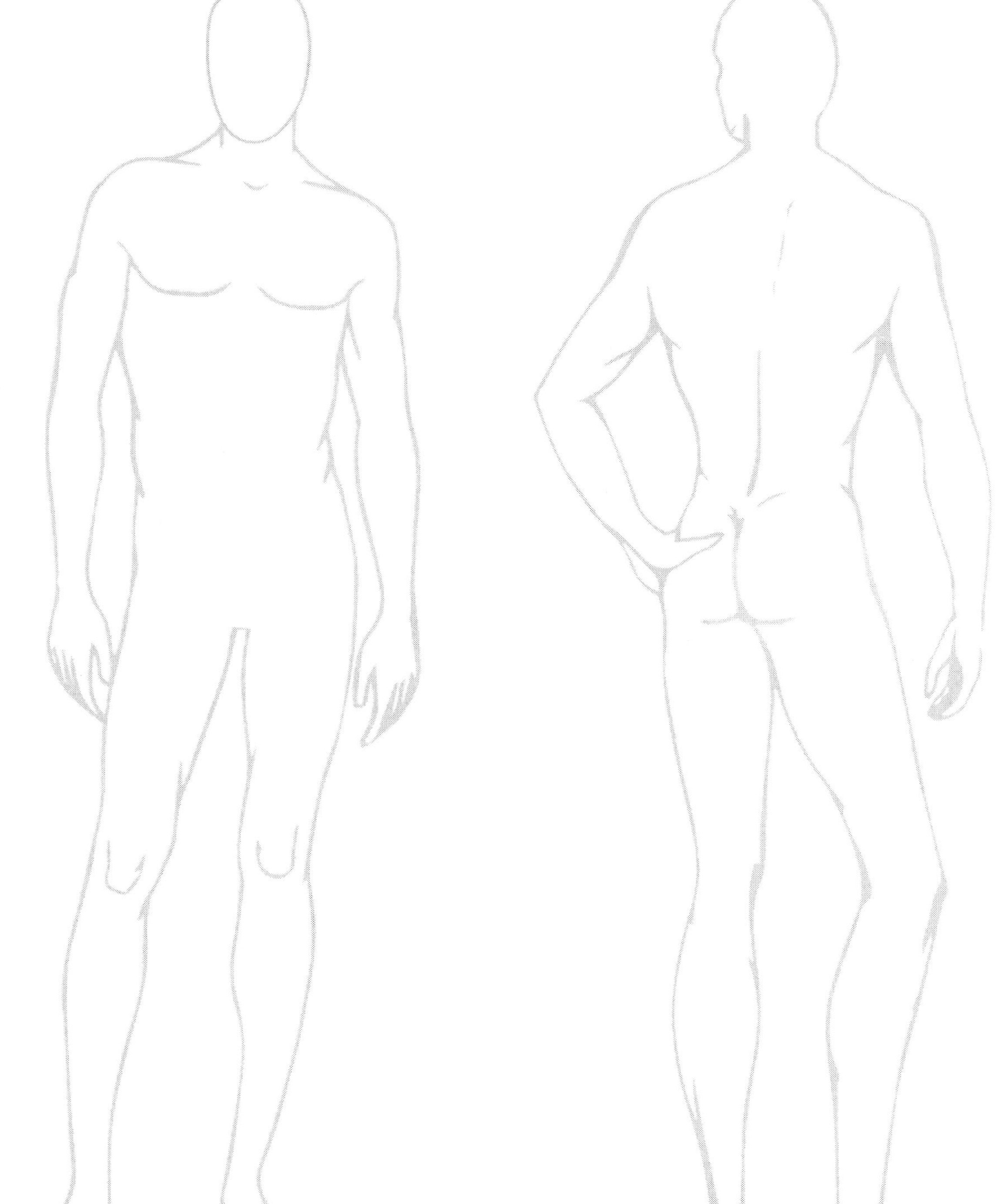

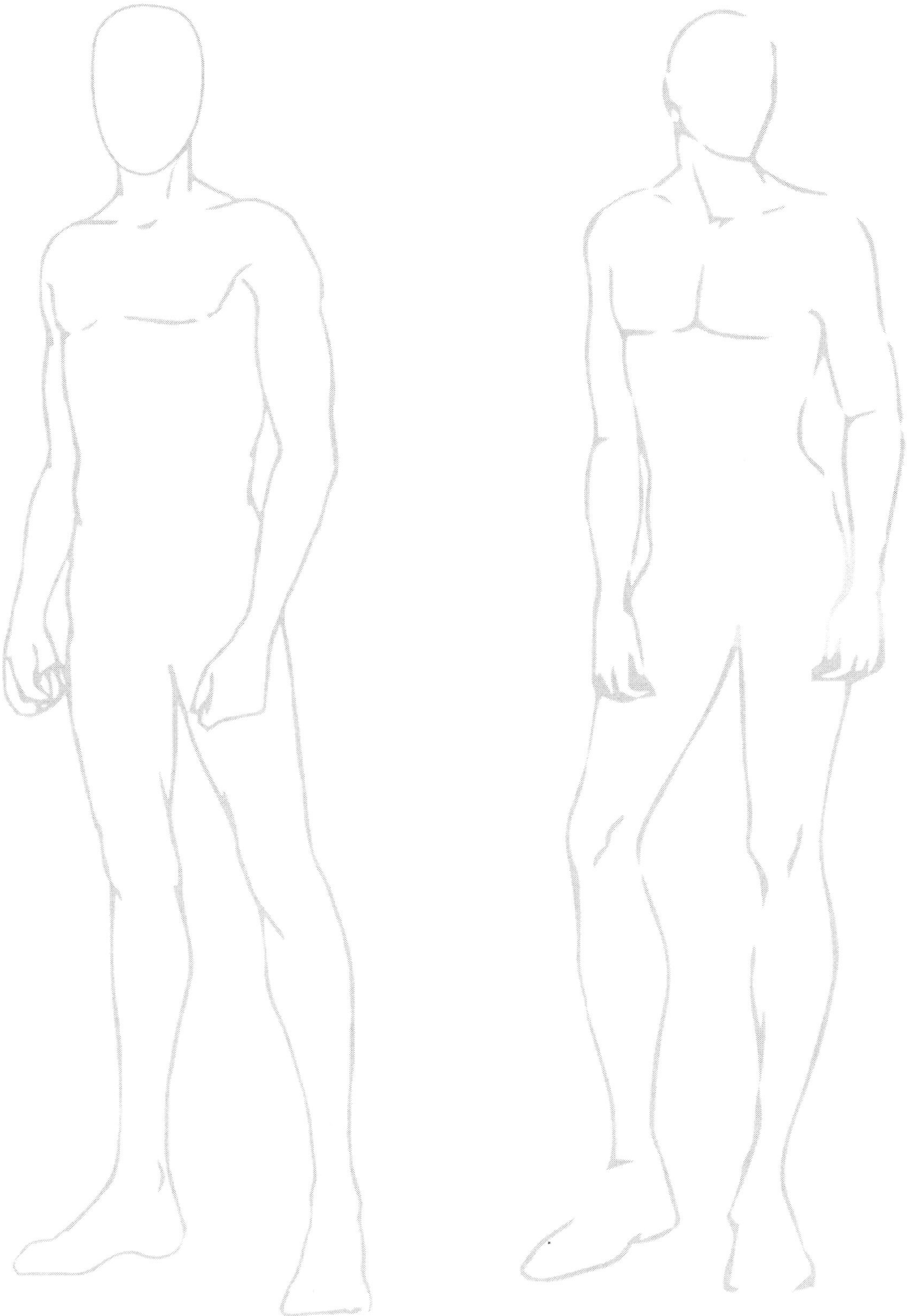

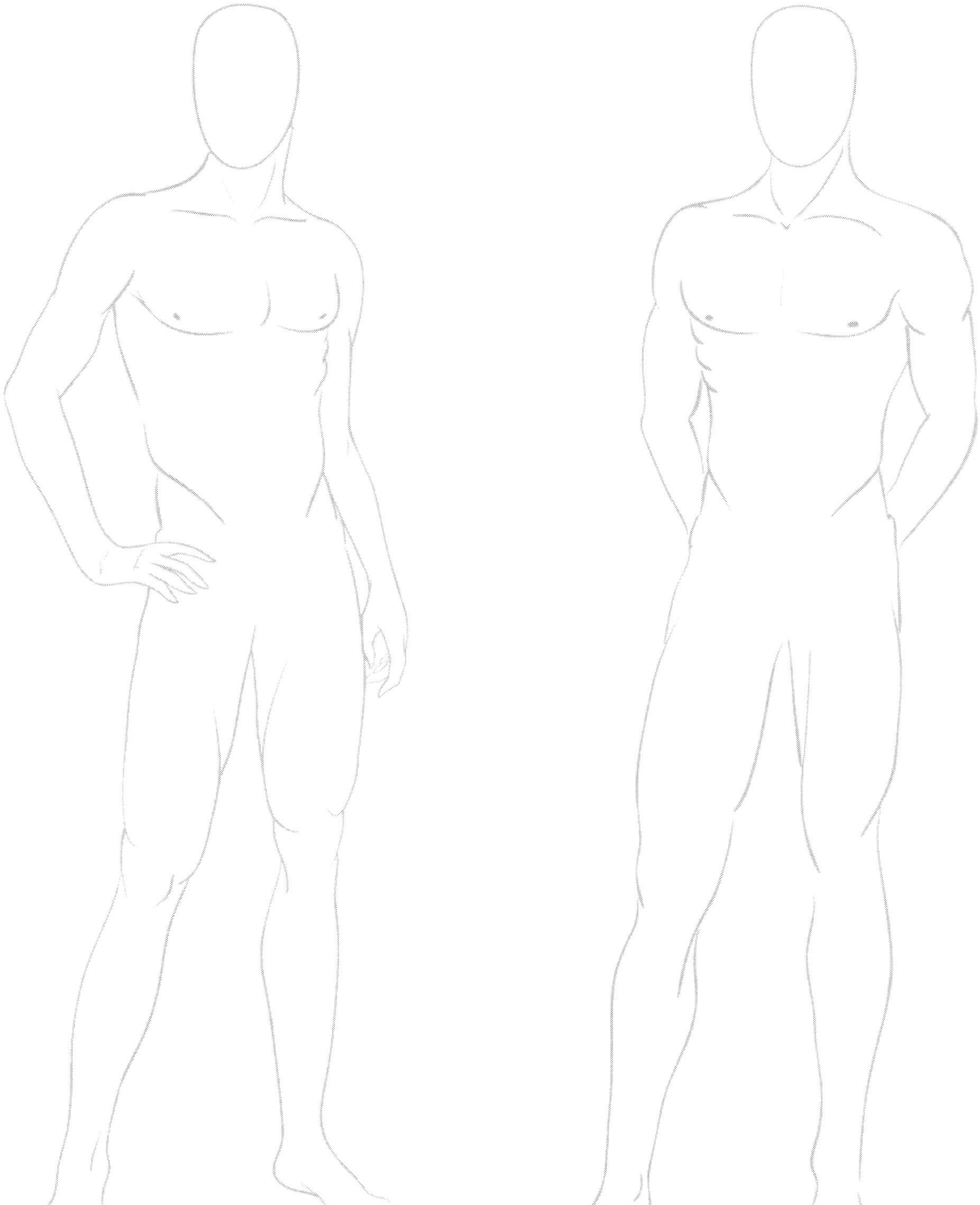

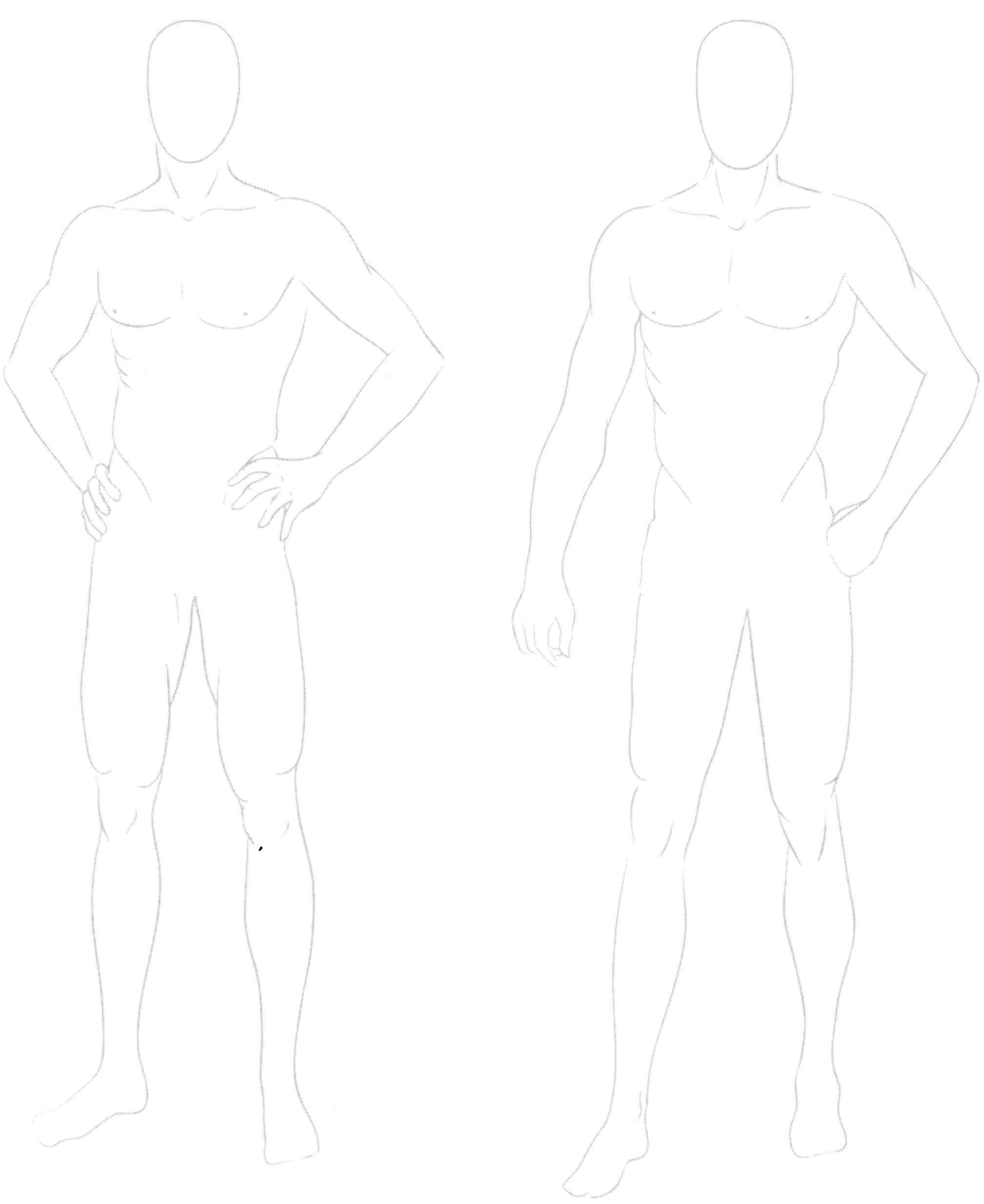

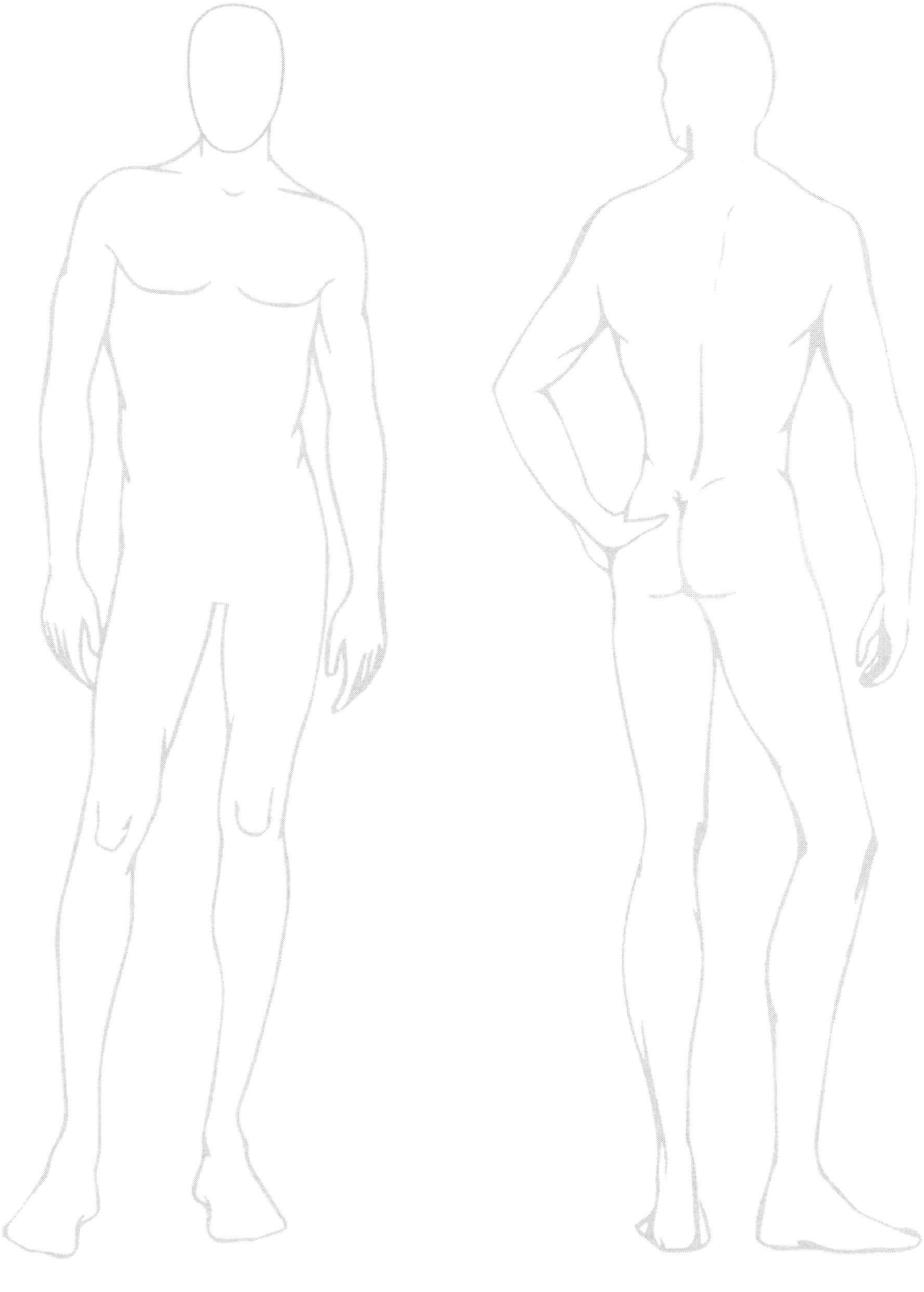

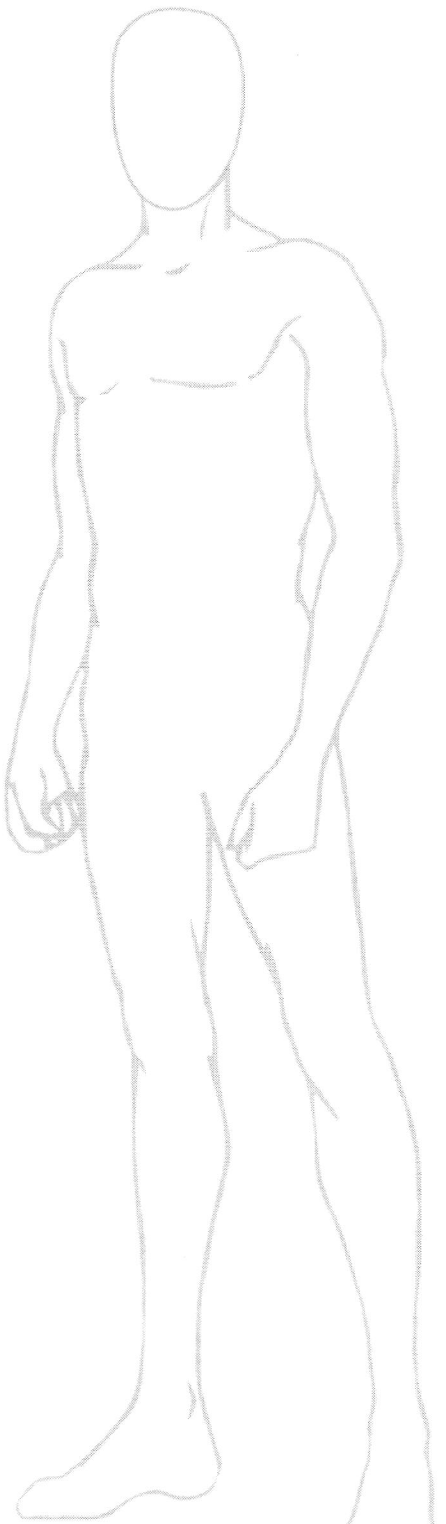

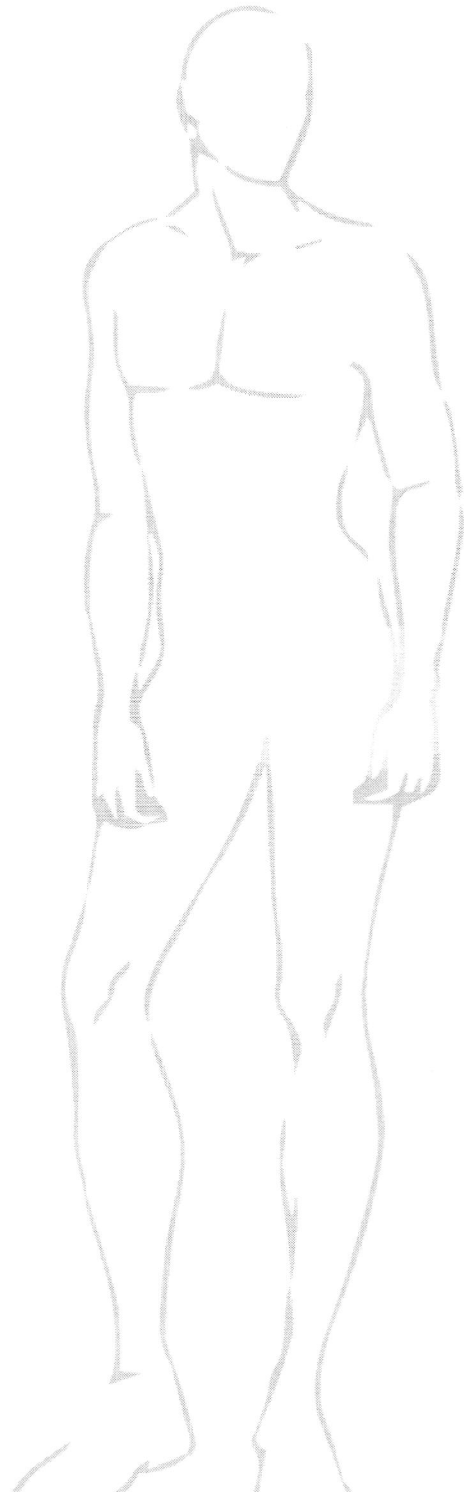

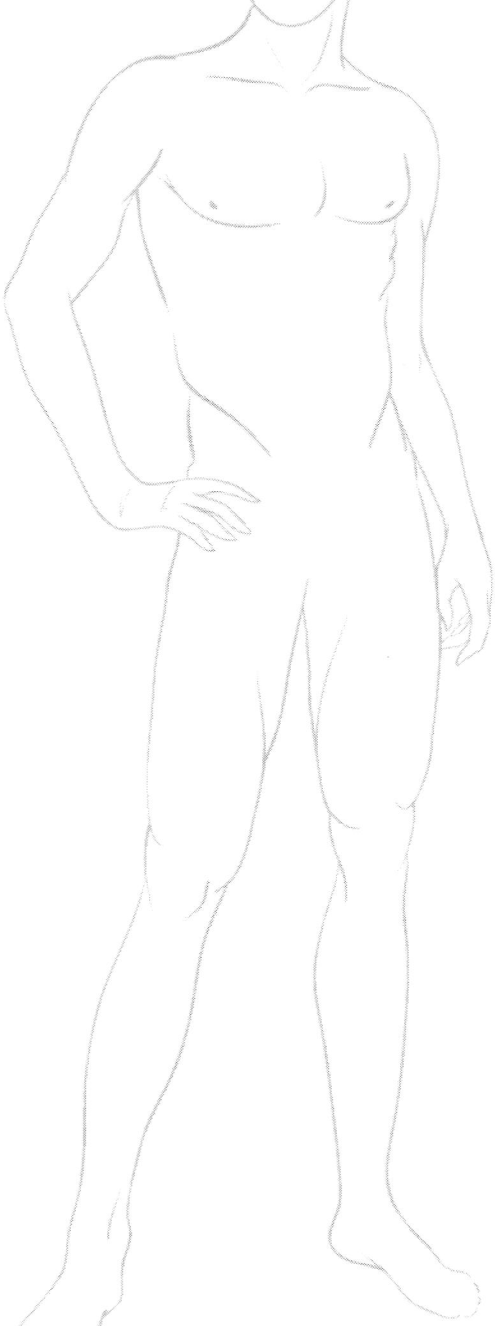

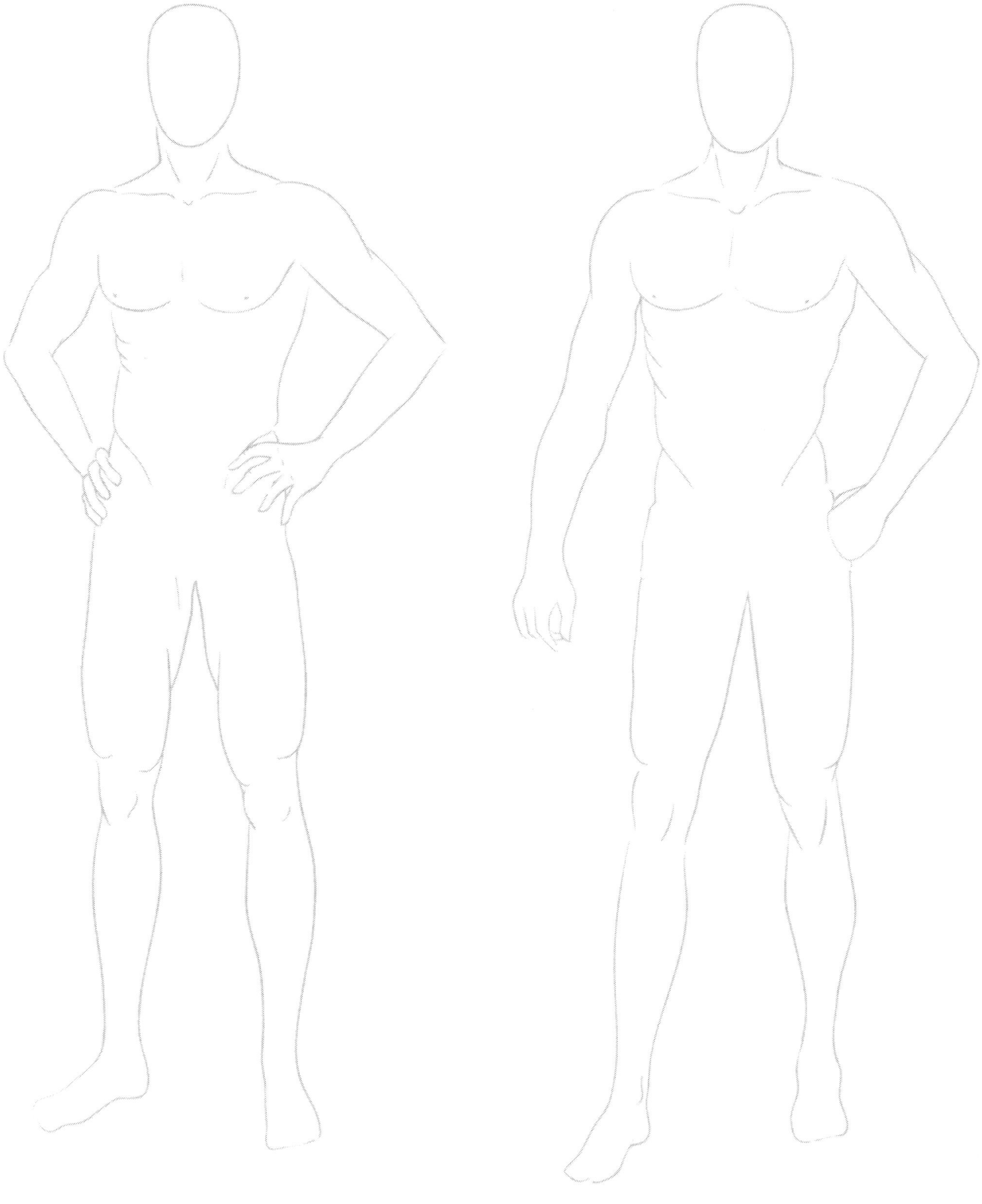

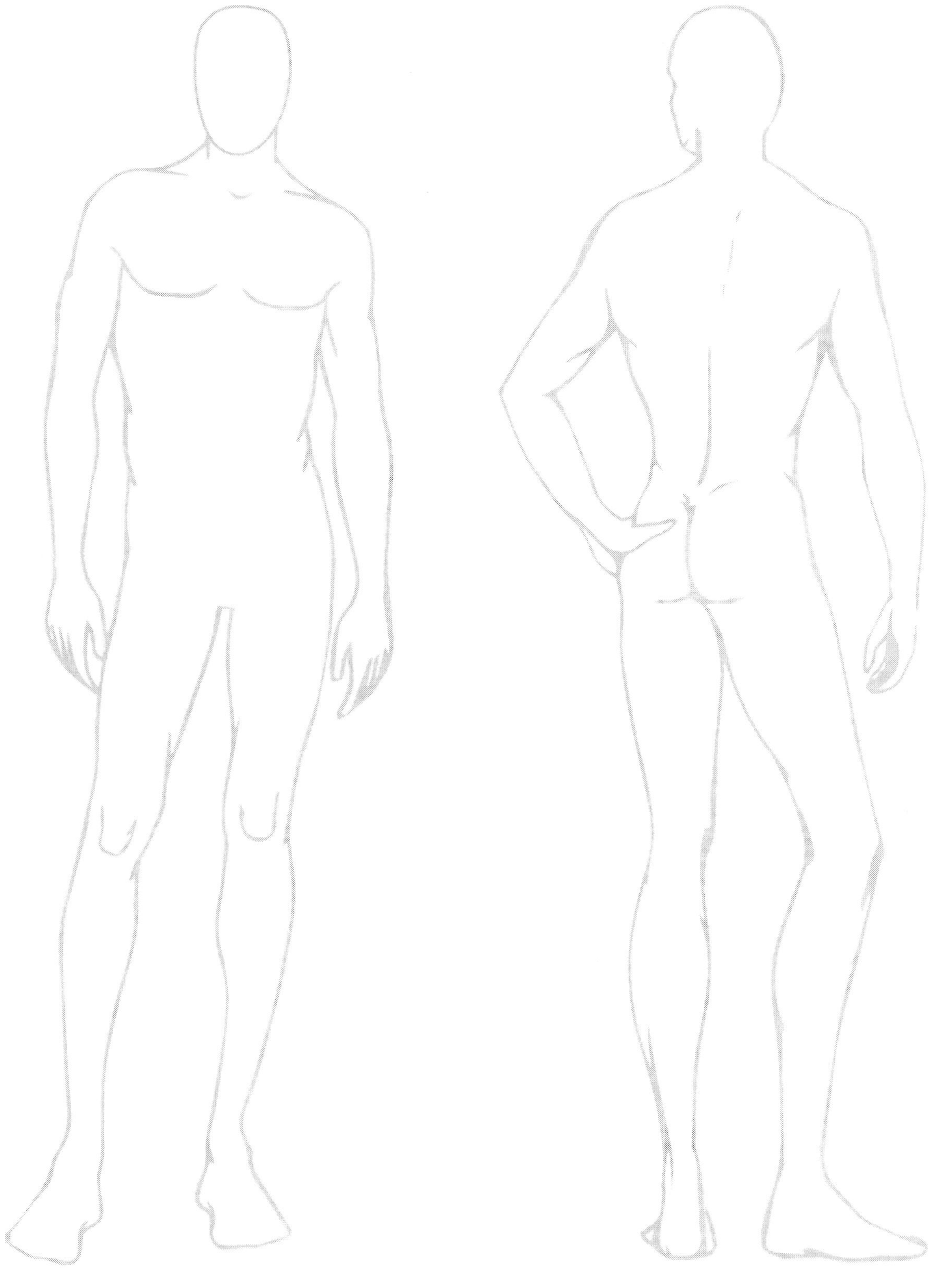

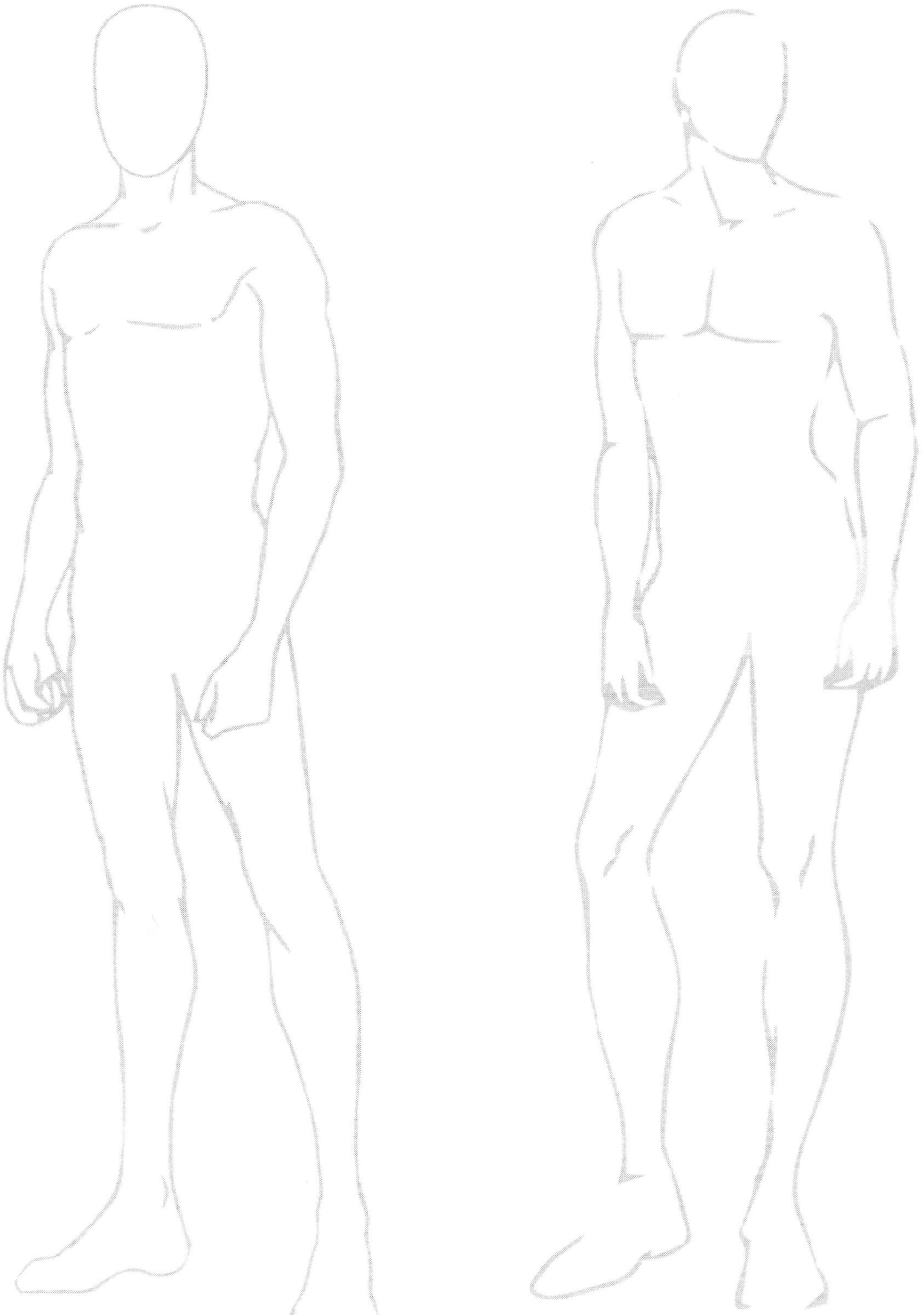

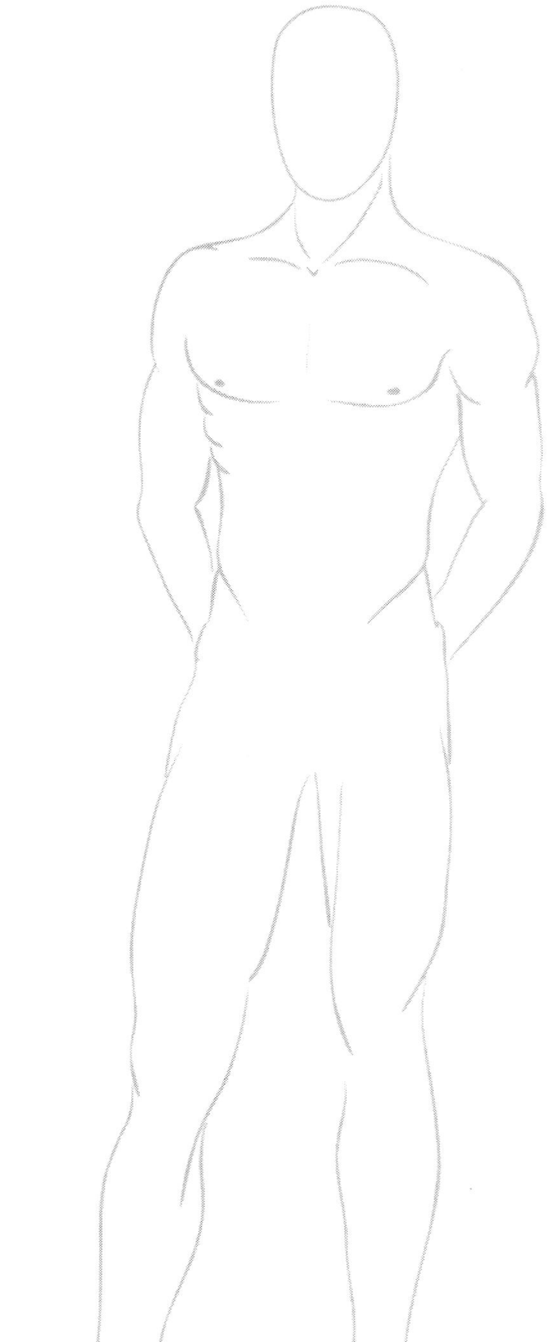

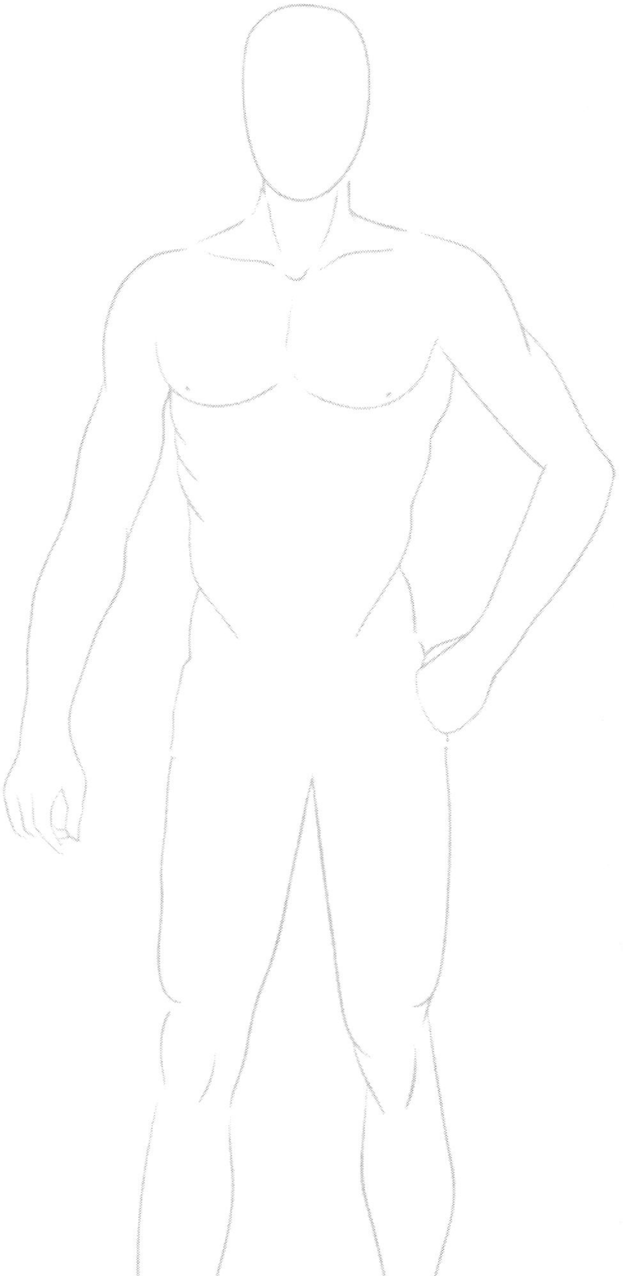

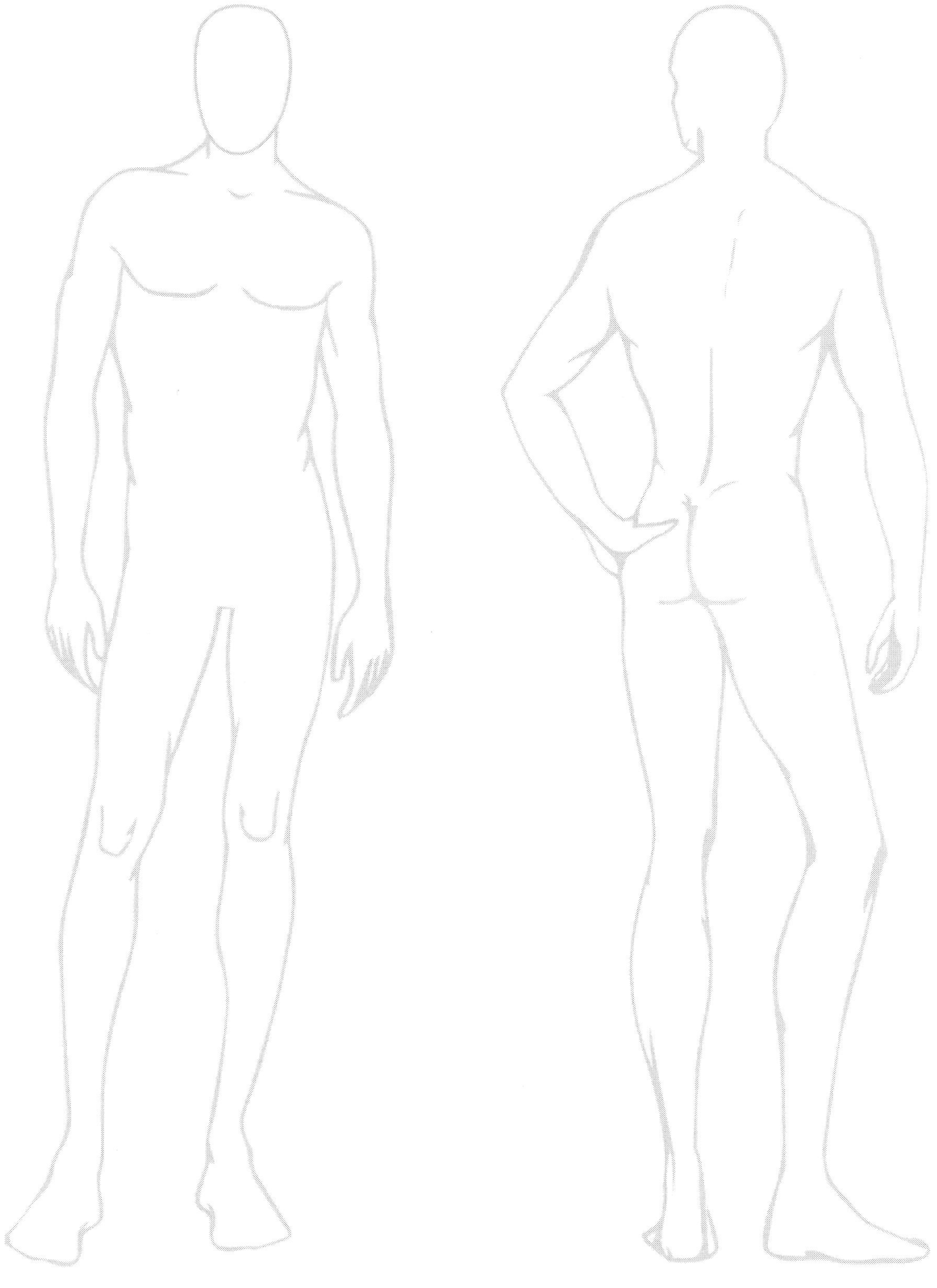

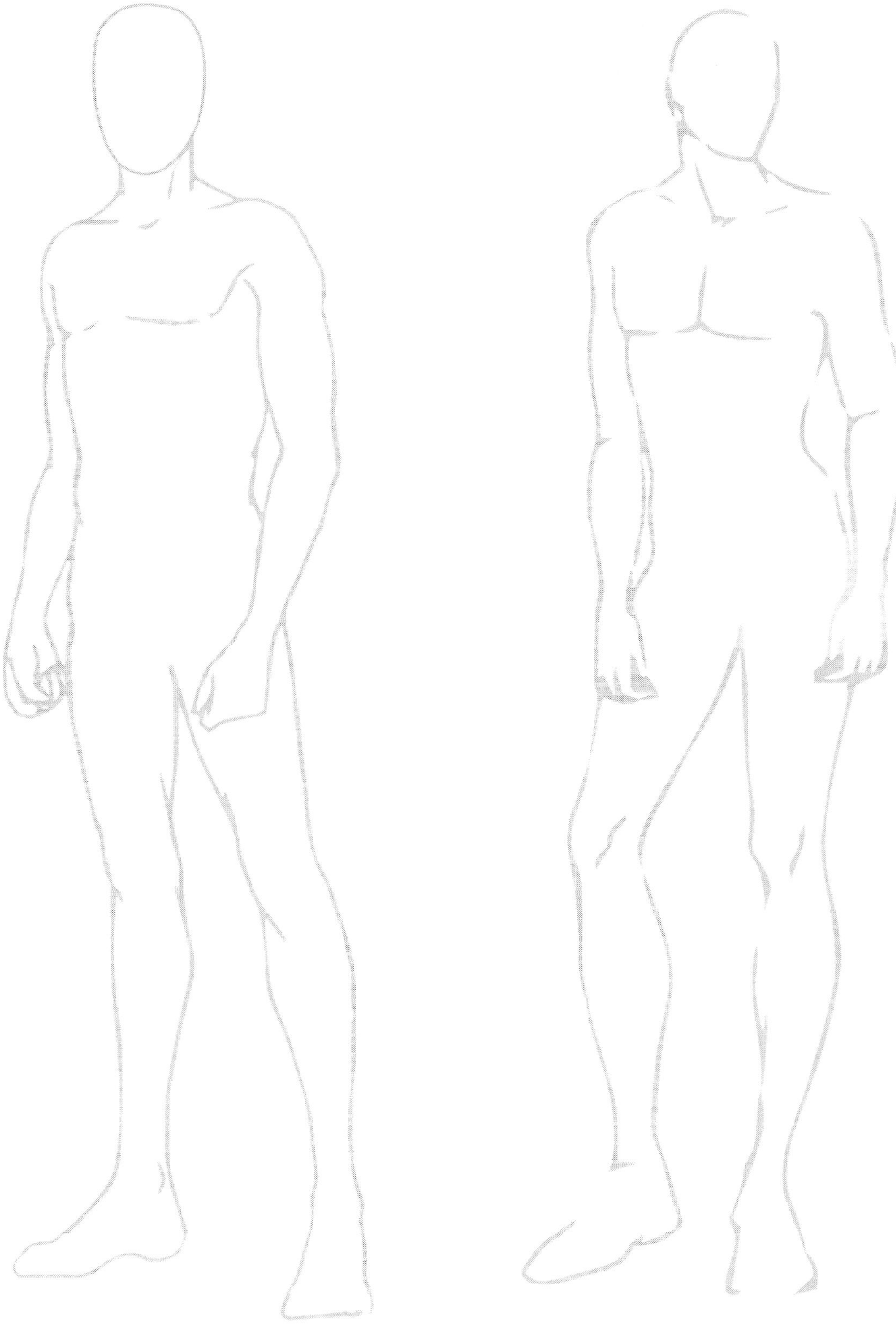

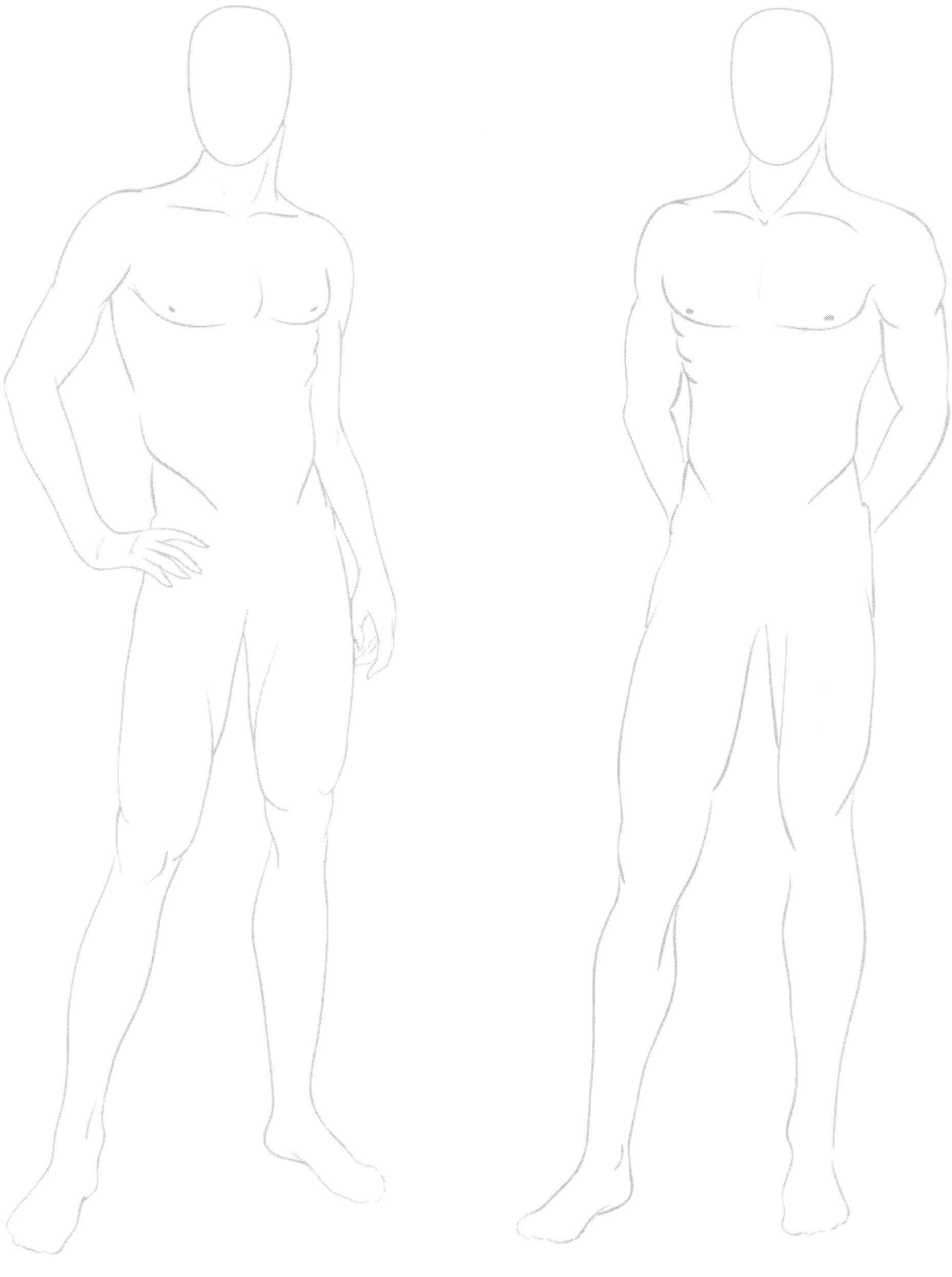

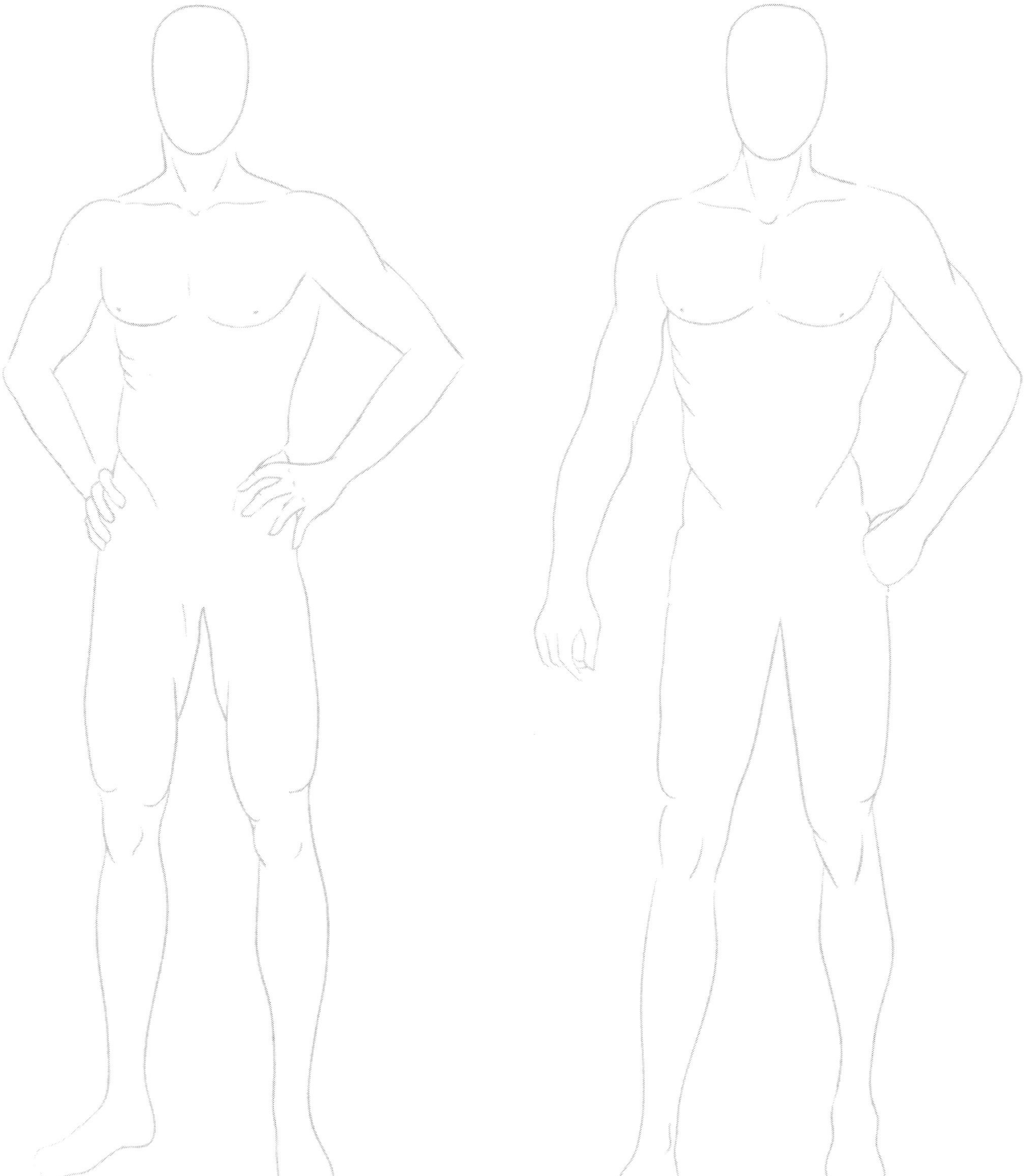

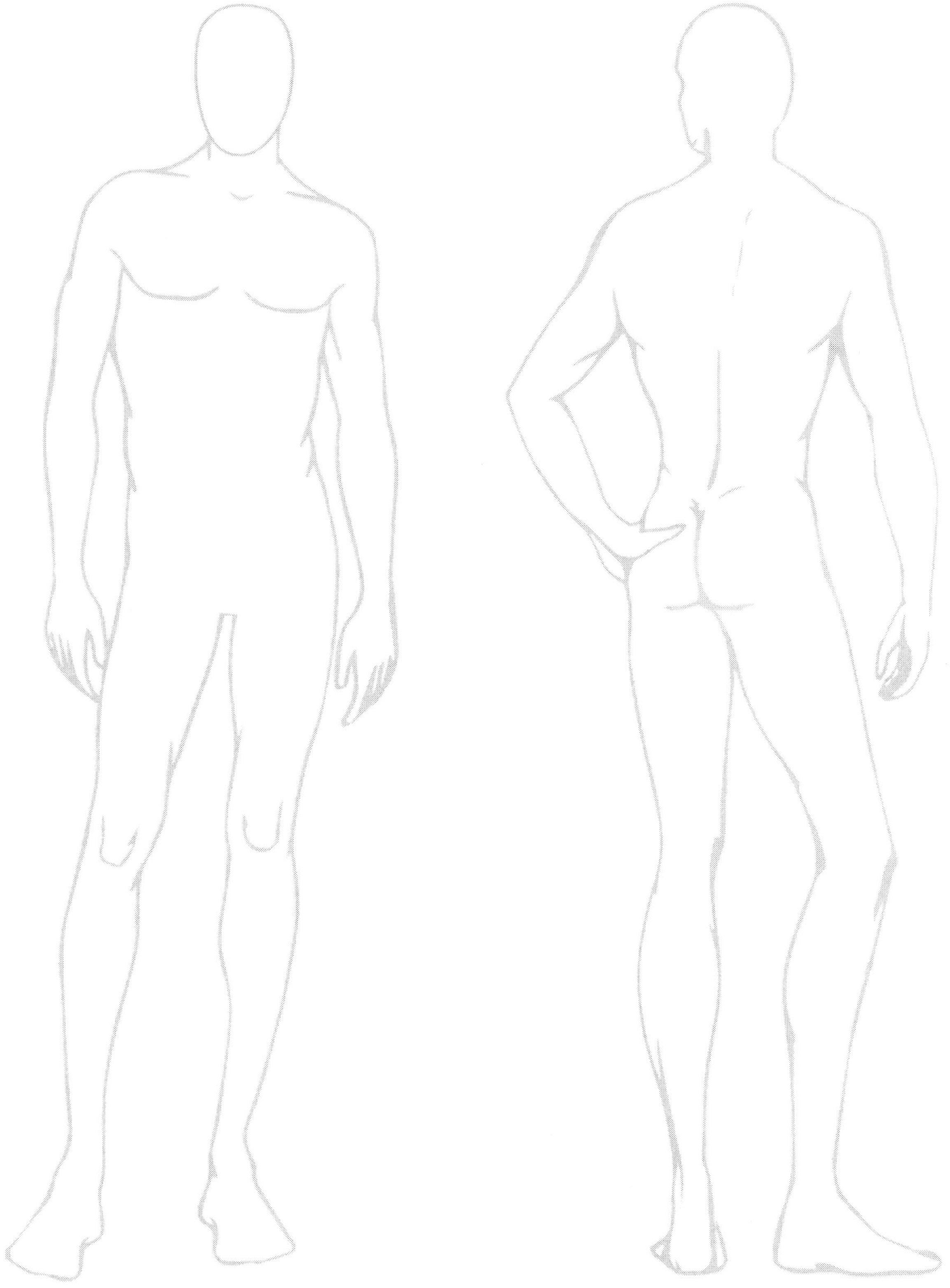

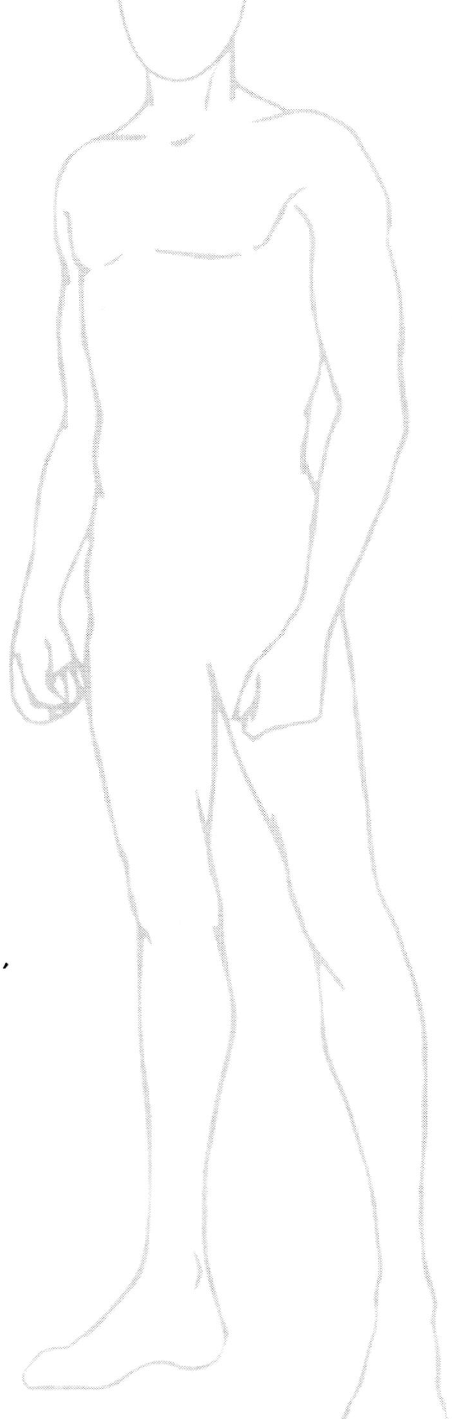
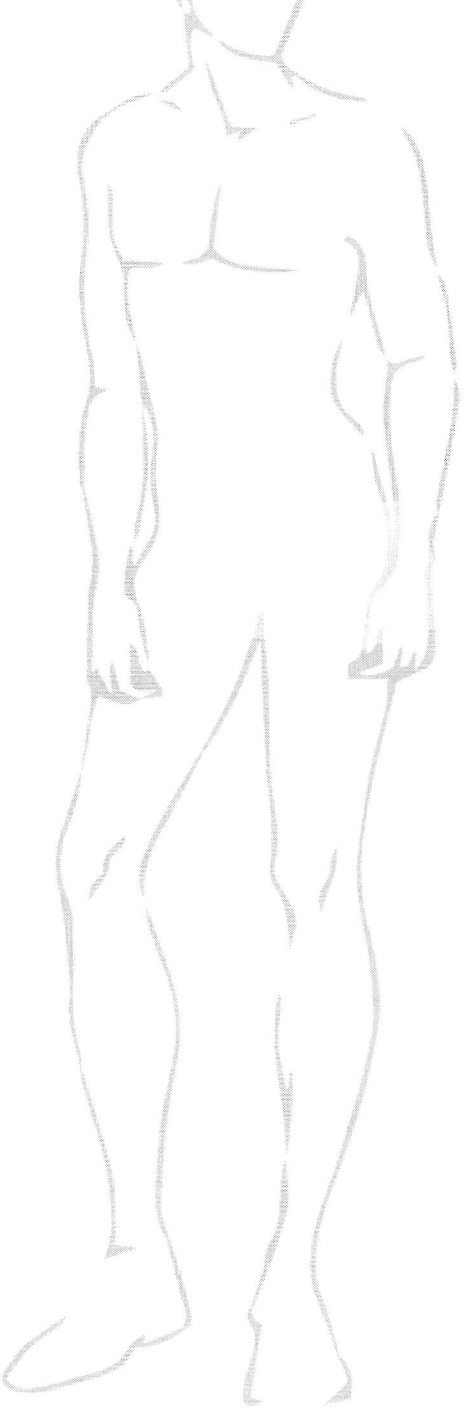

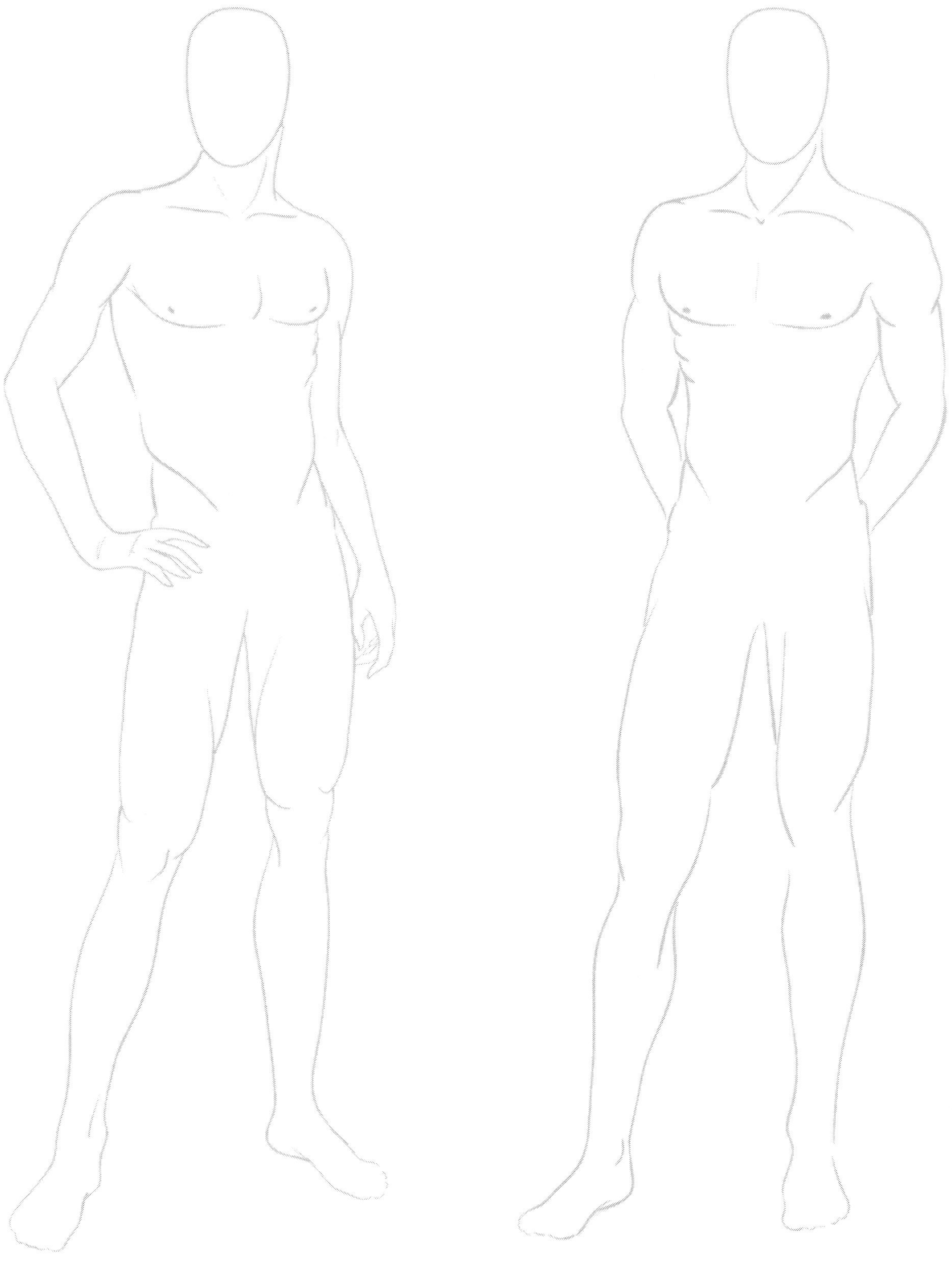

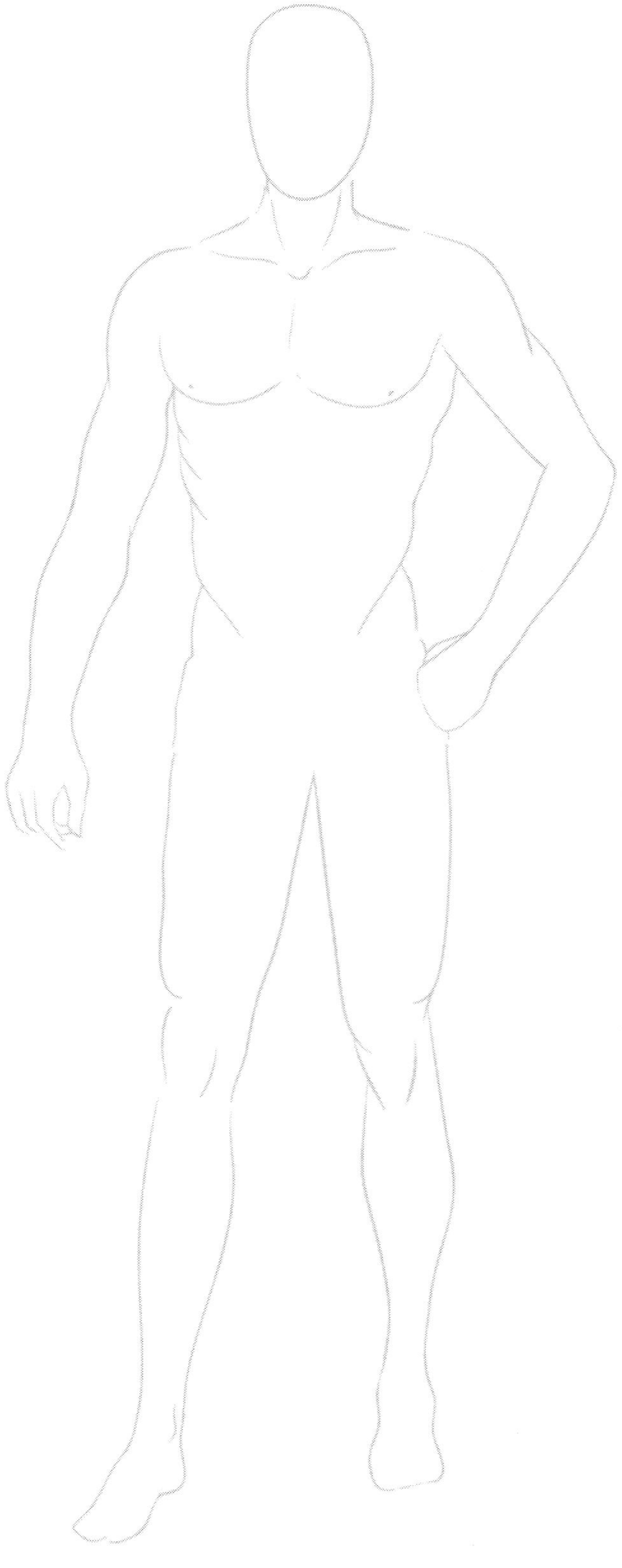

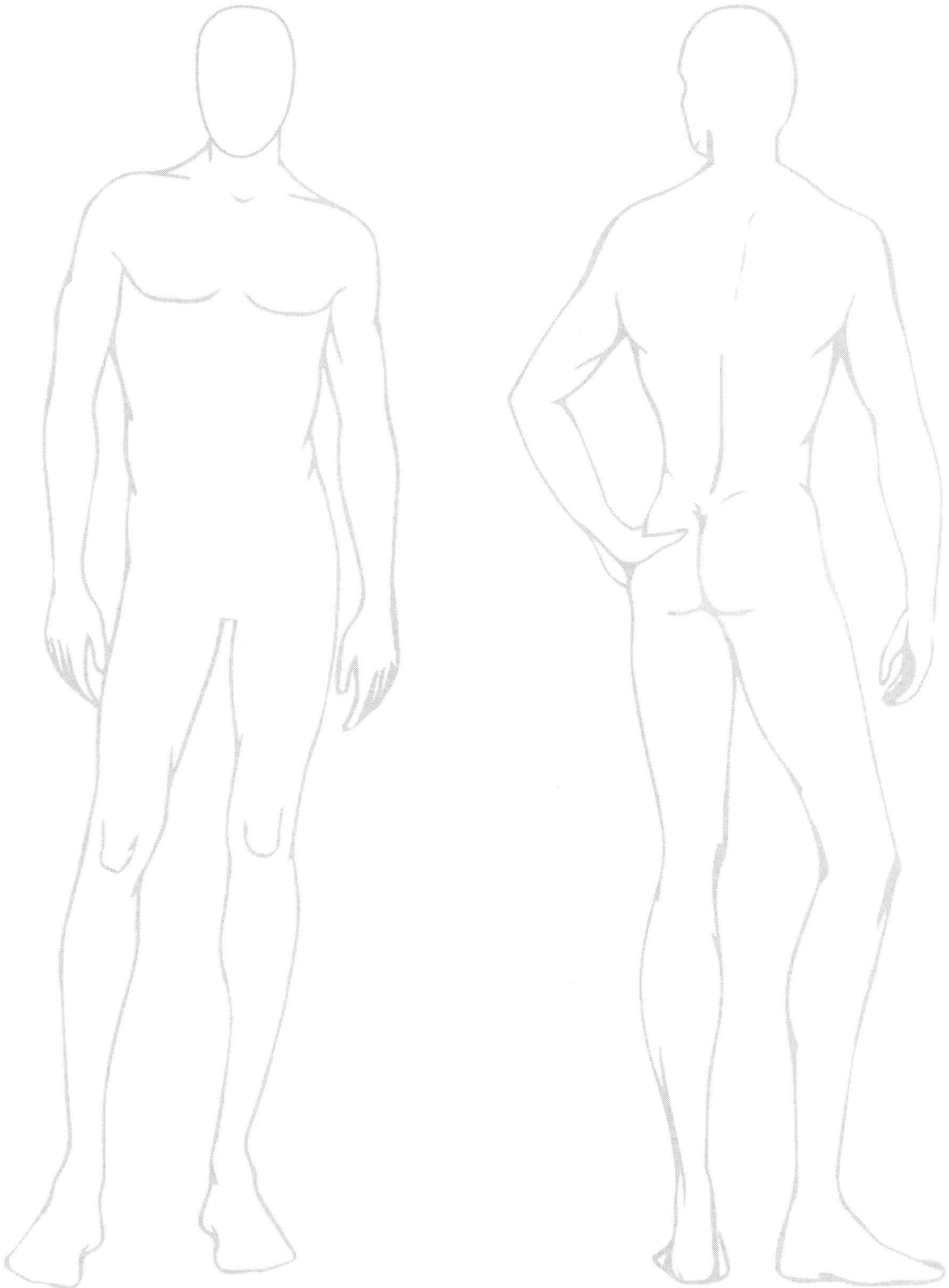

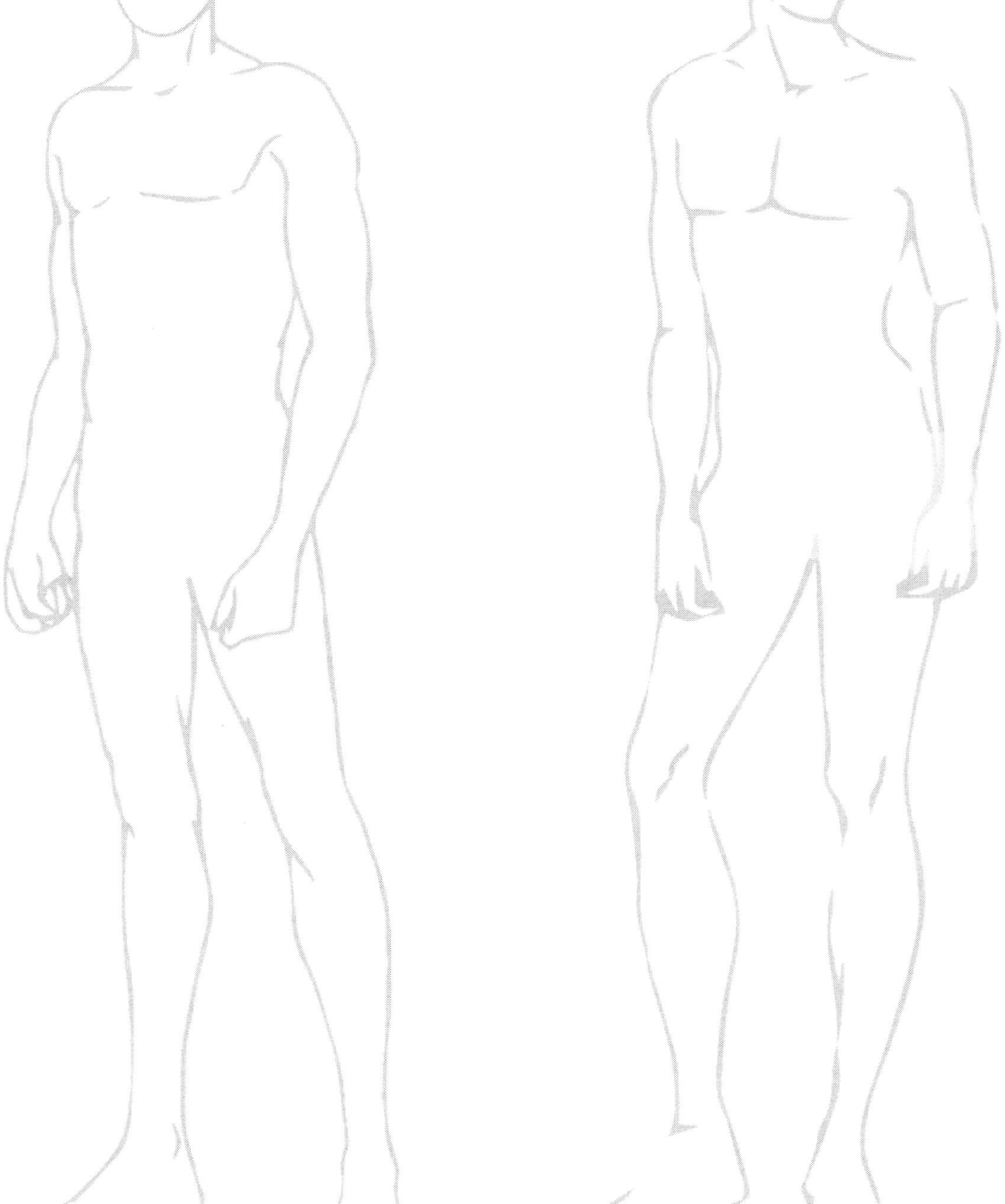

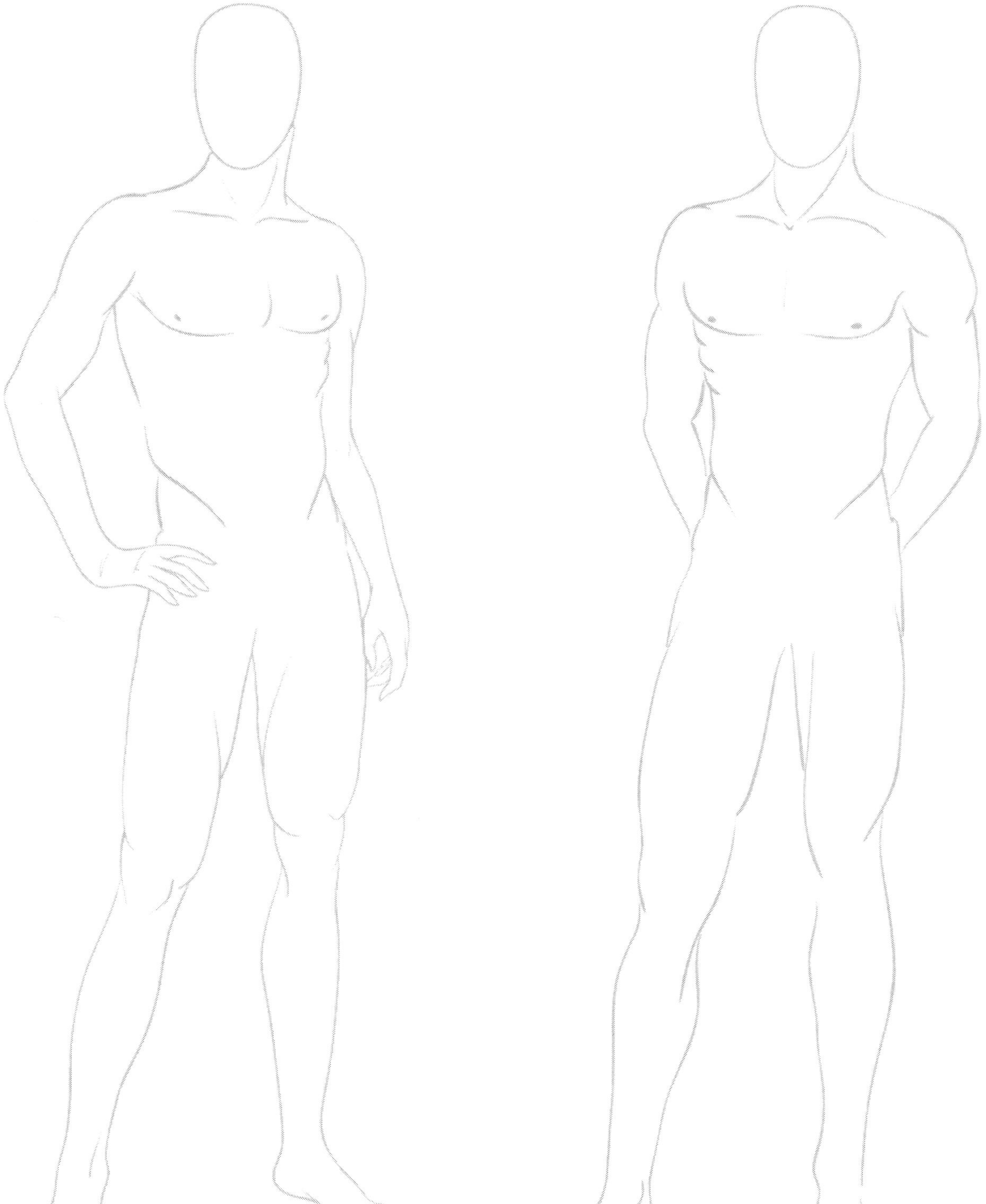

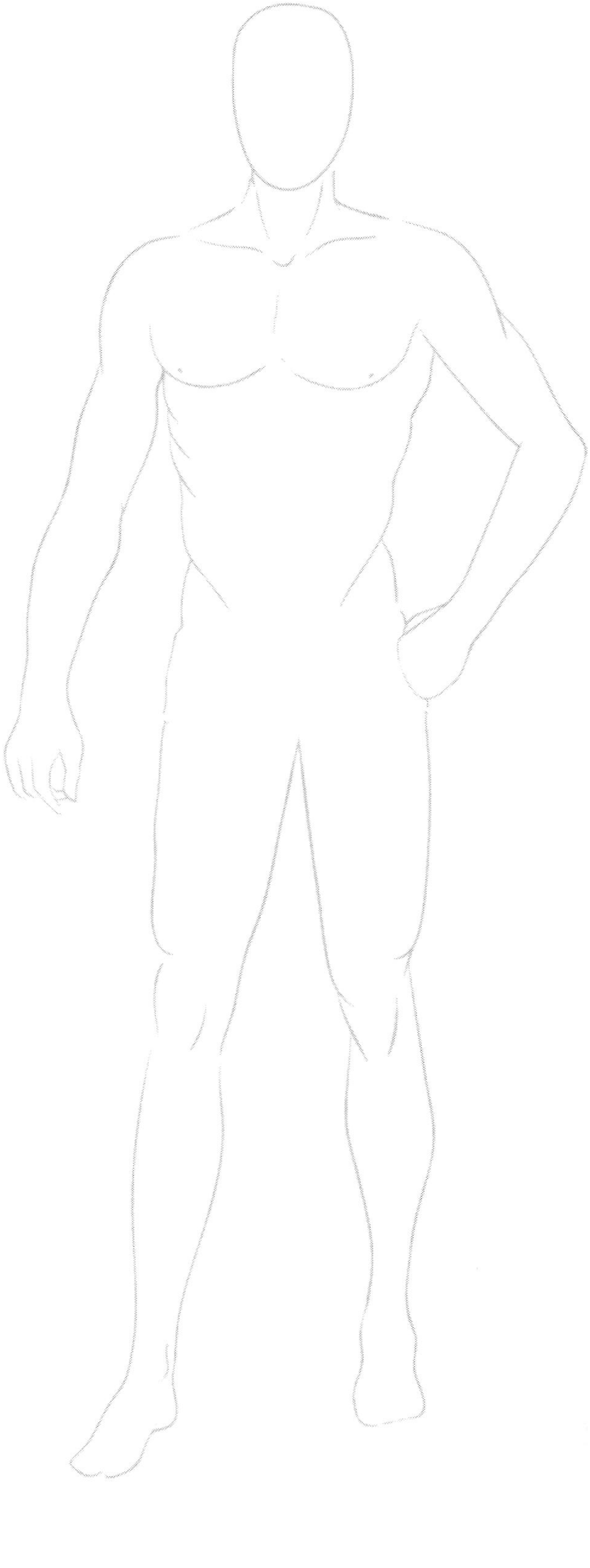

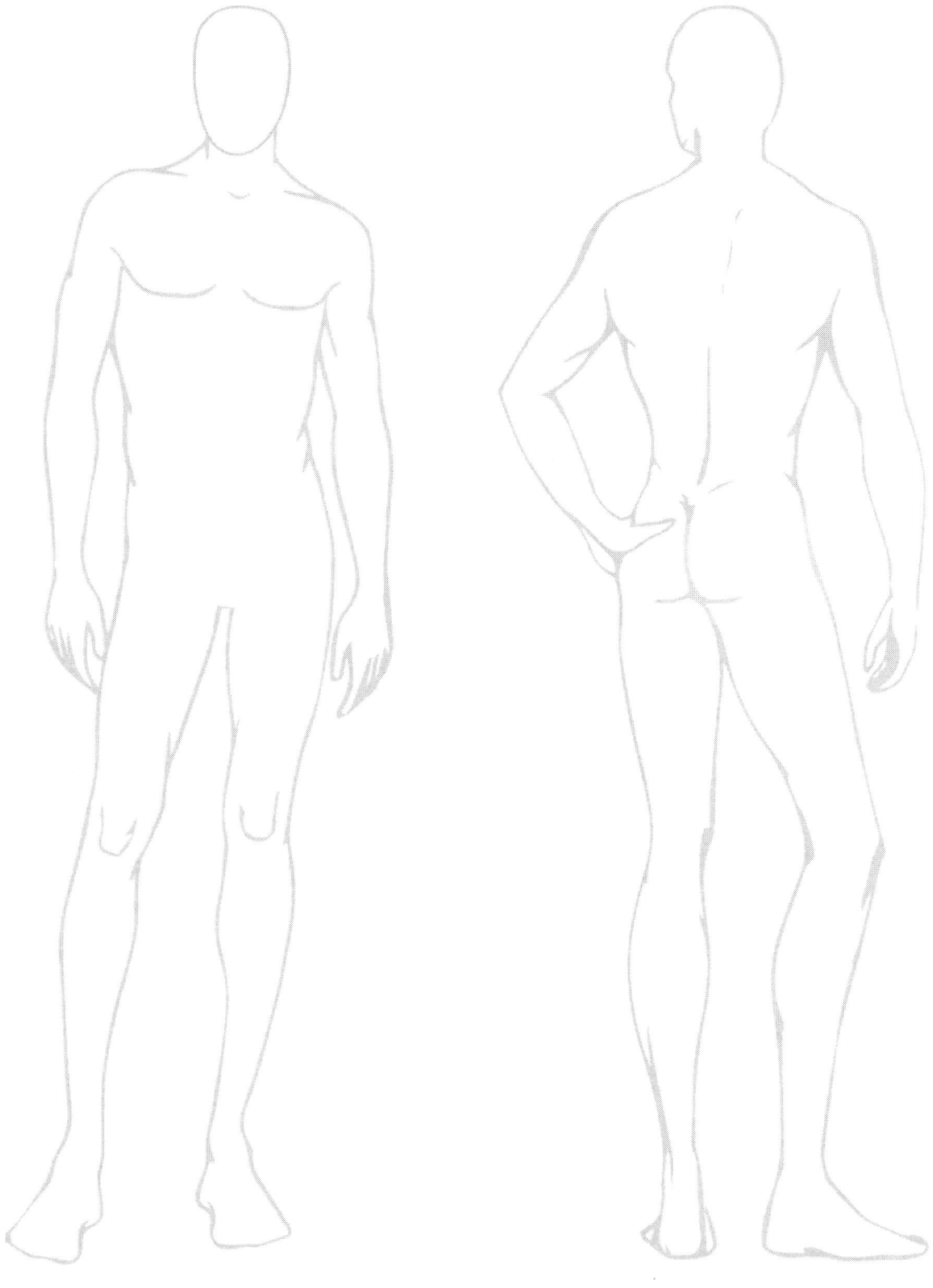

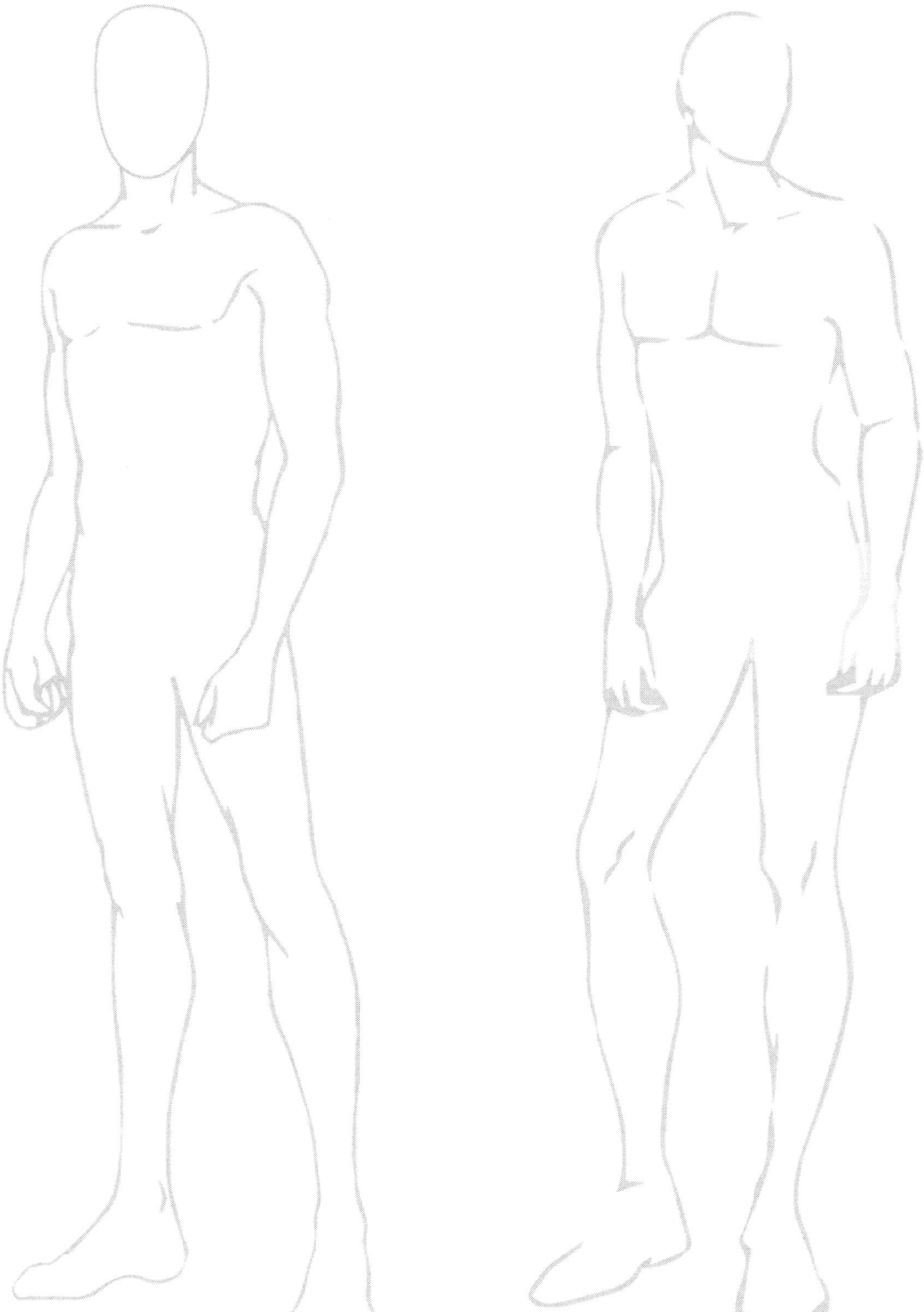

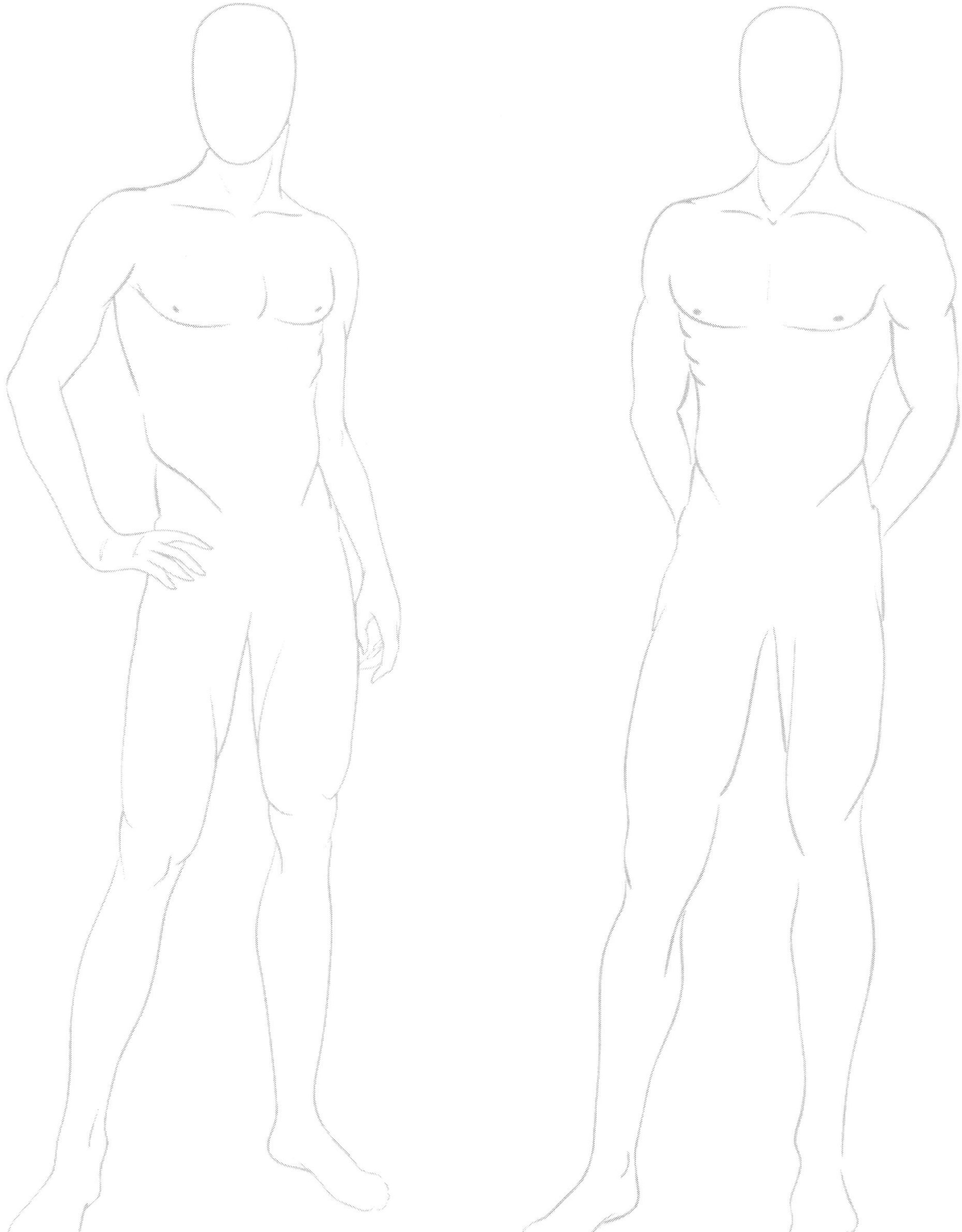

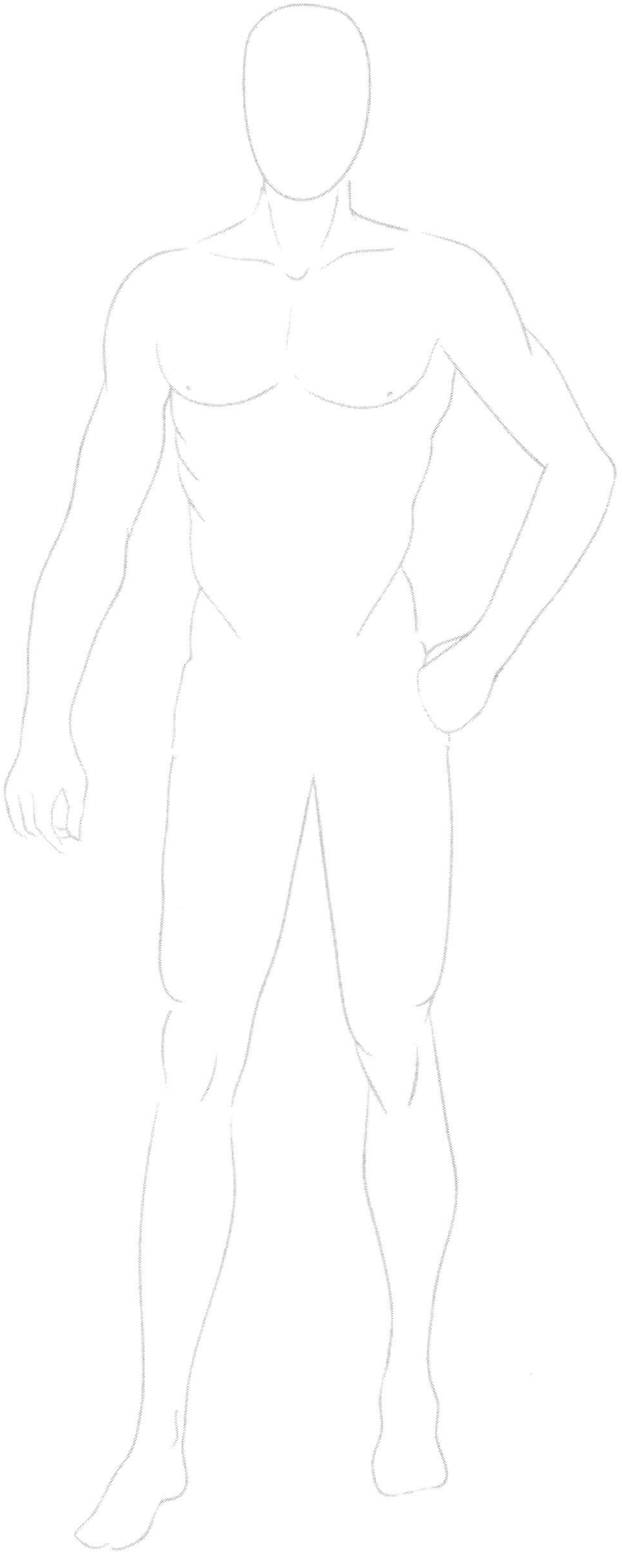

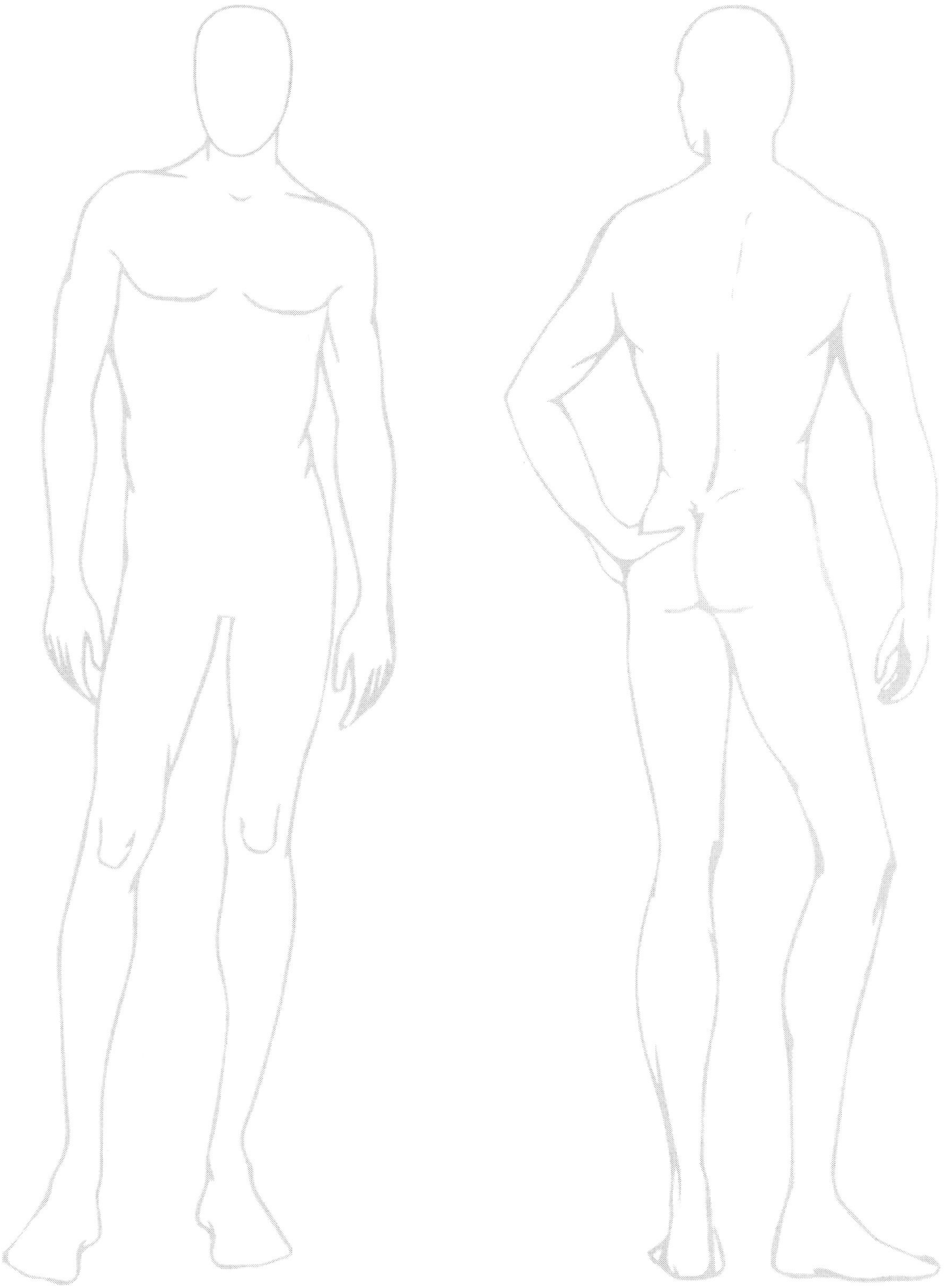

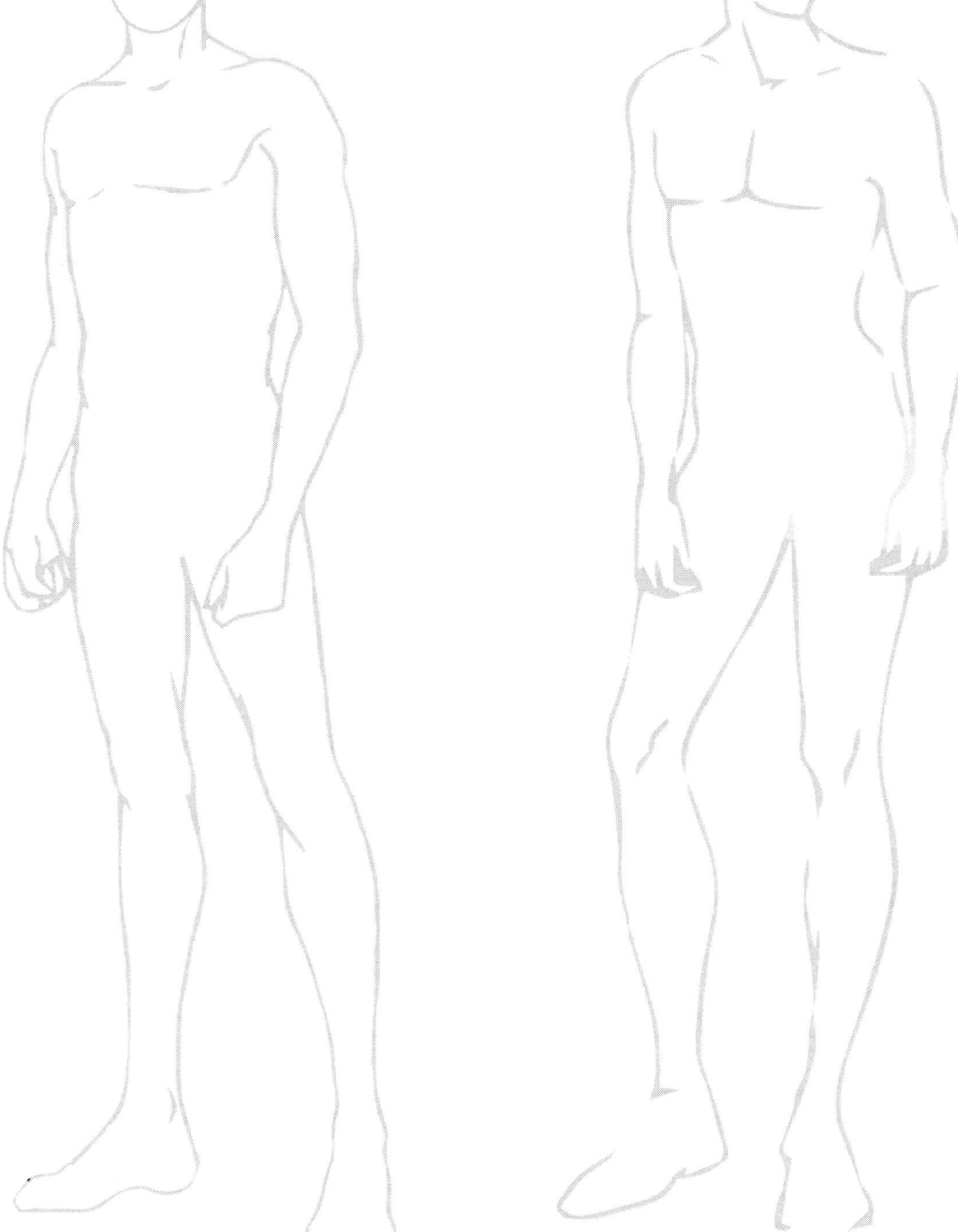

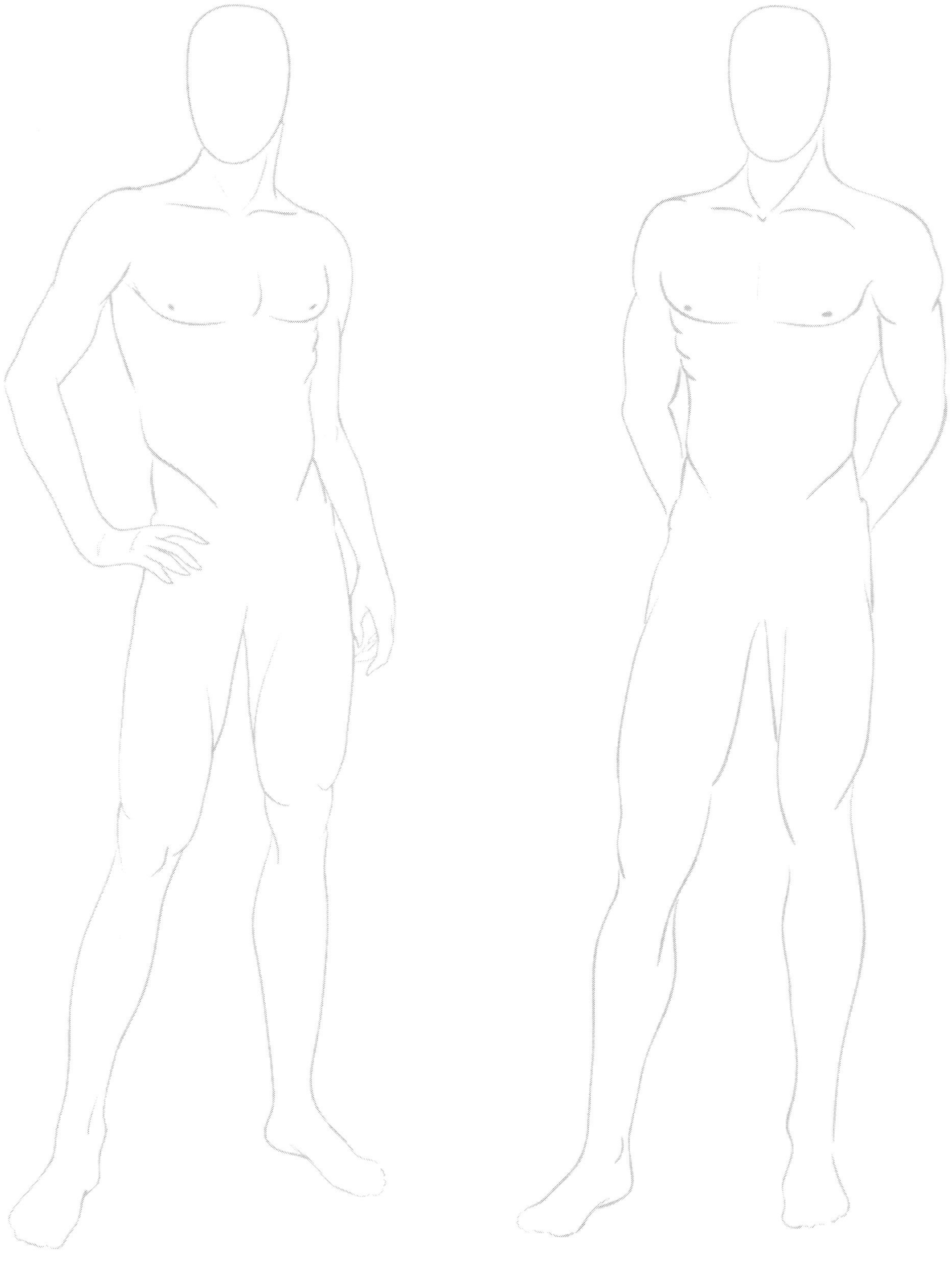

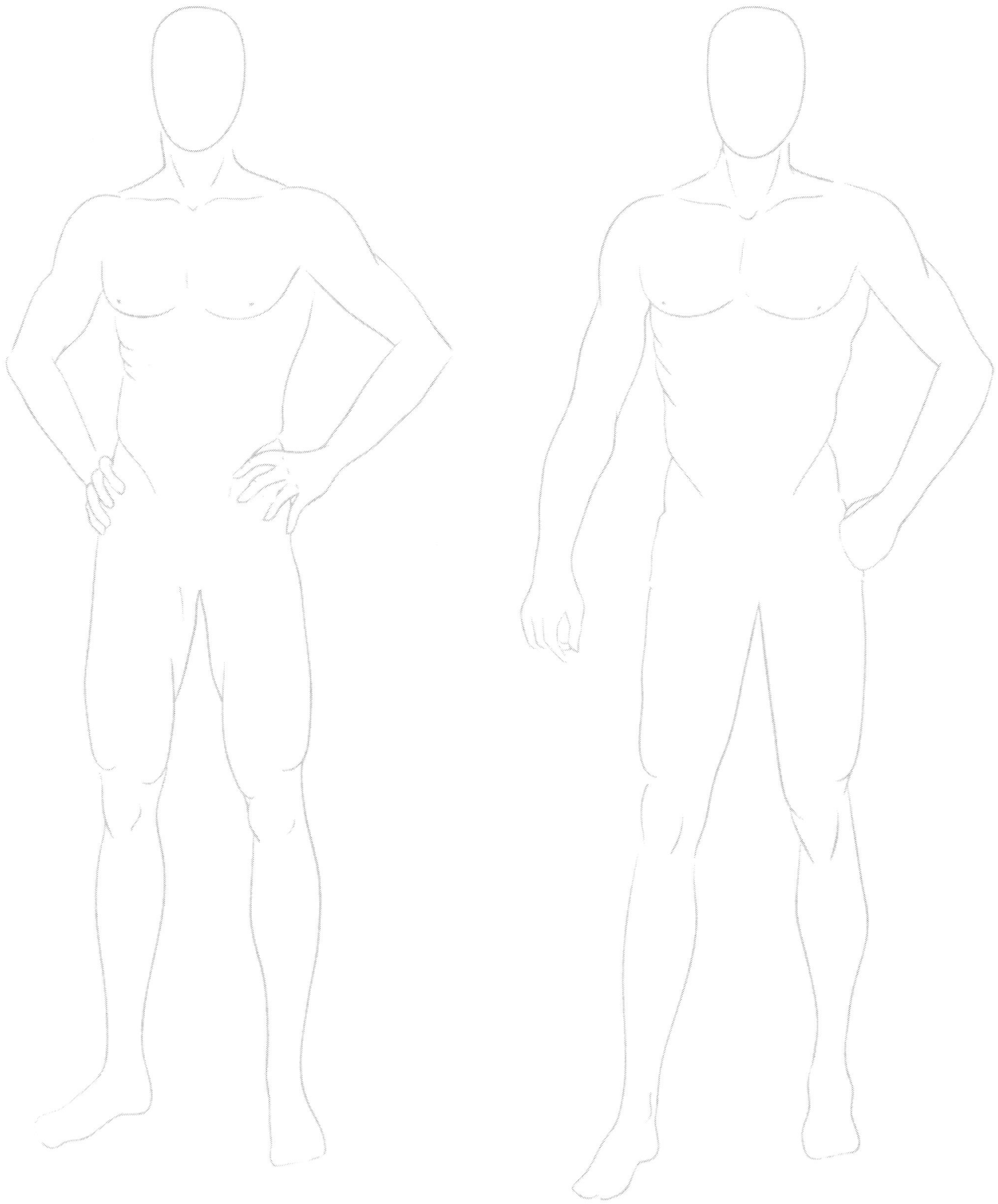

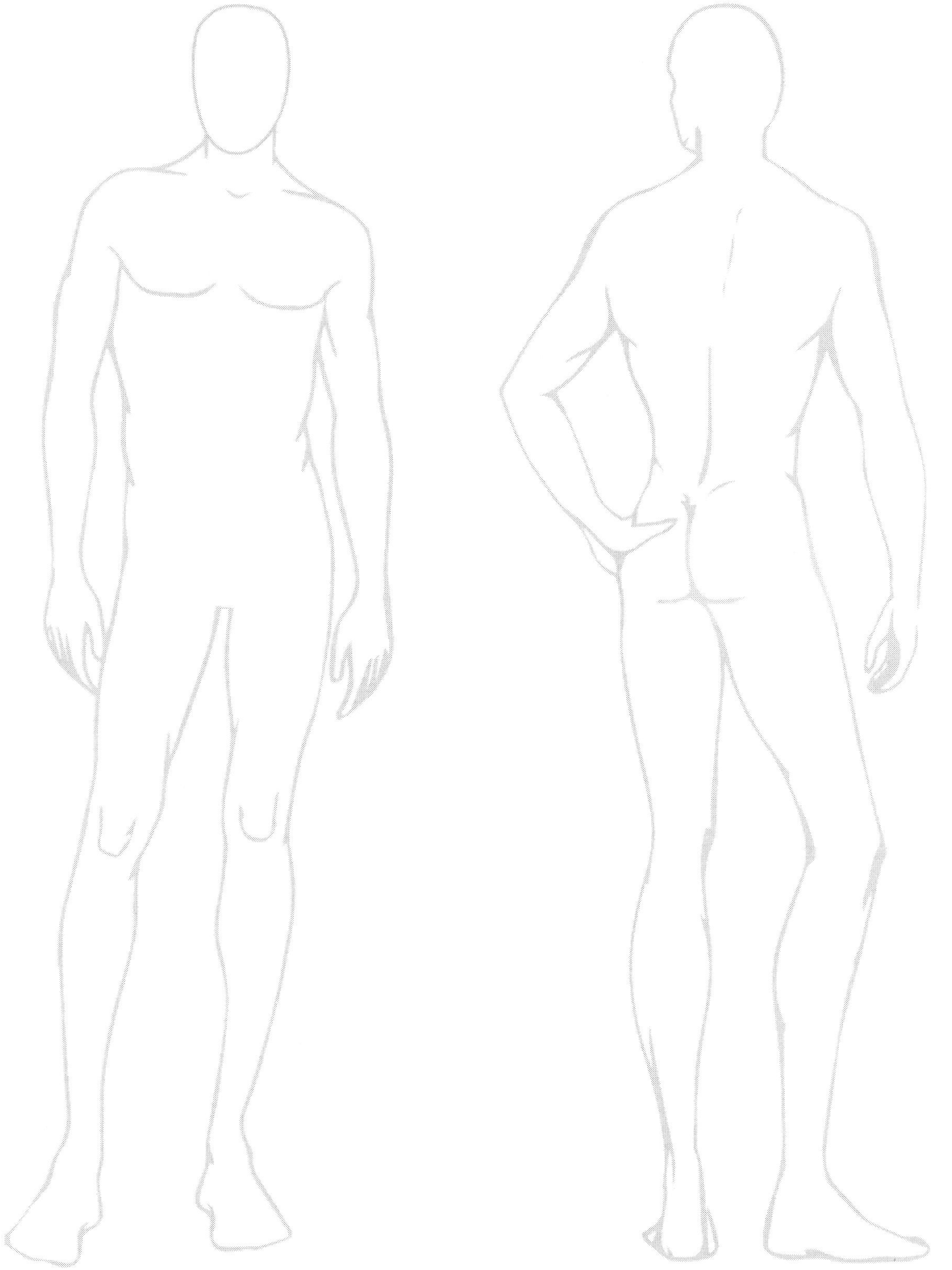

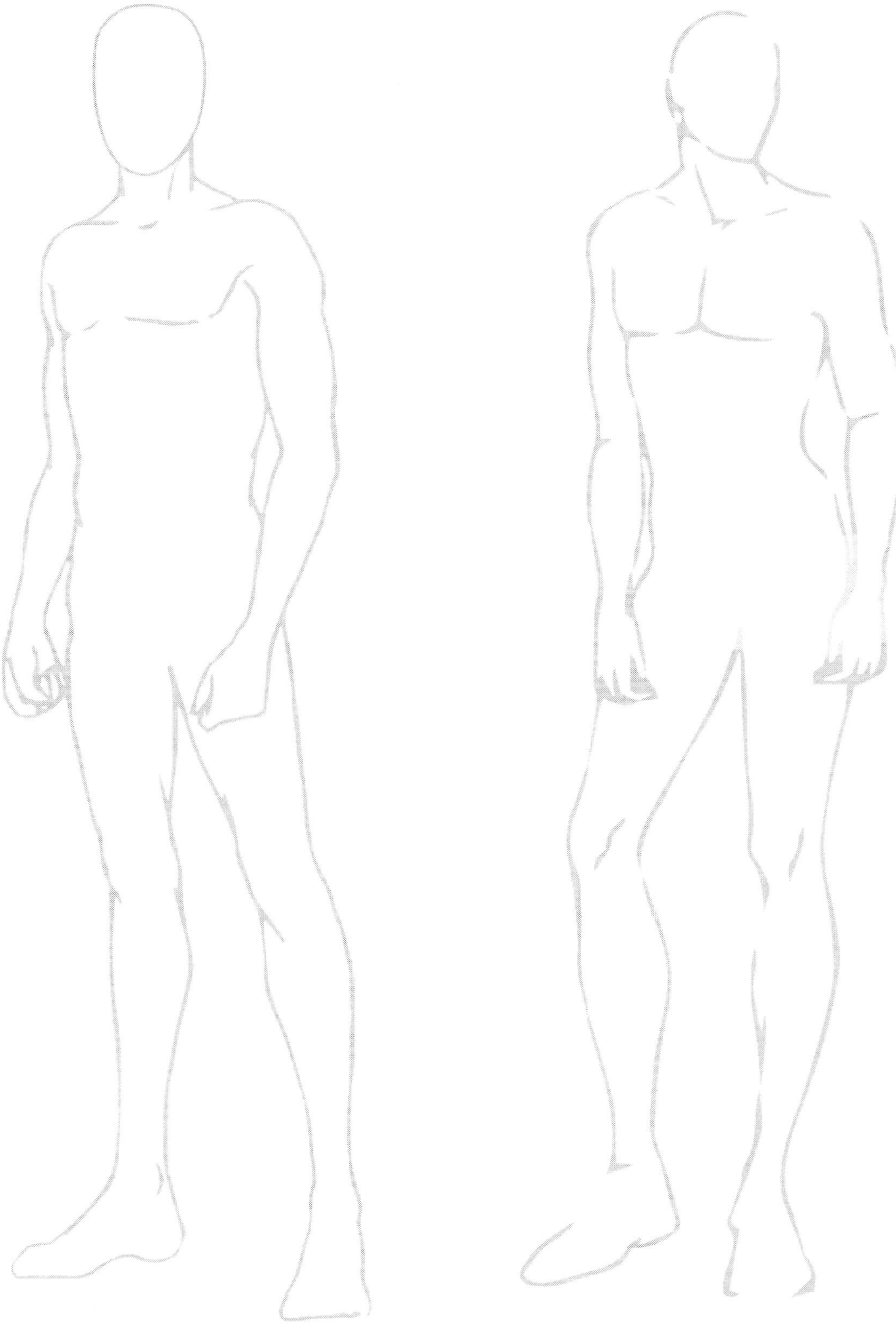

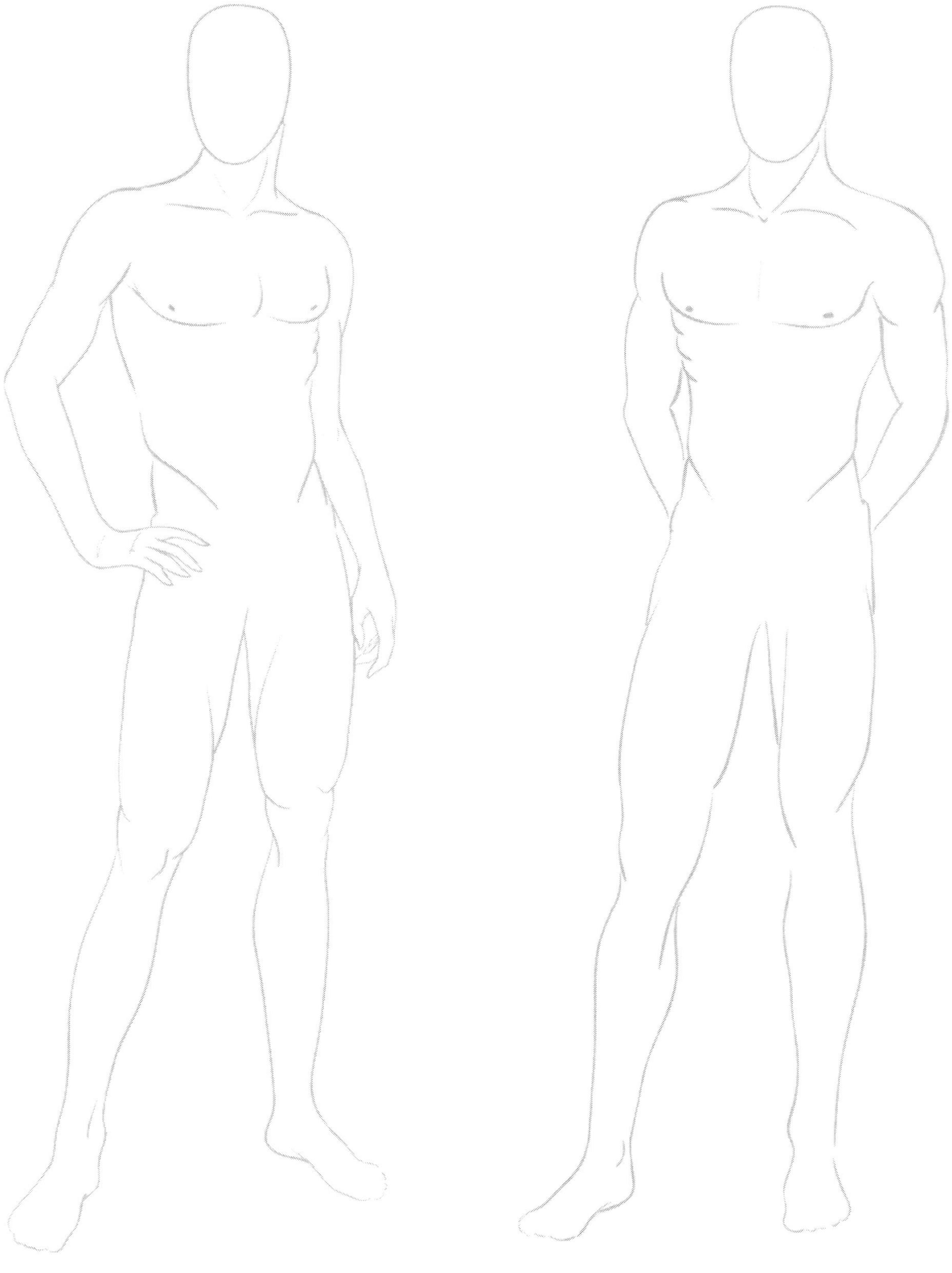

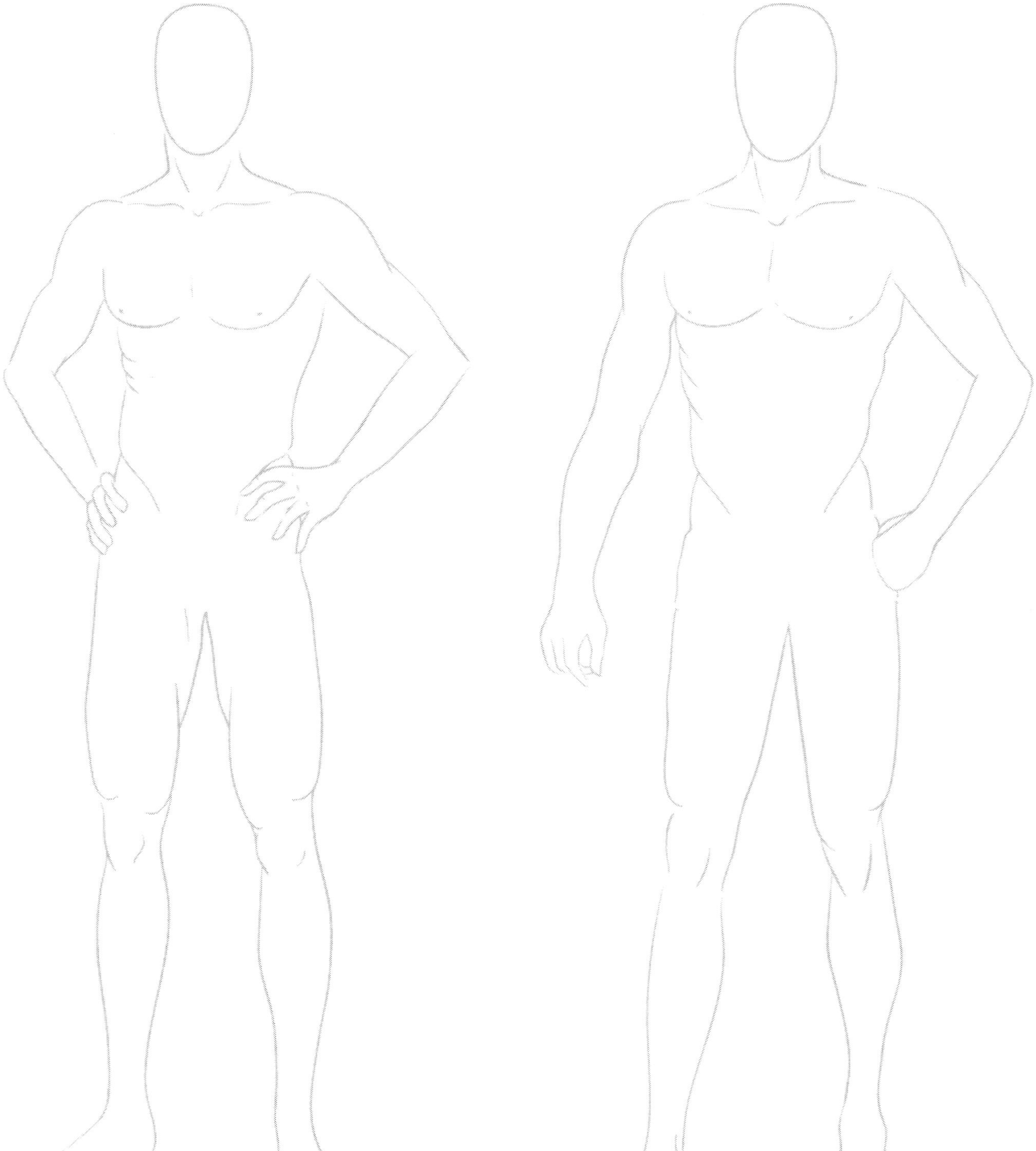

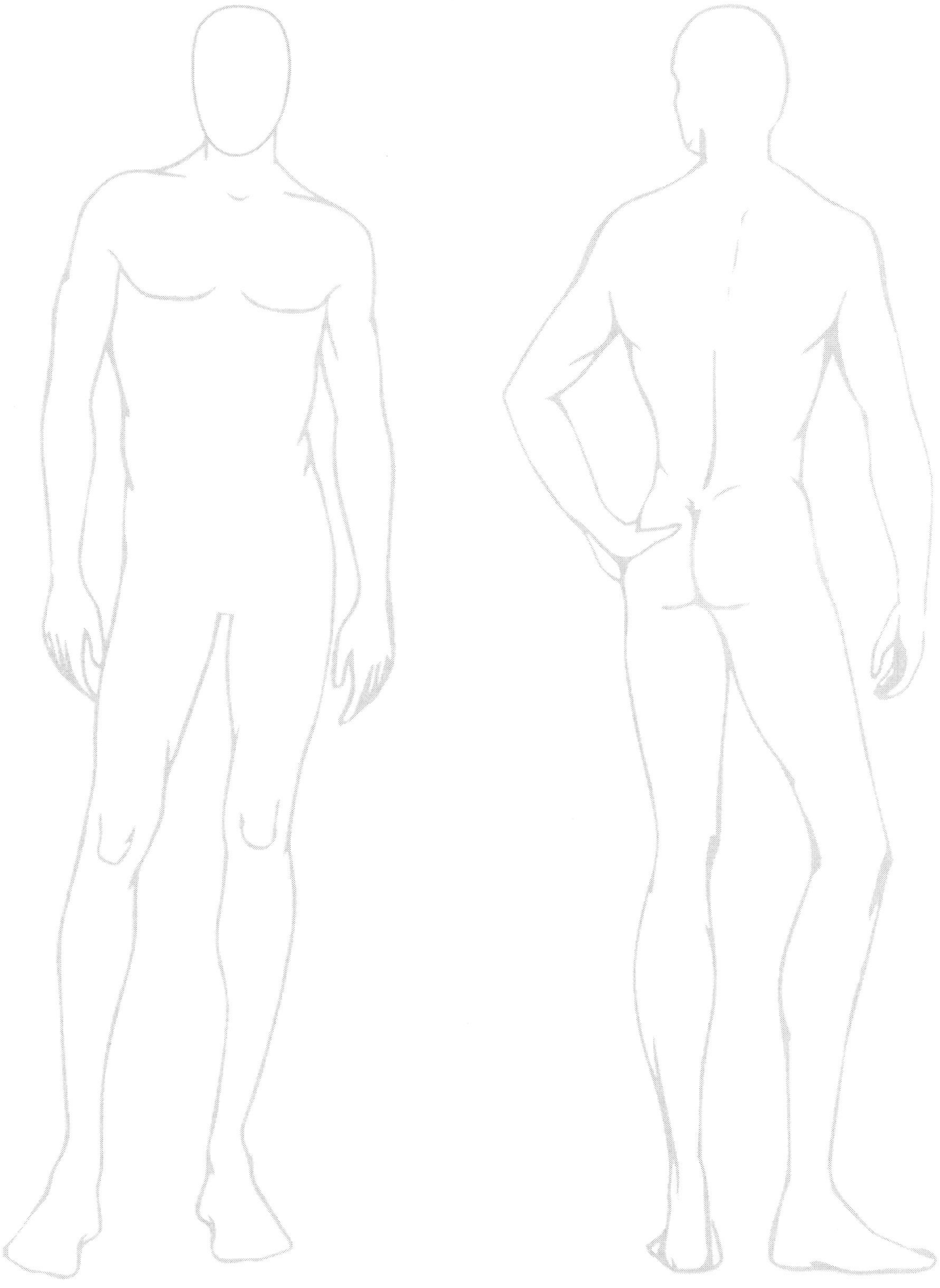

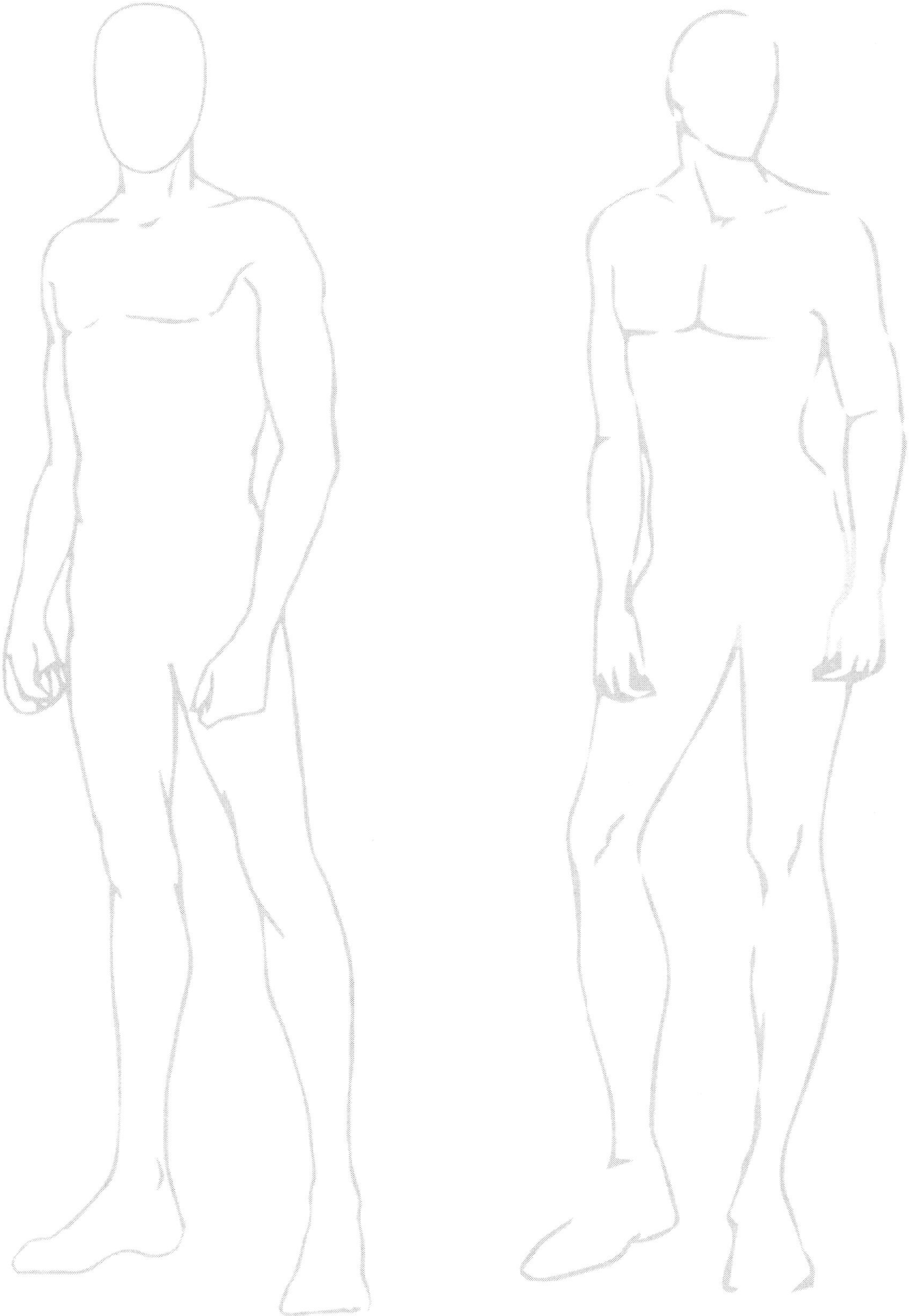

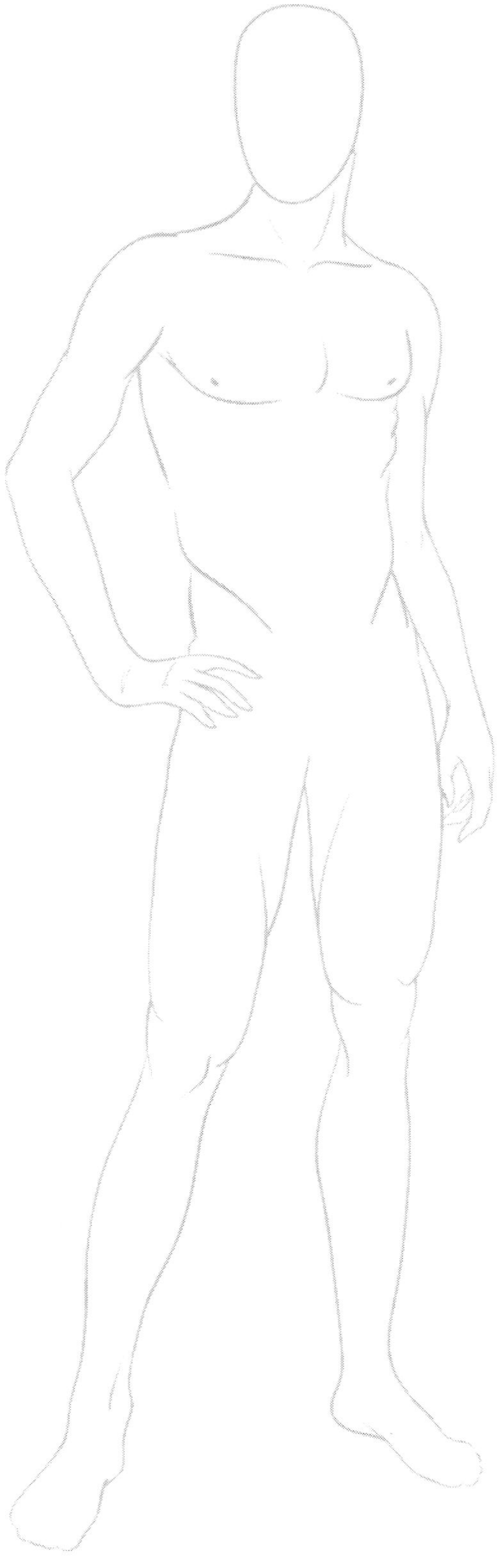

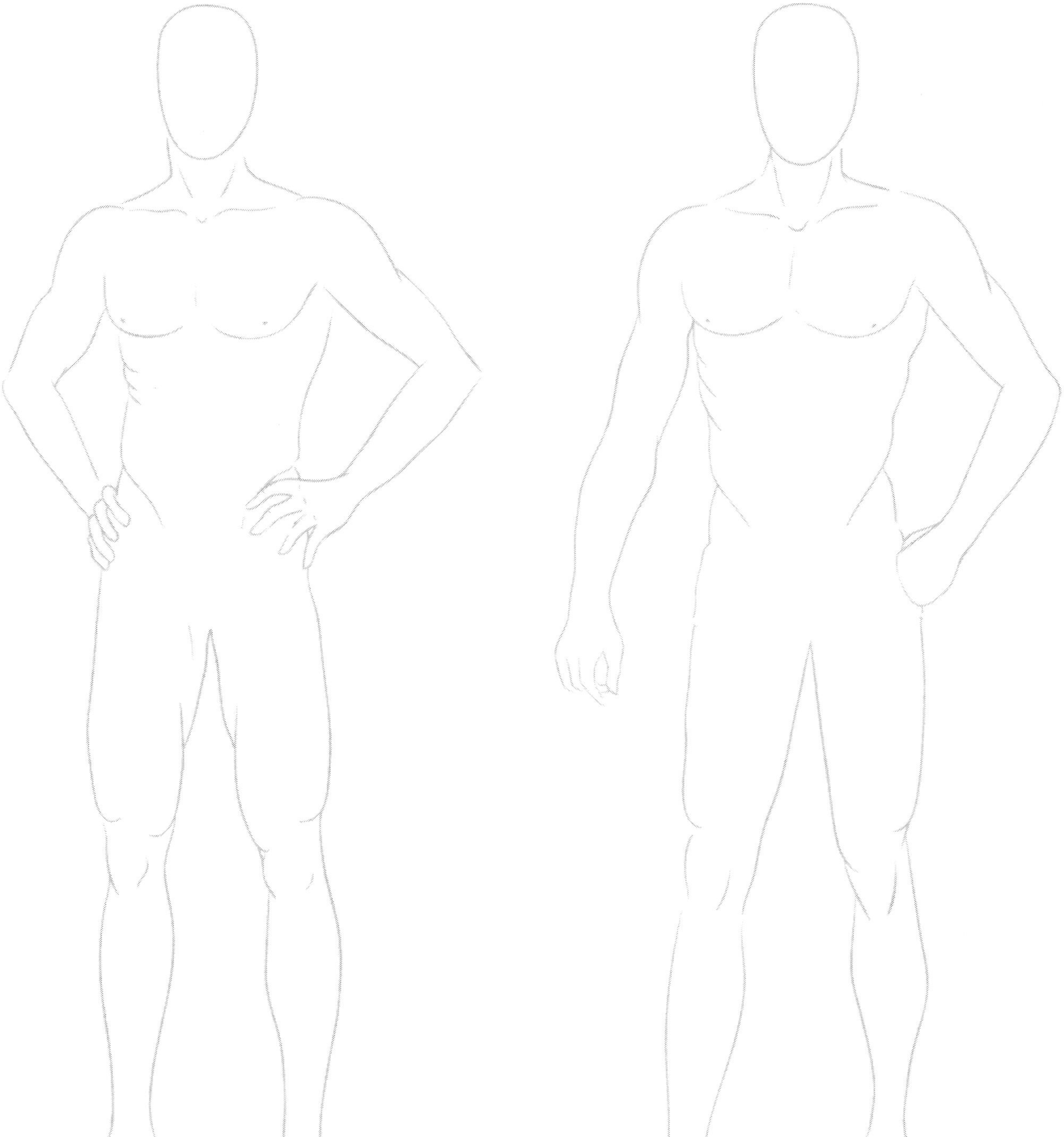

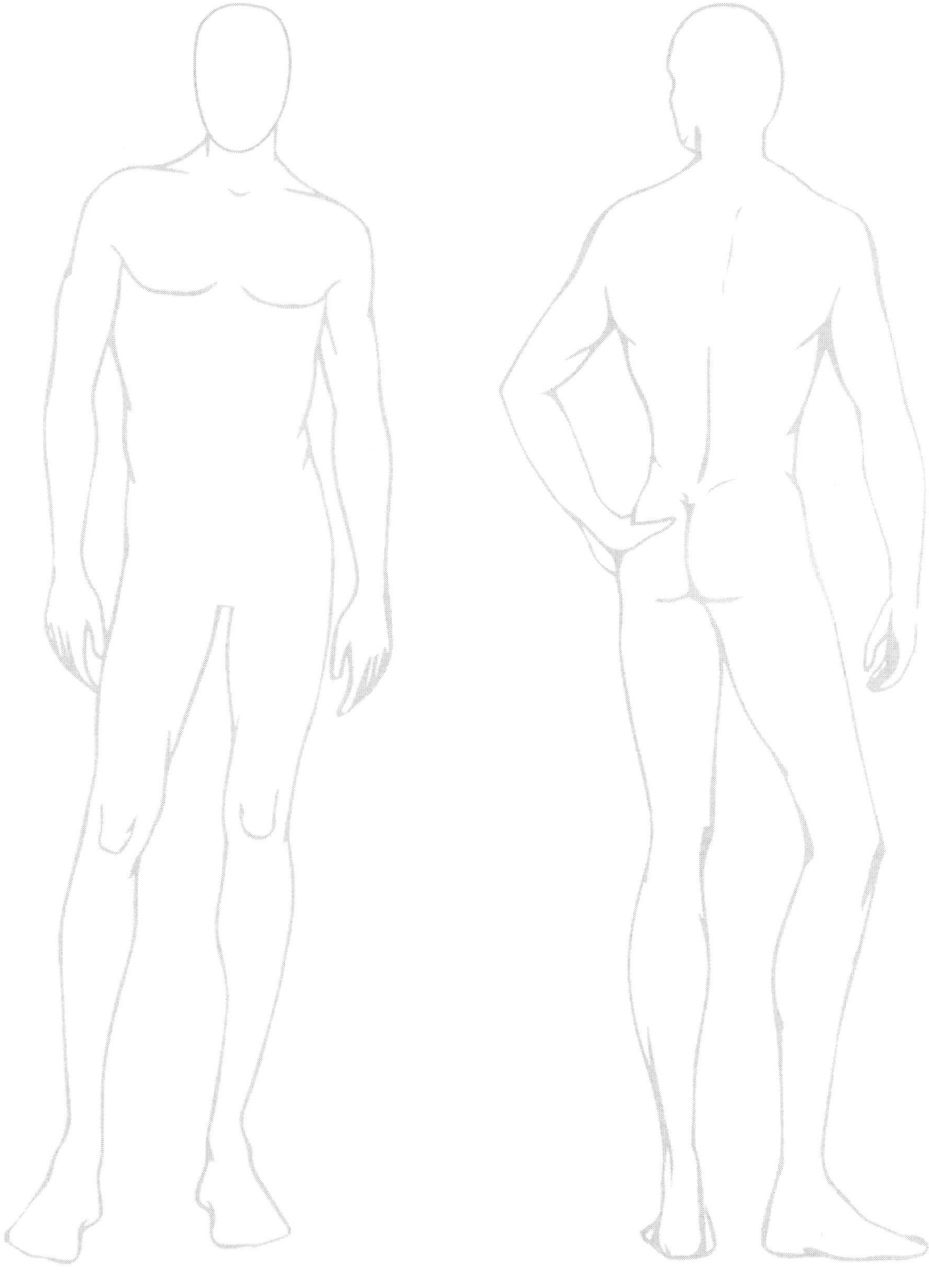

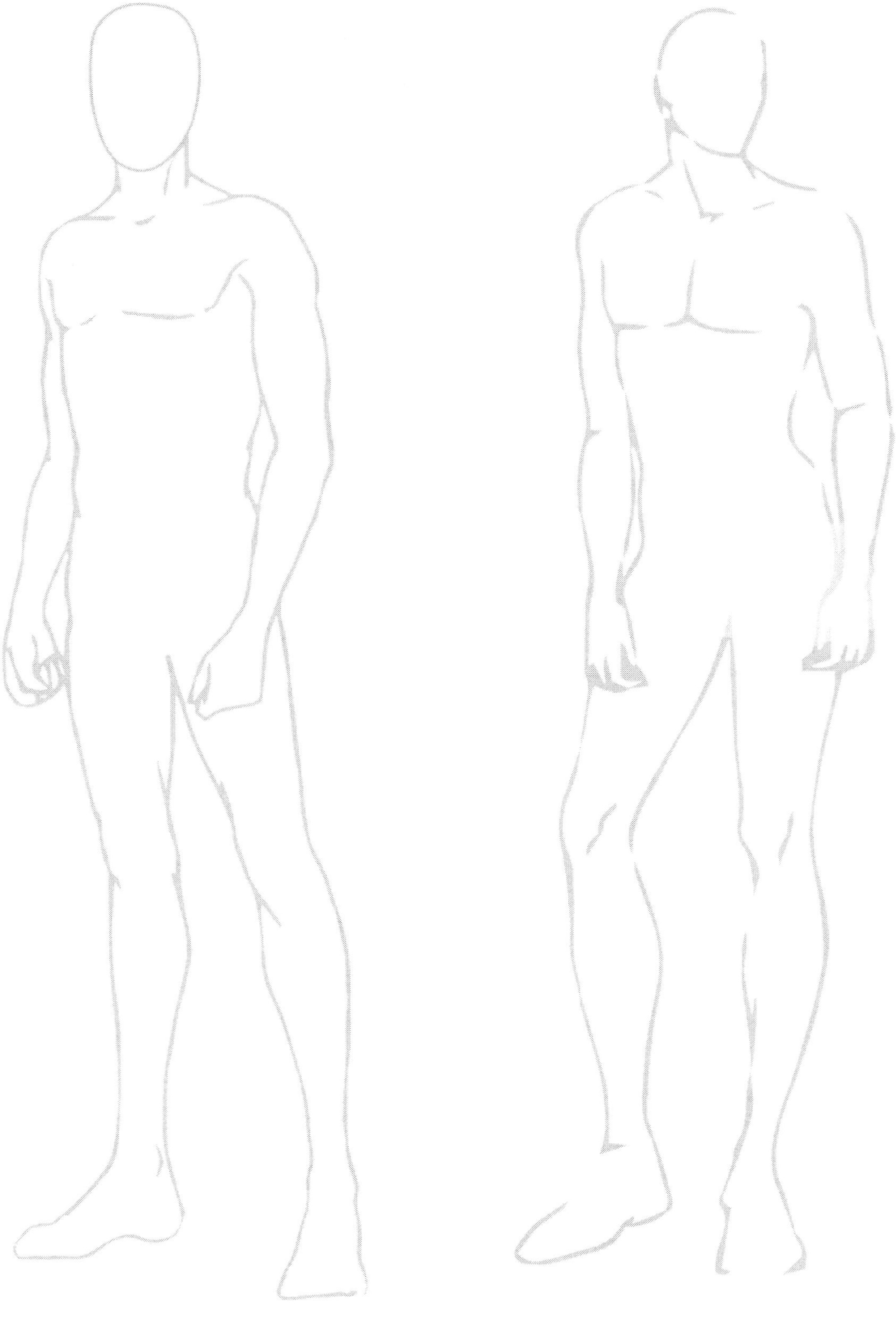

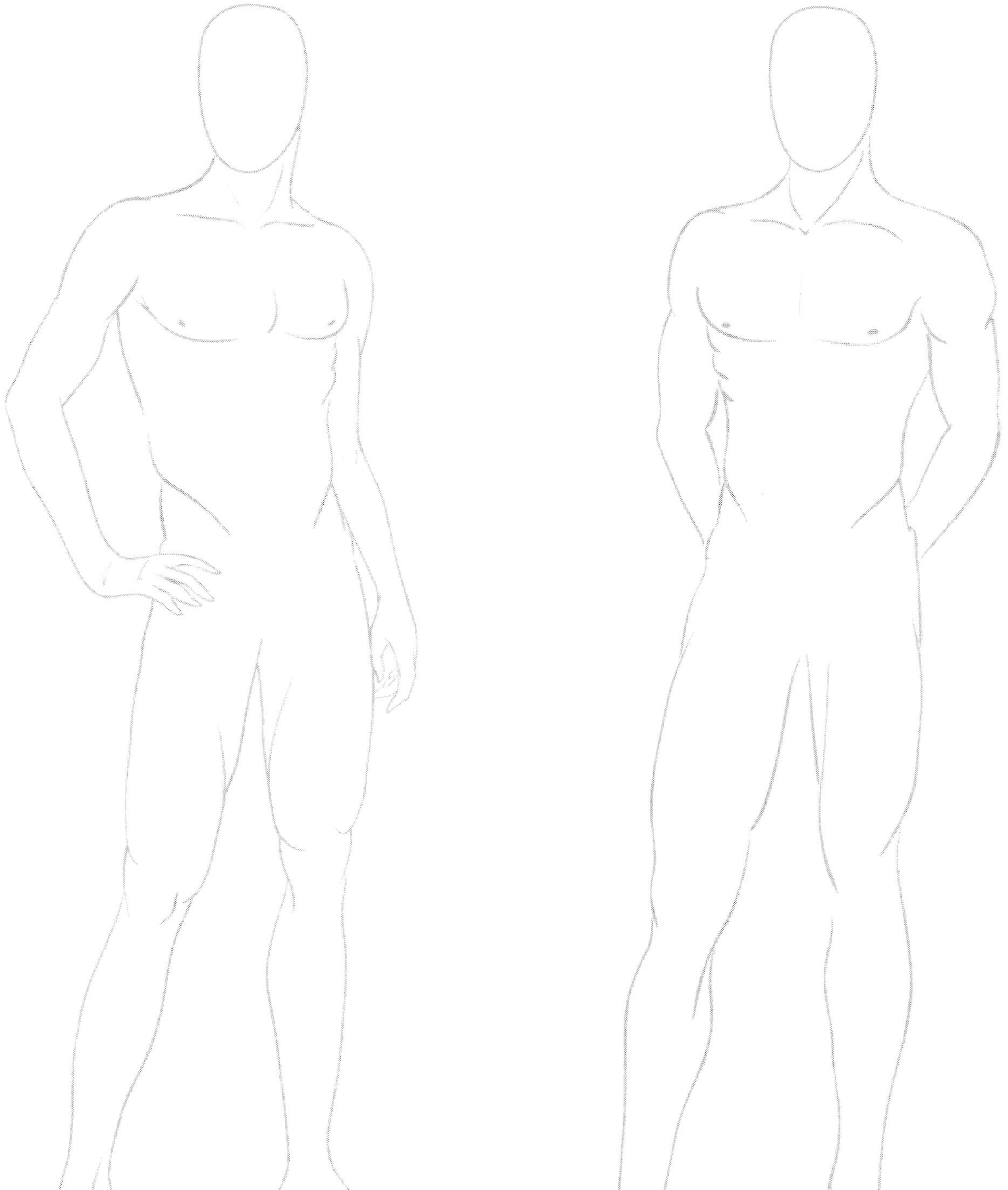

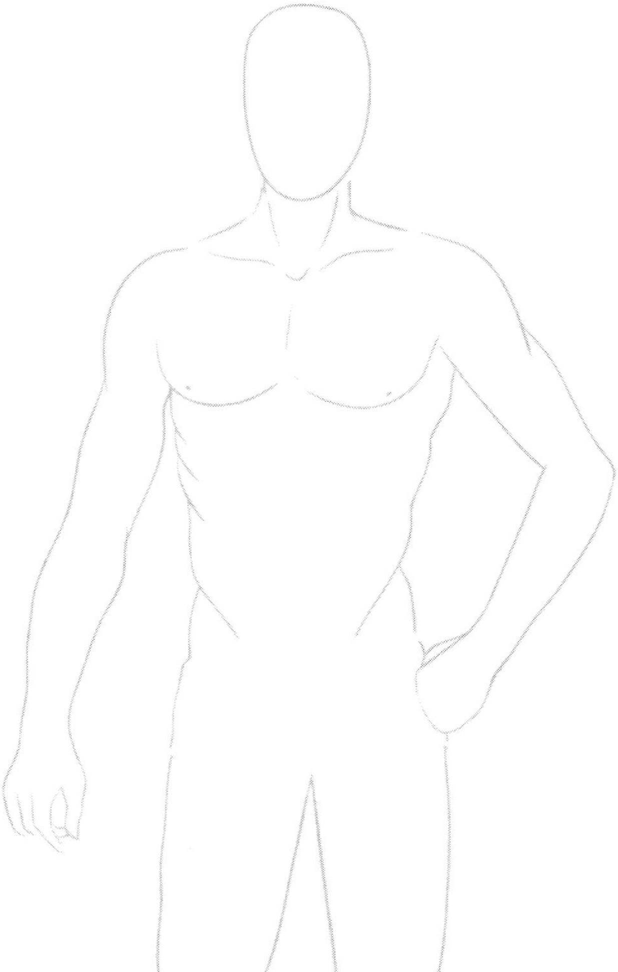

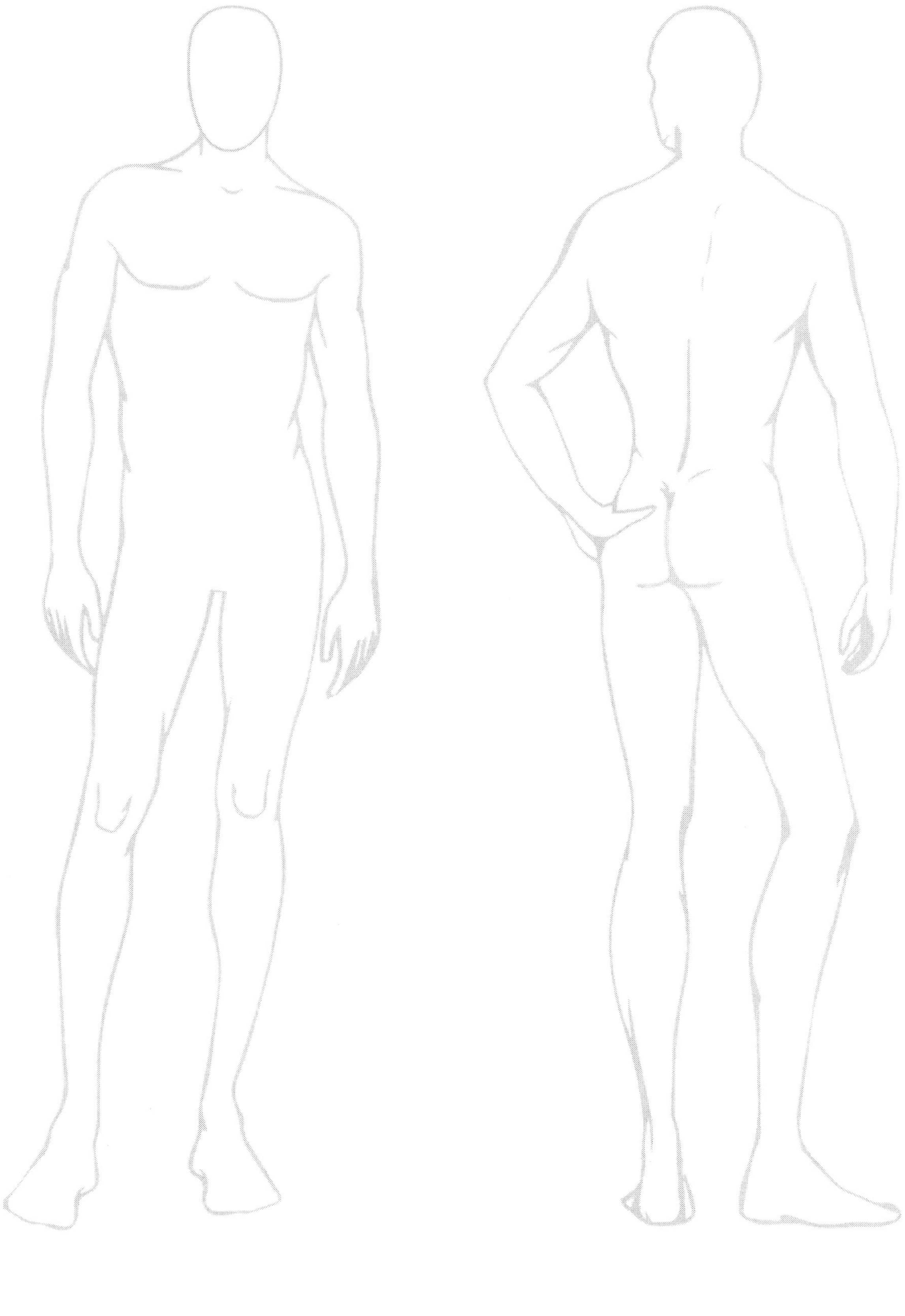

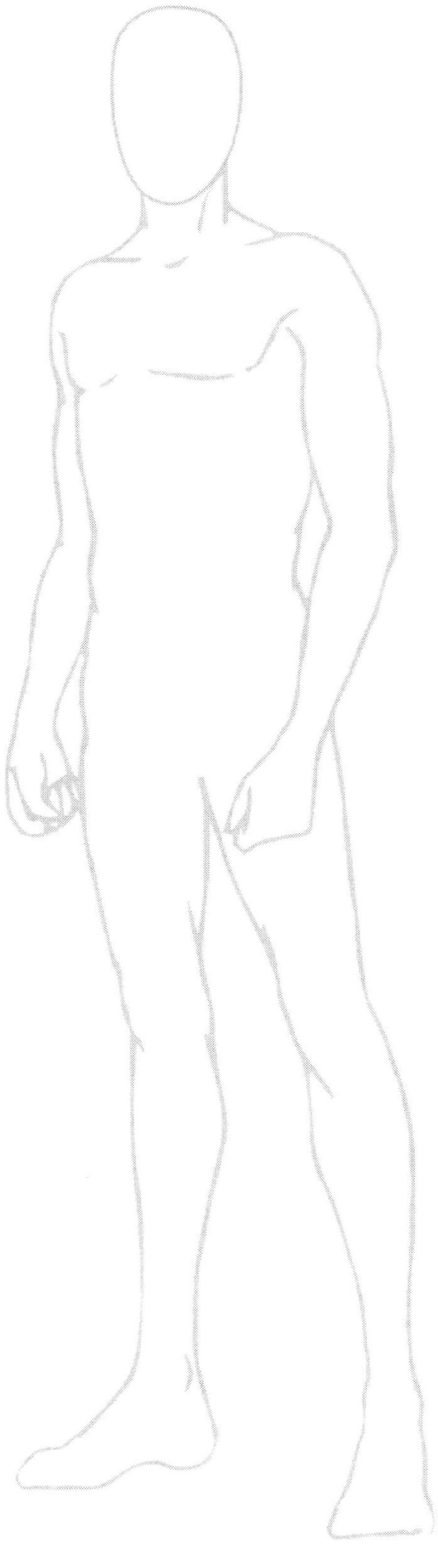

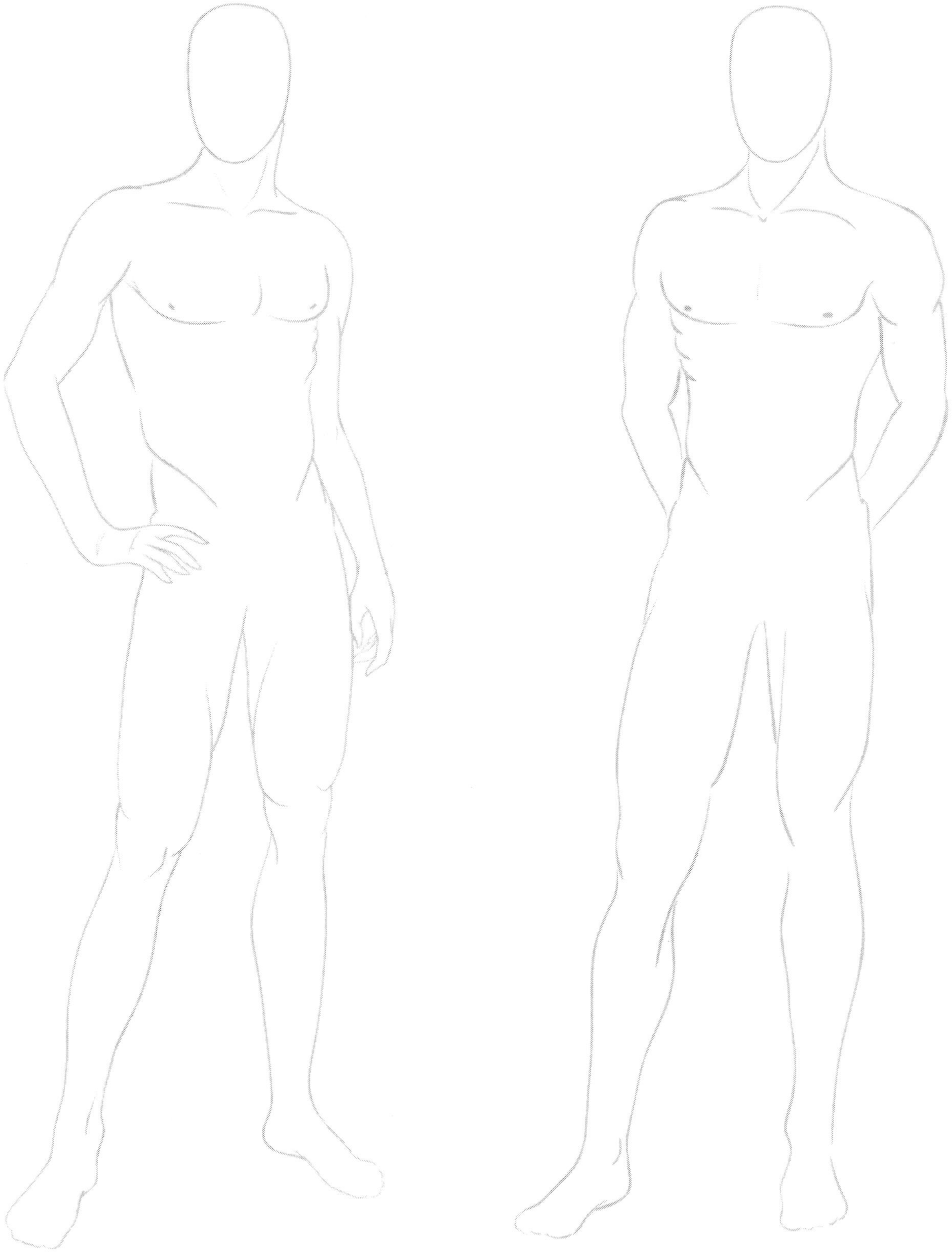

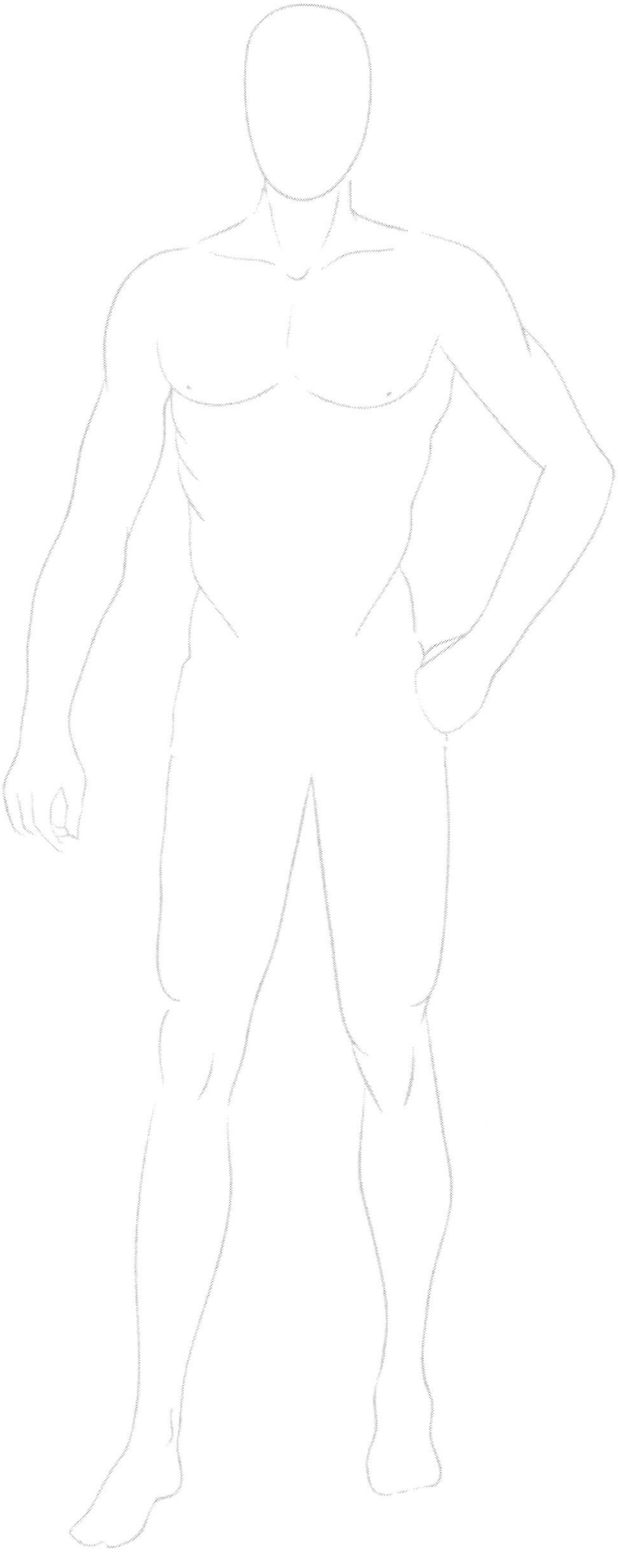

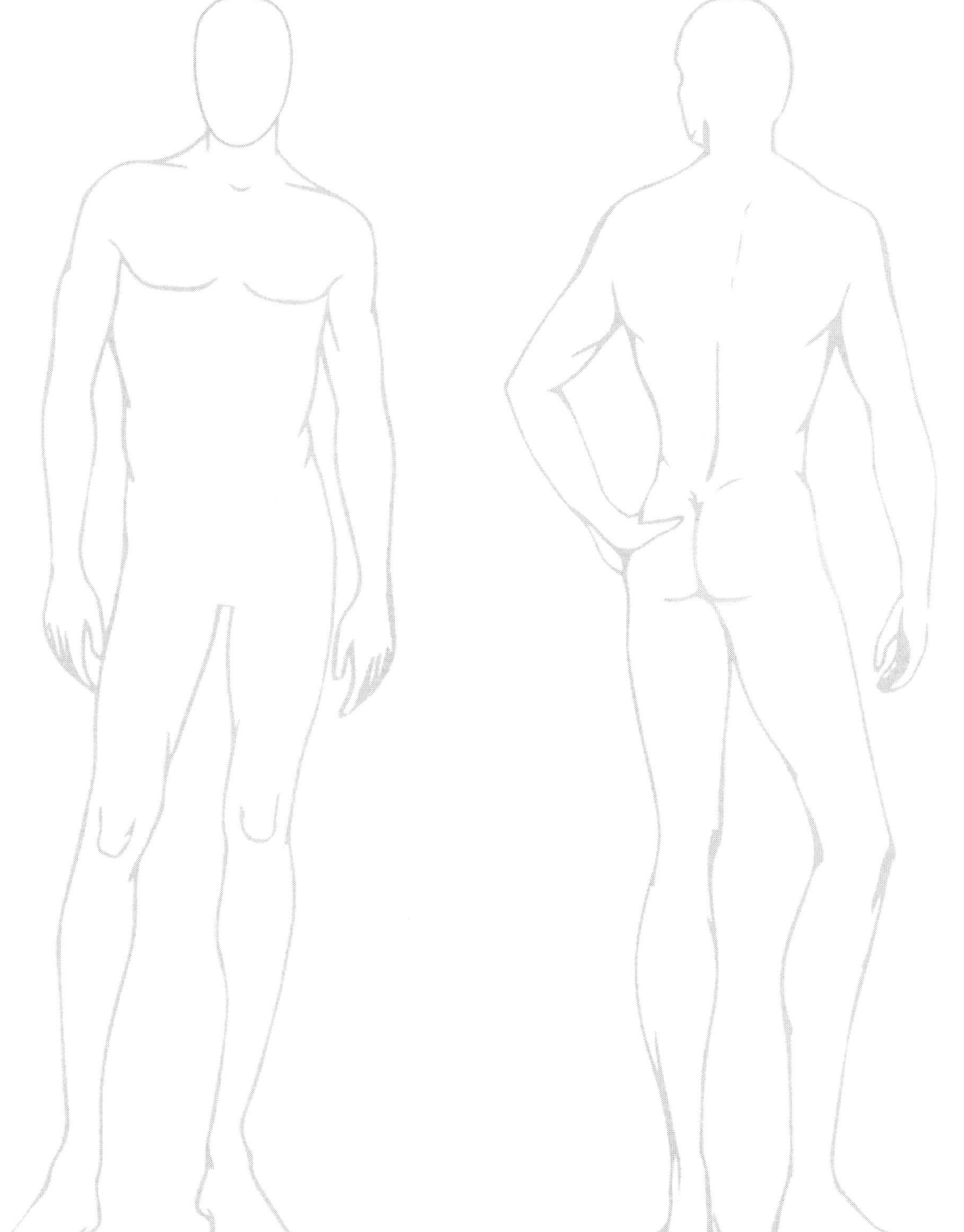

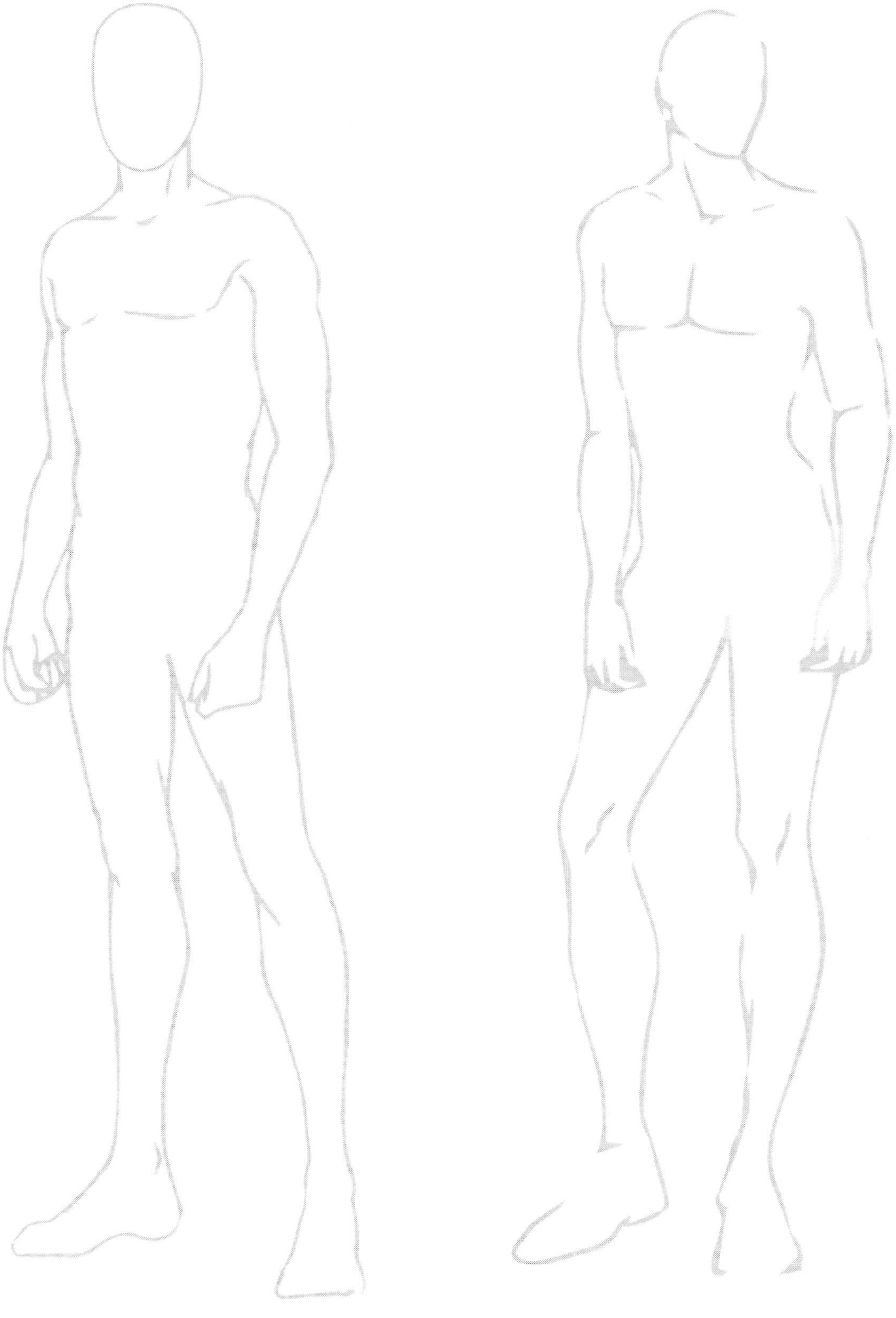

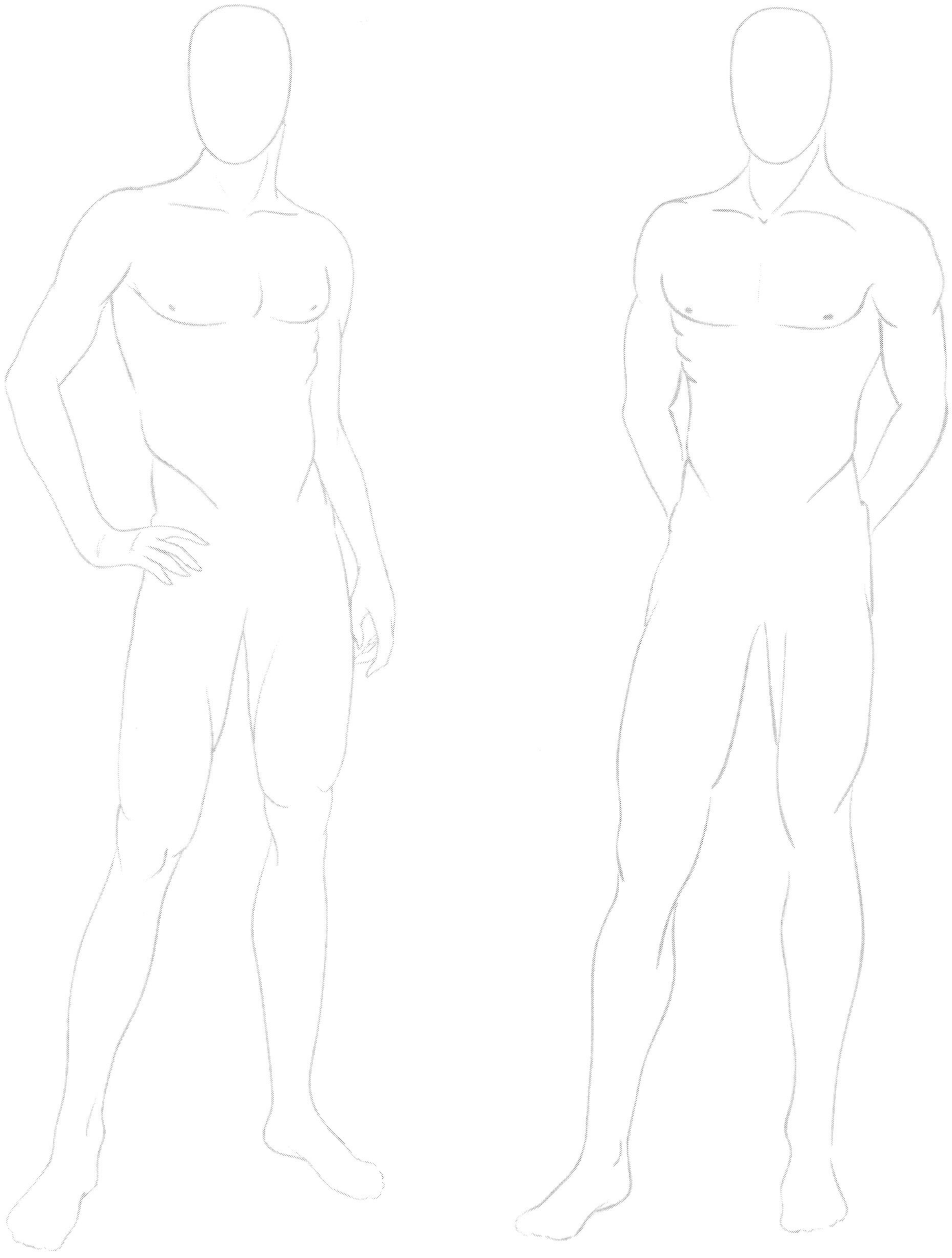

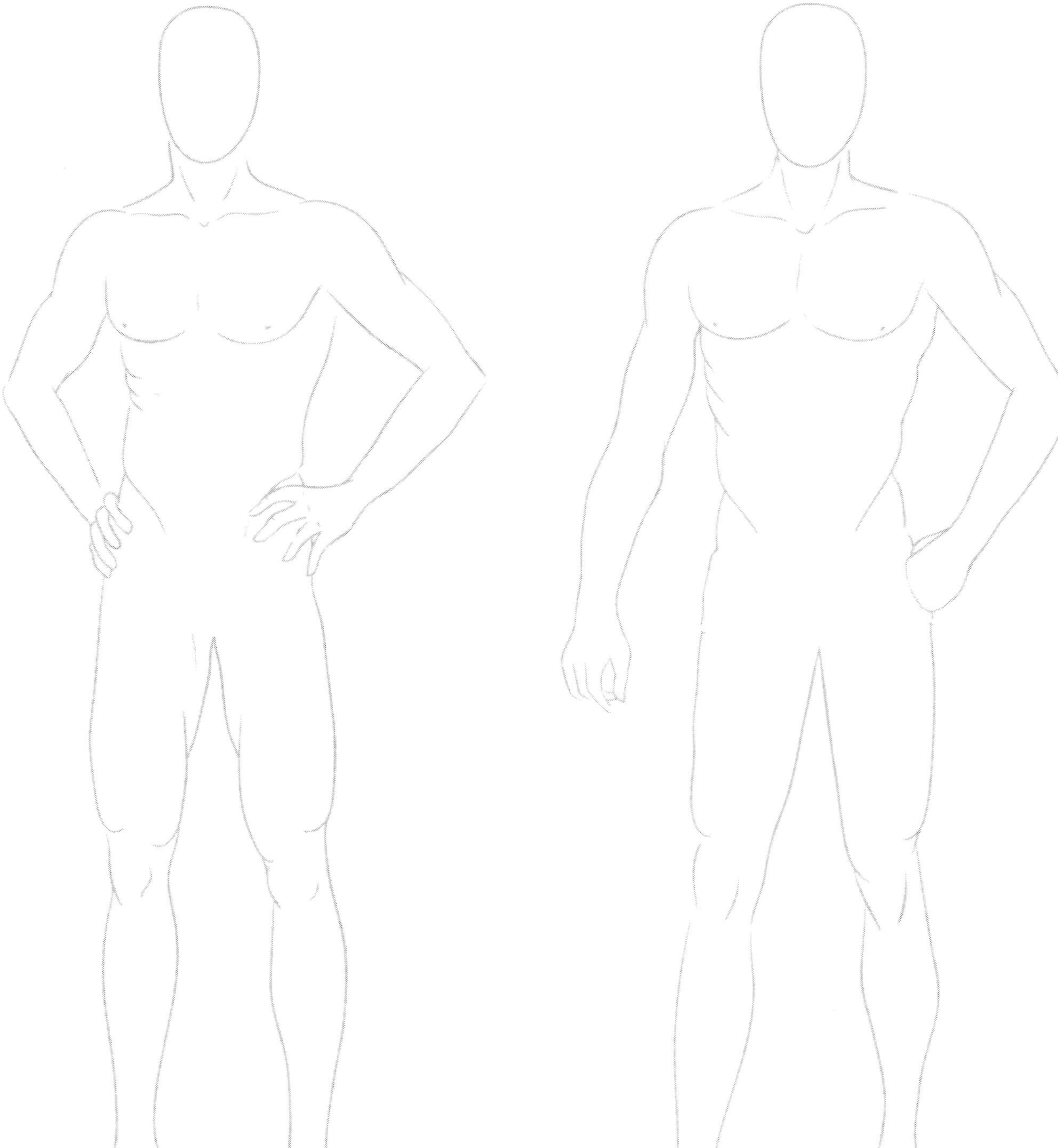

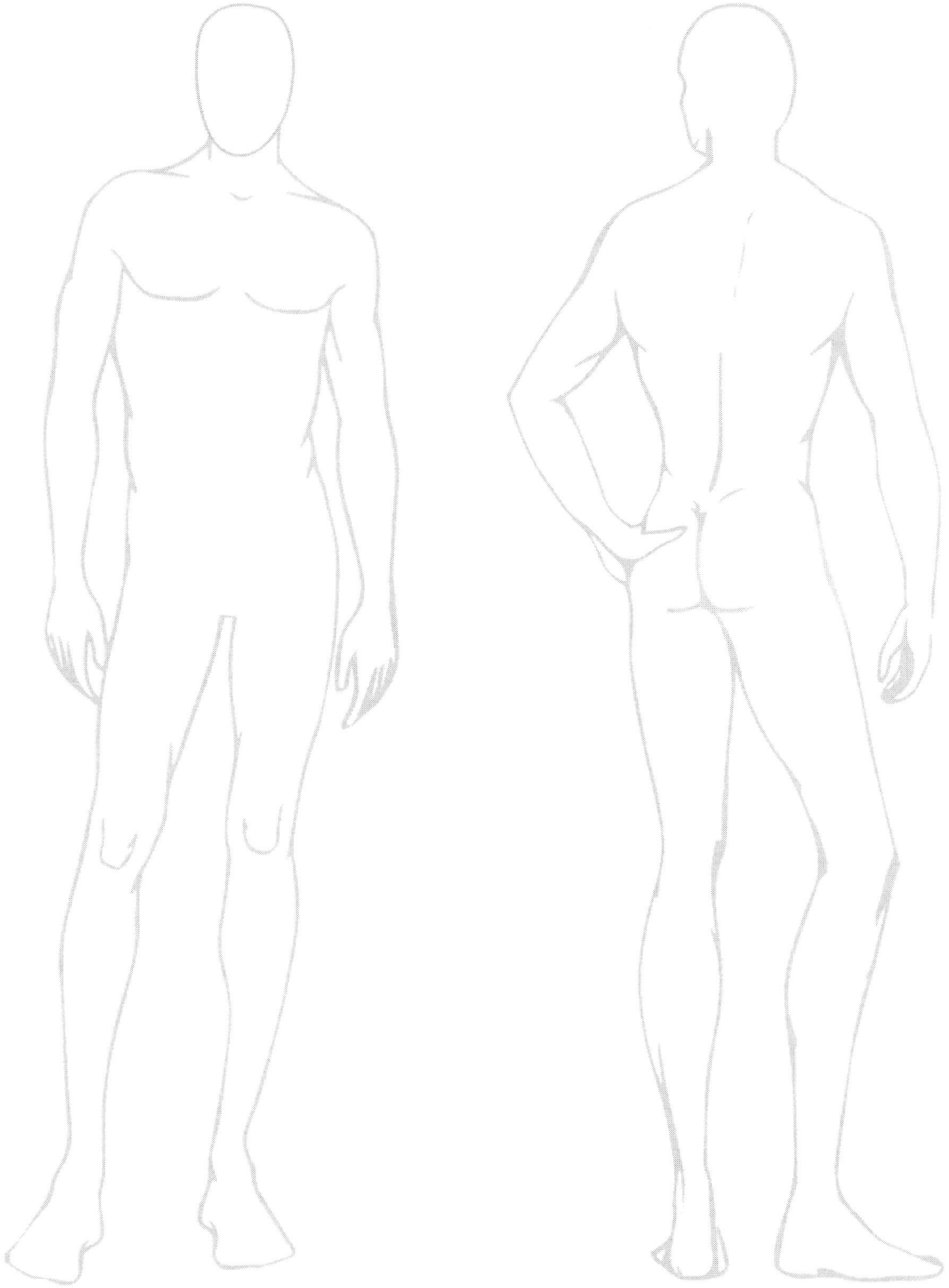

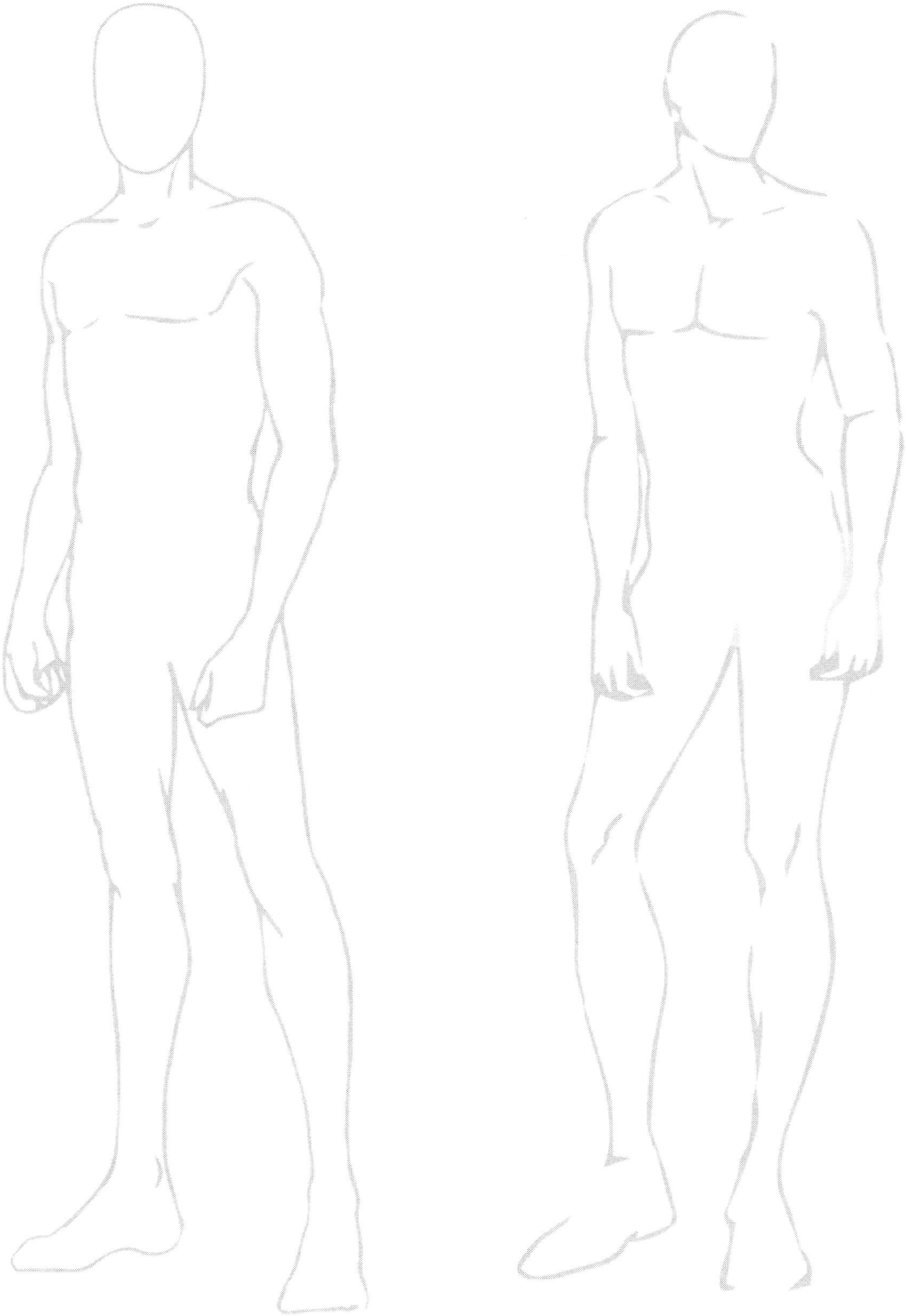

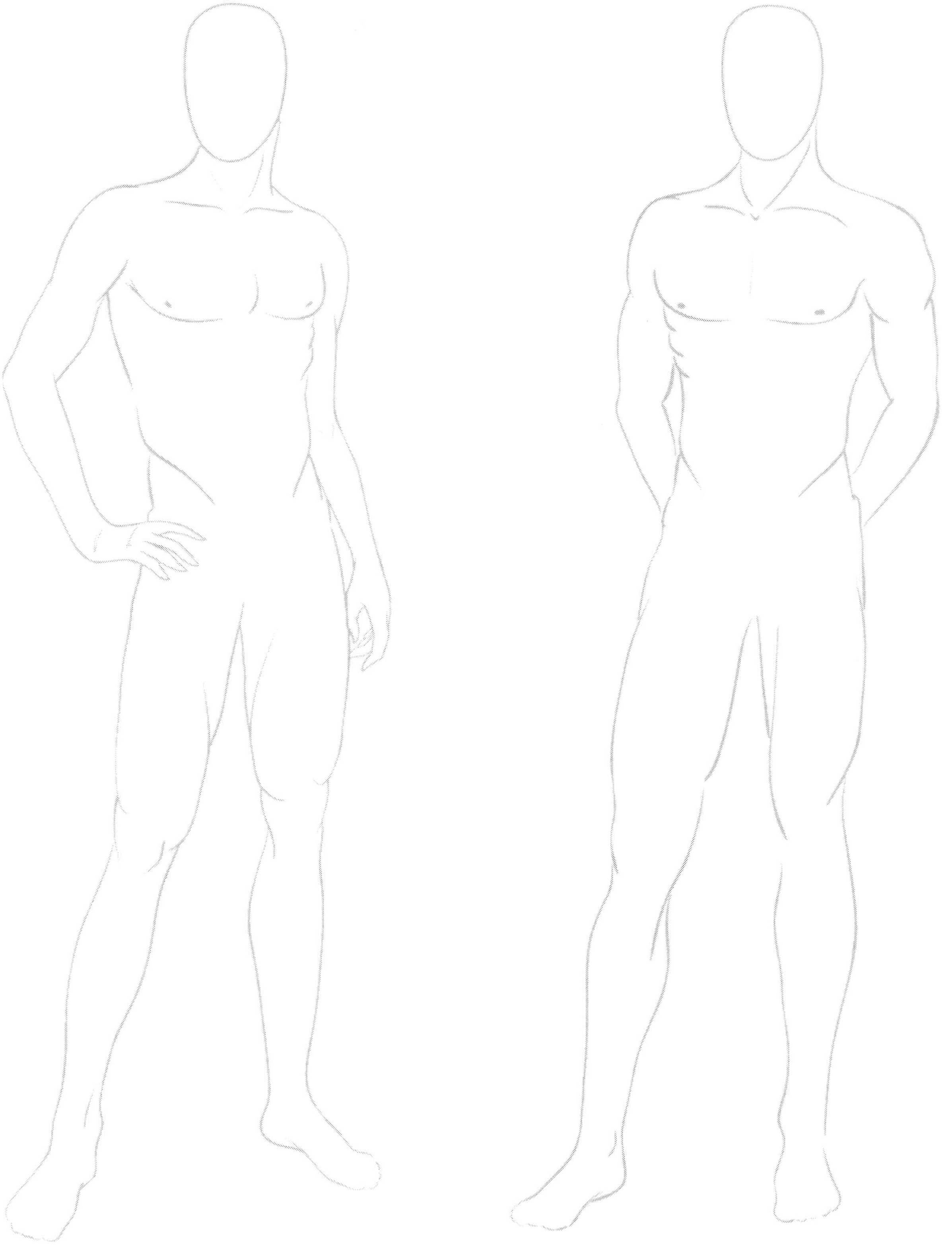

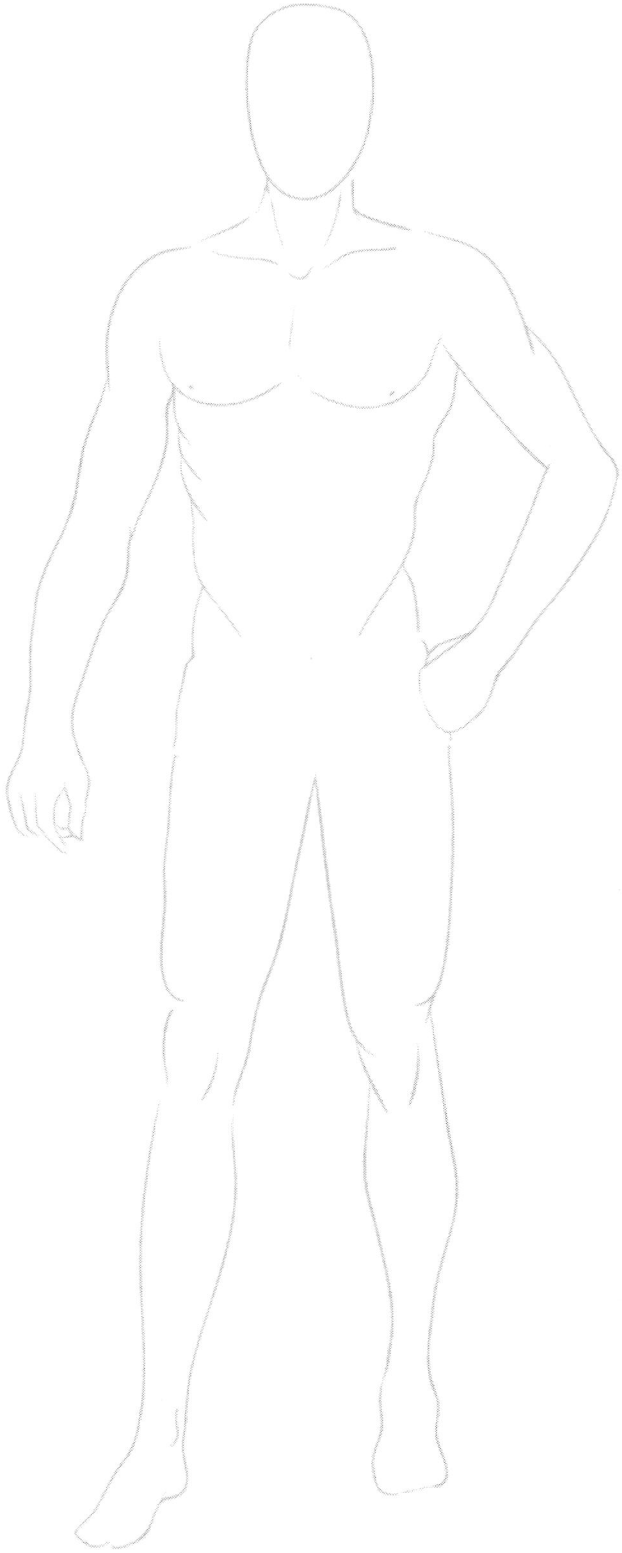

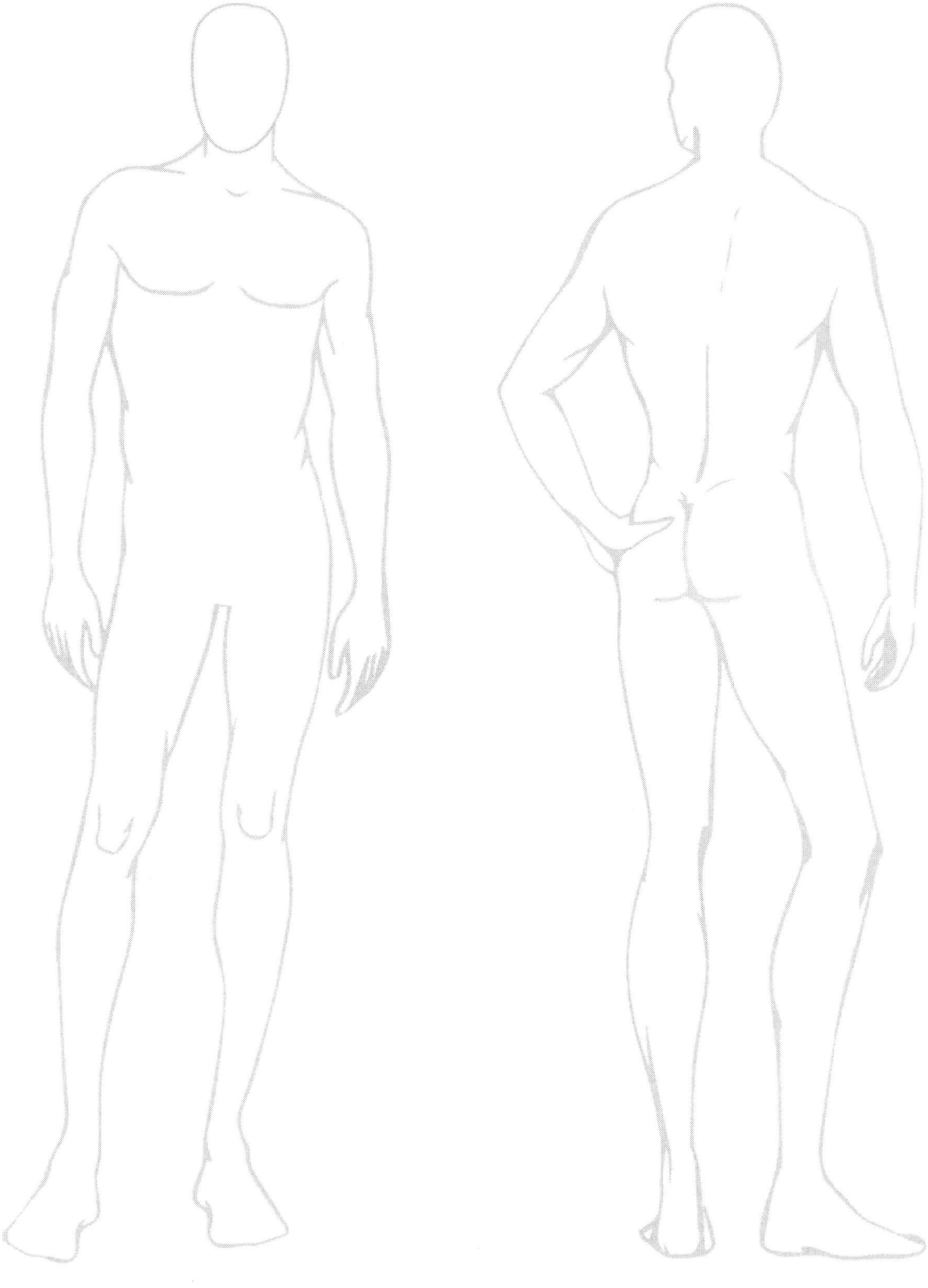

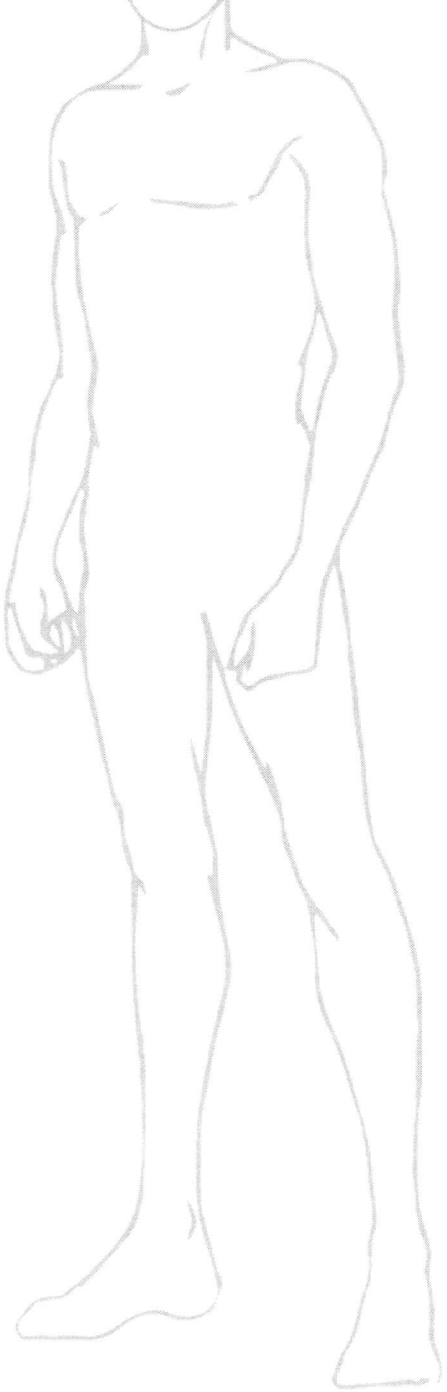
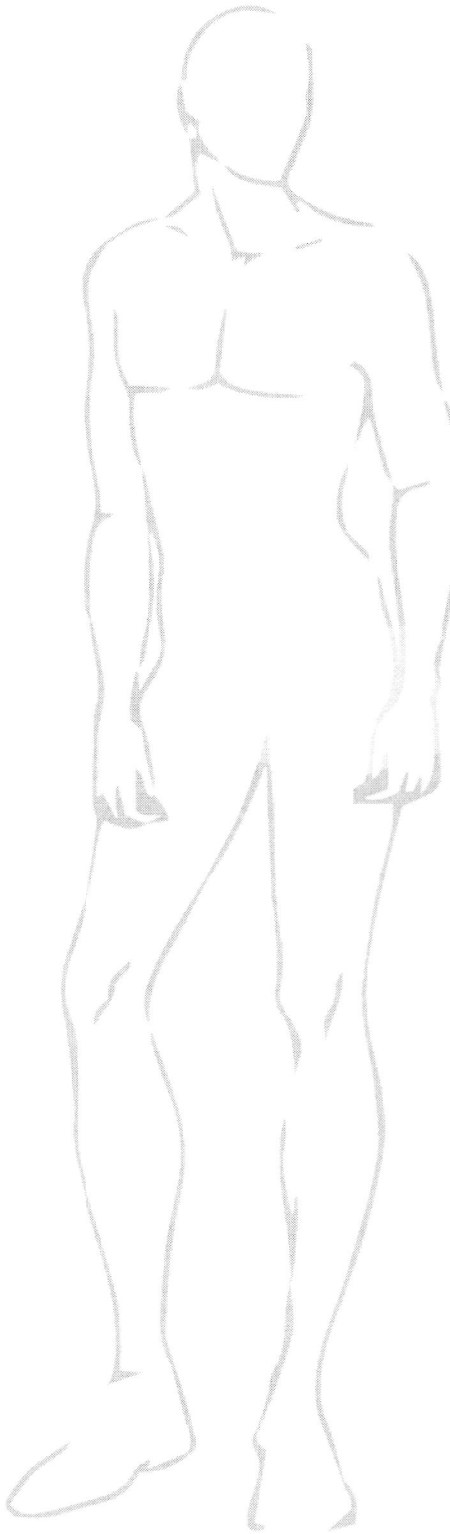

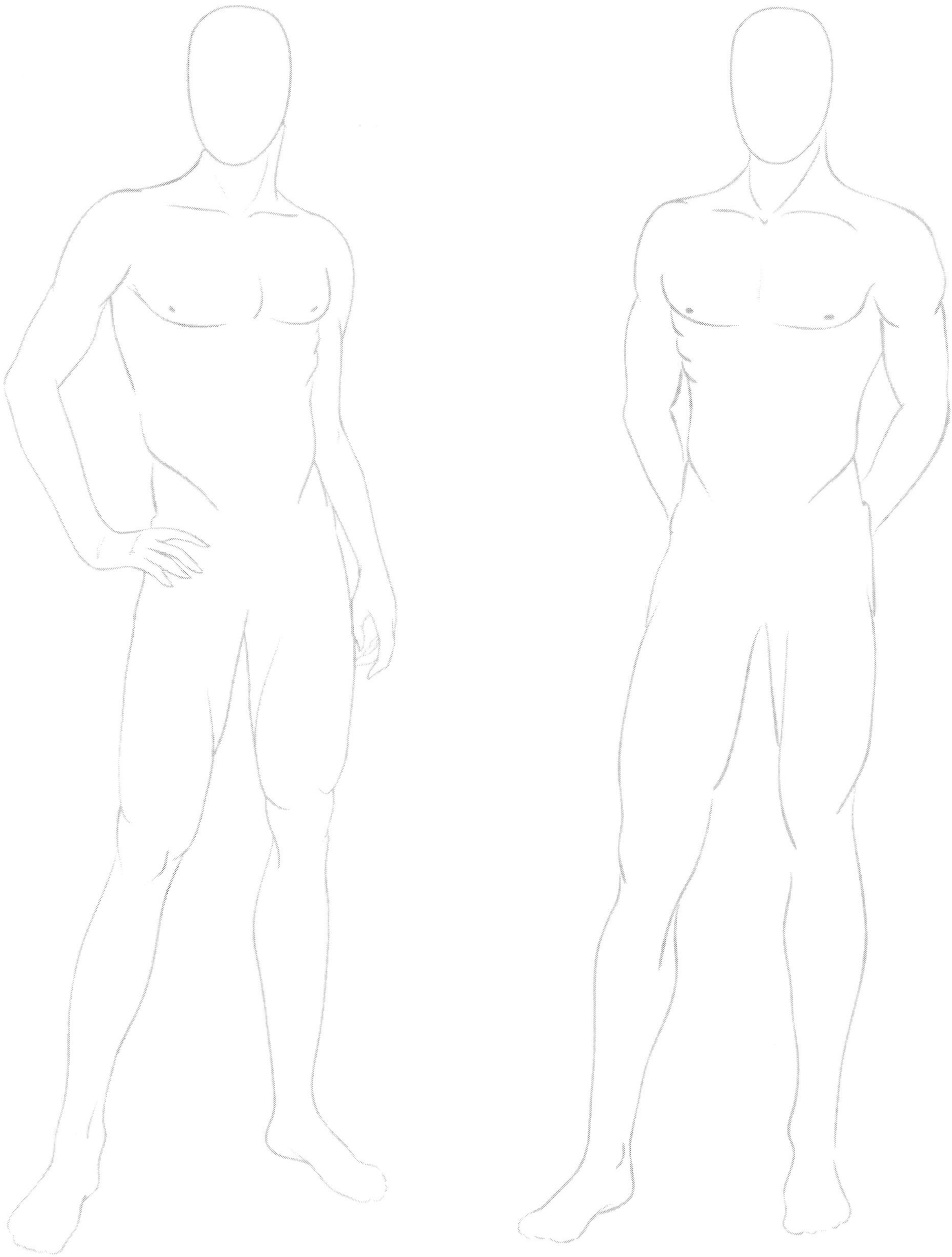

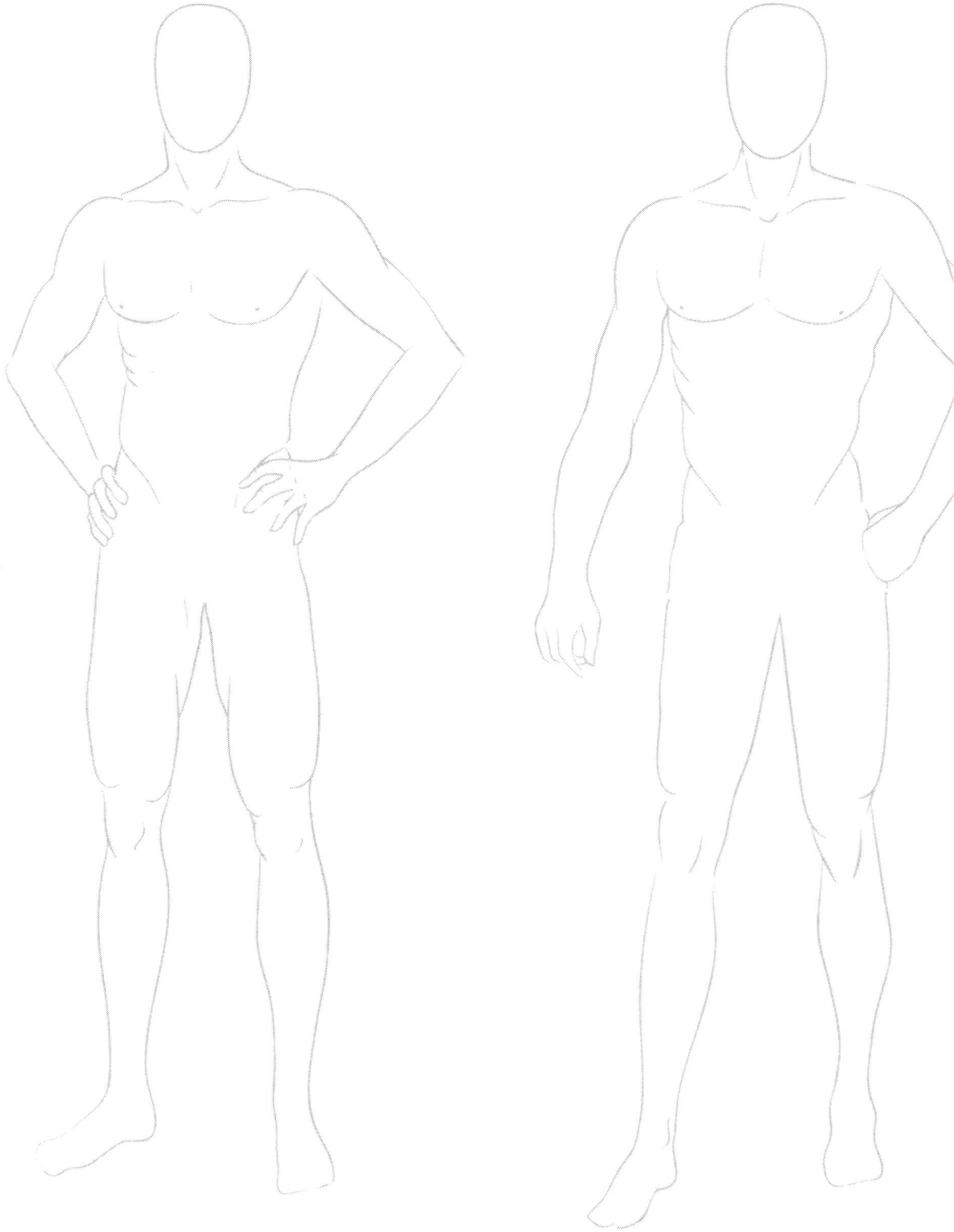

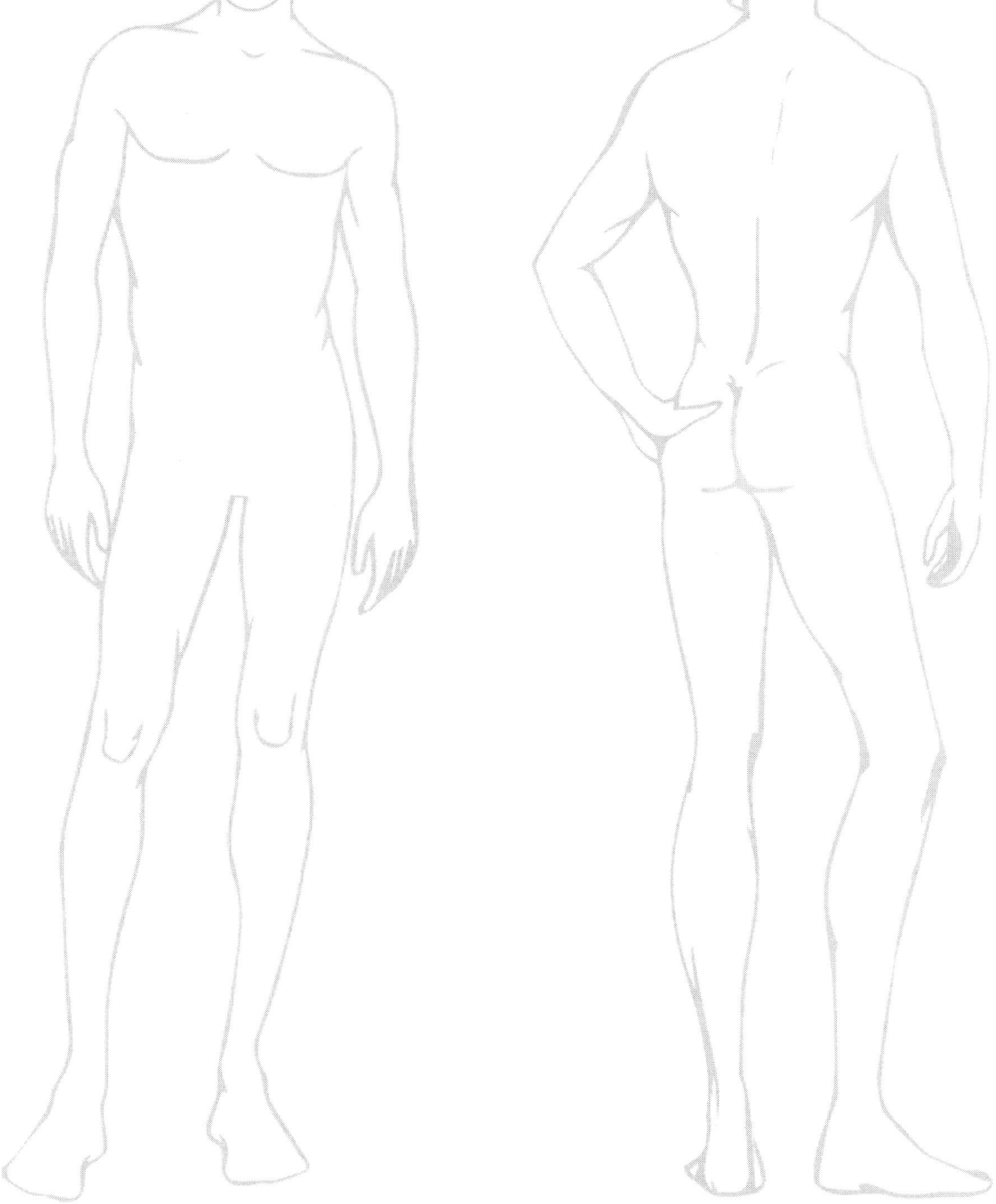

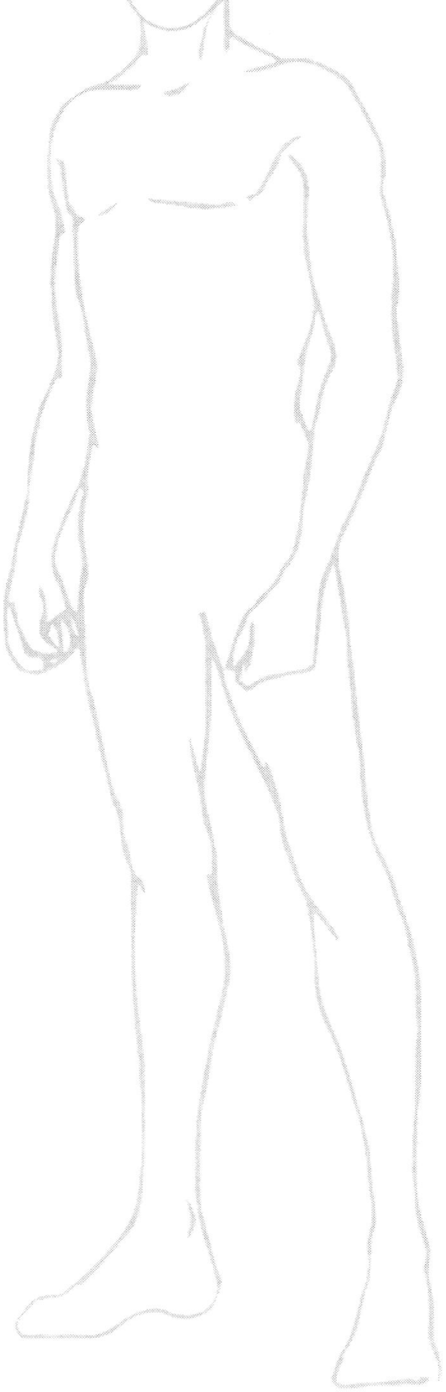
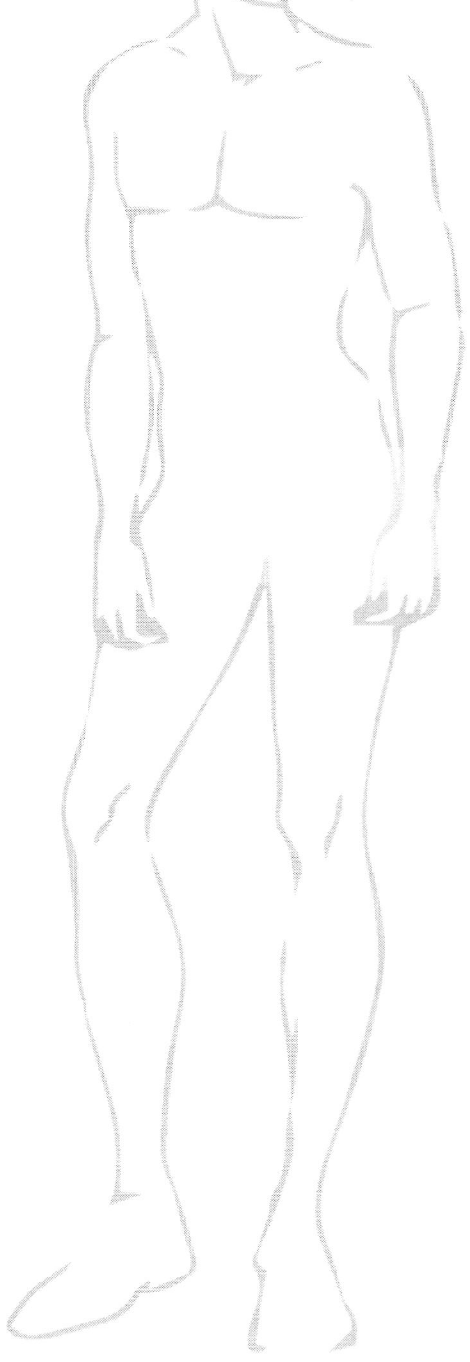

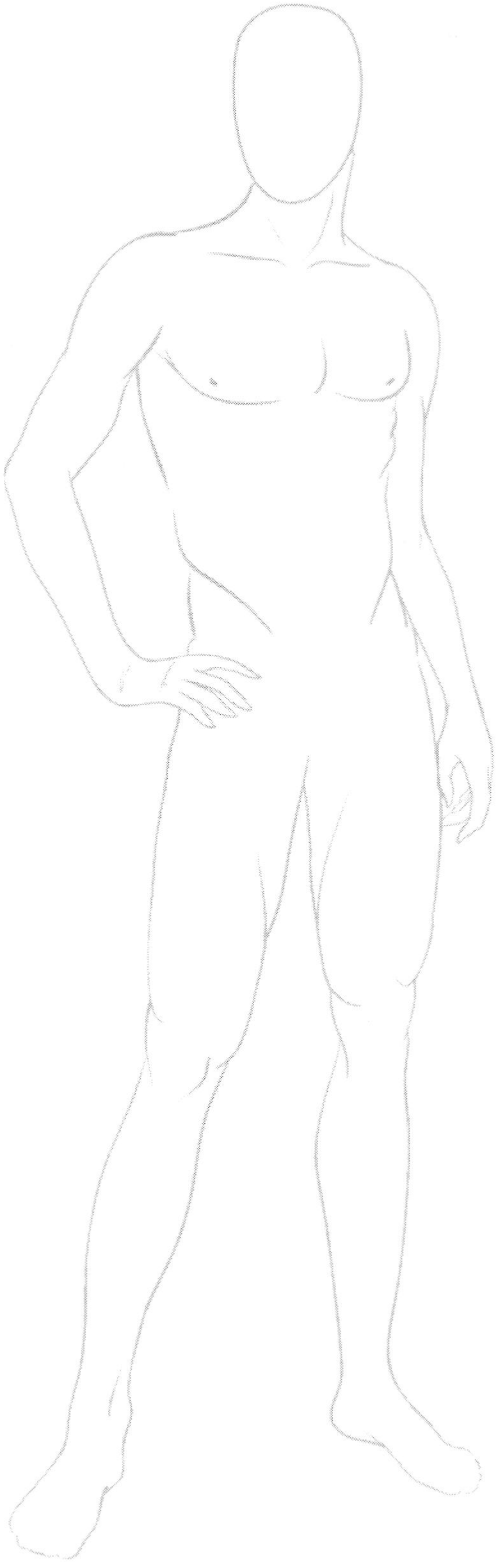

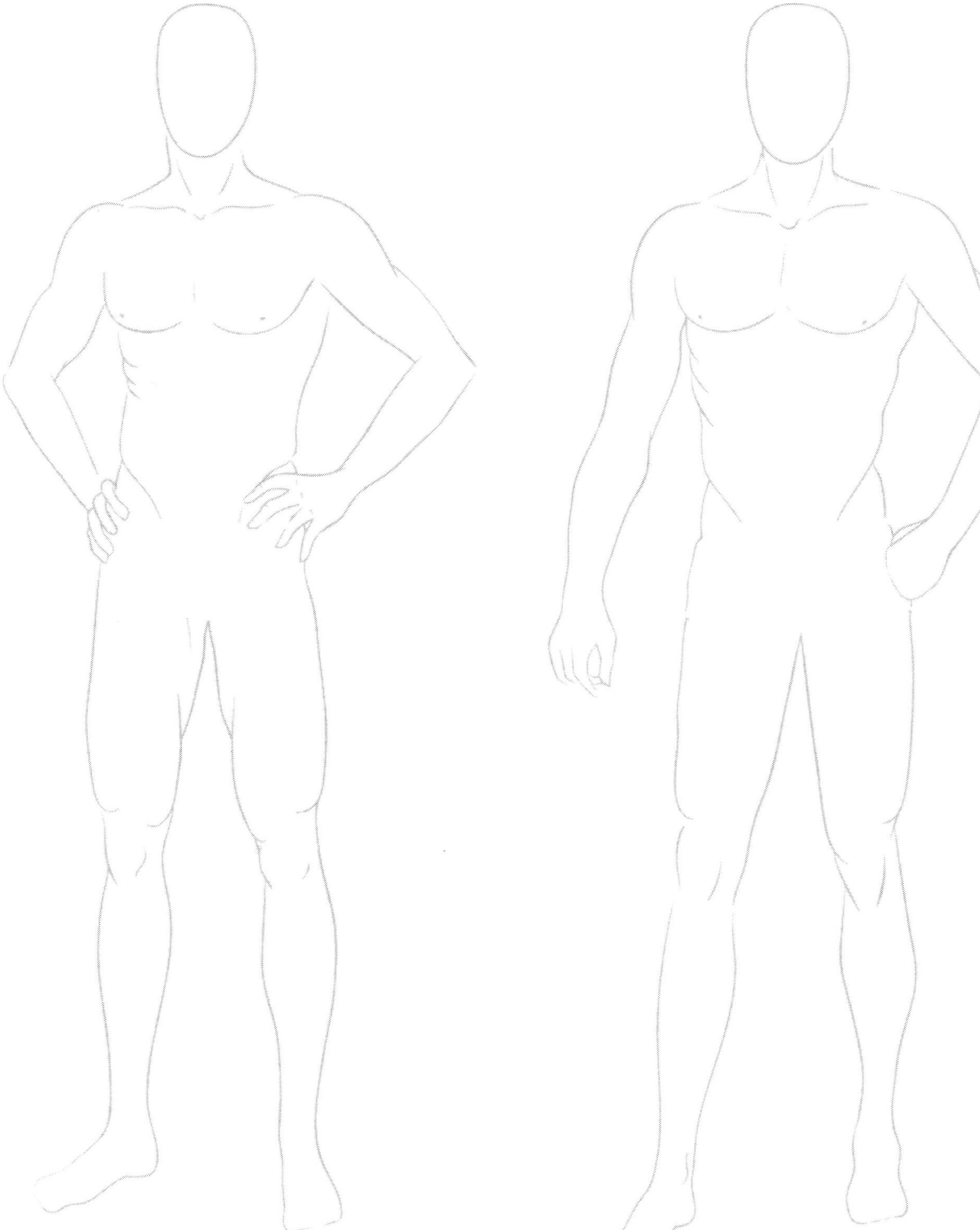

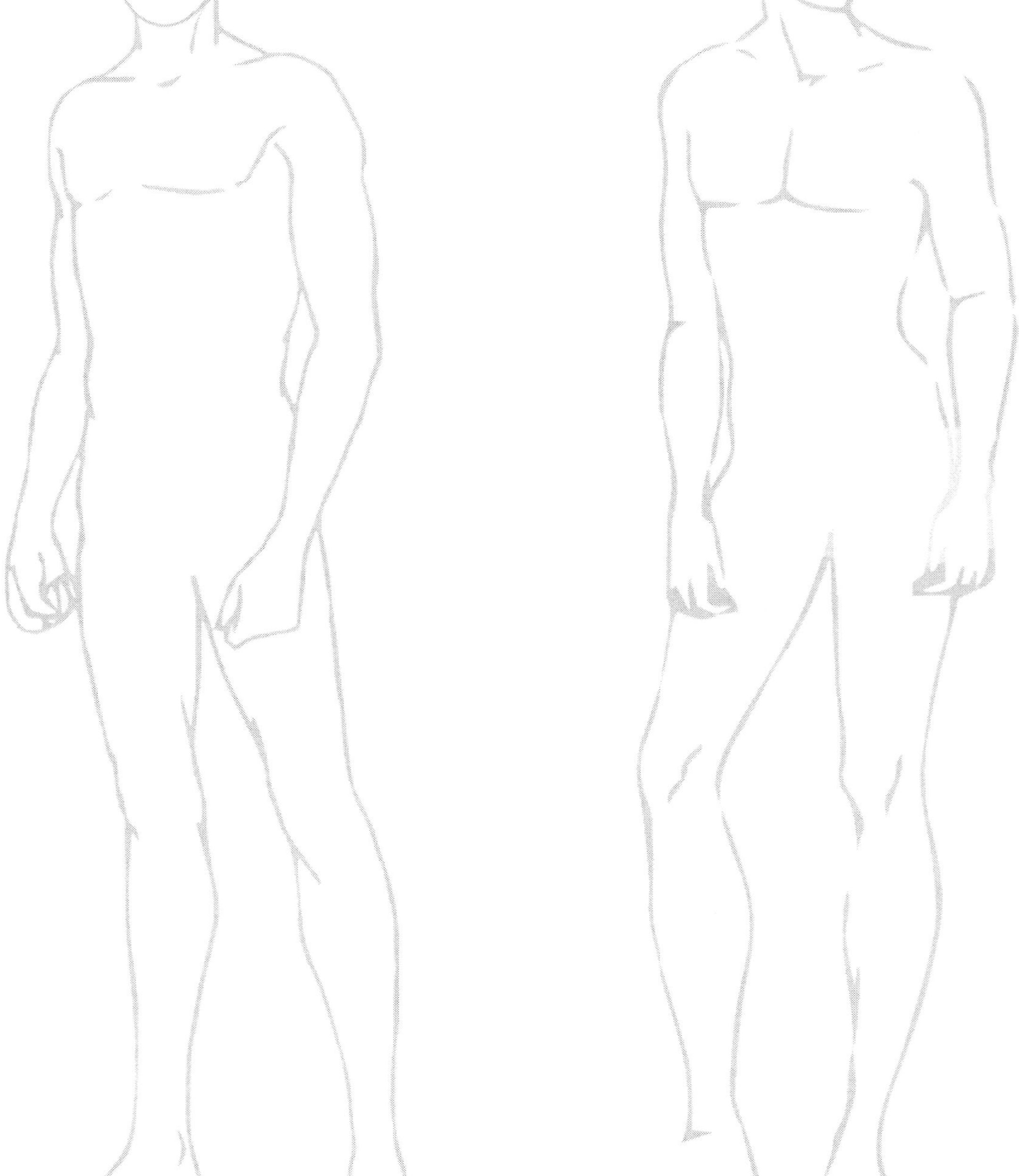

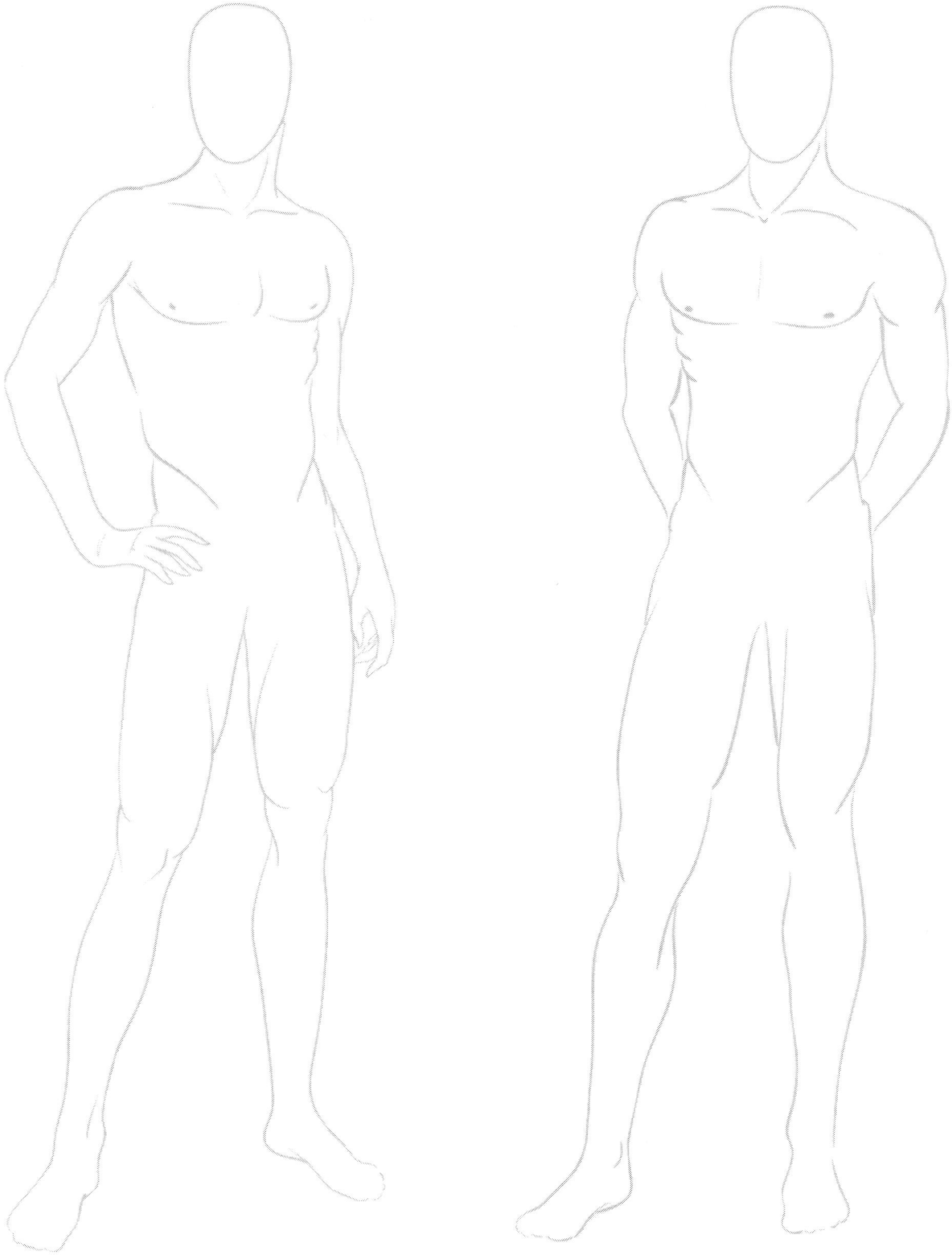

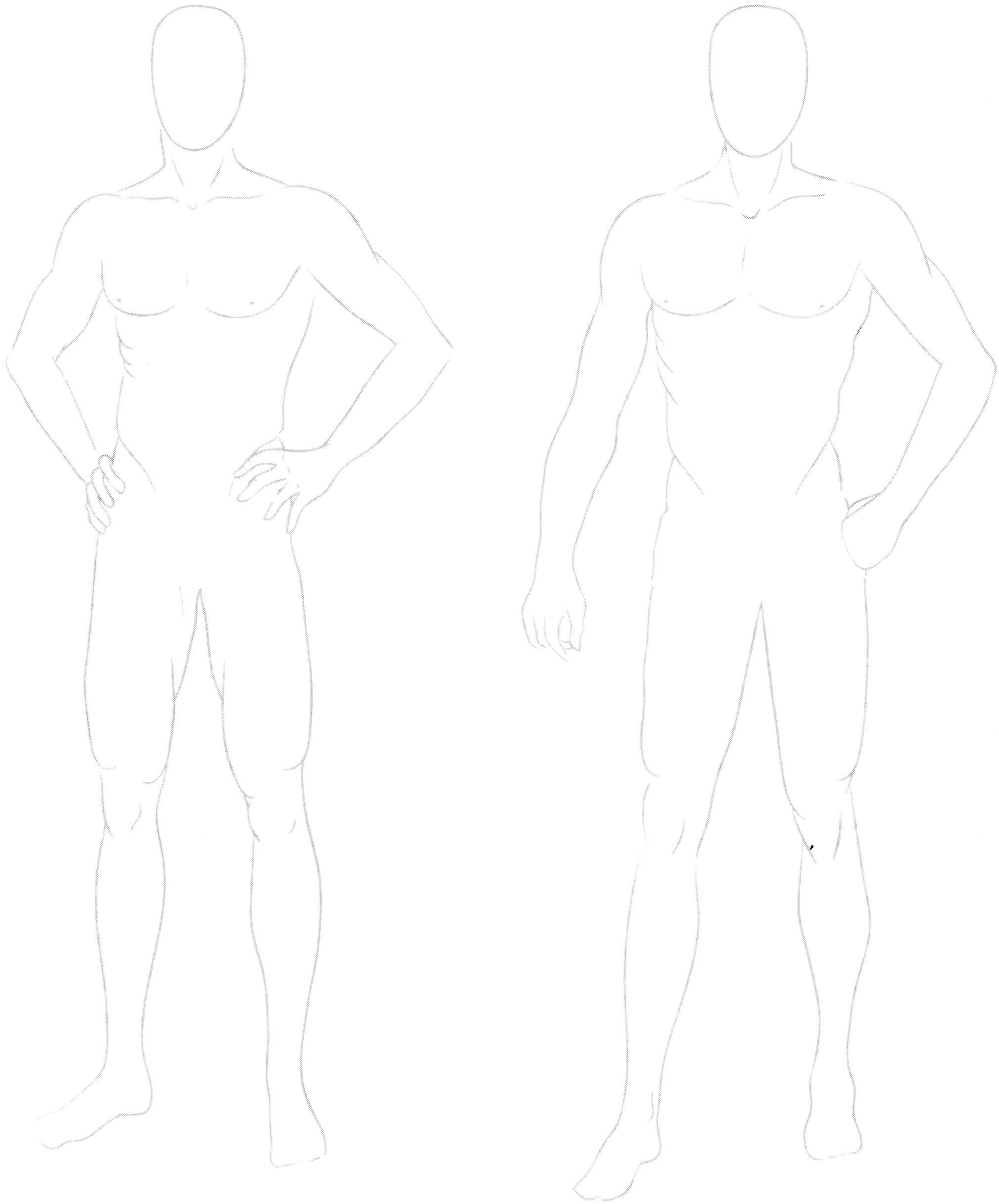

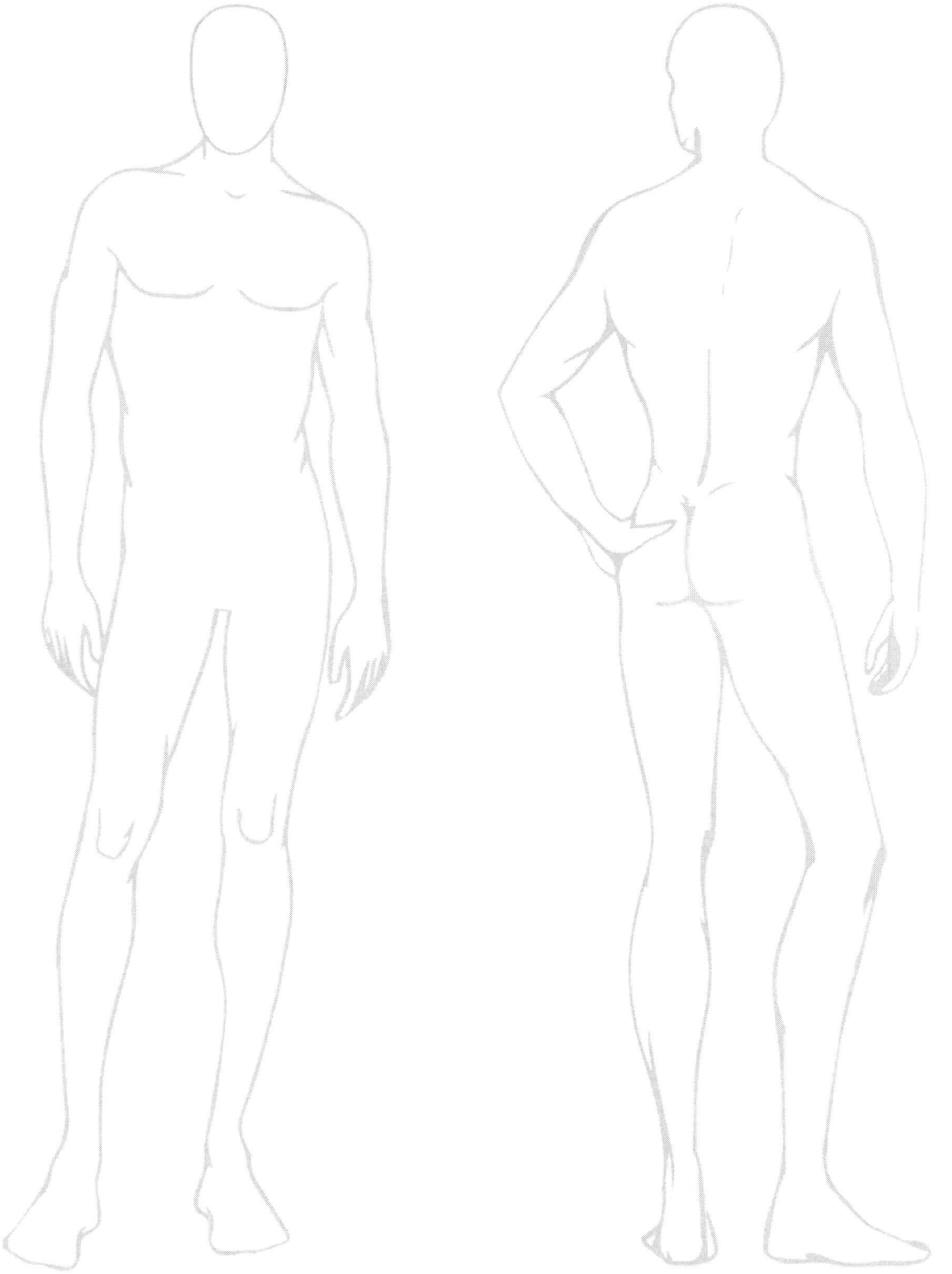

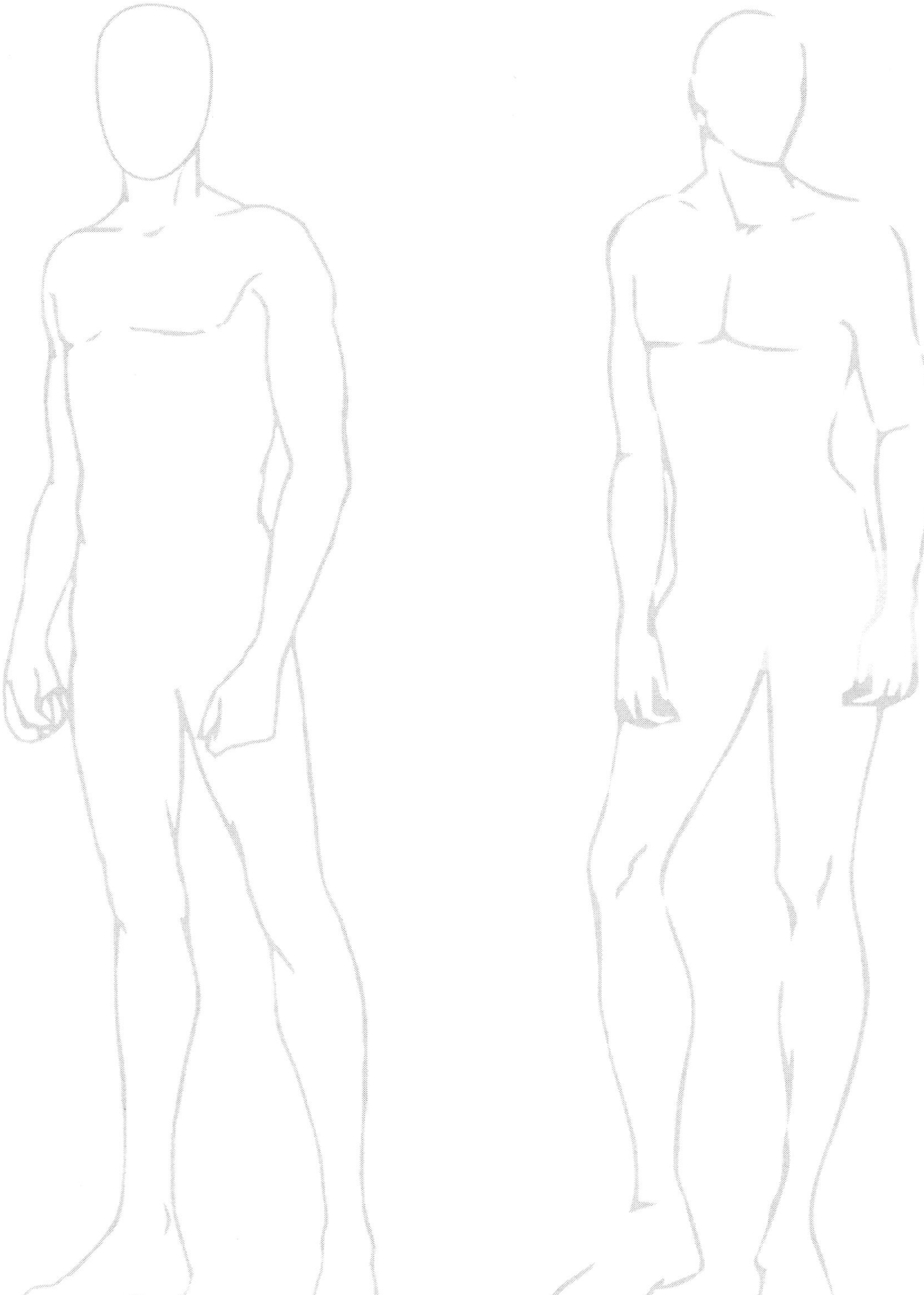